# Ethical Problems in Psychological Research

# Ethical Problems in Psychological Research

### HEINZ SCHULER

*Institut für Psychologie*
*Universität Erlangen–Nürnberg*
*Federal Republic of Germany*

### Translated by

### MARGARET S. WOODRUFF

*Linguistics Research Center*
*University of Texas at Austin*
*Austin, Texas*

### ROBERT A. WICKLUND

*Department of Psychology*
*University of Texas at Austin*
*Austin, Texas*

ACADEMIC PRESS     1982

*A Subsidiary of Harcourt Brace Jovanovich, Publishers*
NEW YORK     LONDON
PARIS   SAN DIEGO   SAN FRANCISCO   SÃO PAULO   SYDNEY   TOKYO   TORONTO

BF
76.5
.S313
1982

COPYRIGHT © 1982, BY ACADEMIC PRESS, INC.
ALL RIGHTS RESERVED.
NO PART OF THIS PUBLICATION MAY BE REPRODUCED OR
TRANSMITTED IN ANY FORM OR BY ANY MEANS, ELECTRONIC
OR MECHANICAL, INCLUDING PHOTOCOPY, RECORDING, OR ANY
INFORMATION STORAGE AND RETRIEVAL SYSTEM, WITHOUT
PERMISSION IN WRITING FROM THE PUBLISHER.

ACADEMIC PRESS, INC.
111 Fifth Avenue, New York, New York 10003

*United Kingdom Edition published by*
ACADEMIC PRESS, INC. (LONDON) LTD.
24/28 Oval Road, London NW1 7DX

Library of Congress Cataloging in Publication Data

Schuler, Heinz.
  Ethical problems in psychological research.

  Translation of: Ethische Probleme psychologischer
Forschung.
    Bibliography: p.
    Includes index.
    1. Psychological research--Moral and ethical aspects.
  2. Human experimentation in psychology--Moral and ethical
  aspects.  I. Title.
  BF76.5.S313        174'.915        82-3886
  ISBN  0-12-631250-8                AACR2

PRINTED IN THE UNITED STATES OF AMERICA

82 83 84 85    9 8 7 6 5 4 3 2 1

*Moral predigen ist leicht,*
*Moral begründen schwer.*

**Moralizing comes easily;**
**Justifying morality is hard.**
—ARTHUR SCHOPENHAUER

# Contents

**Translators' Foreword**   xi
**Preface**   xiii
**Acknowledgments**   xvii

# 1
# The Potential Conflict between Methodological and Ethical Norms

Complexity, Methodology, and Theory   2
The Object of Study and the Need for Rules   4
The Experiment as the Preferred Method for Psychological Research   5
Historical Aspects of the Subject Role   15
Critical Issues Related to the Subject Role   19
On the Psychology of the Experimenter   25
The Psychological Experiment as an Interaction Sphere   32
The Power Differential   44
The Experiment as a Social Contract   48
Scrutinizing Milgram's Experiments   60
Ethical Norms   64

# 2
## Ethical Problems of Psychological Experiments

    History and Background    67
    Problematic Experimental Procedures and Their Consequences    75
    Safeguards and Compensations    98
    Evaluating the Acceptability of Experimental Procedures    113

# 3
## Ethical and Methodological Problems of Alternatives to Laboratory Experiments

    The Conflict between Strength of Method and Ethical Preference    136
    Role Playing    137
    Field Research    147
    Action Research    150
    Nonreactive Research Methods    152
    Social Experimentation    156
    Field Research: A Supplement Rather Than a Substitute    162

# 4
## The Codification of Ethical Principles for Psychological Research

    The Functions of Ethical Guidelines    166
    The History of Regulations for Research with Humans    169
    APA Codes of Ethics    176
    Other Codes of Ethics: A Comparative Survey    185

## Appendix

    USA (1973) and Canada: Ethical Principles in the Conduct of Research with Human Participants    193
    USA (1977): Ethical Standards of Psychologists (1977 Revision)    194
    USA (1981): Ethical Principles of Psychologists (1981 Revision)    205
    Federal Republic of Germany (1978): Berufsethische Verpflichtungen für Psychologen (Ethical Obligations of Professional Psychologists)    218
    Great Britain (1977): Ethical Principles for Research with Human Subjects    221

Netherlands (1976): Professional Code for Psychologists    224
Austria (1976): Berufsverpflichtungen für Psychologen
(Obligations of Professional Psychologists)    231
Poland (1971): Psychologist's Ethical Code    233
Sweden (1975): Ethical Principles in the Conduct of Psychological
and Educational Research with Human Participants    234
Switzerland (1974): Code Déontologique (Deontological Code)    236
France (1960): Projet de Code de Déontologie à l'Usage des Psychologues
(Proposed Deontological Code for Psychologists)    239


**References    243**
**Subject Index    261**

# Translators' Foreword

As discussions of ethics in psychological research have spiraled to an unanticipated high in North America and more generally around the world, an Austrian-born psychologist has assembled a book on this topic that is captivating in its depth. Dr. Schuler's *Ethische Probleme Psychologischer Forschung* makes its first impression by showing the reader the historical path. Beginning with early questions on the subject role in the psychological experiment and the parallel ethical issues in even earlier medical research, the book moves to more recent developments in both fields and ends with a detailed and sweeping look at contemporary ethical and methodological questions in psychology. The book stands alone in another, closely related aspect: It is the only existing book on this topic with a genuine and informed international perspective. Not only are historical trends examined from perspectives on both sides of the Atlantic, but troublesome methodologies and resulting ethical rules are treated with a consistent international flavor. For instance, not just the ethics codes of the American Psychological Association (APA), but also the codes of eight European nations are found here.

One is accustomed to thinking that those with an eye toward history, and especially with an eye toward international developments, are less attuned to the details of the scientific process. With this expectation as a background, the reader will be very much surprised: Schuler currently conducts field and laboratory research in Germany and shows a familiarity with modern theories, methods, and findings that would usually be attributed to someone less concerned with history and philosophy. For example, in discussing and criticizing role playing as an alternative to the deception experiment, Schuler cites over 60 relevant studies or commentaries on the role-playing issue. As another example, in a section on the voluntary nature of participation in psychological research, he introduces over 20 relevant studies or commentaries, in addition to detailing out seven ways to reduce the negative impact of coercing individuals into research participation. The detail is in large part social psychological; it is the social psychologists who will be most impressed by Schuler's sensitivity to the multimethodologies of the field.

Does the author take sides? This is a simple question to answer. Schuler makes a convincing case of having researched the ethical issues to their roots; he makes an equally convincing case of having explored the methodological requirements for making progress in a science of psychology. The recommendations resulting from the juxtaposition of ethical and scientific requirements come across as fair minded; the reader will not sense that Schuler has axes to grind or favorite paradigms to defend.

The translation of German to English necessarily proceeds along the lines of simplification. *Einverständniserklärung* and *Gesetzmässigkeiten* become "consent" and "laws," respectively, and a 98-word sentence constituting a paragraph of its own is dissected into three English sentences. Quite a different problem arises in the course of conveying the precise meaning of terms. For instance, the adjective *kontrollierbar* is normally translated as "controllable," sometimes as "checkable" or "verifiable." It could also be translated as "accessible to supervision or inspection or examination" or "open to audit." In one context in Schuler's book, the word appeared to us to have both English senses of "controllable" and "checkable," so we used two phrases to capture its flavor. *Kontrollierbar* calls attention to the subtle challenges associated with translating cognates and borrowed words from German to English. *Institution* remains "institution," and *experimentelles* becomes "experimental," but *kontrollierbar* is not always "controllable," and translating *Potential* as "potential" can lead to some awkward results.

The reader will find the text to be Americanized, at the very least. The expense of doing this, of course, is that of occasionally leaving aside the color and complexity that would only be possible in the original version.

We appreciate the assistance of Irwin C. Lieb with the translation of technical terms from the field of philosophy; of Peggy Beauvois, Francis Bulhof, and Elizabeth Daverman with the translation of the French and Swiss codes of ethics from the original French; and of Rebecca Woodruff in proofreading at various stages of production. Most of all, we are grateful to Heinz Schuler for working closely with us on the translation, reading our first draft, and patiently clarifying numerous questions. Collaboration with the author is the ideal context for translation.

ROBERT A. WICKLUND
MARGARET S. WOODRUFF

# Preface

For scientists, there is a close tie between involvement in research and readiness to consider the ethical problems connected with their professional actions. Expressed as a correlation coefficient, this connection is high and negative. The most industrious and successful of our colleagues show the least interest in seeing and discussing their scientific work from the standpoint of its ethical implications, and vice versa. To reduce the main concern of this book to the briefest common denominator: It is supposed to help transform that negative correlation into a positive one.

Attempts to impose values involving ethical reflection or even particular philosophical or moral positions are not likely to be effective with those who are not prepared to discuss ethical issues. In fact, such attempts would probably make such a transformation even less likely. This volume is no argument in favor of a particular moral system. At points, however, it is impossible merely to report; rather, it is necessary to argue in favor of some position. At such points, I will try to base these judgments on a minimum of moral values about which there seems to be a consensus and to build on the values and basic moral principles that are a common basis for everyday actions.

The following discussion is intended, then, to inform and to awaken interest rather than to persuade. To be sure, the standpoint from which the information is presented is seldom explicit. But the perspective can be identified, although this is not to suggest that the reader is not at liberty to take other points of view. This study would be a failure if it registered a dogmatic moral credo.

The information presented here focuses on the relationship between experimenter and subject within investigations in the biomedical and social sciences. If this relationship is understood as a social contract, we can weigh benefits and costs against each other for the partners in this interaction, to use the terminology of exchange theory. For this purpose, we need only refer to the general principles of social justice, fairness, and responsibility that govern our conduct in society. Ethical imperatives needing more justification than these principles are not necessary. Studies of the experimental situation, the social psychology of the psychological experiment, can be used in such a way that the responsibilities of the partners are based on an understanding of their motives and expectations in the interaction. The result of this analysis is that the experimenters' responsibility for the welfare of their subjects is determined by the extent of their potential control of subjects' behavior. The extent of this control, in turn, depends on certain characteristics of the topic of investigation, as well as the extent of stimulus control and reaction control and the a priori power differential between experimenter and subject.

In this context, the book discusses problems that can arise in concrete research situations, including deception and manipulation as well as mental and physical harm and danger for subjects. Possible safeguards and compensations are mentioned, such as voluntary participation, information and consent before the experiment, and debriefing. Empirical studies of the consequences of experimental procedures are presented; however, up to now these results must not be credited with far-reaching validity.

The root of the problem faced by experimental psychologists is the special nature of the object of the research—that is, the human subject. It is difficult to infer regularities from the behavior of humans in complex everyday situations. Moreover, human behavior is changed by the act of observation. Thus it seems obvious that we must carry out experiments with strictly controlled conditions and considerably reduced complexity. In addition, it seems necessary to design experiments so that they are nontransparent for the subjects. On the other hand—and here the conflict arises—the behavior of researchers in the biomedical and social sciences toward their subjects is evaluated by the same or similar moral principles as any other behavior of human beings toward each other.

Thus the experiment is the principal research method that leads to a confrontation of methodological and ethical claims. The possibility of reducing complexity and of giving the best possible assurance that causal conclusions are valid encourages the use of research procedures that seem ethically problematic.

It is for this reason that the following discussion emphasizes experimental research, even though the title *Ethical Problems in Psychological Research* is considerably more general. To be sure, several methodological alternatives to experiments are examined, evaluated, and compared with the laboratory experiment, including role playing and various kinds of field research. The results of this comparison can be summarized briefly: Role playing cannot be a genuine alternative to the laboratory experiment, but at most a supplement, for methodological as well as epistemological reasons. On the other hand, one of the field research approaches mentioned here—social experimentation—is seen as a promising, progressive extension of laboratory experimentation.

In another sense, also, the title is perhaps too general, in that the focus of the book is on social psychology. This is in part because social psychology is the author's field and in part because of the particular danger of reactivity in social–psychological research and the consequent impact this problem has had on research designs. Thus we could have spoken of "ethical problems of research in social psychology" or even limited the field to experimental social psychology. On the other hand, the examples are by no means intended to define the problem area. It is no less necessary to consider problems with research procedures in psychopharmacology or in educational psychology, for example, than in social psychology. The ethical considerations in this volume should claim validity beyond the area of psychology, well into a large part of biomedical and social sciences. What is analyzed here as the social contract between experimenter and subject is basically the same in medicine or anthropology. The parameters that define this contract are abstract enough to apply to any research with human subjects. Research studies can overlap and blur the boundaries between the sciences, particularly in the case of interdisciplinary projects. Moreover, the same questions are often investigated by various disciplines, perhaps under different titles. In such cases, whether the research is considered sociology, social psychiatry, or clinical psychology sometimes depends more on the profession of the project leader than on the nature of the investigation.

The research codes, of which the most important are introduced in the last chapter and appear in the Appendix, should also be understood as applying to more than just the field of psychology. Some refer explicitly to research with human subjects in general; they all have common roots in scientific history—that is, the rules of the World Health Organization, which was established in the aftermath of the Nuremberg trials.

The discussion of ethical problems assumes a consciousness of ethical standards and usually originates in observed violations of these standards or in discontent with the standards, as an impulse to change them. In this sense, there are additional problems that could be called ethical and that have attracted more attention than the problems discussed here: How can psychology benefit humanity? Is psychology worth the money that is invested in research? Can basic research be justified? Can applied research be justified? Which is superior, not in terms of economic efficiency but in terms of moral efficiency? Do psychologists have a particular social responsibility, and if so, how should research goals be formulated and research projects be chosen in order to fulfill it? None of these questions is raised or answered here. Nowhere are the products or consequences of psychological research discussed, but only the research process. One section does raise the question of which research procedures can be justified by the expected consequences. This section also warns against steering research too much toward the consequences, given the difficulty of predicting them. It is hard to justify a cost–benefit analysis that balances the contributions and stresses of the subjects with the presumed usefulness of the research project. Thus, except for this line of argument, the discussion is restricted to that for which the researcher is the main person responsible: the research *process*. An altogether accurate title for this book, then, would have to read something like this: "On the relationship of ethical and methodological demands in the empirical research process for the biomedical and social sciences, presented primarily with examples from experimental social psychology."

# Acknowledgments

Even though the present volume seemed like a hermit's work to someone who is accustomed to empirical team research, I was still dependent on the advice, support, and suggestions of others. Much of this work would have progressed more slowly and less adequately without their help. I owe thanks to many people and institutions for their support and consideration, particularly the following.

A fellowship from the Deutsche Forschungsgemeinschaft (German Science Foundation) freed me from everyday obligations for a year. This made it possible for me to pursue a topic that I had previously investigated more as a hobby than a bread-and-butter job. The same society supported the German publication of the present work. I am also very thankful to Bernhard Otto, of the Hogrefe Verlag, for directing the initial publication of this project.

The staff at the information service PASAR (Psychological Abstract Search and Retrieval System) helped me collect material on this subject and turned out to be well informed in the related area of medicine as well. A number of manuscripts that could not be obtained through publishers were sent to me by cooperative colleagues, primarily from the United States.

Vera Bauder, Wolfgang Deibl, and Ingeborg Schnörch helped me with the many tasks that are necessary from the search for relevant literature at the beginning to the creation of indexes at the end. This contributed greatly to the speed with which the book was completed. Ingeborg Schnörch also typed the manuscript diligently and carefully, assisted by Ursula Brutscher.

I would like to thank the national associations of psychologists whose research regulations are reproduced in the Appendix for permission to reproduce them and for information about new developments in their countries. I was kept particularly well informed by the National Commission for the Protection of Human Subjects in Biomedical and Behavioral Research. Thus I would like to thank Miriam Kelty, commission member for the field of psychology, as a representative of the contact persons of all the other associations and institutions. The kindness of Barbara Rosemann, who is in charge of questions of professional ethics for the Polish Association of Psychologists, also deserves personal thanks. She took the trouble to translate her organization's entire set of regulations for professional ethics into English so that part of it could appear in the Appendix of this book.

I owe special thanks to Hermann Brandstätter and Lutz von Rosenstiel, the two professors who approved my monograph in its version as an academic thesis. In Professor Brandstätter, I had a teacher and supervisor who is distinguished not only by being a model and incentive but also by having a second virtue that is rarer or at least seldom coupled with the first: tolerance of independent opinions. This tolerance is particularly necessary for a topic with which rational discourse meets its limits so quickly.

Lutz von Rosenstiel, senior partner in a variety of research projects, criticized this study in the unique manner in which he criticizes any manuscript he is asked to read: with a veritable explosion of stimulating suggestions. I know no one with more contagious ideas or with kinder and more friendly criticism.

I was able to discuss my first ideas for this study thoroughly and profitably with both Donald T. Campbell and Michael Argyle. Campbell's methodological creativity impressed me as a compelling alternative to dealing with ethical problems by means of avoidance.

Unfortunately, I did not meet or begin corresponding with some of the most interesting of my other colleagues until the manuscript was finished. Thus I was able to incorporate only a few of their stimulating suggestions in the last revision of the text. Much of what I owe them will not be reflected until an extension of the present study is undertaken; some of it goes far beyond this topic. I encountered as much interest and personal involvement from colleagues I met recently in connection with this study, above all from Ralph Rosnow, William McGuire, Martin Orne, and especially Otfried Höffe and Robert Wicklund, as I would expect from people I had known for some time. Along with some other outstanding colleagues, these men show a rare combination of sober commitment, intellectual stimulation, and comradely support. It seems that those who concern themselves with ethical problems are particularly pleasant and agreeable people.

HEINZ SCHULER
*Augsburg, Fall 1979*

# 1

# The Potential Conflict between Methodological and Ethical Norms

In addition to the methodological problems that arise in every area of scientific research, the biomedical and social sciences are confronted with problems resulting from the fact that people are attempting to investigate their own kind. Scientific investigation of humans is defined and limited not only by methodological criteria but also by the special norms that regulate human interaction. The ethical problems implied by these special norms are not only added to the methodological ones but also interact with them in a complex manner.

The following two theses will serve as points of departure for some introductory considerations:

1. It is difficult to infer causal relationships from human behavior in the undiminished complexity of everyday life.
2. The behavior of the persons being investigated is influenced by their knowledge that they are being subjected to scientific investigation. Thus, their impressions of how and for what reasons they are being studied have implications for the results of the investigation.

We will try to show that both of these basic conditions encountered by the psychologist as scientist foster the choice of research methods that contradict certain ethical norms. First, however, we will consider the extent to which the biomedical and social sciences, particularly psychology, occupy a special position not only from an ethical but also from a methodological standpoint.

## COMPLEXITY, METHODOLOGY, AND THEORY

Psychologists who are not strict behaviorists might be inclined to add the special complexity of the object of their research to the two original theses, as a third factor determining the special nature of their own research practices. A central aspect of this complexity is the reflectivity and goal-directedness of human behavior. The science of psychology, this "bundle of institutionalized problem-solving processes [Herrmann, 1976, p. 42]," would take a completely different form if humans were stimulus–response automatons; if they were not oriented toward a criterion of meaningfulness for their behavior; if they had no self-concept against which to measure their planned behavior, no plans or areas of action in relation to which they explore how adaptive alternative strategies for action promise to be; and if they did not have a certain amount of freedom to decide among behavioral alternatives.[1]

Human beings are able to control to a certain extent the connection between experience and behavior and thus also between stimulus and response. This "freedom" in responding makes it harder to recognize genetic and other causes and thus to establish nomothetic regularities like those in the natural sciences. The presumed greater variability of human behavior, in contrast with the "behavior" of objects observed in the natural sciences, is partly a function of this capacity for self-control and self-direction. Later we will show to what extent this makes it necessary to employ special methods of investigation. Here it may suffice to say that the first of the above two theses includes the aspect of complexity called "behavioral freedom."

Behavioral freedom is also related to the second thesis, that behavior is changed by observation. Social psychologists did not begin to investigate this problem until the late 1950s (Orne, 1962; Riecken, 1958/1974). Long before this, however, it was known that observation (or, more generally, a social situation) causes people to behave differently, given that they know they are being observed, even when the social situation is created only in order to register their "individual" behavior.

This phenomenon is by no means unusual in other experimental sciences.

---

1. Presumably, psychology would not then have a lesser scope, since every science tends in any case to expand to its methodological limits. But if people were in fact so uncomplicated in their psychological functioning, we would face entirely different questions in psychology today. Since methods are dependent to a certain extent on the formulation of questions, a lesser complexity of the object of investigation would of course be methodologically relevant. Such changes, however, would have no specific implications for the dilemma of the potential conflict between research methods and ethical obligations. There is an even more basic metatheoretical problem: Science in the form in which it is practiced would be unthinkable without the complexity of human action. One could also say that science is one of the manifestations of this complexity. This problem does not need to be discussed further here. It may, however, warn us not to allow the global concept "complexity" too much independence in explaining the special nature of psychological research.

For example, scientists performing a spectral analysis of very small quantities of matter must be sure that secondary effects of the measurement process do not falsify the results. (On the basis of the contamination of instruments, completely new substances have been "discovered.") And an experimenter who wants to determine the photoelectric qualities of certain crystal structures does well to avoid holding his head above the apparatus in such a manner that it changes the amount of light in an undefined way. These are very simple examples, within the conceptual range of the layman, and thus very simple technical solutions suggest themselves. The scientist need only control the measurement process better or perhaps quantify the influence of the error sources and attempt to partial them out from the results. But actually, in many areas of research in the natural sciences, recognizing—to say nothing of correcting—all error sources implied in the observation process is much more complicated and less likely. Thus, mere complicatedness cannot explain the empirical difficulties of the social sciences, even though "complexity" is often plausibly used to console us for the unsatisfactory state of knowledge in psychology. And indeed, some examples from the natural sciences—meteorology, for example—do show that the interaction of many individually familiar variables is often too much for the scientist's predictive ability.

Complexity may thus be related to the difficulty of finding regularities independent of whether we are considering natural or social sciences. The actual difference between psychology and other experimental sciences is not at the level of phenomena but of *explaining* these phenomena. To illustrate this point, we might consider some theories that conceive of human behavior as conscious and goal directed, taking place in a field of active psychological forces (Lewin, 1935) and oriented by means of behavioral plans (Miller, Galanter, & Pribram, 1973). These plans are thought to be carried out meaningfully in a frame of hierarchically structured spheres of action (Kaminski, 1974) by persons who are equipped with the necessary freedom of action or decision. This being so, human reactivity to social stimuli—to the observation process—acquires a meaning entirely different from corresponding processes in inanimate nature. In the context of such an explanatory model, there are further ramifications for the difficulty of the research process. For example, the greater the significance of the observation within the sphere of the actor's behaviors, the more likely it is that the observed behavior will be a function of the process of observation. The process of observation affects observed behavior in proportion to the status of the observer and in proportion to the impact of being evaluated on the actor's self-concept. Another relevant factor is whether people under observation expect their professional future to be influenced by the impression formed by the observer.

We may find cognitive behavior theory a better, more "natural" explanation of the results of human action. Or we may, being skeptical and pragmatic, judge theoretical constructs only by their value for practical, empirical research procedures. In any case, cognitive theory explains a broader class of phenomena than does a mechanistic theory. For example, it can explain why human beings, unlike inanimate objects, react differently depending on the *purpose* for which they are being observed. The same observer provokes different behavior from the same persons depending on whether their style of speech, their achievement orientation, or some other process is being observed. This is true even though the form of observation is identical in all cases. We are of course assuming that the person knows or guesses the goals of the observation.

## THE OBJECT OF STUDY AND THE NEED FOR RULES

The two theses stated earlier, concerning the difficulty of observing (*a*) in a natural environment and (*b*) without affecting the object observed, apply with some variance to the objects observed in all disciplines. A principal difference between sciences dealing with human beings and other sciences is that those dealing with human beings have special, stricter ethical norms with respect to the object of investigation.[2] Social and biomedical scientists must be concerned about the people they study. They are obliged to employ the same ethical principles in research as in their usual conduct with humans. Researchers must be sure that in extending the boundaries of knowledge they do not harm their subjects but rather treat them like all other human beings and preserve the norms of morality and decency.[3]

---

2. Even this rule has an exception, however. In many religions, theological research is restricted by the prohibition of forming a concept of God; in most religions, we find the "prohibition of thinking," as Freud called it, which has been pointed out so often since Voltaire and Marx. And of course all scientists are subject to a whole series of other behavioral norms unrelated to their specific disciplines. We could say that scientists are subject to norms to the degree that their actions have implications for the contemporary view of the world. General guidelines, determined by society and history, influence the work of scientists but are not specifically related to science. In addition, social scientists have some norms in common with other scientists—for example, the obligation to report results accurately or to consider the possible consequences of their own research.

3. Concepts such as ethics, morality, and morals are used in the everyday sense in this book, except when that sense differs significantly from the customary concepts of practical philosophy. In dictionaries of philosophical terms, *ethics* is usually described as the theory of just or moral action (Neuhäusler, 1963, p. 57); *morality* is that "basic normative framework for behavior, particularly to fellow human beings, which is fundamental to human existence [Höffe, 1977, p. 162]." The adjectives *ethical* and *moral* are used synonymously in everyday speech. Some philosophers distinguish between the adjective describing actions or obligations (moral) and the adjective describing the discipline of ethics or moral philosophy (ethical). When obligation and responsibility are mentioned in this book, even without expressly characterizing them as moral, we are using ethical, not legal categories. These moral principles are based on a general consensus ("respect for human

Our central dilemma lies at the crossroads of ethical and methodological demands. If the two original theses are correct, not all research methods are equally suited to studying human behavior. Indeed, some are apparently not at all suited for the social sciences. The most suitable methods are those that allow the experimenter a high degree of stimulus control—that is, reduction of complexity (Thesis 1)—while restricting the extent to which the subjects are informed about the research (Thesis 2). Thus, researchers with human subjects, especially in psychology, tend to develop deceptive and manipulative methods of investigation. Employing these methods, however, involves a conflict with such commonly accepted moral principles as honesty and avoidance of manipulation or harm to others.

The complexity of human behavior intensifies the conflict. The effect of different investigatory measures on different people is as hard to predict as human behavior in general. Statements about the acceptability of research methods and measures are faced with the same difficulties as other statements of psychological laws, if one evaluates them on the basis of their effect on the subjects. These difficulties would remain even if psychologists agreed on the ethical norms to be applied.

In the rest of the chapter, the two initial theses will be developed and substantiated, and on this basis, the relationship between experimenter and subject will be formulated as a social contract characterized by parameters of methods and behavior that simultaneously define a researcher's responsibility for the subjects.

## THE EXPERIMENT AS THE PREFERRED METHOD FOR PSYCHOLOGICAL RESEARCH

Most of today's knowledge in psychology consists of interpretations of the results of experiments—at least that is the part of our knowledge that the majority of us are most ready to trust and to consider valid. In a psychology based on experimentation, psychologists obtain their data primarily by creating the conditions they need for their observations. The experiment is to be distinguished from all other research methods (Carlsmith, Ellsworth, & Aronson, 1976, p. 8); in this respect, psychology is no different from most other empirical sciences. However, this means not only that the scientist's view of human nature is based on experiments but also that the experimentation, like any other method of conducting research with humans, reflects the scientist's view

---

dignity, rejection of coercion, reduction of suffering, etc. [Höffe, 1977, p. 163]"). From the standpoint of cultural anthropology, the function of this consensus is "to protect human life on the basis of mutual trust [Höffe, 1977, p. 163]."

of human nature. The implications are particularly problematic for psychology and the related social sciences. They are less an issue for such sciences as medicine and biology, where mechanistic ideas are no longer considered disturbing. The connection between world view and research methods gives rise to concern because:

1. The experiment can be seen as a global paradigm, in one of the senses that Kuhn used in 1962. In that sense, a global paradigm is a consensus on methods reached by a scientific community, having an arbitrary and modish quality; it is more an agreement among scientists than a God-given principle.
2. Experimental psychologists may find that their work is labeled in terms of a view of human nature to which they do not subscribe.

## The Experiment's Relation to Behaviorism and the Cognitive Revolution

How close is the affinity of the experimental method to the psychology of behaviorism? Is this affinity only historically conditioned, or is it also based on the internal logic of the discipline? Is the identification of the experiment with a mechanistic stimulus–response psychology merely an exaggeration by those who, at a great distance, are trying to reinforce their own position as representatives of phenomenological, interactionist, or hermeneutic psychology?

For a long time outsiders have considered whether taking over a method, say from physics, implied that characteristics like those observed in physics would then be seen in the object of study. Only since the cognitive revolution in psychology, however, has this problem been generally discussed by psychologists. Koch (1959) was either farsighted or premature when he decided that the time had come for an epilogue to the "age of scientific misunderstanding [p. 783]." Phenomenologists, and they alone, have long claimed that the impoverishment of psychology is due not only to the eradication of mentalistic concepts by behavioristic psychology but also to the adoption of methods and research strategies from the natural sciences with their implicit demands of physicalism and operationalism. These methods can be said to restrict the empirical sphere in which psychology operates in the sense that the methods constitute a criterion of admission for empirical data. Graumann and Métraux (1977, pp. 30–31) suggest that experimental psychologists have tended to apply methods from other sciences instead of considering without prejudice the problems involved in their particular area of knowledge. These borrowed methods have made psychological research what it is today. However, using the words of Adorno (1971, p. 211), Graumann and Métraux warn against confusing "that which is brought about by the method with the matter itself."

More and more, psychologists are beginning to focus on "the matter itself" again, from new perspectives. But which research methods correspond to these new perspectives? To what extent will such methods be in a position to supplement or replace traditional experimental research, or perhaps even to lead to evolutionary leaps in psychology? Before discussing these questions, we will outline the logic of the experiment, which has brought our discipline to its present state.

## A Perspective on the Causal Relationship

The concept "causal relationship" has always occupied a very special position among the various kinds of connections among variables—those connections serving to reduce complexity and organize phenomena within science. The special position of the causal relationship has been particularly prominent since the Cartesian shift from the scholastic or philosophical world view to the empirical or scientific world view. Indeed, all attempts to explain events are based on this concept. Organizational relationships basically just divide phenomena into groups of X, Y, and Z, but the concept that causality exists and can be discovered enables us to ask "why Y" and answer "because X." Thus, causality allows us not only to understand phenomena but also to manipulate them. To be sure, the existence of the empirical principle of causality cannot be proven by observing temporal contiguity. David Hume showed this in his famous essay "An Inquiry Concerning Human Understanding" (1748/1964). Hume argued that causality has an empirical meaning only in human thought, as a construct that our intellect applies to reality.

The surest method of determining a causal relationship is either to notice in a natural manner that *A* precedes *B* temporally and that a variation of *A* results in a variation of *B* or to provoke this observation—that is, to experiment. Of course, in a number of disciplines the objects of investigation can hardly be manipulated by the researcher because of their size (astronomy or government) or because they no longer exist (history). In such cases, we must observe natural results of events and conditions or evaluate their symbolic representations (verbal reports or spectral fluctuations). A science can develop extensively without a means of verifying chronology and covariation experimentally. It needs only a symbolism anchored in precise semiotics, such as the language of mathematical formulas, highly developed methods of observation, and regular, observable cyclical processes. Cook and Campbell (1976, p. 226) point to the advantages that astronomy has in this regard. To be sure, astronomy feeds on basic experimental research and on experimental research in other disciplines. We could also say that *because* appropriate instruments were available it was possible to discover cyclical structures, or because *certain* instruments were available, *certain* structures were developed (and others overlooked). We could also ask, very skeptically, whether astronomy did not perhaps merely discover the simplest phenomenon possible (the phenomenon most suitable for the method).

How can we know, then, whether astronomy is closer to its goal than psychology is to its goal? Perhaps it would be better to approach this question from a different angle. We could make the measure of scientific progress the distance from the point of departure instead of the closeness to distant goals—after all, one might doubt the utility of formulating distant goals for any particular discipline. Even if the distance from the point of departure is the measure of progress, however, envious psychologists will have to admit that astronomy has probably already progressed farther. Thus, if the various social, intellectual, and economic conditions are favorable, a discipline can acquire a good reputation even without being able to manipulate the variables relevant for the formulation and testing of its laws. If such favorable conditions are not present—that is, if no simple cyclical structures are to be found in the domain of a discipline, or if these structures cannot be isolated, as in government or history, and if the discipline also cannot formulate and test its laws by manipulating the relevant variables—then its scientific status will be correspondingly low.

Psychology seems to find itself in a middle position. On the one hand, conditions are not favorable, because the behavior of the people who are to be observed is not only difficult to understand in itself but also seems to be inextricable from many-layered, complex external conditions. On the other hand, the objects of psychological investigation have proven to be adequately manipulable and controllable, to a certain extent even divisible into elements. That is, individual functions apparently can be influenced without all the others simultaneously covarying. The implication is that psychology can solve its research problems by creating conditions and controlling—that is, experimenting—instead of waiting until the relevant behavior occurs naturally.

This implication is especially important in that the observation of behavior in a natural context only rarely shows the hypotheses to be unequivocally superior to alternative interpretations. The experiment seems to be the best method not only for observing chronology and covariation but also for excluding alternative interpretations of the results.

### The Role of the Experiment in Dealing with Alternative Explanations

This latter point can be stated more concretely. Ellsworth (1977) lists five basic patterns of alternative interpretations that compete with the research hypothesis $X \rightarrow Y$ ($Y$ is the result of $X$): $Y \rightarrow X$, $X \rightleftharpoons Y$, $Z {<}^X_Y$, $X \rightarrow Z \rightarrow Y$, and $(X + Z) \rightarrow Y$. The first two alternatives are problems of chronology or the functional interdependence of the two variables. $Y \rightarrow X$ really would not play a role in an actual experiment but at the most in a quasi-experimental design in which subjects cannot be assigned to experimental conditions at random (Cook & Campbell, 1976, p. 224). $X \rightleftarrows Y$ is only significant when it is important to exclude the possibility that, while $Y$ can indeed be influenced by $X$, $X$ can *also* be dependent on $Y$. The other three alternatives are conceivable in any empirical investigation and thus in any experiment: that both $X$ and $Y$ are dependent on a third variable without actually being connected with each other ($Z <^X_Y$), that $X$ is related to $Y$ only by means of $Z$ ($X \rightarrow Z \rightarrow Y$), or that $X$ influences $Y$ only when $Z$ is present ($[X + Z] \rightarrow Y$).

Experimenting alone does not guarantee unequivocal conclusions. The experiment is superior in principle to other research methods only in that it excludes the alternative $Y \rightarrow X$. Ellsworth (1977, p. 614) claims that certain field procedures can be better suited than laboratory methods for excluding some of these alternative explanations. She suggests that experimenting in the field offers better possibilities for considering complex causal connections than does experimenting in the laboratory, where so much is typically kept constant that complex causal relationships can hardly appear. To be sure, Ellsworth's claim is valid only when field conditions do not seriously diminish the possibilities of control and measurement precision.

In planning research so as to exclude alternative interpretation through third variables, it is necessary first to lay down theoretical assumptions about the connections among the several variables. This does not necessarily mean that one must use an experiment but instead that the investigation must be organized in a manner that suits the theory at hand.[4] For example, the connection between depictions of violence on television and aggression in children might be such that depictions of violence stimulate aggression only in children who already have a high degree of hostility. In this case, which is the $(X + Z) \rightarrow Y$ variety, an experimental investigation can establish this connection only if the hypotheses (i.e., the theory) determine the experimental design. Further, an experimental design can often exclude alternative hypotheses that are constructed after the fact, although it is rarer that post hoc hypotheses can be substantiated, since the necessary measurements are usually not present.

Thus, the strength of the experiment lies in its ability to test clearly formulated hypotheses, in the realization of research ideas. In potential for generating hypotheses, the experiment is clearly inferior to other research methods, such as participant observation. On the other hand, participant observation and

---

4. Cook and Campbell (1976) discussed four types of validity of conclusions from experimental data. Of the four types they mention, three are directly related to theory: *internal, external,* and *construct validity*. Only for the fourth, *statistical conclusion validity,* are considerations of content and theory less directly relevant. Cook and Campbell's *threats to validity*— threats to the correctness of assumptions about causal relationships—apply at least as much, usually more, to any other scientific method as to the experiment.

other methods that do not permit random distribution of subjects among experimental conditions often cannot solve even the basic question of causality with adequate reliability. That is, they would not address the issue of whether depictions of violence stimulate aggression or aggressive children watch more shows of this sort than other children.

The experiment, then, is uniquely suited to clarifying the problem of causality. In all disciplines in which the object of investigation is such that experimenting is feasible, Boring's statement readily applies: "The experimental method is science's principal tool: $y = f(x)$ is the goal [1969, p. 9]." It is true that some researchers, primarily those oriented toward phenomenology, have expressed doubts that this thesis applies unreservedly to psychology. Graumann and Métraux (1977) were already cited in this connection, and Thomae (1965) argues in a similar fashion. But Elms (1975) describes the attitude of social psychologists to their research methods and theory formation at the time of the second edition of *The Handbook of Social Psychology* (Lindzey & Aronson, 1968) as a "high-water mark in social psychological sanguinity [p. 967]." This sanguinity seems characteristic of the attitude of most psychologists.

## The Experiment under Fire

Signs of crisis or uncertainty regarding the tenability of the experimental approach have been with us for several years. The "discovery" of the subject as a social being is one of the roots of this crisis. For instance, Aronson and Carlsmith's very influential article "Experimentation in Social Psychology" (1968) has undoubtedly contributed to the spread of knowledge about subject-related, experimenter-related, and other types of error in the psychological experiment. Even ethical problems are discussed to some extent. However, the criticism is still based on "internal problems." Deviations from the experimental ideal are described as "interference factors," as errors that can be removed by stricter experimental control. Appropriately, Aronson and Carlsmith end their discussion of ethical problems by suggesting that experimenters should try to avoid deception whenever possible (p. 29). On the other hand, this chapter has actually been called "a guide for deceiving and manipulating subjects [Fishbein & Ajzen, 1972, p. 489]."

Research methods and goals were rarely questioned until after various reflections on the theory of science had been adapted for psychology and critical movements emphasizing social politics had become prominent. Impulses to change have tended to arise from the connection of the theory of science with the more general criticism of society. (In German-language writings, this is clearest in the works of Holzkamp, especially 1970a, 1970b, 1972.) The widespread demand for relevance in psychological research, or in research in general, was probably the clearest expression of this development and the aspect with the most consequences.

The result for psychology of the alliance between the theory of science and the criticism of society has been the impulse for experimental psychologists to consider the spirit of experimentation from a metaperspective. Those with such a metaperspective no longer see deficiencies in the validity of experimental results, particularly results of laboratory experiments, as mere technical inadequacies to be remedied. Now these deficiencies are also seen as an expression of a systematic reduction of the complexity of the human–ecological system, a reduction in line with the stimulus–response behavioral model, which has an affinity to experimentation and resembles the approach taken in physics. The simple principle of causality and the model of thought based on analysis of variance are questioned. Gadlin and Ingle suggest that in order to see a problem in terms of fact or artifact, like Kruglanski (1975), we "must assume a world already divided into independent and dependent variables. Once we define the problem of the experiment in terms of fact or artifact, we accept the experimental method [Gadlin & Ingle, 1975, p. 1006]."

Such observations arise not only from authors oriented toward phenomenology and humanism, such as those just cited, but also from researchers who have become famous for their experimental work. The criticisms of the latter are no less rigorous:

> If we agree that the simple linear sequence model has outlived its usefulness for guiding our theorizing about cognitive and social systems, then we must also grant that the laboratory manipulational experiment should not be the standard method for testing psychological hypotheses [McGuire, 1973, p. 454].

Experiments can no longer be considered particularly suitable for confirming theories, McGuire writes, but only for demonstration. As an alternative, and a way out, McGuire suggests:

1. Emphasizing the creation of hypotheses
2. Accepting complexity
3. Observing people instead of data
4. Using longitudinal data from archives
5. Learning more complex techniques
6. Working in ways that are suited to available resources (less expensively)
7. Not insisting on premature consistency between data and knowledge

Gergen (1975), another experimental social psychologist, argues that the experiment is not an appropriate research method for psychology. It has not solved the problem of external validity, nor can it do justice to the historical properties of psychological and social phenomena.

In cases where the usefulness of the experiment is not actually questioned, the emphases have at least shifted. For example, psychologists are paying increased attention to the representativeness of actions and experiences within experiments. No longer are researchers strictly concerned, as before, with the representativeness of the subjects and the environment. Rather, there is an attempt to make sure that the conditions set by the experimenter are actually experienced and understood by the subjects as the experimenter intended and that the experience resembles an experience in nonexperimental situations (see Holzkamp, 1964; Sader, 1976, pp. 22–23). Of course, this demand has been made for some time by non-behavioristically-oriented researchers but was earlier ignored.

The relatively great dissatisfaction of psychologists with their own discipline corresponds to the questioning of methodological truisms. Psychologists appeared especially skeptical in their responses to a survey by Amelang and Aevermann (1976) and ascribed many errors in planning and interpretation to the work of their colleagues: "We cannot help noticing that the psychologists who responded distance themselves more from any claims for quality in their research than do the representatives of other disciplines [Amelang & Aevermann, 1976, p. 92]." The reasons for this dissatisfaction could lie in a generally more critical position, in the greater difficulty of the tasks involved, or in a genuinely lower quality of research.

Considering this dissatisfaction in connection with the failure of basic truisms within a science that was just beginning to develop a tradition, it seems as if the change in paradigms described by Kuhn (1962) must be imminent. The "sense of malfunction," one of the prerequisites cited by Kuhn for a "scientific revolution," appears to have arrived as a result of experiencing a crisis. Kuhn (p. 90) points out that confrontation with a crisis causes scientists to change their attitudes toward existing paradigms and correspondingly the nature of their investigations. In the transition from one sort of research to another, the number of competing formulations increases rapidly. Researchers are ready to try anything, but they also express discontent openly or take refuge in discussing basic philosophical issues.

If this period of transition described by Kuhn leads to a productive alternative to the experimental definition of the scientific world, the change could be radical. After the domain, methods, and goals of scientists are redefined, suggests Kuhn (1962), scientists will see the same data with quite different eyes, like "a change in visual gestalt: the marks on paper that were first seen as a bird are now seen as an antelope, or vice versa [p. 85]."

In a later section it will be suggested that none of the alternatives to the psychological experiment can completely replace it. No single method seems capable of overcoming the weaknesses of experimental research without simultaneously abandoning its strengths. Rather, the experiment can be improved and refined, and at the same time, creative testing of a variety of other methods should be demanded and encouraged. Radical alternatives have been proposed, such as a return to hermeneutic psychology, so rich in tradition (Gould & Shotter, 1977), or to action research, which goes back to Lewin and is understood within the context of critical theory to be an emancipatory movement (Haag, Krüger, Schwärzel, & Wildt, 1972). However, these alternatives have not been accepted by the majority of research psychologists.

## Carrying the Experiment beyond Behaviorism

The affinity between experimentation and behavioristic theories is impossible to overlook. However, one can say that this is a matter of the history of the disciplines rather than a necessary, indissoluble, preestablished parallel or identity. Experiments are already beginning to help us reproduce more complex realities than in the past and to bring to light causal relationships that are more complex than the one-sidedly deterministic ones. Such an expansion of the experimental process will have to go hand in hand with the elaboration of more exacting methods of measurement and data evaluation and of course with the further development of psychological theories. Both the context for creating the situations to be observed and the context for understanding the data gathered need to be expanded.

Indeed, hardly any psychological investigation in the past has managed to interpret experimental data exclusively within a stimulus–response paradigm, unless the investigation was explicitly concerned with that theory's original domain. R. M. Farr (1976) illustrates this by referring to a prototype of simple laboratory experimentation in social psychology, the classic Asch experiment (Asch, 1952). Although the experiment, which had to do with estimating size under social influence, appears to be an instance of a behavioristic approach, Asch conducted thorough interviews with the subjects for the purpose of fine tuning the data. Thus, his explanations were also based on introspective insights. Farr (1976, p. 229) points out that sensitivity to *demand characteristics* (Orne, 1962) is reflected in Asch's questions to his subjects about their experience of the experimental situation. Comparable work is found in other research efforts, especially those associated with Lewin. Festinger (1953) distinguishes between cognitively real and cognitively experimental orientations of participants in an experiment. *Cognitively real orientations* refers to perception of the experiment as a real social situation. *Cognitively experimental orientations* refers to awareness of acting in an artificial experimental situation.

It is hard to predict what long-range effects the current discussion of scientific theory will have on the methodology of psychology. Such discussions have been inevitable in recent years in other disciplines and are becoming increasingly prominent in psychology as well (Groeben & Westmeyer, 1975;

Schneewind, 1977). It is probable that the experiment will retain its dominant role in the subdisciplines of psychology where the topics under investigation necessitate a close relationship to the natural sciences, as well as in other sciences concerned with humans, such as medicine and biology. In other areas of psychology, the experiment is more likely to be modified, extended, and supplemented by other research methods, but it will probably not lose its basic importance. The coexistence of various methods is especially likely if pluralistic models of science (such as the one formulated by Herrmann, 1976) become dominant in the scientific community.

### *Imprecision in Measurement: Psychology Is Not Alone*

At no time, in no scientific discipline, and with none of the available methods of observation have we been able to claim with certainty that we have made a completely error-free measurement. Presumably this was recognized long before the following incident, which is a familiar anecdote (e.g., Boring, 1957, p. 134). Toward the end of the eighteenth century, Nikolai Maskeleyne, English court astronomer at the Greenwich observatory, noticed that his assistant David Kinnebrook was making errors in his notes on the transit of the stars. When compared with Maskeleyne's own notes, Kinnebrook's records of the movements of the stars showed a systematic time lag of fractions of a second, up to a whole second. The astronomer called his assistant to account, which did not improve matters, and finally dismissed him. Not until 20 years later was Maskeleyne's colleague Bessel able to show by comparison with the records of a series of well-known astronomers that Kinnebrook was apparently not the obstinate fellow his master had thought and that even Maskeleyne's own observations probably did not constitute the last word. Deviations in recording the transit of the stars, Bessel realized, were not the exception but the rule.

Since then we have learned to expect such errors in all measurements and to take them into account. To be sure, instruments of measurement have been refined, but our expectations of precision have also increased. The angle of deflection of starlight, predicted by Einstein to be 1.745 sec of arc, was "confirmed" during the eclipse of 1919 by measurements of 1.61 sec, 1.98 sec, 1.72 sec, 2.20 sec, and 2.00 sec (according to Campbell, 1969, p. 353). The perfection of any measurement is reduced by the imprecision of the instrument, by imprecision in the style of observation, and also by the instability of the objects of observation. Having acknowledged this, we have had to abandon the expectation of perfectly reliable measurements and perfectly valid conclusions from the observed data.

We have also had to accept that measurements, as well as conclusions, are usually more subject to error in psychology than in its model, the natural sciences. We have become accustomed to living with errors of measurement of considerable size as well as with uncertainty about the appropriateness of the nature of the measurements undertaken or of their interpretations. In addition, psychologists have come to realize that experimenters and subjects are not merely apparatuses for recording data and objects of investigation. They also behave as human beings in the experimental situation, with interacting intentions and modes of behavior that can affect the results in unintended ways.

Of course, this insight presumably applies not only to social sciences but to some extent to all sciences. At any rate, it has given us a special perspective on the psychological experiment. Perhaps the results of many experiments are bound up with the special nature of the persons involved or with the idiosyncratic social character of the situation, and thus, the impact of the experimental variables might be overestimated. The exploration of this possibility has become a separate branch of psychological research.

## HISTORICAL ASPECTS OF THE SUBJECT ROLE

### Introspection as a Predecessor of Imprecision in Measurement

One dominant quality of humans is their pronounced sensitivity to observation. This reactivity was perhaps noticed when scientists first began to study human behavior, as suggested by Boring (1954). He points out that the control group was invented by psychologists at the beginning of this century in order to determine the effect of pretests by using as a baseline the results from subjects who were not pretested. In other words, it was recognized early that a feature of the observation process—the pretest—could have a direct impact on the central phenomenon to be observed. Perhaps this was recognized first by diagnosticians because they had always tended to make conclusions that went beyond what was immediately obvious and observable.

It is useful at this point to delve into an earlier period of introspectionism, to illustrate how those who were sensitive to the issues surrounding introspectionism were also attuned to the fact that behavior and experience can be changed by the process of observation. This fact was also recognized by the behaviorists, who were interested only in simple, observable behaviors and saw psychology as "a purely objective, experimental branch of natural science which needs introspection as little as do the sciences of chemistry and physics [Watson, 1913, p. 176]."

Introspection as the "royal road to consciousness," a basic constituent of every phenomenological psychology, had been ridiculed by objectivists in the materialist tradition of the history of ideas ever since Lange (1866). James compared introspection with turning on the light to see what darkness looks like; Wundt compared it with Münchhausen's feat of pulling himself out of the swamp by his own forelock. Wundt was thereby criticizing the "systematic experimental introspection" developed by his former disciple Külpe in Würzburg. In contrast to his earlier work, Wundt had come to believe not only that we cannot observe ourselves but also that this process becomes less possible the more intensively it is attempted. He distinguished "accidental perception" from "observation," in that observation necessarily involves attention being directed toward phenomena before they appear. At the most, Wundt accepted as valid those perceptions of one's own impulses that occur "accidentally," without attention being directed to them. The more accidental a self-observation was, the more reliable he expected it to be (Wundt, 1911, pp. 125–128).

Not only can self-observation influence one's inner behavior, but also observation by others can influence outer behavior (and probably inner as well). This parallel insight was not generally recognized for some time. It seems appropriate, in light of these considerations, to formulate a common principle for both phenomena: Human behavior and experience are changed by awareness of being observed. This is a special case of the more general principle that the object of observation is altered through observation.

### Wundt and the Subject Role in Introspectionism

A history of the role of subjects in the psychological experiment could be drawn from the history of the problems and methods of psychology. To begin with, the early subject as introspector regularly exchanged roles with the experimenter. How then did it come about that the subjects of laboratory experiments today sometimes seem to be mere sources of data, observed only from the outside, often treated as if they were replaceable by rats? Experimenters frequently either ignore the subject's experience of the experiment or else perceive this experience as an interference factor and endeavor to eliminate it. ("Perceive" and "endeavor" remind us that stimulus–response theory has always been a theory for subjects, not for experimenters.)

It is not so easy as it might seem to describe the transition of roles from the subject as introspector to the subject as participant in a traditional laboratory experiment. We could begin by contrasting prebehaviorist and behaviorist psychology, with their characterizations of the subject as a trained and competent observer on the one hand and as an objectified, interchangeable organism and provider of data on the other (Schultz, 1969). This contrast may be basically correct and serve to indicate general tendencies, but it is expressed in a very simplified and crude form, particularly if prebehaviorist is equated with preexperimental and behaviorist is equated with experimental. Unfortunately, many elements of a complex development are necessarily lost in the course of simplification. For example, in the light of this contrast between behaviorist and prebehaviorist psychology, Wundt would be labeled as the father of controlled introspection, thus appearing as a prebehaviorist. This prebehaviorist aspect of Wundt's work is best captured by reference to two of his followers, Külpe and Titchener.

Külpe (1893) stressed the importance of subjective methods (introspection and memory), asserting that they could be applied without objective methods (experiment and language), whereas objective methods could not be used alone. Külpe found introspection ("inner perception") to be the simplest, most obvious method and suggested that "without inner perception the experiment is no more than a frivolous imitation of physics, and language becomes a meaningless image or sound without memory [pp. 8-9]."

Titchener (1901, pp. xiii-xviii) stated that, although some experiments should involve only one person, most experiments require two participants: an introspector and an experimenter in charge of instruments and records. All experiments requiring an experimenter and an introspector had to be repeated, with experimenter and introspector changing roles. Boring (1953) mentions the 10,000 controlled introspective reactions that Wundt's subjects had to complete in order to be allowed to contribute data for published studies. This incredible amount of practice and the emphasis on subjective methods and on exchanging roles allow us to infer a very egalitarian relationship between the roles of experimenter and subject.

Wundt (1862) wrote in his first psychological work, *Beiträge zur Theorie der Sinneswahrnehmung* [Contributions to the theory of sensory perception], that all psychology begins with introspection; however, he simultaneously laid the groundwork for an experimental psychology. The skepticism expressed in many of Wundt's statements contrasts with his emphasis on introspection. According to Titchener (1895b, p. 507), Wundt said that some individuals lacked the power of concentration necessary to become trustworthy subjects for introspection, just as some had no capacity for observation in such fields as astronomy. By no means do Wundt's subjects seem always to have been trusted or always to have shared an equal status with him and his assistants. Seen from another point of view, their extensive practice as described earlier would make the subjects direct forerunners of those student subjects who today in some places reportedly participate in 100 hours of experiments a year as a matter of course (Sasson & Nelson, 1969, p. 429). From this perspective we can even see Wundt's significance as far greater for experimental psychology than for the development of introspection. It is not at all far fetched to consider the physiological psychologist Wundt as an early *functionalist* in the materialistic-behavioristic tradition, as a link between the philosopher Lange and the learning theorist Skinner. From this standpoint it would be less appropriate to accept Titchener's description of Wundt as a *structuralist*.

Just as we have done with Wundt, it is equally possible to cite statements by James that support various alternative schools of thought and to make him responsible for varying developments, as Pongratz (1967) shows. To be sure, the emphasis on the American sort of pragmatism is greater in the case of James.

It is clear from the discussion of Wundt's work that the role of the subject as a mindless organism has no a priori correspondence to the experiment. This role can appear only when specific methods that call for it are developed on the basis of a particular theory. The most important prebehaviorist school in psychology, that of the Wundt Institute in Leipzig, was experimental. If Wundt himself had seen a conflict between introspection and the experiment, the principle of experimentation would have been more important to him in the long run than the principle of introspection.

## Differentiating the Concept "Subject Role": The Entrance of Watson

Not until after the turn of the century can a line be drawn between the different concepts of subjects' roles in psychological research. At that time, new introspectionist schools were founded in Germany, and experimental animal psychology, supported by the reflexology of Pavlov and Bechterev, gained importance in America. In Würzburg Wundt's followers Külpe and Marbe developed a way to approach the processes of thinking, problem solving, and opinion formation by fractionation of experience—a method called "systematic experimental introspection." As already indicated, Wundt took a very skeptical view of this (see also Flugel, 1933, p. 234). The subject's involvement reaches its peak in this method: It is identical with that of the researcher. The colleagues at the institute take turns with the tasks of problem solving and record keeping. There is no separation of the roles of experimenter and object of the experiment.

A movement in the opposite direction, as far as the role of the subject is concerned, may have begun with Watson's behaviorist manifesto (1913). Probably it began even earlier, with Thorndike's observation that captured cats free themselves faster the second time than on the first attempt, and his conclusion from this that one can understand learning as the association of behavior and its consequences (1898). But again, the roots of this movement had been present for a long time in the materialistic history of ideas. The generalization of the regularities found by Thorndike and Pavlov to human behavior and the excessive testing of these regularities with humans encouraged a concept of the human as an organism that merely reacts to stimuli. This development reached a climax as early as 1920 with Watson's conditioning experiments with children, including the well-known formation of a conditioned and generalizing reaction of fear of fur-bearing animals in the boy Albert (Watson & Rayner, 1920). Thorndike did not explicitly formulate the claim that his theory was also valid for human behavior until 1931, when the phase now called "classical behaviorism" was already coming to an end (Pongratz, 1967, pp. 328–333).

According to Pongratz (1967, p. 338), further developments in behavioristic psychology are characterized by a decrease in the importance of physiological reductionism (Skinner, 1938; Tolman, 1936/1950). But a new emphasis around 1930 by Hull and others (Hull, 1943) also affected the role of the subject. Hull emphasized the necessity of testing hypotheses experimentally and employing statistical procedures in order to show connections and ensure that the data do not result from chance. These procedures developed and spread rapidly. For Hull's purpose individual subjects, as in the manner of Watson, are not adequate. Instead, one must think in terms of groups of subjects and series of investigations.

The present role of the subject in experimental psychology goes back to this early period. It is the role of an organism that is by no means mindless, and thus rarely treated inhumanely, but is nonetheless interchangeable with other human organisms and needed in great quantities. The functions of this organism that are unnecessary in testing the hypotheses are ignored for the duration of the experiment.[5]

## CRITICAL ISSUES RELATED TO THE SUBJECT ROLE

Social psychology, which has never been characterized by an all-too-simple stimulus–response concept, has become a focus of methodological criticism in recent years. One reason for this may be that in social psychology it is obvious when "rigorous experimentation" (Argyris, 1968)—that is, the control of a few variables—is achieved at the cost of blatant disregard of the complexity of real environments. Kurt Lewin, who played a large part in determining the form of present-day social psychology, was undoubtedly interested in more than highly reduced behavioral data. The same is true of his followers, through whom the psychology of social behavior has gained much stature. For Lewin (1935) a prerequisite for meaningful interpretation of behavior is knowing how the person involved defines the situation. Rosenberg (1965, p. 28) points out that a similar attitude was found as early as 1918, in the work of Thomas and

---

5. Some German-speaking readers may miss in this historical sketch of the role of the subject the depiction of a second development, which had a quite different intellectual and political background—that is, the development from the Leipzig school's view of the experimental subject to the view of subjects held by holistic psychologists such as Sander. For the sake of simplicity, I am describing only the development leading to the subject role that is typical for current empirical psychology and has become problematic at the present.

Znaniecki. The experiments by Asch have already been cited as an example of how on the one hand an artificial social situation is created in order to observe a particular reaction in isolation and on the other hand theoretically productive interpretations of the results are hardly possible without a thorough interrogation of the subjects. Most experimental social psychologists have been quite aware of this dilemma. Nevertheless, the intrinsic value that many experimental paradigms seem to acquire for researchers through frequent use cannot be overlooked; it seems possible to forget the actual research problem in concentrating on the method.

The blatant quality of the discrepancy between experiment and reality may well be one failing that encourages criticism of experimental social psychology (see Chapter 2). A second factor is the often considerable social distance between experimenter and subject. This difference in power (Kelman, 1972) may be particularly noticeable to those concerned with the study of social behavior. In addition to these first two bases of criticism, one may also criticize social psychology for its recalcitrance in coming to sense that the experiment is very much a social situation. The subject reacts not only to stimuli provided by the experimenter but also to the experimenter as a social stimulus. Thus, the recorded data are potentially confounded, consisting of a combination of the reaction to the intentionally introduced independent variables and the separate reaction to the experimenter. In other words, all data from psychological experiments may be construed as data about social behavior in certain situations. Riecken (1958/1974) has pointed out that gathering data about behavior is a social process and can thus be studied as an interaction in a social situation. Within this context Riecken, Orne, and others set in motion a wave of reflection and experimental investigation of the experiment, which had long before become the most important source of knowledge for psychology.

### *Uncovering Demand Qualities*

In his investigations of hypnotic states, Orne tried to discover the amount of control hypnotists have over their subjects. The tasks he posed to hypnotized as well as nonhypnotized persons were assumed to be those that subjects would refuse to perform in a waking state (Orne, 1959). He found, however, that the degree of hypnotic state cannot be tested in such a way, because the normal experimental situation seems completely adequate for persuading subjects to engage in almost any form of extreme behavior. He could not identify any task that subjects would refuse to perform (Orne, 1962, p. 778). Orne noticed among his subjects the attempt to do everything right, to make themselves useful, and to help confirm the hypotheses of the experiment. He characterized this attitude with the term "good subject" and categorized as "problem-solving behavior" the subjects' attempts to discover the hypotheses of the investigation in order to confirm them. In order to discover what is expected, the subject presumably draws upon all available information: instructions and explanations of the experiment, rumors about the purpose of the research, the personality of the experimenter, the other subjects, the experimental setting, etc. Orne (1959) called such cues "demand characteristics of the experimental situation."

The existence and effect of such demand characteristics in research with human subjects was not a completely new discovery. Medical researchers had already described the placebo effect (Beecher, 1959; Shapiro, 1960), recognizing that a patient's reaction to a medicine is not necessarily attributable to the chemical effect of the preparation. In many cases a reaction occurs after the application of substances that have no chemical or physiological effect, showing that to some extent reactions can be attributed to the expectations of the patient. Orne (1969, p. 164) later pointed out the analogy between demand characteristics and placebo effect. The dependence of the effect of medication on the specific situation indicates the relationship of the demand characteristic concept, or Lewin's *Aufforderungscharakter* (Lewin, 1929), to the placebo problem. Orne (1969, p. 165) cites the work of Beecher (1959), who showed that on the battlefield saline solution by injection is 90% as effective as morphine in relieving the pain of acute injury. In civilian hospitals following operations, however, such placebos are only 70% as effective as morphine and even less effective with subsequent administrations. Thus, though the placebo effect can be very powerful, its effectiveness depends on the situation in which the placebo is administered.

### "Irrelevant" Subject Motives: A Challenge to the Experimenter

The problem of response sets and response bias has long been known in diagnostic psychology (Cronbach, 1946). McGuire (1969, p. 17) cites relevant literature going back as far as the early 1930s. Concern about response bias, conceived of as a personality characteristic, finally led to the construction of social desirability tests (Edwards, 1957).

Response bias is closely related to the problem-solving behavior described by Orne, especially in the social desirability variant that appears in questionnaires. However, Orne, who recognized the subjects' intention to make a good impression, saw this intention as subordinated to their need "to perform well."

Riecken (1958/1974), in contrast, suggests a whole series of motives: self-insight, curiosity, credit and advantages for one's studies, as well as interest in discovering the true purpose of the experiment and the need to make a good impression on the experimenter. He considers this last aim of favorable self-presentation to be the most important, the main goal to which the others are subordinate. From this standpoint, the need to be good subjects (i.e., to perform well) actually serves the purpose of self-presentation. According to Riecken (1958/1974, p. 112), subjects want to discover the hypotheses in order to present themselves in a favorable light. This insight clarifies the relationship between Orne's good-subject motivation and the social desirability aspect of response sets in diagnostic psychology. Problems formulated in early interview research (Hyman, 1954; Rice, 1929), particularly the often observed attempt to answer in a socially desirable manner in a clinical interview (Masling, 1960), can be seen as forerunners of this discovery.

The subject's desire to be favorably evaluated comes to the fore with Rosenberg's "evaluation apprehension" concept. Rosenberg (1965) offers an alternative to dissonance theory's explanation of the inverse relationship between the amount of pay and the extent of attitude change after behavior contrary to attitude. He suggests that the subject interprets the experiment as a test: "They probably want to see whether getting paid so much will affect my own attitude, whether it will influence me, whether I am the kind of person whose views can be changed by buying him off [p. 29]."

Orne's demand characteristics are thus used to facilitate a favorable self-presentation. The "good subjects" only seem to be so altruistic as to concern themselves with the confirmation of the research hypotheses. This effort actually serves the avoidance of fear of evaluation. Rosenberg suggests that subjects tend to approach psychological experiments expecting psychologists to evaluate their emotional adequacy or mental health. Whenever the early stages of an experiment confirm this suspicion for subjects, they may experience evaluation apprehension. Rosenberg (1965) defines this as "an active, anxiety-toned concern" that they receive a positive evaluation or at least "provide no grounds for a negative [evaluation] by the experimenter [p. 29]."

The Hawthorne effect of experimental psychology—that is, the alteration of behavior through measurement—had been generally recognized since Lazarsfeld (guinea pig effect, 1948) and Campbell (reactive measurement, 1957). With Orne and Rosenberg, this principle received its first alternative content interpretations. On the basis of their explicitly formulated concepts of subject motives, subjects could no longer be understood as passive providers of data. These two explanations were the good-subject motive, whereby a docile subject tries to ascertain the demand characteristics of the experimental situation in order to help the experimenter, and the concern with being evaluated positively in the evaluation-apprehending subject.

The work of Riecken, Orne, and Rosenberg quickly awakened interest in the new role of the subject, particularly among social psychologists. Experiments on the nature of experiments were carried out (surveys of these are given by Mertens, 1975, and Weber & Cook, 1972). Expanded concepts of the subject role were proposed (Masling, 1966). Subjects were questioned about their expectations (Shulman & Berman, 1975), and experimental investigations comparing theories of subject behavior were undertaken (Sigall, Aronson, & Van Hoose, 1970). Argyris (1968) pointed out that not only has our notion of the behavior of the subject in the experiment been deficient, but psychologists have also neglected to consider that subjects in their role as students owe loyalty to their fellow students. On the basis of informal norms, they are often obliged to pass on information from the experiment, thereby contributing to the spread of uncontrolled demand characteristics.

## *Voluntary Participation*

In addition to the search for general principles of behavior, a differential psychology of the subject has developed. Connections have been discovered between personality characteristics and the reaction to special measurement procedures (Cherry, Mitchell, & Nelson, 1973) or the readiness to follow instructions (Miller & Minton, 1969). The impact of undergoing an experiment on the subjects' trust (Fine & Lindskold, 1971) and on experimental results (Cook, Bean, Calder, Frey, Krovety, & Reisman, 1970; Turner & Simons, 1974) has been investigated. Rosenthal and Rosnow (1975) assembled an extensive collection of literature concerning the variable "voluntary participation." The differences between voluntary and involuntary subjects (listed by Rosenthal & Rosnow, p. 195) could be a good reason to decide, as researchers often do, not to recruit subjects through voluntary participation. According to Rosenthal and Rosnow's list, volunteers (as compared with involuntary subjects) are characterized by:

1. Higher education
2. Higher social status
3. Higher intelligence
4. Greater need for social recognition
5. More pronounced sociability
6. Greater need for new, exciting experiences
7. Less conventional attitudes
8. Lower authoritarianism
9. Religious affiliation: Jews are easier to obtain as volunteers than Protestants, Protestants easier than Catholics

One of the correlates of these differences is that volunteers would presumably be more ready to adapt to demand characteristics than involuntary subjects. This makes the representative nature of the results with volunteers particularly questionable. To be sure, if we conclude that it is better to avoid voluntary selection and recruit subjects almost by force, a special methodological and ethical dilemma appears. This will be discussed in Chapter 2 in the section on the voluntary nature of participation in an experiment.

The problem is magnified still further by the fact that there seem to be interactions among willingness to participate, sex, and type of task. For example:

1. In general, women are more willing than men to participate voluntarily. However, they are less likely to volunteer for physically and emotionally stressful tasks (e.g., electric shocks, high temperatures, sensory deprivation, interviews about sexual behavior).
2. Male volunteers are in general less conforming than involuntary male subjects. Such a distinction cannot be detected with women, on the other hand, or with men when the conformity has to do with typical clinical research projects (e.g., hypnosis, sleep, and therapy research).

A particularly extreme example of the difference between volunteers and involuntary subjects is revealed in a study by Horowitz (1969) on the connection between fear arousal and attitude change. He found a positive correlation for volunteers and a negative correlation for "captive subjects." That is, volunteers tended to change their opinions more in the case of fear-arousing communication, whereas captive subjects changed more when the communication was free of fear.

## *The Subject-Experimenter Interaction*

It is already clear from some of the investigations cited that the behavior of subjects in psychological experiments cannot be explained solely in terms of the qualities of the individual. To be sure, various errors that threaten internal or external validity can be described as special cases of the general principle that measurement changes the object being measured. Part of the error variance of experimental data can be explained somewhat satisfactorily by the variety of motives and modes of behavior of the subjects, even if the subjects are still conceived of as individuals whose interaction with the experimenter is restricted to the reception of instructions and the "emission" of modes of behavior relevant to the experiment.

But many other aspects of the subjects' behavior and the results of the investigations indicate a more far-reaching dynamic of the experimental situation: an interaction with the experimenter that takes quite definite forms and goes far beyond the exchange of relevant information. The connections between the subject's and experimenter's motives and the roles of subject and experimenter are spelled out quite clearly by Riecken. He suggests that subjects may suffer from "vague and far-ranging" anxieties about what experimenters will think of them. They may expect their performance to become part of their academic record, or they may believe that the experimenters' future treatment of them, should they meet again, will be based on their performance in the experiment. Though the psychologist may reassure subjects that there is no right or wrong answer, subjects are aware or suspect that the psychologist knows how their answers will be interpreted and that certain answers will present them in a way they consider favorable, others in an unfavorable manner (Riecken, 1958/1974, pp. 108–109). The "irrelevant" motives and thoughts of the subjects are thus not only determinants of their own behavior but in part also reactions to the experimenter. The experimenter's behavior and presumed intentions play a major role in determining the demand characteristics of the experimental situation. Logically enough, theories about the behavior of subjects have developed into theories about what takes place in a psychological experiment. This process has necessarily involved a closer examination of the other partner in this interaction, the experimenter.

## ON THE PSYCHOLOGY OF THE EXPERIMENTER

Orne, Riecken, and their successors reactivated forgotten knowledge about behavioral determinants and ways in which subjects react in psychological experiments; they expanded this knowledge with new insights and systematized it. As a result, it is now possible to understand the interaction in a psychological experiment. On the other hand, much less attention has been paid to the experimenter as an object of scientific knowledge. Although astronomers discovered almost 200 years ago that human beings are unable to observe and record data without error, we are even farther from developing a useful psychology of the researcher than from developing a useful psychology of the subject.

When classical behaviorism was in its prime, subjects were seen as organisms mediating between stimulus and response. At that time theories of human behavior applied to subjects, not to experimenters. As experimenters recorded the quasi-automaton-like responses of the subjects, they were quite aware of their own complexity. Experimenters today who have kept up with the literature on subjects in psychological experiments and do not completely deny the findings can no longer treat subjects with the same naiveté as 20 years ago, even if they are committed to behaviorist theories. For pragmatic reasons an experimenter may act as if subjects were stimulus–response organisms; however, it is obvious that the subjects have thoughts about the experiment that do not appear in the experimenter's plans.

Thus, the concept of the subject has changed much more than that of the experimenter. The discrepancy is not accidental but can easily be explained from the logic of the research process. It is not primarily the experimenter but rather the *subject* that is of interest in a psychological investigation—whether the focus is on the subject as a whole, considered from various points of view, or on the subject reduced to certain functions.

To what extent the experimenter attempts to see the subject as reduced to elements, or as a whole, and which aspects the experimenter focuses on depends on the current state of psychological theory. The increased emphasis on human behavior as social behavior—that is, the ground gained by social psychology—has certainly contributed to expanding the concept of the subject. A scientific revolution was not necessary in order for the subject to be seen as a social being or even as a complex being; this is an internal issue for the discipline of psychology. But the behavior of the experimenter must be seen from an interdisciplinary standpoint, from a metaperspective; a psychology of scientific work is required. More radical approaches than those now available must be undertaken in order to expand our view of the experimenter to that of a complex person like the subject, with diverse interests, needs, capacities, abilities, intentions, and plans.

Existing approaches to a conceptualization of the experimenter are based exclusively on the notion of the observation error. This in turn implies a concept, dating back to the days of the astronomers, of the experimenter as a producer of the research situation, motivated solely by a desire for truth. As recorder of the data at hand, the experimenter is replaceable and wherever possible is replaced by mechanical recording. In psychology and certain other social and biological sciences, the experimenter has the additional function of communicating information that is relevant for the behavior of the subjects (patients, people being observed, respondents, individuals). Although Rosenthal and others cited later in this section see these functions as sources of error, their work goes beyond the simple concept of observation error. It enables us to take into account the specific nature of psychological investigation and to develop, if not theories, at least approaches to analyzing the interaction within the experimental situation. But that does not yet constitute a psychology of the scientist.

## Early Observations on the Psychology of the Experimenter

It will be useful here to back up a bit and show how the role of the experimenter has been understood. Titchener (1901) noticed that experiments were often spoiled when experimenters suggested in some indirect way to their introspecting subjects that they should discover a certain fact at a particular time. Introspection became twice as hard, according to Titchener, when introspectors knew that the experimenter wanted them to produce some particular result. Studies from the most diverse areas make it clear that the danger that the experimenter's expectations will influence the experience and behavior of the subjects—whether these expectations are communicated intentionally or unintentionally, verbally or nonverbally—is not restricted to data obtained through introspection. Rice (1929) showed that the attitudes of the interviewer are partly responsible for the answers of the interviewee. Stanton and Baker (1942) added that distortions are produced not only by lay interviewers but also by experienced researchers. Woodworth (1931) pointed out that Pavlov's dogs also reacted to unconscious mimetic expressions and movements of the experimenter and not exclusively to the stimuli intended for conditioning. Kennedy (1938, 1939) interpreted the positive results of investigations of extrasensory perception as effects of unnoticed and partly unconscious communication between the experimenter and the subject.

Pfungst (1911) explained the astounding arithmetic and reading achievements of the horse Clever Hans in this same way. Pfungst experimented systematically with this "prodigy" trained by the mathematics teacher von Osten and controlled for the experimenter's knowledge of the answer. When he also controlled the medium of communication, it turned out that the optical signals were much more important than the acoustic signals. A minimal and unintended movement of the experimenter's head when the horse arrived at the right answer was the sign for the horse to stop tapping his forehoof. This, of course, had not been noticed by the experts on the investigating commission.

Numerous investigations of the influence of the tester on the subject's answers are reported from diagnostic psychology (Masling, 1960, 1966). Projective tests seem to be particularly susceptible to experimenter influence. Gibby and Stotsky (1953) showed that the answers to follow-up questions in connection with Rorschach tests were influenced by the psychologist much more than the spontaneous answers were. This tendency varied considerably among the clients. Finally, Escalona (1945) established in experimental testing of the food preferences of babies that preference for various juices covaried with the preferences of the persons caring for the babies.

## Rosenthal's Studies

The influence of the experimenter on subjects in psychological experiments became a research domain through the work of Rosenthal (summaries 1966 and 1969). He described two kinds of experimenter influence on the behavior of subjects: experimenter effects and experimenter-expectancy effects.

*Experimenter effects* refers to influences due to traits or modes of behavior of the experimenter that have nothing to do with interaction and do not affect subjects' responses (Rosenthal, 1969, p. 182). Among the experimenter effects are errors of observation, recording, and calculating, to which Rosenthal assigns relatively little importance. In addition, there are errors of interpretation, which also play a subordinate role in Rosenthal's discussion, although their importance is probably very great; the same is true of intentional effects (i.e., falsification of data in research reports). Various biosocial factors on which experimenter effects are based form another category. For example, male experimenters were more friendly to their subjects than were female experimenters (Rosenthal, 1967), and male subjects were more ready to expend effort with attractive female experimenters than with unattractive females (Sigall, Page, & Brown, 1971). Rosenthal (1969, pp. 188–189) also describes a psychosocial effect, which refers to the influence of the experimenter's psychological traits, such as emotional warmth, level of fear, or need for affiliation. Among the situational effects listed by Rosenthal are the amount of experience the experimenter has, the experimental setting, and the experimenter's reaction to the subjects' behavior. When the experimenter and subjects are better acquainted, the subjects' achievement scores and their openness increase (Jourard, 1968, cited by Rosenthal, 1969, p. 190). Finally, modeling effects, whereby subjects' behavior mimics the experimenter's style, can be found in all areas of psychological research. Klinger (1967) found more achievement-oriented reactions in subjects when the experimenter gave the impression of being motivated to achieve, even when verbal cues were eliminated.

*Experimenter-expectancy effects,* the second facet of experimenter influence, are considered more important by Rosenthal. "As with mystery writers, experimenters usually have a precise view of the outcome before things even begin," writes A. G. Miller (1976, p. 41). This results in the experiment's being carried out in a way that favors the verification of the hypotheses to be tested, despite acknowledgment of the principle of falsification. The communication of the experimenter's expectations to the subjects is less obvious than the external experimental conditions that favor the hypothesis, and thus the problem of expectations was disregarded for a long time.

Rosenthal (1969, pp. 223–228) cites 57 studies using a standard experiment to test the experimenter-expectancy effect. In all the studies, the experimenters as well as the subjects were students. Each of the (usually 10) experimenters was assigned a group of subjects. The experimenters were asked to show each subject individually a series of 10 photographs to be rated on a scale of $-10$ to $+10$, according to whether the person pictured seemed to be accustomed to success or failure. The photos were chosen by means of a pretest as being neutral on this dimension. The experimenters received uniform instructions for conducting the experiment and were warned not to deviate from the instructions. In addition, they were told that this experiment was testing their competence in reproducing reliable results. At that point two different expectancies were given to the experimenters. One group was told that their subjects would average $-5$, and the other group that their subjects would average $+5$. In most cases, the experimenters produced the results that they were told were expected of them. In a comparable study, the behavior of rats was to be recorded on various dimensions, and the preinformation was either that the animals were from an intelligent species or that they were from an unintelligent species (Rosenthal & Fode, 1963a). The results, just as with the human subjects, were congruent with the experimenters' expectations.

Variations of the basic pattern of these experiments led to positive results in a great number of investigations (Rosenthal, 1969; Timaeus, 1974). Verbal stimuli (Adair & Epstein, 1968), eye contact (Jones & Cooper, 1971), further nonverbal cues (Rosenthal & Fode, 1963b), as well as other modes of experimenter behavior (Masling, 1966) mediated the transmission of hypotheses. Friedman (1967) found that the subjects' ratings depended on the length of the procedure, the length of the instructions, the time given to rating, and the frequency of eye contact.

### Friedman's Proposals

Friedman (1967, pp. 170–179) found the importance of experimenter effects to be so great that he proposed regular use of the following control measures:

1. Like subjects, data gatherers—whether experimenters or diagnosticians—should be chosen from a random sample.
2. Researchers should film random samples of their data-gathering situations.
3. Post hoc control methods (such as analysis of covariance or partial correlation) should be used regularly to eliminate the experimenter's share in the results.

If one agrees with Friedman that because of the presence of an experimenter experiments are basically investigations of social behavior, then even the most random choice of experimenters will not prevent general psychological experimenter effects. Only the last of the three control measures could serve to correct experimental results. It might even be possible to develop a system of corrective measures if the parameters that distinguish certain behaviors during observation from the same behaviors without observation are known. The other two control measures would only be suitable for controlling differential experimenter effects, if one accepts Friedman's view. To be sure, because of economic considerations all three measures seem better suited for training future researchers than for application to current research practices. The need for representativeness in experimenters is a general need, after all, not a problem for just one particular institution. Moreover, we do not know nearly enough about which context variables are really relevant for responses in an experiment or which experimenter traits and behaviors interact with which other variables with regard to which subjects. As long as nothing more specific is known and no more practical control measures have been found, critical replication of interesting investigations seems to offer a better and more economical way of checking for representativeness.

### Rosenthal's Research under Fire

Two critics of the research on expectancy effects, Barber and Silver (1968), consider some of the artifacts obtained by Rosenthal and his followers also to be artifacts. Their secondary analysis of the data produced positive results in far fewer cases than indicated by the original authors. Independent of the strength of Rosenthal's findings, Barber and Silver found that some of the numerous causes of experimenter effects have not been taken seriously enough or sufficiently into account. Included among such causes are making errors in the evaluation, recording, and reporting of the data, reinforcing subjects verbally for "correct" answers, and transmitting expectations in a nonverbal manner, not only unintentionally, but also deliberately.

The suggestions of Barber and Silver were rejected by Rosenthal (1969, pp. 245–249). Nonetheless, those suggestions could well serve as an approach to a psychological view of scientific work that was not present in previous research on experimenters. A brief discussion of an early, classic study will be useful in showing the feasibility of their suggestions.

This study, by Hartshorne and May (1928), investigated dishonest behavior among school children. The subjects were left alone with a difficult assignment and the possibility of cheating, after having been promised relatively high rewards for completing the assignment successfully. Arellano-Galdames (1972) cites this study as an example of an ethically questionable investigation. The subjects were deceived and secretly observed, dishonest behavior was provoked and perhaps even reinforced, and in addition, the subjects might have felt humiliated after they were debriefed. Thus, this study may indeed be considered one of those investigations that can come into conflict with contemporary ethical standards.

However, Barber and Silver's findings would suggest that an even more relevant question here is whether the Hartshorne and May study might not constitute an excellent simulation of the working conditions of scientists. Rosenthal's experimenters, who were actually subjects, behaved dishonestly (some unintentionally falsifying, some deliberately) because of material and immaterial incentives, and they did this in their role as scientists. Is it not true that confirmation of the hypotheses that suit the person in charge (or the hypotheses that seem to suit the spirit of the times) is also a goal for "real" scientists? One would think so, considering the nature of rewards for successful work, the definition of successful work, the corresponding selection for publication by scientific journals, the relationship between publication and chances for employment, and the frequent formulation of post hoc hypotheses. Scientists can be seen as quasi-subjects in an experiment about (dis)honest behavior. They participate in social contracts with the persons in charge: their employers, their colleagues, the institutions where they work, and society. They are obliged to produce "positive" results for them. Many of the expectations of the scientific community are implicit, but some problems are obvious and constitute a difficult test of scientific honesty: For example, the fact that the selection of articles for publication in journals and the acceptance by college professors of studies qualifying students for higher degrees can depend on the confirmation of the hypotheses (Timaeus, 1974, p. 30).

## Further Investigations into the Motives of the Scientist

In this sense, almost against Rosenthal's will, the results of his experiments constitute a point of departure for a theory of the motivations behind scientific behavior. This is especially true of his investigations in which experimenters were rewarded for particular results. The possibility of causing hypotheses to be confirmed through unintentional effects seems especially great in the case of soft data and such methods of observation as are often used in psychology. And of course the presence of such a possibility increases the temptation to falsify.

One prerequisite for genuinely productive theories of human interaction in the research situation would be a revision of the belief, openly espoused by no one but protected by the consensus of all, that the search for truth is the sole motive of the scientist. The role of experimenters in research on humans cannot be understood until we know their motives, interests, expectations, and ideologies as well as those of the subjects. We need to know the plans and structures governing the behavior of *both* participants and the significance of their behavior in the experiment for their general spheres of action (cf. Kaminski, 1974). Probably there is no single way in which experimenters view subjects. Rather, the ways in which experimenters see and treat subjects, as well as the choice of research methods, methods of evaluation, etc., are dependent on such factors as the rewards the experimenters expect in the form of publication possibilities and professional recognition. These rewards are seen in a certain sense as dependent on the investigation as a whole and in particular on the behavior of the subjects. Thus a very differentiated psychology of the scientist or of scientific work is indispensable, though it needs to be different only in certain crucial parts from the psychology of human work in general.

In order to find out which ethical norms scientists feel obligated to acknowledge, we would have to renounce at least in part the assumption that the pursuit of truth is the sole motivation of scientific behavior. This assumption corresponds closely to what Arellano-Galdames has described as "ethical connaturalism": the thesis that scientists are virtuous because of their calling.

Ethical values appear as a more or less innate accompaniment or unintended product of the qualifications for being a scientist, based perhaps on a preestablished harmony among ideals or at least on a miraculous side effect of good mechanisms of selection. The assumption is that scientists will use good sense even in the absence of guiding ethical theories or codes for behavior (Arellano-Galdames, 1972).

## THE PSYCHOLOGICAL EXPERIMENT AS AN INTERACTION SPHERE

Studies on the experimenter effect and the experimenter-expectancy effect, along with comparable information from pharmacology, diagnostic psychology, interview research, etc., lead to a conclusion that is important for our concerns: The experimenter exercises a remarkable amount of influence on the subject. A basic characteristic of the interaction between experimenter and subject is the experimenter's control over the subject's behavior. This essentially one-sided influence is the central concern in most theoretical attempts to expand a one-sided concept of the subject to a situational or role-related concept.

All concepts of the role of the subject proceed from the assumption that this role is defined in relation to the experimenter. Thus, we turn again to the power differential between experimenter and subject, which Kelman (1972) pointed out with particular forcefulness. This status difference, inherent in the psychological experiment, was already plain in the work of Hofstätter. Hofstätter (1957, p. 44) suggested that experimenters may not be aware of their tendency to see themselves as organizers and to see subjects, in contrast, not as active individuals but as anonymous and passive. Subjects, however, are usually aware that their relationship with the experimenter is dual: that of subjects voluntarily submitting to experimenters, often in order to please them, and that of one human being to another. In this relationship the submission and compliance of one of the interaction partners in contrast to the other actually constitutes a definition of the situation.

The structural peculiarities of the experimental situation crystallize into various sorts of subject behavior, to the extent that it can be thought of as role-related behavior at all. Of course, "the experimental situation" exists only as an ideal in any case. Among the conditions determining subject behavior are the person, the experimental task, the specific setting, the extent to which the hypotheses can be recognized, the congruity of the hypotheses with the subject's own motives, the particular experimenter, and the more general plans, expectations, and fears of the subject. Certain kinds of reactions can result from one or the other motive, but the absence of such reactions does not necessarily imply the absence of the motive that is thought to correspond to the reactions. It can also be an expression of the complexity of the situation.

## The Roles of Subjects

At this point, we shall delve more carefully into the details of the various kinds of subject roles, with the purpose of bringing to light the alternative motivations existing in research settings. The categories of roles we will examine come from Weber and Cook (1972) and consist of "good subject," "apprehensive subject," "faithful subject," and "negativistic subject."

### THE GOOD SUBJECT

The first two roles correspond to subject motives that have already been described. Orne (1959, 1962) pointed out that subjects try to discover the real purpose of the experiment and to behave in accord with this perceived purpose, thereby tending to confirm the hypothesis. This gives the subjects' behavior a problem-solving character. For such problem solving, the subject uses all the demand characteristics of the experimental situation. The attention of the subject is centered on the experimenter, the most important source of demand characteristics. Subjects understand their role as that of the experimenter's assistant. They are cooperative and patient; full of trust in the experimenter, they carry out even the most boring, protracted, dangerous, or immoral tasks. The subjects want to be important, to contribute to the investigation. Thus, at the same time as they try to discover the hypotheses and to comply with the experimenter's wishes, subjects try to present themselves as naive because they fear that their data will not otherwise be included in the results. That attempt to seem naive makes it hard for the experimenter to detect a lack of naiveté during the postexperimental interview, and not detecting it may then benefit the experimenter in other ways.

### THE APPREHENSIVE SUBJECT

Riecken (1958/1974) and Rosenberg (1965, 1969) see the subject as wanting to make a good impression on the experimenter and anxiously trying to avoid negative evaluation. (Rosenberg calls this "evaluation apprehension.") While Rosenberg pays particular attention to the need to appear in a good light, Riecken's concept combines this motive with Orne's description of the experimental process. The subject is seen as a status subordinate who listens while the experimenter talks, in order to discover the experimenter's expectations. Experimenters assume that subjects will listen, understand, and follow their instructions (Riecken, 1958/1974, pp. 110–111). Thus, Riecken's theory is an approach to a genuine interaction concept, which is not the case with all role theories. In addition, the aspect of power is addressed very clearly. Experimenters have considerable power, stemming from two sources: their insight into the subjects (as psychologists) and their authority to evaluate students (as professors) (Riecken, 1958/1974, p. 107). Thus, the attempt of the subjects to do their best is also based on avoidance of punishment by someone higher in status on whom they are dependent. Rosenberg's description of the subject's behavior is oriented more toward the usual public image of the clinical psychologist or diagnostician (A. G. Miller, 1976, p. 31). Subjects feel that they are being judged and evaluated, particularly with regard to their mental health and maturity, and want to present themselves in a good light. The psychological research situation appears to them to be a diagnostic situation even when they are assured of the opposite. Subjects differ in the extent of their evaluation apprehension (a personality variable, like social desirability). Thus, when the hypothesis tends in the direction of the behavior for which subjects might expect positive evaluation, some subjects are more likely than others to contribute to a false confirmation of the hypothesis.

## THE FAITHFUL SUBJECT

Investigations by Fillenbaum (1966) and Fillenbaum and Frey (1970) led to the concept of the faithful subject. After the subjects had participated in an initial experiment, one group was debriefed and one was not. In a subsequent experiment it was expected that the subjects' knowledge of the deceptive elements of the first task would be reflected in the results. In fact, the difference between the two groups was negligible. Even when the connection between the two experiments was plainly pointed out, Fillenbaum found no difference with most subjects. This corresponds to McGuire's summary of studies on the forewarning of subjects (1969). The effects are usually not great, do not appear with all subjects, and generally consist only of main effects (which are "annoying rather than misleading [p. 35]"), not of interaction effects with the independent variables.

Fillenbaum interprets his results to mean that subjects allow themselves to be captivated by the task, pay attention seriously and conscientiously, and show trusting eagerness to do what the experimenter suggests. Like A. G. Miller (1976), we can see this as an extension of Orne's thesis of the good subject who is helpful and attempts to do everything right, to comply with the experimenter's wishes, and to contribute the most useful data possible.[6] The role-related behavior of faithful subjects, like that of good subjects and apprehensive subjects, can be characterized by subordination to the experimenter. The subjects are passive and helpful, allow themselves to be influenced, and accept their roles as objects of the exercise of power by their role partner.

A number of investigations have examined competing assumptions about the motives underlying subjects' submission to subtle social pressures within the experiment. Rosenberg (1969) gave two groups of subjects contradictory information as to which mode of reacting was characteristic of emotional stability. The persons in both groups tended to react in the way that would produce "evidence" that they were stable by the definition provided. Minor (1970)

---

6. Miller mentioned this extension of Orne's thesis in the manuscript version of his article, but not in the published version.

produced similar results: An experimenter-expectancy effect occurred only when evaluation apprehension was simultaneously induced. Sigall *et al.* (1970) made it possible for one group of subjects to confirm the experimenter's hypotheses and simultaneously make a good impression. For the second group, these two motives for behaving were placed into conflict—that is, the subjects were able to confirm the hypothesis only if they chose to forgo a positive evaluation. Given this dilemma, subjects acted to their own advantage and behaved in a way that contradicted the apparent hypothesis. They cooperated only when it also benefited their self-image. Rosnow, Goodstadt, Suls, and Gitter (1973) confirmed these results, while also showing that it made no difference whether or not subjects were volunteers.

## THE NEGATIVISTIC SUBJECT

The issue of volunteering played a definite role among the subjects of Cox and Siprelle (1971), whose results can be interpreted in accordance with the concept of the negativistic subject (A. G. Miller, 1976). Subjects whose participation was coerced behaved contrary to the hypothesis. The discovery of the role of the negativistic subject is usually attributed to Masling (1966). However, Masling mentions such a mode of reacting only incidentally, as one of several different modes, distilled from his own and from others' observations of individual cases. Argyris's suggestion (1968) that subjects begin to seek adaptive strategies as their experience increases could better be called a theory of the rebellious subject. A similar tendency can be observed with workers and lower-paid white-collar employees in large firms. Experimenters behave like managers: Concerned with efficiency, they pursue their research rigorously. Among the subjects, the behaviors found are those known in organizational psychology as a mixture of resignation and resistance:

1. Physical withdrawal (absenteeism and turnover)
2. Psychological withdrawal (apparently cooperation, but actually apathy or the pursuit of their own, different goals)
3. Overt hostility (among volunteers)
4. Covert hostility (among coerced subjects)
5. Emphasis upon monetary rewards
6. Unionization of subjects

These modes of reaction—the defense of the powerless—may be characteristic for excessively experienced subjects and especially for disillusioned subjects confronting experimenters who are perceived as inconsiderate, thoughtless, and self-seeking. But they are quite certainly not the modes of reaction of all subjects, nor are they chosen by most subjects. Thus, this analysis is better characterized as a warning of possible developments to come than as a description of reality.

Brehm's reactance theory (1966) has also been used to explain uncooperative or sabotaging behavior of subjects (Grabitz-Gniech, 1972). The feeling of being under pressure, dependent, and unfree to make decisions leads the subject to do the opposite of what is apparently desired—that is, the subject sabotages the experimenter's hypothesis.

With regard to the artifact, both apologists (Weber & Cook, 1972) and skeptics (Kruglanski, 1975) agree that reactance is rarely a source of artifacts and almost never seen in an experimental setting unless it is confounded with the self-evaluation problem. Thus, the same behavior is explainable by evaluation apprehension as well. The strongest evidence for behavior that can be interpreted as negativistic comes from experiments in conformity and conditioning, where behavior contrary to the hypothesis corresponds to a higher social value (not to conform—that is, to be intelligent enough to recognize reinforcement schedules). If negativistic behavior is to be expected at all, it should be expected in the case of coerced participation.

*OTHER ROLES*

In addition to the four roles of "good subject," "apprehensive subject," "faithful subject," and "negativistic subject," still other roles are defined in the literature (cf. Mertens, 1975). These concepts, however, probably have even less claim to validity than the roles described here, and the conceptual distinctions among them are also difficult. More generally, the behaviors of subjects in different experimental settings can probably be analyzed more easily if we think of these actions as based on numerous motives, accompanied and guided by individual differences in cognitive structures, and oriented toward the meaning of specific actions.[7] Thus, for example, subjects will react in one way when the

---

[7] Symbolic interactionism offers a view of the experimental situation that reflects the complexity of human behavior better than isolated role concepts do. This viewpoint, more of an inventory of ideas than a complete theory, can be traced back to Cooley (1902/1967), G. H. Mead (1934), and others. In examining the suitability of symbolic interactionism for analyzing the experimental situation, Mertens (1975) chooses to focus on the interpretive paradigm for describing social behavior. Four important concepts in the phenomenology of symbolic interaction are: empathy with the expectations of the other person, interpretive development of the role, tolerance of discrepancies between expectations and needs, and presentation of self through the balancing of personal and social identity [p. 160]. One of the advantages of this point of view is that it acknowledges the complexity of social behavior. Symbolic interactionism reminds us that social behavior depends less on the objective nature of the stimuli than on the subjective interpretation of the entire situation by the individual. This interpretation is itself dependent on the experiences, attitudes, traits, needs, etc., of the individual. Mertens shows that symbolic interactionism can increase our understanding of various types of subjects, especially those with evaluation apprehension.

However, pointing out that the subject–experimenter interaction is asymmetric, Mertens goes on to claim that, if we apply Lewin's criterion of type of action, we can make relevant statements only about those everyday interactions that are also asymmetric (p. 164). This is the same mistake

good impression that they can supposedly make is only relevant for their own self-image at the moment and in another way when the good impression is experienced as connected with the experimenter's image of them. This is especially true if the subjects are college students and imagine that they might later have an opportunity to take a class from or even be employed as assistants to the experimenter. It makes a difference whether the subjects work conscientiously because they respect the experimenter and do not want to cause problems or because they are interested in psychology as a science and as a possible later career. Finally, it must be added that it is not always so easy to recognize the actual hypotheses, in view of the complexity of most contemporary investigations; more often it happens that hypotheses are invented by the subjects.

## The Self-Concept Approach

If we intend to continue the search for a theoretical principle that integrates the various subject roles, in spite of all the difficulties already mentioned, we should consider one approach that seems even more suitable than the evaluation apprehension concept (Weber & Cook, 1972). This is the self-image approach: *Subjects act according to their self-concept.* This principle, which includes evaluation apprehension, implies a number of roles: trying to help the experimenter (the good subject), trying to make a good impression on the experimenter (the apprehensive subject), behaving honestly in spite of being deceived (the faithful subject), or (supposedly) resisting the (supposed) demand characteristics (the negativistic subject). The specific role depends on the situation, person, experimenter behavior, task, threshold for satiation, degree

---

that is made when the experimental interaction is seen from the perspective of communication theory (see Footnote 9). The difference between the experimenter–subject relationship as such and everyday interactions has no structural significance in Lewin's sense. It is exclusively the influence of this relationship on the behavior to be observed that has structural significance. Only when the experimenter–subject relationship interacts with the modes of behavior that are recorded as dependent variables in a way that is impossible to correct for later does the special nature of the relationship endanger the external validity of an investigation. But if the domain from which generalization is to occur is individual behavior in a strict sense, even the socially most natural relationship between experimenter and subject will invalidate the results.

Symbolic interactionism reminds us that the relationship between experimenter and subject is connected not only with the internal but also with the external validity of the experimental data. This will be considered later in connection with some important experiments (Milgram's obedience study among others).

Even if the viewpoint of symbolic interactionism is correct, it may not be necessary to go as far as Gould and Shotter (1977), who think that symbolic interactionism excludes as a possibility the empirical, nomothetic investigation of behavior in reduced complexity. It may be sufficient to develop more ambitious experimental realizations and, above all, more ambitious interpretations.

of trust–suspicion, values, experiences, seriousness and credibility of the experimenter, etc.

Moreover, a role can change during an experiment. For example, in Masling's conditioning experiment (1966), the learning curve reverses after a sufficient number of trials, suggesting that subjects are "good" or "faithful" until the threshold of satiation is reached. Perhaps they notice early on that the experimenter is always saying "hm, hm" and now decide the experimenter might think they are stupid for not noticing that. Or they decide that being conditioned and manipulated cannot be reconciled with their ideal of a self-directed, critical human being. By suddenly changing their behavior, becoming "negativistic," they could still be trying to make a good impression. They might expect that the experimenter is trying to find out how soon they will see through attempts to influence them. Or subjects might be trying through negativism to behave in a way that suits their self-image.

Self-image seems to be a more generally applicable principle than evaluation apprehension. Some persons interpret their orientations toward the demands of others as clever hypocrisy practiced in order to obtain advantages unrecognized by the others; other persons recognize their own need for positive evaluation by others, disapprove of it, and thereupon act contrary to expectations for the sake of positive self-evaluation. The social desirability behavior in the first example can at least be combined with the self-concept; it raises the feeling of self-worth rather than lowering it. In the second example, the rejection of such behavior takes place quite explicitly for the sake of improving self-evaluation.[8]

## *Foregoing Control*

The relation between the roles of subject and experimenter seems to be characterized most clearly by the power differential between the two, no matter whether the experimenter's power is defined as sheer position power or through evaluation, reward, and punishment. The power differential can be recognized behind all role concepts. It becomes especially obvious in those investigations where the research problem is concerned directly with what subjects will do or allow to be done to them when the experimenter's authority demands it. To name just a few examples: Subjects have been willing to add numbers for 5

---

8. There is something to be said for considering the self-concept to be a central point of orientation when we speak of conscious human action. This idea has been underscored in research stemming from a theory of self-awareness (Duval & Wicklund, 1972; Wicklund, 1975, 1979a, 1979b), in which it has been shown repeatedly that aspects of the self-concept determine behavior to a large extent, but only when the person is made to be self-aware. For example, by placing subjects before a mirror, it has been possible to bring subjects' self-concepts about aggression, sexuality, and creativity to guide behavior (Carver, 1975; Gibbons, 1978; Hormuth, in press).

hours, continually destroying the paper they were writing on (Orne, 1962); to touch poisonous snakes and throw what they thought was acid in people's faces (Orne & Evans, 1965); to eat crackers that were ostensibly poisoned (Kudirka, 1965); to injure other subjects seriously by administering electric shocks (Milgram, 1963); and to eat caterpillars (Foxman & Radtke, 1970) and grasshoppers (E. E. Smith, 1961).

Thus, the experimenter's power is accepted and finds its counterpart in the subject's trust, which goes so far that subjects will undergo risks that they cannot control. Subjects turn themselves over to the experimenter, transferring to the experimenter responsibility for their fate within the limits of this exceptional situation, the experiment. The situation as such, its goals, and the interests and intentions of the experimenter are not transparent for the subjects, and it is not clear to what extent their guesses are correct. In the absence of personal goals for action that would be adequate for the situation and would correspond to their actions in everyday life, subjects fall back on basic motives of social behavior with regard to those who are more powerful. That is, they try "to do a good job" and "to make a good impression," sometimes in the service of a more general effort to sustain a positive self-image. This effort gives their participation in the experiment a gamelike quality. They attempt to understand the experiment by means of metacommunication with the experimenter, through other demand characteristics, or in terms of earlier experiences, so that their behavior in the experiment will have meaning for them. But they behave according to instructions even when their attempts to understand the experiment fail. Their role as subjects is characterized by the renunciation of self-direction. They let things happen to them; they behave as they are told in a situation that they perceive as irreal, as a game, or as a simulation of another, real situation with which they are not familiar. The attempt in a later section of this chapter to conceptualize the experiment with human subjects as a social contract is based on these considerations and their implications. We proceed from the assumption that psychology and other sciences involved in research on human beings will continue to experiment. More precisely, we assume (*a*) that the experiment will not be completely replaced by other research methods; (*b*) that the power structure of the experimental situation will not basically change; and (*c*) that the results of psychological experiments will not need any basically new interpretation as a result of this emphasis on their nature as social situations.

## Models of Communicative Influence

The preceding assumptions seem to be shared by most authors who have concerned themselves with the social psychology of the experiment. Their suggestions consist for the most part of intensified controls on motives and behaviors that are conceptualized as error variables (e.g., Campbell, 1969; Orne, 1969; Rosenthal & Rosnow, 1975). Functionalistic theoretical approaches (Mertens, 1975, based on Holzkamp, 1972) such as that of Rosnow and Aiken (1973) show a corresponding theoretical understanding of the experimental situation. Utilizing McGuire's model of communicative influence (1968), Rosnow and Aiken describe the experimental situation as an influence situation leading to either compliance, noncompliance, or countercompliance. The three variables receptivity, motivation, and capability intervene between the demand characteristics as stimulus and the reaction of the subject. The subjects initially perceive the demand characteristics of the situation appropriately or inappropriately. They are motivated to respond to these characteristics in a compliant, noncompliant, or countercompliant fashion. And finally, they may or may not be able to behave openly in a way that corresponds to their motives.

From the point of view of this model, a particular mode of behavior, such as a reaction against the demand characteristics, need not be attributed to a particular motive or understanding of the role (e.g., negativistic subject). Rather, a mode of behavior is interpreted differently according to the exact constellation of the three components receptivity, motivation, and capability. Other role concepts, such as evaluation apprehension, are also said to be reinterpretable in this fashion. The subject's desire to make a good impression may increase motivation to comply if task- and ego-orienting cues are congruent and receptivity remains constant. If, on the other hand, these cues are incongruent, while receptivity remains constant, then compliance is incongruent with projecting a favorable image and evaluation apprehension may decrease motivation to comply (Rosenthal & Rosnow, 1975, p. 181). To be sure, Rosenthal and Rosnow seem to be reintroducing into the model as an additional assumption a factor that was supposed to be given an alternative interpretation with the help of the model. In the effort to reinterpret evaluation apprehension, they postulate just this factor as a constant, set in a somewhat more complex network of variables. Nonetheless, such a model could contribute to a more differentiated understanding of the behavior of subjects, and it could also serve to eliminate distorting demand characteristics.

At present only the first of the three components of the model, receptivity, seems to offer effective possibilities for the elimination of distortion (Rosnow & Davis, 1977). For example, nonreactive research methods can be employed (Webb, Campbell, Schwartz, & Sechrest, 1966). The experimenter can be eliminated as the principal source of these demand characteristics through a blind design (Aronson & Carlsmith, 1968). Or subjects can be given explanations of the experimental procedures that are false but credible and presumably do not interfere with the internal validity of the experiment. It is with such technical control measures that a potential conflict between methodological and ethical claims arises.[9]

## Participatory Research

Kelman's critique of manipulation and deception in psychological experiments (1965, 1967a, 1968) has played an influential role in the discussion of ethical problems. Kelman advocates an approach with the goal of abolishing the deficit of power of subjects in research in the social sciences (1972). His view of the experimental situation resembles the one presented here: Experimenters have the power to define and form the situation according to their interests and do so at the cost of the subjects' behavioral freedom. The voluntary nature of the subjects' participation is often very questionable. Kelman calls for the development of emancipatory research methods, suggesting that participatory research would tend to reduce the naiveté of potential subjects and increase their sophistication (1972, p. 1003). In interviews, for example, the respondents should be treated as elite members of their group, who have something

---

9. Mertens (1975) points out that communication theory (cf. Watzlawick, Beavin, & Jackson, 1969) helps explain one kind of hindrance to dominance-free interaction in the experiment. From the perspective of communication theory, communication between experimenter and subject is inherently faulty, for two reasons. First, subjects may suspect that the experimenter's explanation of the purpose of the experiment involves deception. And second, there can be no communication about the relationship: Explicit discussion of the nature of the subject–experimenter relationship is suppressed (Mertens, 1975, p. 156).

Mertens also suggests that in order to create sufficient structural similarity between the experimental situation and everyday situations—particularly in social psychology—one must consider the basic nature of communication and interaction among humans (p. 153). This suggestion is based, however, on a confusion of the interaction that constitutes the object of research in social psychology with the interaction in which the subject and the experimenter find themselves. The experimenter observes the interaction of the subject with other (perhaps even fictive) persons. It is this interaction that should show structural similarity to interactions in the extraexperimental reality about which statements are to be made. Whether the interaction with the experimenter resembles any other interactions is methodologically irrelevant to the investigator as long as it does not change the behavior being investigated in an unreconstructable manner. Indeed, the interaction with the experimenter is usually not intended to be an interaction, but rather it constitutes a more or less necessary condition for carrying out the research.

Thus, Mertens' suggestion involves the contamination of a methodological demand with a moral demand. The methodological demand concerns the representative nature or external validity of the experimental event to be investigated; the moral demand concerns the relationship between experimenter and subject as an interaction sui generis. There is a contradiction between the methodological necessities of the experiment and the moral claim of a right to dominance-free communication. If this right is held to be unconditional and without exception, alternative research methods must be chosen. On the other hand, we can give the method priority and allow certain peculiarities of the interaction to exist for the sake of research. If we do this, we are confronted with the fact that the experimental situation is an exceptional situation as far as communication about the nature of the interaction is concerned. As such, it requires special rules of interaction.

important to communicate. Margaret Mead (1969) made this a basic principle of anthropology. Experiments connected with deception should be replaced by role playing with fully informed participants wherever possible. (The validity of this method is discussed in Chapter 3.)

Kelman also proposes that subjects should be included in the research process and in the formulation of research goals. To be sure, he recognizes the difficulties and limits of this approach, unlike the radical representatives of action research (e.g., Klüver & Krüger, 1972). He calls for institutionalized control measures, in order to get a grip on the remaining power advantage of the experimenter. These measures would be designed to ensure that power is used legitimately and prevent its misuse with regard to the subjects, who are generally of lower social status than the researcher. For Kelman, the central norm of the relationship between experimenter and subject is informed consent. The problems of risk of harm to the subject and deception are subordinated to this principle. That is, measures that are otherwise ethically problematic seem acceptable to him if the subjects are fully informed about the nature and degree of risk, or about the presence of false information, and freely consent to participate in the experiment.

## Conclusions

No single one of these theoretical approaches impresses us as being a satisfactory explanation of what goes on in an experiment, but they all contribute to our understanding of the experiment as a social interaction. Friedman (1967) finds it so helpful to view the experiment as a social interaction that in summary of his own and other investigations he claims that all psychology is basically social psychology. He states that social psychologists are actually metascientists, on whose insights and on whose approval the competence of colleagues in other areas of psychology depends. This is comparable to the significance of epistemology for philosophy. Friedman writes that social psychologists are "no mere gadgeteers applying out there in the real world the empirical generalizations developed in the antiseptic environment of the laboratory by an 'individual' psychology [p. 169]." Rather, the insights of social psychologists can help us understand the social situation in which data for individual psychology are gathered, and they can help us generalize from these data. Moreover, Friedman suggests, advances in social psychology will help us develop an adequate understanding of such areas as learning, memory, and perception, by explaining the social context in which they develop.

Friedman may be exaggerating the significance of social psychology and the possibilities of its general application. He may also be overly optimistic about the possibility of combining our present knowledge of social psychology, or even that which will be attained in the foreseeable future, with our other knowledge of human functioning. Yet even if we consider Friedman's statement too extreme, we cannot overlook the phenomenon of the interaction of experimenter and subject. The concepts of experimenter-artifact and subject-artifact have turned out to be too simple and too one sided; their significance can be questioned (Barber & Silver, 1968; Kruglanski, 1975). But in the course of our attempt to see the experiment as a whole, we inevitably observe that it involves complex human interaction. The results of this interaction can be seen in several ways: as additional error variance, as behavior that was supposed to be individual and has turned out to be socially influenced, or as a basically appropriate kind of communication and distribution of roles for human social behavior.

A number of conclusions can now be drawn. We can decide to experiment more rigorously—for example, to create still more effective deceptive measures or even to make the experimental situation as such unrecognizable for the subjects. Or we can turn to other research methods, for example, to role playing or to field studies, which will be examined more closely in Chapter 3.

Many psychologists seem to have decided that the experiment is still the most important method of psychological research. Those who have prefer the most strictly controlled laboratory experiment over attempts to realize experimental and quasi-experimental research designs in undiminished reality (Riecken & Boruch, 1974). Insight into the social psychology of the experiment is the beginning of a more critical examination of empirical research rather than a closed chapter. The beginnings of this insight have not yet disqualified the experiment as such; attempts at reorientation have not yet led to any equivalent substitute. The chosen approach seems more likely to be a methodologically pluralistic research program than a rejection of the research techniques that have become traditional. Instead of attempting to discover and apply radical new techniques, we are likely to focus on better control and on replications with varied methods. We can expect simultaneous, parallel efforts to develop research procedures that combine the advantages of the experiment, especially its internal validity, with the merits of externally valid methods. Liberalized positions on the theory of science, which are concerned with the interconnection of various sources of knowledge (e.g., Bunge, 1967), may prove to be helpful in this regard.

Along with Boring (1969) or Buss (1975), we may see this concern with the artifacts of scientific research as a higher state in the evolution of a science. Or, more cynically, we may join McGuire (1969) in seeing this concern as a part of the dynamics of the research process, in which something that was originally a source of interference finally becomes an end in itself. Whichever attitude we adopt, it is plain that the attention of researchers in the behavioral sciences needs to be tuned in to one more wavelength from among the sources of interference and to avoid at least the clumsiest misinterpretations of this problem.

## THE POWER DIFFERENTIAL

Closer examination has shown that the experiment is not a normal social situation. Compared with the social relationships that characterize commonplace human interaction, the interchange between experimenter and subject is unique in some ways. If we were to overlook these unique characteristics and see the experiment as a perfectly ordinary interaction, we could easily conclude that the researcher's responsibility for subjects is no different from the responsibility we all have for everyday interactions. At most there might be a difference that could be offset by the payment of a small honorarium, by educational benefits expected for the subjects, by the fact that participation helps fulfill requirements for some psychology courses, or merely by the voluntary nature of participation in the experiment.

But on the contrary, the typical experiment involving human subjects—in psychology as well as in medicine—is a very special situation, an interaction characterized by an extreme power differential. Trust and surrendering of identity on one side correspond to control and regulation on the other. This results in a very special responsibility for researchers, because the unique nature of the experimental situation gives them a status and role in the interaction more like that of a physician with a patient than like that of a partner with equal status. This will be substantiated in the following paragraphs.

### *Power and the Necessity for Internal Validity*

The internal validity of an experiment is the sine qua non of work in the experimental sciences (Campbell & Stanley, 1963). It is the minimal basis and indispensable prerequisite for the interpretability of an experiment. In order to achieve high internal validity, the experimenter must have as much control as possible over the design and execution of the experiment. This control should ensure that in the decisive moment the subjects can choose their behavior freely and will elect a behavior that fulfills the prediction of the experimenter (Argyris, 1975). In order to enable the subjects to decide freely at the appropriate moment, the purpose of the experiment and its basic structure must be kept secret from them. Thus, special constraints must be placed on the situation—constraints that would not be acceptable in the course of everyday human interaction. The method by which subjects come to participate must be controlled systematically in order to avoid selection effects and make the results more representative. In the interest of excluding alternative interpretations, assignment to the experimental conditions is either random or else based on some other principle that is not transparent to the subjects and operates independently of their preferences. The subjects are misinformed about the purpose of the experiment, about the nature and significance of the stimuli to which they are exposed, and about the significance of their behavior as a reaction to these stimuli. Subjects are left in ignorance of what kind of reactions they can be expected to show in the course of the investigation, in order to prevent deliberate behavioral control as well as social desirability effects. For the same reason, observations are sometimes made in secret. Highly confidential data are gathered. Finally, subjects are restricted in their possibilities of behavior through the investigator's use of certain limited stimuli and by the fact that only a few selected dimensions for reaction are feasible; in short, the subjects are influenced or manipulated.

We can see that the experiment is planned so that the subjects' behavior can be interpreted as a consequence of the control of the variables and by no means as a reaction to the direct influence of the experimenter. Thus, a good experiment—that is, a valid experiment—is one that subjects cannot see through, one in which they tacitly accept the investigator's definition of the situation. Most subjects agree to these conditions as rules of the game, as surveys have shown (Epstein, Suedfeld, & Silverstein, 1973; Sullivan & Deiker, 1973) and as experimenters know from their own experiences. Subjects, like experimenters, recognize the game rules as necessary prerequisites of experimentation and reconcile themselves to aspects of the experimental situation—the power imbalance, the lack of transparency, and the renunciation of autonomy—that they would refuse to accept in almost any other situation.

## *Submissiveness*

The submissiveness of the subjects constitutes the experimenter's power and is in turn maintained by this power. The evaluation apprehension that motivates subjects is a function not only of the power relationship defined by the situation but also of the diagnostic competence of the experimenter as a psychologist. Argyris (1975) shows very plainly that one of the most powerful forms of social control consists of unilaterally determining the criteria and significance of what one will accept as valid information. One of the most effective uses of social power occurs when one of the interaction partners is allowed to evaluate the behavior of the other or to interpret behavior and attribute characteristics to the other partner. The more powerful partner determines the rules and criteria for conclusions and need not expose the results to the criticism of the other partner or even make the results accessible and comprehensible. Although the evaluation of the subjects' behavior is often only apparent, the extent to which evaluation apprehension determines the behavior could actually be a suitable measure for the experience of power differential.

It is no accident that first-year students are the most popular subjects. Their image of psychology and of psychologists is apparently quite similar to the image most prevalent among laymen, with their orientation toward diagnostic and clinical psychology and their characteristic overestimation, or at least erroneous estimation, of the experimenter's diagnostic competence and interest in diagnosis. To a large extent psychologists are seen publicly in the context of this evaluation apprehension, combined with an uncertainty about the criteria for evaluation and about the content and structure of the theories on which explanations are based. Who is not familiar with the feeling of defenselessness that can arise in response to psychoanalytic interpretations? The image of the psychologist is formed by such associations, and such associations may even furnish a motive for the choice of psychology as a career.

In everyday life, we have various possibilities for avoiding and preventing interpretations and evaluations of our behavior, but the subject is completely at the mercy of the experimenter. Participation in an experiment implies temporary but complete renunciation of the right to understand the conditions under which one is to behave. This distinguishes the role of the subject from most of the other roles that people assume in the vast majority of interactions. The right to give orders and the right to evaluate are combined in a unique way in the role of the experimenter as interaction partner and determine the subject's experience of the situation and certain aspects of the subject's behavior. But probably not all aspects of the subject's behavior are affected by the experimenter's right to give orders and to evaluate; thus, external validity is not necessarily threatened.

### Subjects' Perceptions of the Experimenter

What leads subjects to place themselves in this unique situation? Which expectations justify the renunciation of autonomy? Epstein *et al.* (1973) asked subjects what obligations experimenters and subjects had to each other. The results suggest that subjects ascribe to the experimenters the obligation to give clear instructions, to ensure the safety of the subjects, to warn them of dangers, and to inform them about the nature of the experiment. Experimenters are expected to fulfill these obligations even without having expressly promised to do so. Subjects see themselves as obligated in return to cooperate with the experimenter and to be honest, although honesty ranked tenth and last in the subjects' list of the experimenter's obligations. Whereas Epstein *et al.* were asking about ideal behavior, Shulman and Berman (1975) asked subjects what actual behavior the subjects expected of the experimenter and of themselves. The results are similar to those in the experiment by Epstein *et al.* Professionalism, warmth, and attentiveness are the factors of experimenter behavior expected by subjects, while faithfulness is the first factor subjects expect of themselves. Apprehensiveness and skepticism, the two other actual subject behaviors expected, of course did not appear among the ideal behaviors cited in Epstein's survey.

## FALSE ATTRIBUTIONS

The subjects' perceptions of the experimenter probably consist of a number of blatantly false attributions. For example, the experimenter's personal interest in the subjects' individual behavior is usually overestimated; the role of therapist or diagnostic psychologist is ascribed to the experimenter. This attribution corresponds to the subjects' notion that the experimenter has a quasi-therapeutic responsibility to protect them from danger and unpleasantness and, in the case of unforeseen events, to do the right thing. The experimenter is expected to do whatever is good for the subjects. The magical components of this image resemble those of a patient's image of the physician. The ascribed power to prevent disaster corresponds to the ascribed ability to see through behavior, to recognize traits, motives, and moods. These expectations cannot always be corrected by the experimenter, even through explicit reassurance. Every experienced experimenter is familiar with this problem. After a long and thorough explanation of the purpose of the experiment and after repeated reassurance that the data will be evaluated only on the factor and group levels, some subjects are still prone to inquire anxiously as to whether anyone will think badly of them because of the way they answered item $X$ in the personality test. In this situation, attributions to the role partner are bound up with the subjects' perception of their own roles. The listener interested in the content of a lecture often does not notice the lecturer's evaluation anxiety—indeed, the listener may have no concept at all of the lecturer as a person capable of feelings. Similarly, the basic motives and interests of the experimenter are not accessible to the subject and are replaced by motives relevant for the subject's own sphere of action. If the subject perceived the experimenter more realistically, the experimenter would have less responsibility for the subject's well-being. To be sure, there might also be fewer subjects.

## MISUNDERSTANDING ONE ANOTHER

The "subjective sphere of action" of the subject overlaps only slightly the "quasi-objective sphere of action" of the experimenter (in the terminology of Kaminski, 1974). The experimenter is aware of and indeed is responsible for inducing part of this lack of overlap; internal validity depends on this. Other aspects of the lack of overlap, however—for example, the subjects' trust that the experimenter will ensure their well-being—escape the experimenter's notice and thus are apparently not the experimenter's responsibility.

## BLIND TRUST

The responsibility of experimenters is actually no less than the trust their subjects place in them and no less than the influence they exercise over their subjects. Orne and others have shown how great this trust is and how extensive the influence can be. Rowland (1939) asked his subjects to bring him a rattlesnake. The subjects thereupon approached the snake and were prevented from grasping it only by an invisible pane of glass. Frank (1944) tried in vain, just as Orne did later, to find tasks that one can *not* persuade subjects to perform. He attributed his lack of success to the subjects' unwillingness to violate the implicit agreement—made by volunteering to participate—that they would do whatever the experimenter asked. Orne's experiments have shown most clearly how great an experimenter's influence on subjects can be. Subjects must trust the experimenter and the rules of the game in order to be ready to endanger their life and health and the life and health of others. Orne summarizes his experiences with the following comparison: If we ask someone to do five pushups, the person will ask, astonished, "Why?" If we have first invited that person to participate in an experiment and then mention the five pushups, the response will be "Where?" (Orne, 1962, p. 777). The quasi-magical statement "This is an experiment" made by a reputable scientist radically changes the subjects' readiness to behave in certain ways and leads them to act and let things happen to them in ways that they would find quite unacceptable in any other situation.

## THE EXPERIMENT AS A SOCIAL CONTRACT

### Identifying Costs and Benefits within a Scientist–Subject Contract

Let us attempt to understand the peculiar social situation of the experiment by considering the relationship between experimenter and subject as a social contract. Characterizing the situation with various parameters, primarily on the dimension self-determination versus control by others, should show that certain norms of social obligation based on a broad consensus are appropriate and applicable here. Terms from the domains of economics and exchange theory can help us formulate criteria for the appropriateness or justice of the contract as a whole and for some of its elements.[10]

Which elements are recorded in the cost–benefit ledger as benefits or costs

---

10. The concept of justice as exchange, as we understand it today and as psychologists have formulated it in the theories of social exchange (above all Adams's equity theory, 1965; also Homans, 1961, and Thibaut & Kelley, 1959), can be traced back in the history of ideas to the Enlightenment, with its concept of natural law; to Hobbes's social contract (rooted in egotism and understood in the context of political theory); and to Rousseau, with a similar but already democratic orientation (cf. Windelband, 1957, pp. 371–374, 443–453). These ideas and their further development in Kant's practical philosophy are also the basis of more recent attempts in ethics to go beyond the contrast between utilitarian and deontological principles for action and to base something like a "philosophy of positive social behavior" on the idea of justice—with an emphasis on the principle of fairness by Rawls (1958) and on the principle of benevolence by Frankena (1963).

**TABLE 1**
**Costs and Benefits of the Experiment**

| Benefits | | Costs | |
| --- | --- | --- | --- |
| Subjects | Experimenter | Subjects | Experimenter |
| Satisfaction of interest or curiosity | Satisfaction of scientific interest (i.e., of curiosity or desire for knowledge) | Time | Time |
| | | Forgoing other activities | Forgoing other activities |
| Increased understanding of the science of psychology | | Investment of effort | Investment of effort |
| | | Various risks | Various risks |
| Feeling of having contributed to science | Scientific success, other professional motives | Submission (relinquishing control) | |
| Self-presentation | Power | Psychological stress | |
| Recognition | Recognition | Physical stress | |
| Increased status | Career benefits | Anxiety | |
| Social contact | Social contact | Embarrassment | |
| Material rewards | Income | Loss of trust | |
| Course credits | | Disappointment | |
| Stimulation | | Impaired self-esteem | |
| Self-insight | | | |

for the persons involved and show the contract to be an overall profit or loss? The psychology of the psychological experiment has provided us with little that is definite. The subject motives explored have been primarily those that explain the subjects' behavior *in* the experimental situation. Motives that would explain the subjects' participation in the experiment or their evaluation of the situation are given little attention, and even less information is available about the experimenter. Thus, if we are to enumerate tentatively the costs and benefits of the experiment, intuition and nonscientific experience, introspection and speculation must supplement the scanty hard empirical data that the scientific community has agreed to consider more valuable.

Since the reader may find it interesting to see what sorts of costs and benefits we are talking about, a sample list is provided—for experimenter and subjects only, not for science or humanity (see Table 1). Costs and benefits vary among and (temporally) within individuals. The elements overlap and to some extent are hard to classify—for example, risk taking can also be experienced as a reward. Nevertheless, the list can at least indicate the variety of possible motives for and effects of participation in an experiment.

In the following pages, then, the experiment in the social sciences will be considered as a social contract within which elements of cost and benefit are exchanged by the partners—that is, costs are "invested" and benefits "consumed." The situation bears little similarity to simple zero-sum systems. By no means does one partner have to lose or even invest everything that the other partner gains. Rather, the benefits tend to result from complex transpositions of investments on both sides, combined with investments by other parties. For example, many benefits for the subjects (such as self-insight or the possibility of self-presentation) can hardly be related to particular contributions (investments) by the experimenter. Other benefits, such as money, are usually not contributed by the experimenter. And still another class of incentives (social contact, for example) can benefit both partners in the interaction.

### TO WHOSE ADVANTAGE?

Not only is the division of power unequal, the experimental situation is also unbalanced in that the experimenter calculates the possible profit or loss before beginning a series of experiments and will carry them out only if the balance is positive for the experimenter. The subject, on the other hand, has to be satisfied with very uncertain expectations. Classifying the elements as cost or benefit is more difficult for the subject than for the experimenter, and calculation of profits or losses is practically impossible for subjects. For example, how useful is risk taking as a reward? What is the cost–benefit value of taking risks in an experiment? Certainly the elements are not all weighted the same.

### COMPENSATING FOR THREATS TO SELF-ESTEEM

Research on subjects indicates that the preservation or reinforcement of a positive or negative self-image can be assumed to be a particularly significant benefit or cost. The need to make a good impression on the experimenter and thereby gain self-esteem can also be interpreted in this manner as the product of a situation that has no other clear benefits for the subject. This need is an attempt to derive additional benefit from a role or interaction that is inherently disappointing and does not in itself compensate for the subjects' investments. For this reason, the manipulative impairment of self-esteem that is arranged in many experiments in social psychology may be experienced as a particular disappointment, or even as a betrayal. This tendency to feel betrayed may be illustrated by the fact that the only case this author has ever heard of in which legal proceedings were instituted against an experimental psychologist was when subjects were misinformed, as part of an experimental manipulation, that they had low IQs.[11]

11. When surveyed, subjects usually report that they find psychological experiments quite interesting. To the extent that these are first-time subjects, that does not contradict the emphasis in the preceding discussion on the tendency for subjects to find experiments disappointing. In the first place, the experimental situation can be interpreted in so many different ways by inexperienced subjects that they are free to attribute interesting purposes and goals to it. Subjects are prone

Seen from the standpoint of the subjects' difficulty in calculating profit or loss, the proposal that the subject be renamed the "participant in the experiment" is primarily a demonstration by the experimenter of goodwill and modesty, of readiness to do without a certain status. Such euphemistic assurances of the partnership and equality of the role relationships in the experiment are sometimes even a sign of opportunism in the area of social politics and, as a side effect, an attempt to be relieved of responsibility. In fact, though, the ideal experimental situation is unambiguously defined as a constellation of stimuli created by the experimenter for the subject. The subjects have to put themselves at the experimenter's disposal in many ways. They take the risk of "placing their fate in the experimenter's hands," which should go down in the book as a significant cost.

This cost may seem to the subjects to be balanced by a benefit: their delegation of responsibility for their behavior to the experimenter, so that they need not worry about the consequences. Deliberately and more or less of their own free will, the subjects have become involved in a relationship that is structured quite differently from the usual interactions among adults. In hardly any other situation would people waive the right to react with aggression, defensive action, or retreat, and put themselves at the disposal of another person, intentionally demonstrating their complete submission. Such voluntary submission implicitly demands in return that the partner refrain from aggressive, harmful behavior. The investigations of subject expectations cited earlier showed this very plainly. "The experimenter may lie to me," thinks the subject. "That's part of the experiment. But he may not hurt me. On the contrary, he must warn me of any dangers and protect me from harm."

## The Dynamics Seen from a Theoretical Perspective

The dynamics of the experimental situation can be approached in terms of various theories of social dynamics. Using psychoanalytic terminology, for example, the subject role calls for regressive behavior. Subjects must refrain

---

to evaluate an experiment in terms of their general attitudes toward science, particularly when they do not understand the purpose of the experiment. Those who have a basically positive attitude toward science, moreover, will find it easy to interpret their experiences in any particular experiment positively because they themselves, as subjects, are in effect supplying the raw material for progress in this empirically oriented scientific discipline. Second, participation as such has an activating effect, and activation encourages positive evaluations. And third, the most convincing confirmations of the hypothesis that dissonance is reduced through raising the value of the stimulus situation have been supplied by just those experimental realizations that forced subjects into subsequent justification of their participation in a worthless or tiring experiment (Festinger & Carlsmith, 1959). Thus, certain simple mechanisms often lead to subsequent positive evaluation by subjects even with problematic experiments.

from activating the secondary processes necessary for successful mastery of reality by adults. In exchange, subjects firmly expect the protection and goodwill of the parent figure to whom they have submitted. Experimenters are considered guilty of a serious violation of this implicit agreement—guilty of a blatant breach of trust—if they seem unjust or if they supply punishments in exchange for effort and submission. Put in economic terminology, the experimenter would thereby be offering additional costs instead of benefits in return for the subjects' investments.

Of course, by no means does the inequality of roles necessarily imply any sort of contempt for the subject. The therapeutic situation shows very clearly that a power imbalance between interaction partners does not exclude the possibility of high esteem for the less powerful partner. The success of therapy, regardless of which school of thought, seems to depend to a considerable extent on the therapist's expression of goodwill and high regard for the client.

### Four Characteristics of Experimental Interactions

As we have said, the experimental situation leads to a distribution of power that distinguishes it from the usual social interactions. The extent to which the experimental situation differs from everyday interactions in this regard covaries with the characteristics of the experiment. Four of these characteristics that seem particularly important are the *familiarity and danger* involved (dependent on the nature of the object of investigation and the special arrangement of the situation in which it is investigated); the extent of *stimulus control* and *reaction control* found necessary for the investigation; and the *power differentials* between experimenter and subject that exist independent of the experimental situation.

#### FAMILIARITY AND DANGER

The responsibility of the experimenter for the subjects and the difference in roles from which this responsibility stems are determined by the nature and situational context of the object of investigation. Suitable parameters for differentiation are the familiarity and the danger involved in the situation or in the behavior that is induced. Sometimes the experimental situation or the behaviors induced in it are so far removed from everyday experience as to be unfamiliar or even dangerous. To students, for example, discussing conditions at the university with other students is familiar behavior, whereas punishing another subject with electric shocks would be an unaccustomed behavior. One familiar situation is a classroom setting; a padded cell might well be an unfamiliar situation. Filling out a biographical questionnaire is generally a safe behavior for subjects, but touching a poisonous snake may not be. Long-term sensory deprivation is an example of a dangerous situation, whereas talking to another subject is a safe situation.

Familiarity and danger should always be considered together, since the degree of familiarity determines the degree of objective danger (when subjects are operating a buzz saw, for example) as well as the degree of subjective danger (when subjects are taking hallucinogenic drugs, for example). We could pretend for the sake of simplicity that the objective danger of taking certain drugs would be equal for all subjects. Even then, however, the subjective costs would be greater for persons who are not familiar with such substances than for habitual drug users. Thus, the subjects not familiar with the drugs would be surrendering or entrusting themselves to the experimenter to a greater extent than the habitual users would be. The responsibility of the experimenter varies correspondingly.

## STIMULUS CONTROL

Stimulus control is the extent to which the experimenter controls the stimuli for the subject. High stimulus control, for example, occurs in the case of experimentation with thresholds of acoustic perception, especially when other perceptions are simultaneously screened out. Low stimulus control often appears in the design of field research—for example, with the lost-letter technique (Milgram, 1969). In this technique, the percentage of deliberately "lost" letters to fictitious political organizations that are received at the address given is interpreted as an indicator of political positions.

## REACTION CONTROL

In the present context, we define reaction control as the determination of the behavioral possibilities of the subject. For example, reaction control is low in the investigation of the effects of aggressive behavioral models on interaction in children's groups; it is high in the playing of matrix games.[12]

## POWER DIFFERENTIAL

The power differential that already existed before the experiment began is based on such factors as age, social role, and occupational status. As a rule, this power differential carries over to in-role behavior and to the exchange of rewards during the experiment. Agreement to participate in the experiment is easily obtained, and readiness to relinquish power is high, if the subject is dependent on the experimenter. With a lesser power differential—for example, when students volunteer for the experiments of their fellow students—the experimental contract is less stable. Less is invested, and if the cost–benefit

---

12. Although reinforcement by the experimenter is occasionally an independent variable—for example, in examining the question of awareness—the behavior of subjects is seldom supposed to be influenced by reward or punishment. Reaction control as defined here is quite different from reaction or response control as defined by learning theory.

relationship turns out to be unfavorable, the subject finds it easier to break off participation in the experiment.

Control over reinforcers belongs in this category even when it is not coupled with direct dependence. The experimenter controls behavior by establishing incentives for the subjects to participate in the experiment and to follow the instructions as closely as possible. In this sense we could say that the less the subjects' behavior is influenced by the experimenter, the more independent the subjects are. One example of control over reinforcers can be found when prisoners are used for medical experiments. The prisoners anticipate that their sentence will be shortened or made easier as a result of their participation. In addition, they have an urgent need for material goods and may even be motivated by a need to do penance. Power of reinforcement surely also includes the gentle pressure that results from promising students course credits for their participation in experiments.

*ILLUSTRATIONS*

Let us consider an experiment in which the unfamiliarity and danger, stimulus control, reaction control, and power differential were all low. Külpe, Marbe, Bühler, and their colleagues carried out investigations of thought processes at the beginning of the century in Würzburg. All of these thought processes were part of the daily lives of the subjects—one could say, part of their work habits. As far as anyone could tell, the thought processes were completely harmless. The experiments were carried out at a psychological institute, in surroundings that were just as familiar for the subjects as for the experimenters. Thus, familiarity and absence of danger characterized the situation as well as the behavior induced. The control of stimuli was limited to assigning problems to be solved; otherwise, the situation was not restricted. The reaction control was even less. The behavior of the subjects was not evaluated, and it was controlled only in that the subjects were asked to solve the problem and say everything that occurred to them in relation to it. Asking them not to withhold anything did constitute minor reaction control, of course. The subjects were just as interested in the results as the experimenter was, so there was no extrinsic reinforcement. Finally, the subjects were as close to the experimenters in status as possible: All were instructors or professors of psychology. In this case, the inequality of roles was minimal. In fact, the subjects were actually able to exchange roles with the experimenters. In such a situation, the experimenter has very little responsibility for the subjects.

An example at the other extreme would be an experiment in long-term sensory deprivation, carried out with children in a physiological institute. In this hypothetical experiment, the children's consciousness is reduced to one perceptual dimension, and the only possible reaction is pressing a button. The object of investigation, the location, the equipment, and other characteristics of the situation are as unfamiliar as possible to the subjects. The stimuli and reactions are almost perfectly controlled, and the power differential between experimenter and subject is extremely great. In order to ensure reinforcement power as well, the children could be rewarded for their participation by being allowed to skip one major test. The experiment might be dangerous, depending on the object and method; the extent for individual cases is unknown. The roles of experimenter and subject are completely different, and the responsibility of the experimenter for the subjects can be assessed as extremely high.

## Cost-Benefit Analysis

The costs that the experiments (or experimenters) described in the preceding section impose on the subject are the unfamiliarity and danger of the experimental situation and the behavior induced in it, the stimulus control, the reaction control, and the power differentials. Subjects will expect benefits from the experimental contract that are as great as their investments. Costs are low for the subjects when they are told while in familiar surroundings to do something that is not dangerous, when they are not restricted to a few stimuli and reactions, and when they are required to surrender only a little of their behavioral freedom to an experimenter of equal status. That is, costs are low when the *preliminary* investment of effort required is not substantial. In such a case, a relatively small reward—perhaps a small amount of money—suffices to persuade the subjects to take the time necessary to perform the tasks required for the experiment. For additional rewards, subjects are perhaps ready to endure certain "damages"—physical or psychological stress, pain, deprivation, etc.—up to the point where the cost-benefit equilibrium becomes unbalanced to their disadvantage. For example, the pay might be better than average or they might benefit from the intrinsic interest of the experiment. The more transparent the situation—that is, the more easily subjects can calculate costs and benefits—and the more behavioral freedom subjects have, the less responsibility the experimenter bears for this calculation.

When the experimenter has high control of the situation and of the subjects' behavior, the situation is different. The subjects must invest so much merely by virtue of this definition of the situation that the experimenter would actually have to offer them decidedly positive experiences in order for the contract to be balanced. If the subjects had not already renounced their freedom of action through the contract, the increase of costs to them during the experiment would lead them to dissolve the relationship. But the subjects are not able to perceive their right to a balanced cost-benefit relationship. (This interpretation is supported by the low proportion of refusal when there was no model who refused, and the high proportion with such a model, in the experiments conducted by Milgram.) Therefore, the experimenters themselves are responsible for ensuring the balance of the relationship, assuming they do not want to be accused of misusing the definition of the situation and their power advantage for exploitation of the subjects. Every burden placed on the subject beyond the amount already determined by the four basic dimensions could then be characterized as an excess contribution from the subject, not balanced by the rewards that are usual in psychological experiments.

COSTLY RESEARCH PRACTICES

A number of relatively common practices tend to lead to excess costs for the subjects. These would include inducement of criminal behaviors or behaviors that contradict the subject's own moral standards, concentration on behaviors or data that are thought of as belonging to a very narrow area of the private sphere, and long-term change in attitudes or readiness for behaviors. Possibilities for reducing such costs for the subjects in the context of debriefing include offering exonerating possibilities of attribution and labeling, encouraging insight into the research and its usefulness, and emphasizing the subject's contribution to scientific progress.

THE EXPERIMENTER CONTROLS THE BALANCE SHEETS

In contrast to this, experimenters carry out their own cost–benefit analyses before deciding to experiment. As one might expect, this analysis is generally favorable to the experimenter. The numerous ways in which the experimenter can benefit contrast with the relatively low costs. The experiment's significance for the experimenter's scientific career tends to be the most important benefit.[13]

## The Pursuit of Equity

What is the relationship of the experimenter's cost–benefit analysis to that of the subject? When their roles are nearly equal, we may speak of two scales that need to be balanced, one for the experimenter and one for the subjects, in order for a social contract to come into being at all. If conditions are favorable, each scale will show higher benefits than costs. On the other hand, when the roles are decidedly unequal, the experimenter can increase benefits at the expense of the subject—that is, only one scale is involved. An experiment that

---

13. Of course the experimenter, like the subjects, weighs investments against profit. The number of publications of experimental studies indicates that in most cases the calculation had positive results. That does not mean, however, that researchers who do not conduct experiments have necessarily reached other conclusions. Rather, from their point of view, the other forms of research might offer even greater rewards and even fewer risks. Among the costs these researchers would undoubtedly take into account would be the low esteem in which nonexperimental psychologists are held by influential colleagues.

creates a sensation in the scientific community requires only a little more effort from the experimenter than a boring investigation. The experimenter need merely furnish original ideas, which could be thought of as costs only in a very restricted sense. However, impressive experiments are often bound up with high costs for the subjects, who are not compensated for these by equivalent benefits. For example, in the Stanford prison experiment (Haney, Banks, & Zimbardo, 1973; Zimbardo, Haney, Banks, & Jaffe, 1973), the compensation for what the authors themselves called "pain and humiliation" suffered by subjects was said to be that the subjects apparently increased in self-knowledge (Zimbardo, 1973, p. 243). Such "enrichment" of the experimenter's outcomes at the expense of the subjects tends more often to occur when roles are unequal.

A fair exchange is possible only when all participants have the right to decide whether a transaction is to take place—that is, to refuse to participate if they want to. That refusal is never possible when participation in experiments is forced or made a matter of course by means of more subtle sanctions. The result is a conflict between the methodological demand that the representativeness of the results not be limited by self-selection on the part of the subjects and the moral demand that subjects not be forced to participate in an experiment.

Improving the techniques for recruiting subjects is sometimes seen as a way out of this dilemma. Rosenthal and Rosnow (1975, pp. 198-199) recommend such techniques as using clever rhetoric and persons with high status, giving little presents, emphasizing the normative nature of participation, representing the research as interesting and significant, and aiming for public obligation to participate. It should be clear by now that this would help only in a very limited sense. These techniques would probably not change the basic characteristics of the experiment or the resulting social contract. The transparency might remain low, and the subjects might still be influenced far beyond their possibilities of control. Thus, the experimenter would be relieved only very superficially of responsibility. In fact, responsibility actually increases in proportion to the effectiveness of the recruiting methods. Influencing self-selection in this way is justifiable only when we can expect the results of the subject's cost–benefit analysis to be positive or at least balanced—or if the subject has all the prerequisites for performing the calculation unaided, which is rarely the case.

## The Experimenter as Scientist: A Second Contract

Up to this point, we have been developing a characterization of the experimenter–subject relationship as a social contract. This characterization would be incomplete without consideration of the experimenter's responsibility as a scientist. As scientists, experimenters are obligated to do justice to the special values of their profession: to serve truth, science, and society through useful work. Indeed, the costs to the subjects are usually justified by reference to these values. In expectation of such benefits, society has made certain investments in scientists and their work. Financial means, possibilities of employment, and a number of freedoms and privileges are invested by colleagues, the university, the institution furnishing financial support, and society in order to make scientific research possible. Finally, members of the scientific community, and to a certain extent also other authorities, evaluate the results of the scientist's work and consider whether the achievements are equivalent to the investments. Further investments are dependent on this analysis. If the results of the researcher's work are particularly valued—that is, if the benefits to society are considered very high—the scientist derives additional profits: fame, promotion, influence, prizes, etc. These additional profits are equivalent to the added value that is ascribed to the results of the scientist's work in comparison with the original investments.

This relationship, then, can also be understood as a social contract, one in which the partners can take the form of supraindividual social units. The contract partner of a young research assistant may be above all, but certainly not exclusively, the leader of the research project. The latter, however, will not feel responsible to any single person, but primarily to the organization that supports the research, and will be evaluated by professional colleagues (i.e., the scientific community). In order to meet the conditions of this contract, the scientist must find methods for fulfilling research obligations appropriately. One of these methods for social scientists is to fulfill contractual obligations to employers with the help of the subjects.

Thus, the researcher is a partner in two different contracts—the first with the scientific community and the organization supporting the research, the second with the subjects. The second is based on the first contract, and fulfillment of the first is based on the success of the second. Researchers who do not succeed in entering into subject contracts under the usual conditions will turn to other means. For example, they will increase their efforts at recruiting or perhaps offer higher rewards to potential subjects. If these costs exceed their readiness or ability to invest, they will seek alternative research methods—for example, carrying out field studies or modifying the question under investigation.

While researchers are trying to balance out one of their two contracts, they must simultaneously keep in mind the balance of the other one. For example, it is not possible to decide to do without control groups for pharmacological investigations in order to avoid ethical problems, since such investigations are worthless without control groups. Often subjects in a control group receive only placebos in spite of their need for treatment, but eliminating the control group would disturb the cost–benefit balance for the other partner. Instead, the scientist may decide to administer a similar, competing medication to the control group, if it is held to be an appropriate substitute.

Researchers can also proceed quite differently, however. In order to fulfill the contract with their employers, they can neglect the balance of the contract with their subjects. Instead of making the investments themselves—through more intensive attempts to win subjects, thinking up alternative research methods, etc.—they can transfer the burden to the subjects. For example, they can refrain from mentioning significant characteristics of the experiment that would prevent subjects from participating. After all, experience has taught them that subjects hardly ever decide not to participate once the experiment has begun.

How is the researcher able to do this? In contracts with their employers, experimenters have equal or inferior rights and must go along with relatively predetermined criteria, such as standards for the appropriateness of their methods. In contracts with their subjects, however, they have a considerable power advantage over their partners, based on the specific nature of the experimental situation and on their status as scientists. The sanctions for disregarding their responsibilities are therefore very different in the two contracts: severe for one and minimal for the other. When in doubt, scientists often give in to the temptation to neglect the balance of the contract with their subjects. This was suggested by a survey of young medical researchers conducted by Makarushka and Lally (1974), who found that during training, the importance of research was emphasized more than the welfare and rights of patients. Some researchers found themselves under pressure to take excessive risks with their subjects or to disregard the practice of obtaining informed consent. Not all refused to submit to this pressure.

Thus, the conflict between the two contracts—the difficulty of fulfilling obligations to both sides—is intensified by social pressure on scientists from their colleagues and supervisors, by demands for proof of achievement, by norms established by the scientific community, etc. Because of this pressure, the conflict tends to be resolved by burdening the weaker partner with the costs.

Sometimes scientists find it necessary to justify questionable practices with regard to their subjects. One popular and widespread argument is that scientific progress requires sacrifice, and the benefit that is to be expected from the investigation easily compensates for the burden placed on the subjects. (Some examples of this argument are cited in Chapter 2 in the context of weighing costs and benefits.) In the first place, this line of argument constitutes dishonesty or rationalization; at best, it is incomplete. We can assume that in most cases the sacrifice made by the subjects contributes to fulfilling the scientist's personal desires no less than it contributes to scientific progress or the welfare of humanity. In the second place, this argument connects—in a sense, short-circuits—two contracts that have nothing to do with each other except that the scientist participates in both of them. The experimenter imposes on partners of one contract, the subjects, the costs that are incurred in the course of fulfilling obligations to the partner of the other contract, the employer. Combining the two contracts is justified only when the subjects support the goals of the research as their own and are integrated into the research process as participants, as in the case of the experiments on thought processes conducted by the Würzburg school. It is not justified when the role relationship between experimenter and subject is the one that has become typical for experimental investigations.

## SCRUTINIZING MILGRAM'S EXPERIMENTS

By now we should have the concept of the experimental contract clearly enough in mind to consider a series of actual psychological experiments from this standpoint. This is the series of obedience studies published by Stanley Milgram, starting in 1963. These experiments have been criticized as widely as they have been recognized. Today, after a long series of follow-up investigations, they are counted among the most popular studies in social psychology. Thus, they should be sufficiently familiar that a brief summary will be adequate here.

The subject's task was to punish another subject for failure in a learning experiment by administering electric shocks of increasing intensity. The victim reacted with visible or audible expressions of pain when the electric shocks were administered. Nevertheless, most subjects (in the basic form of the experiment approximately two-thirds) continued with the punishment even after the initial pleas and cries, and even after the screams of the other person gave way to a silence from which the subject could conclude that the other person had fainted or possibly even died. The experimental arrangements also gave the impression of a high degree of danger. For example, the buttons for the strongest electric shocks were marked with danger signals. Almost all subjects attempted to break off participation in the experiment one or more times during the punishment phase. However, they were prevented from doing so by the experimenter with such demands as "Please continue," "The experiment requires that you continue," "It's absolutely essential that you continue," or even "You have no other choice, you *must* go on" (Milgram, 1963, p. 374; italics in original).

The basic elements of the experiment were of course fictitious. The lots that "determined" whether the subject would be the teacher or the learner were prearranged. The subject who was punished was an actor, and the actor's learning failures were simulated. And finally, the equipment did not in fact deliver electric shocks.

## The Milgram-Subject Contract

We can apply to this experiment the terms used earlier to describe the social contract between experimenter and subject and the characteristics of the experiment that distinguish it from an everyday interaction. Milgram's experiment can thus be characterized by low familiarity of the experimental situation and of the behavior induced, as well as by danger—at least subjective danger—of the behavior. There is a high degree of stimulus control and an even higher degree of reaction control. The power differential between experimenter and subject is great. It is based on their extraexperimental status and also made plain during the experiment by situational characteristics and experimenter behavior.

The experimental situation, then, is characterized by high disparity of roles and low self-determination of the subject's behavior. Thus, the experimenter has a high degree of responsibility for preventing additional costs for the subjects and for offering positive experiences that might balance their investments. But actually the disparity of roles and the lack of transparency are used to create experiences for the subjects to which few of them would submit voluntarily. Deceiving the subjects about the actual nature of the experiment and the nature of the behavior induced makes it possible to have them act in a way that can have considerable influence on their self-image. The debriefing can certainly change the nature of the burden placed on the subject, but it does not always diminish it. In the context of the contract model, it is not acceptable to cite the scientific significance of the results as a justification for these high costs to the subjects. With the extreme disparity of roles that prevails, this would constitute an illegitimate connection of the experimenter's two contracts. The subjects are burdened with the costs of financing the benefits. Yet it is not they, but the researcher's scientific reputation, and perhaps also science and society, that receive the benefits. To be sure, the subjects are part of society—but we must consider the proportion of benefits they would receive in this way. In any case, we cannot call this a voluntary sacrifice. It would also be a rationalization to claim benefits for the subjects by asserting that subjects always profit from being enlightened through self-insight, even when this sort of therapy has not been requested.

### EXPERIMENTER DEMAND AS A SCIENTIFIC VARIABLE

The following phenomenon is especially remarkable. We pointed out earlier that in order for an experiment to be internally valid the subject's behavior must be interpreted as a consequence of the control of the two variables, not as a reaction to direct influence by the experimenter. Milgram's experiment, however, is a special case: The experimenter's influence *is* the independent variable. What this experiment is actually designed to show is what subjects are prepared to do under the influence of an experimenter. It therefore belongs to that category of experiments in which subjects show themselves willing to undergo hardships that should really seem senseless to them and to behave in ways that endanger themselves and others (some are cited by Orne, 1962, and Orne & Evans, 1965).

## THE MAXIMAL GOADING OF SUBJECTS

Milgram's experiment combines all the prerequisites for high experimenter influence. In addition, his experimenter contributes to the maintenance and renewal of the influence during the experiment. When the subjects, showing all signs of nervousness and fear, want to stop administering the punishment, the experimenter demands that they continue (Milgram, 1965, pp. 66–69). The experimenter's intonation is designed to emphasize the power differential and reassure the subjects that by no means is the experiment out of control. It is suggested that this is nothing more than a normal procedure for an experiment in the social sciences, even though the subject cannot understand it. From previous impressions as well as from the characteristics of this experimental situation, the subject must conclude that the experimenter is a responsible person, capable of fulfilling and ready to fulfill all responsibilities as always. That is, the subject expects the experimenter to fulfill the terms of the social contract that they previously made.

## RESPONSIBILITY TRANSFERRED

Fulfilling the terms of the contract is precisely what the experimenter does not do. The subjects are made to do something that contradicts their understanding of the situation, something that they would perhaps not do under any other circumstances. In effect, the experimenter offers to assume the costs and then suddenly says, "We didn't even make the contract you were relying on. What you thought was a game was serious. You yourself must bear the responsibility." This would be comparable to a magician using a vaudeville setting along with the authority inherent in the definition of the magician's role to persuade a guest to cut the girl in the coffin in half. Then, when the blood flows out, the magician says in horror: "God Almighty, what have you done? She's really cut in half."

The magician asked that the instructions be carried out on faith, without anyone actually understanding how they could be reasonable and appropriate. In exchange, it is the magician who really should be considered responsible for everything that happened. Similarly, most of us would be willing to follow the instructions of an auto mechanic who told us to rev the engine up to 8000 revolutions per minute if the mechanic said it emphatically enough and appeared to be sufficiently competent. We would probably hesitate if the red line on the tachometer began at 6000. But if the resolute answer were "Do what I tell you if you want me to repair your car," certainly most nonmechanically inclined customers would obey and thereby possibly ruin the engine. Likewise, the captain of a volunteer fire unit would find it easy to persuade newcomers in the unit to set fire to a shed as part of a firefighting exercise. Even if the newcomers doubted whether the resulting fire could be kept under control and thought that it seemed as good as certain that the entire premises would burn down, they would probably cooperate. Nor would the head doctor of a clinic have a hard time persuading a young nurse to administer to a patient a dose that the nurse felt was extremely dangerous.

All these situations have one thing in common—an implicit contract that reads: "To be sure, you don't understand why I'm making you do this. You think it's foolish or dangerous, immoral or even completely insane. But my position proves that I can make the right decisions, that I am competent to judge the results of my actions. I'll be responsible, and you do what I say."

## THE FREEDOM TO REFUSE

In order for Milgram's subjects to refuse to cooperate with the experimenter, it would have been necessary for one or more conditions such as the following to prevail: certainty that the person in charge would not be competent to control the consequences of the behavior in question much longer, general distrust of social contracts, habitual denial of social obligations, great flexibility in redefining social situations, or intense fear of the behavior required. These conditions are seldom found; in fact, it is fortunate that such conditions as general distrust of social contracts are rare. Thus the "obedience" of Milgram's subjects is nothing more than behavior that is appropriate for the subject role. They act contrary to their own doubts and concerns in a situation outside their own realm of experience, trusting that the experimenter will also assume appropriate role behavior. But the experimenter acts like the magician after the unsuccessful trick that has such a bloody end. Stepping out of the role and out of the situation that was supposedly defined by consensus, the experimenter says: "Now look what you've done. I was just pretending to bear the responsibility. Actually you were responsible all along."

This experimenter failed to keep his word. The terms of an implicit social contract were not observed, and the trust of the subjects was misused. Attention was distracted from this breach of contract by means of spectacular association of the subjects' behavior with crimes committed in concentration camps. Milgram's strategy aims at stirring up excitement among the readership. If the strategy succeeds, it is hard for readers to think about the experiment from another perspective. Excitement of course does not necessarily invalidate the experiment.

*GENERALIZABILITY*

We always wonder whether the subjects' behavior can be generalized; in the case of Milgram's experiments, the generalization is particularly problematic. The extent to which the subjects' behavior can actually be generalized to behavior outside the experimental situation depends on whether the relationship between experimenter and subject is equivalent to social relationships in nonexperimental situations. Although the assumption of a generally high readiness to obey is quite plausible on the basis of certain mechanisms of socialization, and probably also on the basis of biological conditions, it is nevertheless rather daring to make this assumption on the basis of Milgram's experiments. This is rather like asserting that subjects lacked cognitive complexity because they never checked anything but yes or no on a dichotomous scale.

Milgram's own data support our interpretation of his results. In one of his experiments (Milgram, 1974, Experiment 15), all subjects broke off participation immediately or with only a slight hesitation as soon as they had reason to believe that the experimenter was no longer master of the situation. A second experimenter who was present expressed doubts about continuing with the punishment, and this contradiction made it clear to the subjects that the experimenter was no longer filling the role flawlessly. Thus, the experimenter could no longer assume complete responsibility. Responsibility returned, in a sense, to the subjects, who immediately realized this and began to behave "normally" again. Another factor was probably that the break in the dynamic tension of the situation encouraged cognitive restructuring and rethinking of the situation.

## ETHICAL NORMS

The concept of the social contract as proposed here seems thus to be capable of offering alternative explanations for some experimental results. Its main purpose, however, is to help us understand the experimental situation in such a way that we can develop criteria for evaluating the behavior of social scientists. Naturally, this also assumes agreement about certain ethical principles, as we will show later. The evaluation of specific experimental measures such as the deception of subjects or the secret observation of their behavior varies considerably with the ethical standards applied and has thus given rise to long and sometimes quite unproductive discussions. But an important basis for agreement would be consensus on the widespread social norm of staying within the framework of social contracts—or, to express it somewhat more generally, agreement on a norm of social obligation.

This viewpoint is based on exploration of aspects of the experiment that had not been considered before. Experimenters could hardly recognize the expectations directed at them or the responsibilities they were to fulfill without reflecting on the social nature of the experiment and without knowing what motivates subjects, how subjects see the role of the experimenter, or in what way the behavior of subjects is dependent on the behavior of the experimenter and on the situation. Only on the basis of such knowledge can the relationship to the subjects be understood as a binding social contract. Moreover, once this basis has been established, it is hard to deny the social contract point of view.

If we accept the perspective that the experiment is a social contract, then determining whether certain measures are justifiable is no longer optional. Highly relevant here is Frankena's (1963) theory of moral obligation. The existence of some such norm of social obligation can hardly be denied, no matter what one's point of view. The social obligation norm can be justified by Kant's categorical imperative, by Bentham's happiness formula, and by the Christian command that we love our neighbor. It can, in fact, be described as a composite of utilitarian, teleological, deontological, and other theories of philosophical ethics (cf. the two sections in Chapter 2 on the philosophy of weighing costs and benefits).

Not only the range covered by such a norm, but also its practicability will determine whether it proves to be a principle suited to guide research in the social sciences. Thus, we will occasionally explore this problem in connection with subsequent discussion of specific cases and principles. But first it is desirable to present some specific ethical problems as they have been considered in the past and not to impose more structure on this presentation than is necessary for such a summary. Therefore, we will refrain from applying the social contract principle explicitly until the end of the next chapter, when we will attempt to reconstruct basic philosophical positions from the arguments that have been used in the past in debating the morality of research.

# 2

# Ethical Problems of Psychological Experiments

## HISTORY AND BACKGROUND

### Vinacke's Indictment of Psychological Research

In a letter to the *American Psychologist,* Vinacke criticized his colleagues' lack of concern for the well-being of their subjects: "In various ways the psychologist conceals the true purpose and conditions of the experiment, or positively misinforms the subjects, or exposes them to painful, embarrassing, or worse, experiences, without the subjects' knowledge of what is going on [1954, p. 155]." At the same time, he observed that no one besides himself considered this lack of concern a problem, but that, on the contrary, accounts of subject manipulation contributed to amusement at conventions.

The situation described by Vinacke, which was particularly noticeable in experimental social psychology, contrasts with earlier established principles. In 1938 the American Psychological Association (APA) founded a committee for the discussion of ethical aspects of psychological research. One of the principles that the committee formulated, in "Ethical Standards in Research" (1951, Principle 4.31-1), suggests that psychologists should not withhold information, misinform subjects, or cause them emotional stress unless the research problem is important and cannot otherwise be studied. It also suggests that harmful aftereffects should be anticipated and prevented and that, if they nevertheless arise, psychologists must deal with them. To be sure, this principle is general enough to allow justification of almost any concrete research project. Even the authors acknowledged that it is often hard to decide whether a procedure might harm a subject and when, if ever, a project is significant enough to risk harm or difficulty for subjects (APA, 1951, p. 441).

Vinacke proposed two measures for clarifying the extent to which it is necessary to mislead subjects and for ascertaining the subjects' views of practices that had become standard in psychological research laboratories. The two measures, which were eventually applied a decade later, were ($a$) to try out a variation of role playing, and ($b$) to question subjects, researchers, and others on the acceptability of various research procedures. Interest in the subjects' views apparently did not begin until psychologists came to see the experiment as a social situation.

## Precedents in Medical Research

In the field of medicine, on the other hand, a wide variety of views on ethical problems with experiments were exchanged considerably earlier. After all, medicine had been developing into an experimental discipline since the middle of the nineteenth century. Bernard, a famous French physiologist and pharmacologist, argued in 1856 that medical experimenters must never risk hurting a human being, even if their experiment would result in a contribution toward healing others (Pappworth, 1968, p. 37). Many of Bernard's contemporaries seem not to have considered the stringency of his deontological ethical principles in any way binding. To be sure, long before the turn of the century, the administration of justice in America proceeded from the principle that the risk and responsibility for all medical procedures that had not yet been adequately tested belonged to the physician. Ladimer (1955) reports on a large number of cases that were discussed at that time and cites the opinions of professional and legal authorities on this issue. Nevertheless, individual researchers apparently had considerable freedom of decision. For example, by referring to the benefits of scientific knowledge, von Hubbenet was able to justify the deliberate experimental transmission of syphilitic infection to young girls without their knowledge or consent, though syphilis was not curable at the time. When in 1860 he reported on his 6 years of experiments in syphilitic infection, he had every reason to expect sympathy and understanding from the readers. Weighing the costs and benefits of his experiments, von Hubbenet concluded that establishing the contagious nature of the secondary stage of syphilis would be so beneficial for humanity that it would justify the suffering of the few victims of his experiments (Veressayev, 1972, p. 288).

### THE EARLIEST ETHICAL PROTESTS

Long before the formulation of the first ethical guidelines, there was occasional opposition to various medical experiments. For example, the first ex-

*History and Background*                                                                                   69

perimental psychosurgery by the Swiss Burckhardt in 1891 is said to have inspired violent attacks (National Commission, 1977b, Appendix, I-5), and even earlier experiments in 1874 by the American Bartholow (Veressayev, 1972, pp. 290-291) had also encountered criticism. Yet the benefits for humanity that were expected from the continued development of medical knowledge and techniques lent sufficient dignity to even the most daring and dangerous experiments. Though the significance of any individual experiment may have been almost impossible to determine, it was possible to claim for each individual case the generally recognized value of research and to use this to justify nearly every procedure.

*DISTINGUISHING THERAPY FROM RESEARCH*

Paradoxically, the difficulty of separating research and therapy has made it easier for medical researchers to obtain subjects. Often this difficulty arises because in a given case an experiment actually is identical with an attempt at therapy. But often, too, the experiment is *made* to seem identical with therapy: The nontransparency of the procedures chosen—to the patient and to outsiders—is deliberately used for the benefit of research goals. The seeming identity of experiment and therapy may encourage patients to consent to a procedure that would be rejected if it seemed merely part of a research project. It is hardly possible to adapt to the public image of the physician the notion that a particular procedure might be of questionable value, or at best beneficial only to future patients, or even dangerous for the patients involved. Least of all can patients believe that a physician is not concerned solely with their welfare. They will consent to an experiment because they believe in the accepted public image of the physician, even if the physician openly attempts to enlighten them to the contrary. Thus, the a priori power differential between physician and patient favors the patient's consent to research participation.

*MAKING A CYNICAL ATTITUDE EXPLICIT*

The combination of a lack of transparency, a power differential, and the possibility of justifying harm to individuals by means of collective benefit are the foundations of the carte blanche that experimenters in the biomedical and social sciences occasionally claim for their work. Sasson and Nelson report examples of this attitude in contemporary experimental psychology, such as Sinick (1954), who "submits that experimenters be free to induce emotional stress and let general discomfort exist when there is some justification for it [Sasson & Nelson, 1969, p. 421]."

Allowing individuals to suffer hardships in the interest of better research or a better future is occasionally even made a qualifying criterion for scientists, as Ring (1967) complained with regard to psychology. This is clear from the line of reasoning expressed in 1961 at an international medical convention by the physician Szent-Györgyi:

> The wish to relieve pain has little value in research. Whoever cherishes this desire should be advised to devote himself to charitable works. Research needs egotists, confounded egotists, who are out for their own pleasure and satisfaction and find it in solving the mysteries of nature [cited by Pappworth, 1968, p. 19].

Thus in a miraculous way, the greatest happiness for the greatest number of people is in a sense supposed to result automatically from the accumulation of the efforts of egotists, just as the aggregation of the profit seeking of all individual members in a free-market economy is supposed to result in the greatest possible benefit for all participants.

### Justifying the Means: Some Medical Examples

Because of the possibilities of concealing and justifying even the most questionable procedures, problems in the biomedical and social sciences have continued up to the most recent times. Thus at the Nuremberg trials after World War II, Nazi doctors, accused of having experimented with human beings in the most cruel fashion, pointed out that quite similar experiments had been carried out at all times and in all countries, even in those of the victorious forces (Katz, 1972, pp. 292–305; Pappworth, 1968, pp. 85–88). Indeed, their work was also dedicated to a higher goal, or even two higher goals, since the decimation of "worthless lives" was connected with the benefits expected for humanity.

Still with the Nuremberg trials as a background, Guttentag suggested in 1953 that most physicians who conduct experiments agree that it is not justifiable to use force on even one person. They feel that such an amoral act would be wrong even if it could save millions of lives, since it might lead to millions of other amoral acts. According to Guttentag, although these physicians might not be completely aware of the actual nature of the relationship between physician and patient, they share the democratic notion that morals are more important than science (cited by Beecher, 1959, pp. 29–30). Pappworth (1968) presents an impressive collection of evidence that the hoped-for reformation did not occur. Described in the following paragraphs are two examples (pp. 81–82, 187).

One example is a typhoid experiment carried out in the Philippines, published in 1963 by Lantin, Geronimo, and Calilong. They treated only 251 out of 408 typhoid patients with an antibiotic known to be effective, in order to study side effects of the medicine in these patients compared with the control group. The experimental group did in fact show certain side effects, though not severe ones. The important observation from this study is that 23 deaths in the control group can be attributed to the control subjects' not having been treated.

Pappworth also cites Biermann, Miller, Dod, Kelly, Byron, and Black, who reported in 1951 experiments involving new procedures for heart catherization. They tried out methods of inserting catheters against the flow of blood in arteries far from the heart. Four severe complications resulted from this, and two ended fatally. The justification was that the percentage of complications was not high enough to warrant prohibiting such procedures and that new methods always involve problems at the outset. The authors pointed out that, after all, most patients chosen to undergo these procedures were already very severely ill.

This attitude does not seem to be limited to a few individual cases. Pappworth estimates that his collection of problematic medical studies comprises more than 500 publications. We must also consider the success bias of published studies, which is surely no less here than in other branches of science. That is, published studies generally report relatively positive results; many more investigations with negative or questionable results were undoubtedly conducted than published reports indicate. Beecher (1972) considered 12 of 100 investigations published in a professional journal in 1964 to be ethically questionable and found on the average 3.7 references to similar experiments in each of these. To be sure, criteria for what is to be considered ethically questionable can be formulated in a relatively unambiguous way only for extreme cases; distributions cannot be derived from these figures.

## Ethical Illiteracy among Scientists

There is reason to think that researchers receive no systematic instruction in ethical questions. Barber, Lally, Makarushka, and Sullivan surveyed 307 researchers who had experimented with humans in various biomedical areas. They asked when in the course of their training the researchers had become aware of ethical problems (1973; excerpts also published in Makarushka & Lally, 1974). Only one of the researchers had ever taken a course on this subject; 57% had never heard anything about ethical problems during their studies, neither in lectures nor in seminars nor in discussions of actual experiments with people and animals. Nineteen percent of the respondents became aware of ethical questions through problematic cases in their own research, 5% through the influence of their colleagues, 3% through the increasing control exercised by ethics committees, and 47% were never made aware of ethical questions in the entire course of their research.

As part of the survey, some cases were submitted to the respondents for evaluation. One of the cases involved the testing of a new antidepressant drug in a psychiatric clinic. There were some indications that the antidepressant was more effective than the standard medication, but it also seemed to have serious side effects. The depressive patients in the control group, which was to include some of the suicidal patients, were to be administered a placebo medication. Written consent of the patients would be required. Sixteen percent of the respondents rejected the investigation flatly; some of the others accepted the investigation with reservations, suggesting better control of the side effects, special precautions with suicidal patients, or use of the standard medication in the control group. But the largest single group consisted of those who approved of the investigation without reservations: "50% of our respondents saw no ethical problem whatsoever in doing the study as we wrote it [Barber *et al.*, 1973, p. 38]."

## The Demography of Ethical Commitment

The results of the few available studies on the relation of ethical principles to demographic and other attitudinal variables indicate that research commitment is inversely related to the rigor of individual ethical standards. Hamsher and Reznikoff (1967) found quite consistent results in the answers of 251 psychologists from a variety of institutions:

1. The more intense the commitment to research expressed by the respondents, and the more extensive their research experience, the less they were concerned about stress manipulations of their subjects.
2. Commitment to research and opposition to external control of research showed a perfect positive (rank) correlation.
3. Beginners attributed greater significance to ethical problems.
4. Commitment and expenditure of time to inform subjects were correlated with the importance attributed to the principle of free consent.
5. Women showed more interest in all ethical questions than men did. (The same result appeared in the survey of laymen by Hillis and Wortman, 1976.)
6. Eight occupational groups were identified; school psychologists showed the most commitment to ethical questions, whereas psychologists at universities attributed the least significance to such questions.

The construct "hard-headed scientism of researchers" (Hamsher & Reznikoff, 1967, p. 204) is supported by an investigation by Shapiro and Struening (1973). They asked 240 physicians about their position on the use of placebos in therapy and research and found a clear connection between extent of research activities and lack of concern about use of pseudomedicines with patients in need of treatment.

## Explaining the Effect of Research Commitment

From the point of view of exchange theory, these results are hardly surprising. The more scientists are committed to research—and the more their own interests are connected with the results of their research—the more likely they are to balance their first contract at the expense of their second contract. The first contract, of course, is the scientists' commitment to the scientific community and to the organizations supporting their research. The second contract is their commitment to the welfare of the subjects. Since the two parties to either contract do not have equal power, the scientists can impose increased costs on their subjects (patients) in order to finance the increased benefit expected from the other contract. Corresponding expectations of benefits on the part of the public are useful to scientists, making it easier to conceal personal motives (cf. the quotation from Szent-Györgyi earlier in this chapter). Revealing motives, on the other hand, might further the closing of balanced contracts.

Less benefit is expected by the public and by the researchers themselves from psychological research than from medical research. This could be responsible for the fact that psychological experiments rarely involve such serious danger and harm to the subjects as some of the medical experiments cited: The benefits are not expected to be great enough to balance high costs. To be sure, this impression may also result from the fact that it is harder to establish mental damage than physical damage. Some studies in the interdisciplinary area of psychological physiology are found among the relatively spectacular experiments that have contributed to the development of the discussion of ethical problems in psychology.

## *Illustrations of High-Risk Research*

One example of a high-risk investigation is a study of the intraarterial injection of adrenalin, which is said to involve greater risks than intravenous injection (Glover, Greenfeld, & Shanks, 1962). Subjects were placed under psychological stress by being led to believe that they had been given the wrong dose and were in considerable danger. After 10 anxious minutes, subjects were reassured to the contrary (Pappworth, 1968, p. 96).

Reactions to life-threatening events were also investigated by Berkun, Bialek, Kern, and Yagi (1962). Five different situations that were suitable for arousing fear of death, including a simulated airplane crash, were realized experimentally, some of them with considerable effort. The subjects were soldiers in the American army. In order for the experiments to succeed, it was impossible to inform the subjects in advance; nor had the soldiers volunteered to participate in the experiments. Rather, they were uninformed about the experimental nature of the situations.

An experiment with the induction of fear of death was described at the West Coast Conference for Small Groups Research in San Francisco in 1959. According to Argyle, who raised a protest against this kind of experiment and thereby initiated what was probably the first major public discussion of a psychological experiment, the experiment proceeded as follows:

> In this experiment, young G.I.'s, who were not volunteers, had a sample of blood drawn by an allegedly inexperienced medical orderly. In the middle of the operation, the orderly quickly withdrew the syringe, dropped it, and ran cursing and screaming from the bunker. Immediately afterwards the experimenter rushed in, told the subject that the untrained

orderly had accidentally injected a bubble of air, and that the subject would shortly die as a result. The subject was left alone but kept under observation for a period, later claimed to be half an hour. It was reported that all subjects tested had sat apathetically waiting for the end [1960, p. 1].

The authors of the investigation were attacked violently in the public media; in professional circles, Argyle was attacked and accused (wrongly, according to him) of being responsible for the campaign in the press. The threats and attacks on Argyle, who had to justify himself in writing to his British professional organization, subsided very slowly (Argyle, personal communication, August 1976).

Milgram's series of experiments must certainly be mentioned in particular among the experiments that have contributed to our sensitivity to ethical problems in psychology. Milgram described the first of his experiments on obedience to authority in 1961 in an unpublished research report, which received little notice. The wave of discussion did not start until the project was published in a series of articles beginning in 1963. It continued to an extent that was almost unprecedented for professional circles in psychology. This publication may be considered the actual beginning of the development that is presently leading to—or, as in the United States, has already led to—stricter professional and governmental regulation of research.

In a series of experiments already outlined in Chapter 1, Milgram investigated the extent to which subjects were prepared to obey the experimenter. He related these experiments explicitly to the crimes that were committed in obedience to commands in the Nazi period. As we know—contrary to the expectations of experts (Milgram, 1974)—he was not able to find any limits to willingness to obey in most subjects.

Milgram's study, which was awarded the prize of the American Association for the Advancement of Science in 1964, was criticized first by Baumrind (1964) and then by numerous other professional colleagues. Finally, a considerable number of replications and variations of the study were undertaken. The most important points of criticism, the replies of Milgram (1964) and others to these points, and various attempts at empirical testing of the arguments that were exchanged are all mentioned in the following sections. The central point of discussion was the problem of the deception of subjects. Kelman's comments (1967a and 1968) were particularly influential for subsequent discussions. The development and testing of alternative research methods (presented in Chapter 3), particularly in social psychology, originated primarily in connection with this discussion.

### Rewarding a High-Risk Procedure

To close these introductory remarks, let us cast some light on the system of rewards for researchers, which contributes significantly to the dilemma of research in the biomedical and social sciences. The following case, reported in detail along with a transcript of the court records by Katz (1972, pp. 9–65), speaks for itself.

With the physician Chester M. Southam in charge, 26 chronically ill patients at the Jewish Chronic Disease Hospital in New York received an injection of live cancer cells in July 1963. The experiment had no relationship to the patients' illness and was carried out without the patients' being informed about the nature of the experiments. Instead, the patients were told it was a harmless skin test. The goal of the experiment was to investigate resistance to cancerous tissue that was foreign to the body of the patient.

Experiments with over 300 healthy volunteer prisoners had already shown that cancer cells, like healthy tissue foreign to a person's body, are eliminated after some weeks. In addition to the experiments at the Jewish Chronic Disease Hospital, Southam had also carried out experiments with nearly 300 cancer patients at Memorial Hospital and determined that the expulsion of injected cancer cells by cancer patients is delayed past the usual period shown with healthy persons. Cancer cells that had been injected into one patient who died a half year later (presumably from his original illness) were found to be still alive and present at the time of his death.

The question now under investigation was whether chronically ill patients with lowered resistance who are free from malignant tumors react like healthy persons or like cancer patients or whether in certain cases they are perhaps no longer even able to expel the cancer cells. The result was that they reacted like healthy patients and expelled the cancer cells relatively quickly.

The hearing before the Board of Regents of the State of New York (a legal authority created by the New York legislature as the governing body that makes decisions with regard to all licensed occupations except law) ended in 1965 with the withdrawal of medical certification for the period of one year for the two physicians in charge, Southam and Mandel. This sentence, however, was suspended.

In 1967, at the Fifty-Eighth Annual Meeting of the American Association for Cancer Research, Chester M. Southam was elected vice-president of the association; a year later he was chosen president.

## PROBLEMATIC EXPERIMENTAL PROCEDURES AND THEIR CONSEQUENCES

Let us suppose that psychologists are not the persons whose own research possibilities could perhaps be limited by the open discussion of ethical problems. Instead, imagine them diagnosing the attitudes, statements, and behavior of others with regard to ethics, perhaps as expert witnesses. How much interest and discernment they would apply to identifying the reinforcement systems and motives of experimenters and labeling technical arguments as rationalizations! How much patience and empathy they would apply to classifying the subjects' reactions and interpreting them in connection with the subjects' personality and environment! As we will see in the following pages, not much of this distance and willingness to differentiate can in fact be observed in the exchange and evaluation of arguments by psychologists on this subject. Kelman's demand (1967a) that experimenters should be sensitive to danger signals in their subjects' behavior encounters boundaries that are drawn quite narrowly by the self-concept and self-interest of those involved. In private hardly anyone seems to subscribe to the ethical values suggested by the official guidelines to the extent that these values would influence actions even if the regulations did not exist. Yet the guidelines are influential, especially because the value systems involved can claim public recognition.

Some may question whether it is appropriate to refer to opinions on ethical issues that were expressed in the late 1960s and early 1970s, since later developments may have affected the opinions of those involved in the discussion. However, the arguments that arose in connection with the adoption of ethical principles will always be of historical interest, and in addition, they may be particularly interesting in areas where problems of this sort have not yet begun to be discussed. Principles of historical writing suggest the need to restrict our report of these discussions to the most important arguments and to present the arguments in summary, focusing on a few important aspects.

## Deception or Misinformation

The problem of the deception of subjects, particularly for experiments in social psychology, has undoubtedly received the most attention of all ethical problems in psychological research.

The question of whether to communicate information to the subjects or to keep it secret begins as a methodological question. Awareness that they are being observed and that the observer is interpreting their behavior can change the behavior of persons being observed. Thus, three possibilities suggest themselves. The subjects can be observed without their knowledge. We can arrange for observation in such a way that the subjects are not aware of any characteristics of the investigation that might lead them to alter the behavior that is being investigated. Or, finally, we can arrange for observation in such a way that the subjects interpret these characteristics incorrectly. This involves giving the subjects a certain amount of incorrect information or at least withholding correct information. Any of these strategies fulfills one of the conditions on which the internal validity of an experiment is believed to depend—and of course, every other kind of validity, including that defined by the usefulness of the results, is dependent on internal validity.

The same problem arises in medicine, wherever effects analogous to those in psychological investigations can be assumed. In pharmacology, for example, researchers work with double-blind experimental designs in order to prevent so-called placebo effects. In such designs neither the subjects nor the person administering the medication knows which medication is being used in any individual case. In other sorts of medical experiments, such as those involving surgery, it is believed that knowledge of the experiment will have only minor effects; in the cases where relatively high risks are involved, researchers are almost forced to give complete information.

Researchers designing psychological experiments usually dispense with experimenter blindness, attempting only to keep the subjects naive. For example, subjects may be given a cover story, an explanation of the experiment that is supposed to seem plausible to them and influence their behavior either not at all or to a lesser extent than would knowledge of the actual hypotheses.

The invention of such deceptive maneuvers once seemed unobjectionable to most psychologists. In many branches of psychology, it took on quasi-sporting forms: "a game of 'can you top this?' " as Ring (1967, p. 117) called it in his criticism of the "fun-and-games approach to social psychology." Giving misleading information seemed essential, above all in social psychology and particularly in experiments directly related to Festinger's theory of cognitive dissonance (1957) or inspired indirectly by this theory.

## COUNTING UP THE DECEPTIONS

Various counts have been taken of the frequency of deceptive procedures. Menges (1973) examined various APA journals published in 1971, including a total of approximately 1000 reports of investigations, and found that complete information had been given in only about 3% of the cases, false information in 17%, and incomplete information in 80%. In Stricker's statistics (1967), 19.3% of a total of 457 studies reported active deceptive procedures. The percentage of the studies involving deception varied greatly according to specific area of research. Conformity studies were the highest, with 81.2%. Seeman (1969) found relatively few reports of deception experiments in journals for experimental and clinical psychology, in comparison with publications in the area of personality and social psychology. In addition, he documented an increase in frequency of deception from 18.47% to 38.17% by comparing the 1948 and 1963 volumes of the two publications *Journal of Personality* and *Journal of Abnormal and Social Psychology*. Finally, Carlson (1971) cited as an extreme case an experiment by Kiesler, Pallak, and Kanouse (1968) with 18 deceptions and 3 additional manipulations.

## AN EXTREME COUNTERPOSITION: BAUMRIND AND KELMAN

Some of the discussion about the admissibility of these procedures has been conducted with arguments of principle for which the specific nature of the deceptions was not particularly relevant. For example, Baumrind (1971, 1972) condemned every kind of deception and secret observation as a serious violation of human rights that could result in the subject's losing trust, not only in the experimenter, but by generalization in partners for all future social contact. Moreover, Baumrind feared that the scientist might be seen by the subjects as a model, thus promoting subsequent dishonest behavior.

Kelman (1967a) suggested that things happen in psychological experiments that contradict all widely held human values. He asserted that psychologists have forgotten that their interaction partners are human beings and that the obligation to be honest with them cannot be abandoned at will. It is a violation of human dignity even to create situations in which one of the interaction partners is free from this obligation, he claimed. This last argument, a basic postulate of humanistic psychology, was elaborated into a theory of power in social research by Kelman in 1972. Deception and manipulation will always stand in the way of a partnership that can be characterized by mutual respect, argued Kelman. His call for the development of fundamentally different research methods was based on this argument.

## METHODOLOGICAL ISSUES IN CONNECTION WITH DECEPTION

Methodological as well as ethical arguments can be detected in the work of Kelman, Baumrind, and most other critics of deception: namely, that deceptions are seen through by many subjects and make the subjects useless for future experiments because of their mistrust. Understandably, the methodological side of the discussion is emphasized by advocates of the opposite point of view. Hendrick and Jones (1972) referred to the absolute necessity of giving false information if the results are to have the value intended. (Similar references are found in Flanagan, 1973; Weber and Cook, 1972; and many others.) Otherwise, warned Hendrick and Jones, the results from investigations of attitude change, for example, would give information about subjects' values rather than about the variables that influence attitudes. Rubin (1973) not only feared the effect of evaluation apprehension and demand characteristics but also warned that complete information would necessarily be very confusing to subjects. Gergen (1973a) added ironically that subjects can also be bored when given too much information and that to bore subjects is not unproblematic from an ethical standpoint.

In 1962 Argyle had taken the position that harmless deceptions in themselves were insignificant, just as debriefing of the subjects did not make much difference if the subjects were not bored, confused, or otherwise harmed by the experiment. But few of the participants in the subsequent discussion of deception claimed point blank, as had Argyle, that they still found nothing really problematic about the deception of subjects. Gergen (1973a) attacked the custom of placing the labels "deception" and "manipulation" on actions that everyone carries out daily and calls by other names. McGuire formulated a similar point of view in this way: "Were we to list the moral problems of psychology, we would cite those who are doing experiments which involve deception far below those who are doing too few experiments or none at all as a source of ethical concern [1969, p. 53]." He amplified this statement through a metaphor: "It seems to us that the angel of death is likely to come upon more of our colleagues in idleness than in sin [p. 53]." Elsewhere McGuire supplemented this appeal with the reflection that renouncing the deception of some subjects might in certain cases amount to a deception of colleagues and the public—that is, a deception with regard to whether the results could be generalized (McGuire, 1972, p. 237).

## COUNTING UP CATEGORIES OF DECEPTION

Thus, the deception of subjects was assigned a central role in the discussion of ethical problems. Correspondingly, a number of attempts were made to systematize the kinds of deception that are found among psychological research methods (Arellano-Galdames, 1972; S. W. Cook, 1976). For example, Arellano-Galdames distinguishes between passive and active deception. The various kinds of *active deception* (deception by commission) include:

1. Misrepresentation of the purpose of the investigation
2. Untrue statements about the identity of the researcher
3. False promises
4. Violation of the promise of anonymity
5. Incorrect explanations of equipment and procedures
6. Use of pseudosubjects
7. False diagnoses and other reports
8. Pseudointeraction
9. Use of placebos and secret application of medications and drugs
10. Misleading settings for the investigations and corresponding behavior by the experimenter

On the other hand, the following procedures are classified as *passive deception* (deception by omission):

1. Unrecognized conditioning
2. Provocation and secret recording of negatively evaluated behavior
3. Concealed observation
4. Unrecognized participant observation
5. Use of projective techniques and other personality tests

Some of these deceptive procedures are used chiefly outside of laboratory experiments, but most are used primarily in such experiments. Arellano-Galdames's classification provides no clear boundaries. Assigning procedures to one of the two basic categories is difficult, and the subdivisions are not sharply distinct. Nearly all the experiments that contain any kind of deception, as well as most concrete deceptive measures, fall into several of the divisions enumerated. Moreover, the enumeration is probably not exhaustive, despite its comprehensiveness. These weaknesses are equally true of all other existing taxonomies. Nevertheless, the list may serve to remind us of the variety of misleading procedures inspired by concern for internal validity.

## AN ATTEMPT TO EVALUATE THE PLACE OF DECEPTION

How, then, are these various processes to be evaluated? Is it more justifiable to state a false purpose for the investigation than to let pseudosubjects interact with the real subjects? Are false promises more objectionable than false feedback? Is it more problematic to withhold from subjects the information that they are participating in a conditioning experiment or the information that they are receiving a placebo instead of the expected medication? Or are all these procedures equally acceptable or unacceptable because they all involve giving incorrect or incomplete information? S. W. Cook (1976, p. 211) gives examples of investigations in which the subjects were chosen on the basis of particular characteristics: because they were particularly low achievers, had feelings of inferiority, or had certain prejudices. One might add to the list: because they were especially unattractive or had only a low life expectancy. Are experimenters also obliged to give the subjects complete information in such cases? Or rather are they obliged to do the opposite? Or are they obliged to abandon the investigation because of this conflict?

These questions lead us to consider whether it may be inappropriate to make overall judgments about the acceptability of a class of behaviors that do not have much more in common than a very general name for the class. Craftiness and self-interest can be the source of a deception, but so can compassion. The form of a deception can be the incidental suppression of an insignificant bit of information or the presentation of a distorted image of reality, planned over a long period. The consequences of a deception can be harmless or catastrophic. In deceiving subjects, for example, an experimenter can have them playing matrix games with a computer program instead of a partner, or, like Bramel (1962), can tell them that a psychological instrument shows unquestionably that they have strong homosexual tendencies.

The word *deception* has connotations that should not be associated with a regularly used research method. *Webster's Third New International Dictionary* lists the following words as meaning the same as *to deceive*: to mislead, to delude, to beguile, to betray, to double-cross. Without exception, the implication is the deception of another person to one's own advantage and that person's disadvantage. But this certainly does not apply to all experiments in the social sciences, and it should not apply to any of them. Occasionally one can even assume the opposite. S. W. Cook (1975) and Kelman (1975) discuss the acceptability of the deceptive measures in a study by Levendusky and Pankratz (1975), who administered therapy to an unwilling patient.

*Drawing Finer Distinctions.* To a large extent, the evaluation of actions is dominated by the implications of the words in which the actions are described. Considering this, the term *deception* could prove to be inappropriate for the procedures in most psychological experiments. It is not enough to differentiate deceptive measures by their form—for example, deception by omission versus deception by commission (Arellano-Galdames, 1972), or, similarly, withholding of information versus active deception (McGuire, 1969), or white lies (nonverbal deception) versus black lies (verbal deception) (Campbell, 1969). Campbell points out that it is the "liar"—the experimenter—and not necessarily the subjects for whom white lies are less unpleasant than black lies. He adds, "Lying of either sort is less painful and less immoral when occurring in a setting where it is both expected and justified by convention [1969, p. 370]."

An appropriate evaluation of deceptive procedures in experiments, like the evaluation of modes of behavior that are unrelated to science, can result only from a synoptic presentation of intentions, consequences, forms, and—connected with these—conventions. In experiments in social psychology, unlike medical experiments or experiments in clinical and therapeutic psychology, the statistics cited seem to indicate that certain kinds of dishonesty are part of the usual procedure and thus are also covered by conventions. This dishonesty is a part of the social contract between the experimenter and the experienced subject and can easily be made a part of this contract in the case of inexperienced subjects. This agreement need not be restricted to a single experiment. Rather, as Campbell (1969, p. 370) suggested, subjects can be informed at the beginning of the semester that some of the experiments in which they will participate will include, for the sake of validity, deceptions that will not be revealed until the end of the entire series of experiments.

*Taking the Sting out of Deception.* The deception thereby becomes a part of the agreement, which can be made voluntarily. Indeed, voluntary agreement is necessary in order to make deception unproblematic. In such a case, the deception should not be burdened with a connotation of betrayal but should be called "misinformation" or something similar. This misinformation is only part of the lack of transparency of the experimental situation for the subject. It should be evaluated within the parameters of the contract, like other behavioral events that are made possible by and simultaneously define the inequality of roles between experimenter and subject. The term *misinformation* is appropriate for a deceptive procedure comparable to the deceptions that are part of a social activity such as a party game or a magician's act. The experimenter's deception is no more offensive than the social deception, but subjects must be sure that dispensing temporarily with complete information will not lead to consequences that they will perceive as aversive. If damage or harm to the subject results from or is made possible by a deception or even seems remotely possible, we should speak not only of deception but even of betrayal. In such a situation, subjects are persuaded by means of a trick to make a contract that they would have had good reason to refuse to make if they had had complete information. Similarly, sleight-of-hand artists who do not return gold watches borrowed from members of the audience are guilty not only of theft but also of betrayal, because they deliberately took advantage of the owners' faith in the implied harmlessness of all procedures and thereby broke the contract.

### THE SUBJECT'S POINT OF VIEW

It has been difficult for psychologists to agree on the acceptability of false or withheld information. Moreover, as experience with the ethical codes of the American Psychological Association has shown (see Chapter 4), it is impossible to combine clear imperatives for action with the concept of deception. These two difficulties are based partly on the lack of semantic precision reflected in the use of this term both for procedures that resemble betrayal and for procedures that resemble rules of a game. It seems appropriate to reserve the term *deception* for describing the first set of procedures and to describe the latter set with a neutral word such as *misinformation*. To be sure, we would want to be certain that both partners in the contract were employing the same principles of classification, thus making it impossible for a specific procedure intended to guarantee lack of transparency in the experimental situation to be perceived as a rule of the game by the experimenter and as a betrayal by the subject.

Naturally, the opinion of the subjects cannot be ignored in the process of evaluating actions as misinformation or deception. It is their opinion that determines whether it is appropriate to speak of a convention or of an extraordinary procedure. The first survey of subjects on this matter, a direct reaction to Vinacke's suggestions (1954), was reported by MacKinney (1955). MacKinney's respondents had previously been subjects in a decision experiment. They had been falsely promised that they could decide whether they would be given an essay or a multiple-choice test. The participants were then divided into two groups, which were debriefed in different ways. The first group was partially debriefed: That is, they were informed about the most important goals and procedures of the decision experiment. The second group was informed very thoroughly about all details. A control group consisted of persons who had not participated in the experiment and who received only the "Satisfaction Questionnaire." This questionnaire consisted of 13 items on subjects' attitudes toward the experiment, their reactions to the experiment, the presumed attitudes of the experimenter toward the subjects, and their desire for debriefing.

On the whole the results were positive and showed hardly any differences among the three groups: "We found very little evidence that *these subjects* were disturbed by deceiving [MacKinney, 1955, p. 133]." The emphasis is MacKinney's and expresses uncertainty about the representative nature of the subjects. Of course, the generalizability of the contents of the experiment is equally uncertain. In all three groups, negative opinions were expressed by approximately 14% of the subjects. If we choose to interpret minor differences as well, we can conclude that the opinions of the partially debriefed subjects were the most favorable. However, 75% of the subjects indicated that they preferred complete information about the experiment.

All later surveys of the attitudes and expectations of subjects, as well as the observation of their behavior in experiments, corresponded basically to MacKinney's results. For example, Fillenbaum's subjects were called "faithful" because they performed their tasks docilely in spite of their awareness of the misinformation and did not behave any differently from naive subjects (Fillenbaum, 1966). The obligation to be honest was ascribed to the experimenter by only 6.7% of the subjects surveyed by Epstein *et al.* (1973), whereas 39.7% considered the experimenter obligated to give clear instructions and 27.2% saw an obligation to guarantee their safety (see also the section in Chapter 1 on the subjects' perceptions of the experimenter). When Resnick and Schwartz (1973) wanted to carry out a conditioning experiment with a group of fully prebriefed subjects for the purpose of comparing methods, the participants in this group were so skeptical or mistrustful that half of them did not appear at the prearranged time; some even claimed that they considered the whole experiment a joke.

Thus, we cannot deduce any need for a general condemnation of misinforming or partially informing subjects on the basis of the attitudes and expectations of the subjects themselves. Instead, the subjects seem, just as much as the experimenters, to consider some lack of transparency to be an essential part of an experiment. Resnick and Schwartz (1973, p. 137) even speculate that psychological experiments are considered uninteresting without this element of uncertainty and that therefore its absence would discourage many subjects from participating. Nor does it seem unjustified to argue that we could expect psychology students, our future colleagues, to tolerate this kind of uncertainty. After all, for them participation in the experiment is also a kind of introspection exercise that would not always be possible if they were completely informed, or at least would not always have the same results.

## DECEPTION FROM THE METHODOLOGICAL PERSPECTIVE

The discussion of the admissibility of deceptive procedures has also inspired a series of investigations on the effect of these procedures from a methodological point of view. Baumrind (1972, p. 1084) cites evidence summarized by Wahl (1972) that deception is not effective, since it does not ensure the naiveté of subjects or guarantee an increase in experimental realism. If deception offers no methodological advantage, suggests Baumrind, it is also no longer justifiable in terms of a cost–benefit analysis.[1]

What evidence is there that the widely practiced deceptive procedures have not even reached their goal of guaranteeing the validity of the experimental results? Baumrind's contention is not supported by Stricker (1967), who screened 88 investigations in which misinformation was implied. In 23.9% (21) of the investigations, signs of distrust were noted among the subjects. However, the number of subjects who were distrustful in each case was low: 3.7% on the average, with male subjects (4.4%) clearly more distrustful than female subjects (1.6%). Assuming the presence of appropriate methods for eliciting distrust (which, to be sure, cannot simply be assumed), it is impossible that the percentage of error resulting from the distrust could be very high. Even if all distrustful subjects had reacted differently from the subjects who were acting in good faith, the resulting error would presumably still be far lower than the percentage contributed by other variables to the error variance. Indeed, it seems that distrust alone is not responsible for any errors that can be localized, at least not in all cases.

The investigations reported by Cook et al. (1970), Cook and Perrin (1971), and Stricker, Messick, and Jackson (1969) show an uneven pattern with regard to the problem of distrust. The dominant impression is that in most cases there is no difference or no great difference between the data of distrustful and naive subjects. An experiment carried out by Cook and Perrin showed a complex interaction of distrust with the subjects' opinions about the legitimacy of deception in an experiment, as was to be expected. Unequivocal results, like those reported by Silverman, Shulman, and Wiesenthal (1970), are rare in such

---

1. Such a conclusion is somewhat problematic, however. If we assume a strict ethical standpoint, it can be dangerous to rationalize our arguments and support our recommendations with operational or predictive statements. Such statements make it possible for one's position to be falsified. More precisely, the statements may appear to weaken that position; they can falsify it when descriptive and prescriptive parts of the argumentation are irremediably contaminated. Thus, if someone opposes increasing penalties for crime on a strictly ethical basis, that person may be tempted to cite the argument of the ineffectiveness of increased threats of punishment. It is not wise to do so, however, because this concession to those who accept only empirical arguments can turn out to be a point scored against the person's own side. Confounding a specific positively valued empirical outcome with a broad philosophical principle reduces the philosopher to a level of arguing about facts. Moreover, the operational or predictive statements could be disproved, and thereby the ethical principles might be called into question prematurely.

situations. Silverman *et al.* found that subjects who had experience with deception in a preliminary experiment differed from control persons on all measures in a subsequent experiment.

Thus, previous experience of subjects can play a certain role, although the exact character of this role is not yet clear. Cook *et al.* (1970) found that mere participation in several experiments did not lead to distrust; however, behavior contrary to the assumed hypotheses did tend to appear more often in subjects with experience in being deceived. On the other hand, Holmes (1967) observed the opposite tendency in his subjects. That is, they did their jobs as well as possible and no longer concerned themselves at all about detecting the hypotheses. It seems plausible that both the nature of the variables investigated and the nature of the behavior expected could be moderator variables for the connection being sought, but even here the relationship is not simple. While Schuler (1975) found that quantified speculations of the subjects about the hypotheses had no recognizable relationship to their decision behavior in a group situation, the conformity of the subjects classified as distrustful by Stricker, Messick, and Jackson (1967) was lower than that of the subjects who were considered naive. Stricker *et al.* also found a connection between distrust variables and a number of personality traits, such as social desirability, self-esteem, and intelligence. The investigation by Turner and Simons (1974) indicates that previously deceived subjects were less ready to punish other subjects with electric shocks.

Wahl's study (1972), on which Baumrind's arguments are based, actually shows above all that usable results can be attained even when the subjects are prewarned that not all the information they will receive in the course of the experiment will be correct. This corresponds to McGuire's (1969) experiences. On the other hand, the subject group that was completely prebriefed by Wahl showed behavior in a conformity experiment that differed from that of the uninformed group. We will consider this difference again when discussing role playing as an alternative research method. When one examines the relevant investigations, the summary by Weber and Cook (1972) seems on the whole to be justified: "The effects of prior deception seem to be surprisingly few in number and small in magnitude [p. 286]."

*DECEPTION IN PERSPECTIVE*

From the standpoint of deontological rule theory, it is always reprehensible to give other persons false information, to withhold complete information, or to expose them even with their consent to situations that lack transparency in certain aspects. Assuming that one does not share this viewpoint, it does not seem inappropriate to conclude from the results summarized here that deceptive procedures in psychological experiments can only be evaluated in the context of the particular situation, with knowledge of the goals and consequences for the persons involved. Restricting the discussion of ethical problems to the question of the deception of subjects has in some ways distracted us from more important questions rather than clarifying them.

Instead, the problem of deception is a general problem in the following sense: Deceptions make it possible to use other procedures or encourage other developments that are questionable either in themselves or in connection with the lack of transparency of the situation. For example, lack of transparency can be used for invasion of privacy, or it can facilitate exposing subjects to stress, lowering of self-esteem, and other experiences that they would not undergo voluntarily. In view of the consideration that all experimental procedures must be evaluated from the standpoint of how well informed the subjects are, the principle of informed consent has increased in significance considerably, in medical and biological research even more than in psychology.

The deception of subjects has often been considered as an isolated, one-dimensional problem rather than in connection with other parameters of the investigation. The possible consequences of such a limited consideration may be illustrated by an experiment mentioned by Argyle (personal communication, August 1976). In this experiment on provoked aggressive behavior, subjects had the opportunity to attack their partners with electric shocks. In order not to be guilty of deceiving the subjects, the experimenter used real subjects, not pseudosubjects, as victim–partners. Also, the electric shocks were not simulated, as is usual in such cases; rather, for ethical reasons, they were genuine.

## Psychological and Physical Harm and Danger

The variety of the phenomena that can be experienced as psychological or physical harm and the procedures that can result in such experiences would certainly justify an attempt at detailed categorization. An exhaustive list of such phenomena and procedures, however, would be neither very useful nor practical. Later we will discuss the possibility of a taxonomy of experimental procedures from an ethical point of view, but here we have another goal: to show the connection of the relevant procedures and their consequences with other parameters of the experimental situation and to indicate the possibility of evaluating such procedures in the context of the proposed concept of the experiment as a social contract. We will also cite some of the most important statements published on this subject. These arguments have generally not been limited to taking a position on the acceptability of specific procedures, but rather have claimed a more general validity.

Several investigations that led to debates on the acceptability of certain kinds of procedures were reported at the beginning of this chapter. We should note that very few psychological investigations are as spectacular and as clearly questionable as the many examples obtainable from the field of medicine. This contrast may be attributable to differences in the state and the object of research for the two disciplines, and the greater danger in medicine may be inherent in the discipline. But the contrast may also be due to a difference in the stringency of ethical standards or to the ease of diagnosing physical damage compared with the uncertainties of diagnosing psychological damage resulting from research procedures in the social sciences. And surely a considerable part of the contrast can be traced back to cost–benefit analyses. The benefits expected from medical research are probably greater than those expected from psychological research by precisely the degree that corresponds to the difference in the risk to which the two disciplines expose their subjects. This difference is encouraged by the higher proportion of applied research in medicine. Connected with this is the presumed or actual coincidence of individual benefit (that is, therapeutic effects on the subjects as patients) with the collective benefits of knowledge that can be applied. However, the figures of Barber and associates (1973, pp. 44–57) show that the proportion of medical research that benefits individual subjects is considerably overestimated by the public.

## RESEARCH THAT RAISES THE ISSUE OF BEARING COSTS

Let us assume that we do not merely accept the need to balance costs and benefits for an individual bearer (person) and to balance overall costs and benefits to be expected from a particular research project. Rather, we also expect individuals to bear the costs for possible later collective benefits (without necessarily consenting to this decision). If so, the fact that medical research seems more problematic than psychological research at the moment may merely reflect a temporary lead of medical research on psychological research. Therefore, the relatively low number of psychological experiments with spectacularly questionable ethical aspects could be explained by the fact that the value of psychological research is perhaps not yet considered high enough to justify higher risks and potential harm. If psychology should succeed in making its research more obviously relevant, the model of medicine would suggest a concomitant increase in the burden of risks expected for each subject. It would be shortsighted to discuss the admissibility of individual kinds of harm without seeing the principle behind them.

Nevertheless, some psychological investigations have been challenged, and quite a few more would have been worth challenging. Some of these experiments have already been mentioned here, including the experiments by Berkun et al. (1962) on the behavior of soldiers under fear of death and Milgram's experiments on obedience to authorities. Other examples that deserve to be named are the manipulation by Bramel (1962), who made subjects believe they had strong homosexual tendencies, and by Bergin (1962), who led subjects to think that their scores on the masculinity factor of a personality test were typical of the opposite sex. In another study, a group of students was graded very severely in order to determine the effect of test anxiety on exam grades (Goldberg, 1965); these grades were not corrected until after the exam in the next semester. French (in 1944) investigated reactions to stress by confining a group of subjects in a room and letting smoke pour into the room through the crack under the door (cited by S. W. Cook, 1976, p. 222). Coe, Kobayashi, and Howard (1973) persuaded hypnotized subjects to sell heroin. Heacock, Thurber, and Vale (1975) investigated, like many before them, readiness to behave aggressively in reaction to aversive stimuli (electric shocks). West, Gunn, and Chernicky (1975) induced subjects to declare their readiness for a burglary similar to Watergate; long before, other experimenters had already managed to provoke their subjects to steal, lie, and swindle, to perform acts of violence, and to endanger themselves.

## THE PHYSICAL VERSUS THE PSYCHOLOGICAL

In the preceding list, which could be made much longer, procedures from which psychological harm can be expected undoubtedly outnumber procedures involving possible physical harm. Physical harm and risk seem to be relatively rare in psychological research. Electric shocks, deprivation of food, consumption of alcohol, nicotine, and drugs, injections of adrenalin, acoustic and optical stimuli that reach the threshold of pain, removal of blood, and certain kinds of physical strain occasionally appear, but most of the effects do not have nearly the intensity required to be genuinely dangerous or heavily stressful. In their usual intensity, they are generally perceived by subjects as unproblematic (Farr & Seaver, 1975); however, various effects, such as those of drugs, are hard for subjects to assess themselves.

It is said that in military and secret service research there are quite a few exceptions to the usual absence of physical danger in psychological experiments. Occasionally, incidents such as lethal drug experiments commissioned by the CIA are reported in the press (*The New York Times, International Herald Tribune,* and others, cited by Haaf, 1977, and supplemented by personal information). Another example is the research of Soviet military scientists on the neurological and behavior-altering effects of microwaves and extremely high voltage (Lützenkirchen, 1977). As important as these reports can be for public awareness, our present discussion must be limited to those research activities that have been made public in the profession.

The effects of psychological stresses and risks and of the provocation of immoral or illegal behavior that have been induced or feared include various kinds of fear (fear of pain, test anxiety, fear of death, phobic fears, etc.), frustration, harm from sensory or dream deprivation, damaged self-esteem, self-doubts, insecurity, change in the self-image, embarrassment, feelings of guilt, reinforcement of immoral behavior, habituation to aggressive behavior, loss of trust and other changes in social attitudes and orientations, confusion, disillusionment, and many kinds of emotionally negative reactions to specific experiences.

*Baumrind on Milgram.* The discussion of the justifiability of exposing subjects to the risk of such harm did not begin on a large scale until after Milgram's experiments (1963). Baumrind (1964) was the first psychologist to take a position publicly on these experiments, proceeding from some considerations that also form the basis of the contract concept outlined here. She called on experimenters to offer just compensation for subjects' investments by providing pleasant experiences and pointed out the right of the subjects to expect security and the preservation of their self-esteem when they commit themselves to voluntary dependence on the experimenter. She called for procedures that would prevent subjects in experiments involving risks "from leaving the laboratory more humiliated, insecure, alienated, or hostile [p. 421]" than when they arrived. Baumrind criticized severely Milgram's exposure of the subjects to a high degree of stress, citing two incidents reported by Milgram (1963) himself: "Within 20 minutes he was reduced to a twitching, stuttering wreck, who was rapidly approaching a point of nervous collapse [p. 375]." And, "On one occasion we observed a seizure so violently convulsive that it was necessary to call a halt to the experiment [p. 377]." Above all, Baumrind doubted that it was possible in all cases for debriefing to prevent long-term changes in the self-image, damage to self-esteem, or loss of trust. She suggested that naive, sensitive subjects would continue to feel deeply hurt for quite a while and that sophisticated, cynical subjects would grow still more alienated and distrustful (Baumrind, 1964, p. 423). Contrary to her later views (1972), Baumrind would have considered such consequences bearable if the results had been of "inestimable value for mankind." However, she was not prepared to assume this; rather, she expressed doubts about the validity of these experiments in particular and about the validity of psychological experiments in general.

*Milgram's Reply.* Milgram (1964) justified his investigations with the claim that these results could not have been predicted. Indeed, surveys of colleagues had resulted in totally incorrect prognoses (Milgram, 1974). The first reactions of his subjects, he said, seemed interesting and important enough to justify continuing. By no means could permanent damage by the stress during the experiment be assumed, he asserted, especially since the debriefing was very thorough. Rather, he expected the subjects to benefit from the warning not to submit unthinkingly to authorities. As proof, Milgram cited thank-you letters from some of his subjects, as well as data from a subsequent survey indicating that most subjects were glad they had participated (83.7%), relatively few regretted very much having participated (15.1%) or expressed mild regrets (0.8%), and hardly any were indifferent (0.5%).

Milgram's coworker, Errera, reported similar impressions, though not in statistical form. After a year had passed, Errera conducted thorough interviews with Milgram's subjects. Errera found no cases of permanent damage and only short-term effects of the experience. Within a few days, most distress was relieved; a letter explaining the experiment and some preliminary findings dispelled any remaining discomfort, according to Errera (1972). To be sure, some subjects expressed anger toward the experimenter, but suitable attribution made it possible to record these reactions as unproblematic. Errera found that the angriest subjects seemed to be chronically discontented with their environment and with any available authority figures (1972, p. 400).

*Aftereffects: Ring, Wallston, and Corey.* On the other hand, a replication of Milgram's experiment by Ring, Wallston, and Corey (1970) cast doubt on the complete elimination of negative aftereffects. To be sure, the "model subjects" proved to be grateful for this experience because they had the feeling that they had learned something new about themselves, although their irritation about the successful deception remained. Some subjects, however, reported persistent disappointment and irritation with themselves or expressed self-doubts. And "several suggested that while they themselves were not that deeply affected by their experimental experience, they knew certain other people who would be and that 'they wouldn't have been able to take it' [Ring *et al.*, 1970, p. 82]." Projection is probably not the only defense mechanism to be expected in such cases. Moreover, it turned out that the mode of debriefing was significant. The subjects' stress was reduced more effectively when debriefing included a justification of their behavior than when it did not.

### SUBJECTS' OPINIONS ON EXPERIMENTAL STRESSES

An investigation by Walster, Berscheid, Abrahams, and Aronson (1967) also led to doubts about the dependability of debriefing. This study shows that there are considerable individual differences in reaction to experiments. Persons with high assessments of their own social competence or acceptance by others (defined by the Minnesota Multiphasic Personality Inventory fear of rejection scale) reconstructed their experimentally damaged self-images after the debriefing. However, this did not happen to persons with lower self-assessment. The damage caused by manipulative confirmation of their self-doubts could not be repaired by the debriefing, although the subjects reported that they understood the purpose of the investigation and the inappropriate nature of the manipulation. The debriefing was quite long and unusually thorough in the Walster *et al.* experiment and in an experiment by Abrahams (1967) that was mentioned by Walster and associates (1967) in this context; yet to some extent, subjects still seemed unaffected by the debriefing. The authors expressed their concern that debriefing often seems to leave residual effects that are complex and hard to interpret (p. 300).

Thus, the basically favorable results—those that indicate that the danger of permanent damage tends to be small—could be attributed in part to insufficiently differentiated measurements as well as to dissimulation by subjects. Giving the impression of being healthy and mature is one of the strongest needs of subjects (cf. Chapter 1).

Sullivan and Deiker (1973) were also able to produce partially favorable results. In evaluating the acceptability of four experiments under suspicion of being harmful (stress/pain/self-esteem/immoral behavior), psychologists who were surveyed almost always applied stricter ethical standards than did the student respondents. To be sure, the students also indicated, in some cases by a high percentage, that forewarned subjects would not participate voluntarily (for one of the experiments described, 61% of the students felt this way) and that they perceived the implicit deception as unethical (up to 51%). These results suggest that the stricter ethical standards of the psychologists may serve more as a warning against leaving the evaluation of the acceptability of experiments up to students than as an exoneration of those who expose subjects to risks.

The investigation by Farr and Seaver (1975) should probably also be considered with reservations. In this investigation, subjects rated various physical and psychological stresses on a 5-point scale. Whereas none of the procedures connected with invasion of privacy was rated higher than 2.93, and only one higher than 2.19, physical work accompanied by the smell of rotten eggs was rated 3.48. At an average value of 3.29, it seems that the subjects would have been more willing to have a 4-ounce steel weight fall on their fingers from a height of 12 inches. None of the mental discomforts was rated higher than 3.51, with one exception: to spend 10 minutes in a room with the object one fears most.

In a survey by Epstein *et al.* (1973), 32.6% of the respondents felt that subjects should have the right to break off an experiment when it is connected with invasion of privacy, pain, unpleasantness, confusion, or humiliation. In comparison with the ratings in the preceding paragraph, this figure seems rather high. But as a rule these subjects are not any more likely to discontinue participation than the 23.3% who felt that discontinuation was justified in the case of false or insufficient information.

## RATIONALE FOR MODERATE STRESSES AND DECEPTIONS

Gergen (1973a) argues that permanent harm to subjects in psychological research has not yet been demonstrated and thus that professional regulations controlling research projects are unjustified. This can hardly be denied, at least empirically, although some studies do indicate some harm. To be sure, the counterargument to Gergen's seems more convincing: Subjects, or experimenters representing their cases, cannot be held responsible for proving suspected harm. Rather, the experimenter responsible for the project in question is responsible for proving the harmlessness of a procedure or at least demonstrating high plausibility that a procedure is harmless.

It would lead us too far afield to list individually all arguments for and against risk of damage. Thus, they will be categorized into several groups, and thereby doubtless shortened, in the following pages.

One argument occasionally presented for the admissibility of a certain amount of harm points out the risks and dangers to which one is normally exposed in life and the stresses that one must withstand in other contexts. For example, Steiner (1972) remarks ironically that students face a much higher degree of stress and lack of transparency in academic tests than in psychological experiments. The appropriate counterargument against Steiner's position is customarily found in the field of law and social ethics: Minor evils cannot be justified by the fact that greater evils already exist elsewhere (S. W. Cook, 1976).

A more frequently heard argument with regard to risks—specifically, with regard to psychological stress—emphasizes a positive aspect, the educational benefits for the subjects. According to Kaufmann (1967), human beings benefit from the stresses to which they are exposed; experiments like Milgram's offer them the chance to correct what is apparently a false self-image. Gergen's variation (1973a): Even if the effect were long-lasting self-doubts or insecurity, on the basis of what standards could we say that this was a disadvantage? And the counterargument to Gergen: If we were to stipulate as a prerequisite for establishing ethical standards that they be derivable logically from absolute truths, we would have to renounce all evaluation of human behavior. (How, for example, would we prove that it is wrong to take someone's life?) A more concrete counterargument: We have no right to subject people without their explicit request to educational or therapeutic procedures. A further counterargument: Knowing and changing oneself is a complex process; useful experiences may perhaps be expected in a therapeutic context, but not from a short and threatening laboratory experience (S. W. Cook, 1976). One more counterargument, mentioned by Arellano-Galdames (1972), is that the alleged learning experience is not necessarily positive. According to research based on dissonance theory, it can be expected that immoral behavior carried out in an experiment would subsequently be evaluated more positively and practiced more frequently in the future by the subjects.

A third group of arguments, advanced less often, denies the responsibility of the researcher for the experiences or behaviors of the subjects. After all, it is the subject and not the experimenter who lies, steals, or tortures others.

Indeed, such a concept of behavioral freedom was originally assumed by Milgram in 1963. May (1972), in direct opposition to Baumrind (1971), points out that subjects are chosen at random from a population that has not been screened for emotional disturbances. How can we hold a researcher responsible for contributing to the emotional instability of an individual if the university as a whole cannot master this problem? A resolute counterposition was expressed in the APA's *Ethical Principles in the Conduct of Research with Human Participants* (1973) and has been considered binding for the members of this association ever since.

The final and perhaps most decisive focus of the discussion is the question of balancing costs and benefits of scientific knowledge. This is relevant not only to the problem of harm but also for deception, invasion of privacy, and all other problems. Many arguments on individual questions are based on this cost–benefit analysis, which is the foundation of most research guidelines. Such analysis has often been questioned in the field of medicine; rarely, however, has the risk–benefit approach been rejected by psychologists as rigorously as by Baumrind (1971). At that time the APA committee's draft of *Ethical Principles* already existed. It was based on this approach, as were the attitudes of most of Baumrind's colleagues (which were indeed supposed to be mirrored in *Ethical Principles*). This problem will be discussed separately in the sections of this chapter on the philosophy of weighing costs and benefits.

## THE SUBJECT ROLE: CONNECTING THE METHODOLOGICAL ISSUE TO THE ETHICAL ISSUE

Only rarely have those who concern themselves with risks to subjects attempted to examine connections among the various problem areas. It might be helpful to devote more attention to the connections of possible harm with the voluntary nature of participation in experiments, with the possibility that the subject might break off an experiment, and with methodological questions. Even when subjects give their consent, their participation is often voluntary only in appearance or in a limited sense. Discontinuation by subjects must be examined in the light of insights into the social psychology of the experiment. And finally, one relevant methodological question is whether the risk of harm is just as "necessary" as misinforming the subjects or whether it can be prevented by finding another way of implementing the independent variables, by choosing other methods, or even by modifying the research question. Attempts to evaluate individual experimental procedures have proved to be nearly hopeless, except in extreme cases. We will discuss in Chapter 4 the extent to which the research guidelines that have been formulated by the psychological associations of a number of countries in recent years do more justice to the complexity of research ethics and to what extent this complexity has been reflected in subsequent discussion and research.

One central problem remains unresolved: the need for reliable empirical testing of the consequences for subjects of experimental procedures that are not within the realm of everyday experience. Surely we will never be able to anticipate all possible consequences and determine all effects that can be expected, although sensitivity, patience, and consideration may be able to reduce the probability that side effects will appear. S. W. Cook (1976, p. 242) gives an impressive example of unexpected consequences in an experiment involving the Galvanic Skin Response (GSR) measure with children. By chance the electrode fastened to each child's hand had a red plastic end, and the instrument recorded the response in red ink. Suddenly an 8-year-old subject jumped up and ran distractedly out of the room. Later it was discovered that the child had thought the electrode was drawing blood from his hand. Independent of such unlikely turns of events, testing those effects that can be predicted—in a more differentiated and more valid way—is a task that seems at the moment to be beyond the realm of perceived obligation and beyond the realm of competence of most experimenters.

*Idiosyncratic Reactions of Subjects.* The effects of particular procedures, such as giving false information about abilities and tendencies or provoking aggressive behavior toward other subjects, are effects on individuals. The variance of the consequences of such manipulations must be far greater than is acknowledged by the experimental psychologists whose designs are intended to examine the difference between means of groups. The variance owing to individual idiosyncrasies usually appears in the data analysis only as error variance. This may be due to the low opinion of differential psychology held by experimental and particularly social psychologists.

*An Illustration from Research on Homosexuality.* Male subjects in Bramel's (1962, 1963) research were connected to a GSR machine. They were told that the galvanometer, which they were to watch for the purpose of recording the reading, was especially suited for indicating unconscious sexual response. After an attempt to reinforce their negative cognitions about homosexuality with some additional statements, the subjects were shown pictures of naked men. For some subjects, the GSR reading was manipulated in such a way that they would necessarily conclude that they had strong homosexual tendencies. The second group received values that indicated the absence of such tendencies. The dependent variable was the attribution to others of homosexual tendencies, conceptualized here as a defensive projection. From this attribution measure, inner processes were inferred—namely, a need to defend oneself against unacceptable self-cognitions. Other inner processes that could result from this manipulation, as well as their variance, were ignored. For example, no attention was paid to the change in self-image with respect to probable homosexual tendencies or with respect to the effects on other facets of the self-image. Nor were the effects of probable homosexual tendencies on the related alteration of self-esteem considered. The differences in sensitivity among the subjects were unknown and not an object of interest, nor were their varying abilities to resist information or integrate it safely into their self-images. The following aspects were also ignored and not measured: the significance of the variables for the previous self-concept of the subjects, subjects' tendency to reinterpret previous experience in light of their possibly altered self-concepts, possible change in the structure of their attitudes and values, implications for future behavior and for the classification and evaluation of their own and others' behavior, altered perception of their own and others' behavior as normal, effects on what sorts of behavior they would notice in the future, effects on actual sexual behavior, and so forth.

*Naiveté on the Impact of Debriefing.* Our only purposes here are, first, to illustrate the breadth of inter- and intraindividual variance in reactions and, second, to note the naiveté of assuming that debriefing can reverse all of these complex, interdependent changes in all subjects or that it can reverse those considered undesirable. We are very far from knowing what goes on in an individual. It is not certain what form of debriefing can reverse or re-form in a positive direction the aspects of changed behavior or attitudes that might be evaluated by subjects as negative. Subjects' reactions to the non-open-end dependent variables can enlighten us very little about this. If the two groups should happen not to differ on these dimensions, that in no way implies that no differences exist in the individuals that constitute the group.

It is no accident that most measurements in psychology can explain only a fraction of the observed variance in behavior. The relationships between independent variables, dependent variables, and all the moderating and intervening processes that lie between are still largely beyond our understanding and control. Precisely because the reactions of the subjects are so varied, because so many variables are unknowingly confounded with what we would like to measure, we experiment with larger numbers of subjects in the hope that the uncontrollable quantities will balance each other out. We declare ourselves content with a "significant" fragment of the total variance, perhaps out of behavioristic innocence (or modesty). Because of their contribution to the total sum of experimental results, these procedures can be of some use in connection with the economics of research. Their disadvantages surface in the form of lack of insight and in simple, undifferentiated theories. Both disadvantages are the concern of the researchers and should be taken into account by them. But the effect on the subjects is of interest not merely to the researchers, but also to the subjects themselves. The subjects, with whose help researchers carry out their studies, actually do function in more complicated ways, despite the simplicity of the research theories. Researchers are in danger of transgressing against the responsibility that we all bear toward human beings whose experiences we have manipulated.

## Manipulation

The questionable nature of Bramel's experiment, described in the preceding section, seems at first glance to consist only of subjects' exposure to the risk of changing their self-image in a *specific* way—that is, in the direction of internalizing cognitions about homosexual inclinations. This experiment would not be problematic if less central facets of the self-image had been manipulated or if homosexual orientations did not contradict widely held values. In that case the experiment would not run counter to the guidelines formulated by Kelman (1965) and others that no subject should feel worse after an experiment than before.

But how much leeway does the experimenter rightfully have to change the subjects permanently with respect to values, traits, and aspirations through scientific experiments that do not actually pursue a therapeutic goal (which would be agreed upon, as a rule, with the patient as a contract partner)? The question still seems to be hypothetical. Only in a few cases can permanent changes be traced back to experimental manipulations. Even where permanent influence has been sought—in attitude research, for example—most changes have turned out to be unstable and their measurements to be dependent on the methods used (Nuttin, 1975). But this consolation is deceptive, since the goal of many investigations is indeed to develop *effective* methods. Research efforts will be considered successful when more reliable possibilities of influence have been found.

### VALUE JUDGMENTS IN ATTITUDE CHANGE RESEARCH

In the area of attitude change, we have not progressed far with short-term influence attempts. On the other hand, control of stimuli over a longer period has certainly produced successes. One example is the change in mutual liking among students that occurs as a function of the distance between the rooms assigned to them in a dormitory (Newcomb, 1961). Another example is the successful removal of racial prejudice through manipulated cooperative efforts over a long period (S. W. Cook, 1976). No one will find these examples problematic. The first takes place in the context of normal experience; the second serves a good purpose. But how good is the purpose in drug investigations, for example? In the context of the so-called Harvard drug controversy, Benson and Smith (1972) criticized the experiments with LSD-25 and psilocybin (mescaline) conducted by Leary and Alpert, in which permanent changes in the personality of the subjects were risked. Leary and Alpert (according to Benson & Smith, 1972, p. 391) did not deny that such personality changes really occur; however, they argued that these changes are for the good, in the direction of increased empathy and self-insight, creativity, and love of one's fellow human beings.

In contrast with psychological research in the field, the danger of manipulative influences from laboratory experiments may be relatively low. It is surely low in comparison with the danger in other sciences concerned with humans. To mention one horrible example from genetics: Remington (1972) proposed an experimental design for crossing human beings with anthropoid apes. In addition, he had already developed a proposed ethical code to regulate the treatment of these hybrids: For the sake of scientific progress, they were to be treated like apes. In psychology, the problem of manipulation is more salient in the area of social experimentation (Riecken & Boruch, 1974) or in areas that employ psychological insights for behavioral control, such as educational (Arellano-Galdames, 1972) or organizational research (Argyris, 1975). The usual laboratory experiment cannot compete with the foregoing ones for potentially dangerous consequences.

## THE DANGER OF "EXPORTING" METHODS

Argyris (1975), extending his criticism of the psychological laboratory experiment (Argyris, 1968), pointed out that the problem is not merely the continual degrading manipulation of subjects in psychological experiments. He also believed that experimental research, which is constantly elaborating its manipulative, deceptive techniques, calls for the application of its results in the form of manipulation. In reading such criticism, however, we must be sure not to confound contents and methods more than they already are by the nature of things. Insights attained through manipulation need not be used for the purpose of manipulation. If psychology "exports" its methods to be exploited for the purpose of manipulation in other areas, such as political propaganda or advertising, this is a different problem.

## REINFORCEMENT OR FREEDOM?

An ethically rigorous position like Kelman's (1965, 1968), in which control and restricting freedom of choice are inherently below human dignity, is rare in psychology. In the dispute between Rogers and Skinner (Rogers & Skinner, 1956), Kelman takes the same position as Rogers, who considers the restriction of human behavioral freedom to be questionable in principle, no matter what methods are used. In contrast, Skinner's basic position is oriented toward the *goals* of behavioral control. He asks whether it is not in fact acceptable to use positive reinforcement as a means of moving toward agreed-upon goals that have been found worth attaining. This should be preferable to punishing or threatening punishment for undesirable behavior (which is de facto responsible for a considerable part, perhaps the greatest part, of social control). Let us assume that a condition is perceived as inherently pleasant and worth striving for. Why and how, asks Skinner, could this condition become questionable merely because someone has planned its occurrence? We need only be sure that no one misuses the power of control for selfish ends.

Kelman, on the other hand, argues that the freedom and opportunity to choose are fundamental values that every social system needs to defend and protect from manipulative techniques. Kelman postulates freedom of choice as a basic human need that is manifested under the most diverse historical conditions. In his opinion, it is an irreplaceable component of other concepts that are generally evaluated positively, such as love, creativity, control of one's environment, and maximization of one's capacities. Freedom of choice also preserves humanity from tyranny, which often enough appears under the guise of intending the best for all in order to take power by means of force.

Kelman (1968, pp. 19–31) shows how easily psychologists run the risk of being manipulative and limiting other people's freedom of decision. It is not only in applied research that the psychologist's goals or values might infringe on others' freedoms but also within the context of basic research. It is difficult to reflect on and evaluate the consequences of one's actions. With regard to research in opinion change, Kelman argues, it is easy to see how application to advertising, political propaganda, and other influence attempts (which the researcher could not prevent in any case) can be interpreted as oriented toward restricting human freedom of decision. On the other hand, however, some effects and areas of application of opinion change research can be positively evaluated—for example, the liberating power of increasing our understanding of human behavior and the possibilities of better counteracting manipulative forces, building up resistance against manipulation, or serving accepted goals, such as racial integration or international understanding.

Here, in the area of basic psychological research, the position opposing Skinner seems to lose strength. The contrasting views of human nature are clear-cut in their basic positions but not in their conclusions about the consequences of concrete research practices. In any case, even Kelman does not exclude the possibility that research techniques that are in themselves manipulative can be used to explore the conditions for increasing individual freedom of decision and the possibility of realizing individual values. In order to prevent inappropriate and above all involuntary sacrifices for the sake of goals that are considered worth attaining, Kelman and others have emphasized the principle of informed consent, which was borrowed from medical research.

## SAFEGUARDS AND COMPENSATIONS

Along with research designs, or in connection with the discussion of experiments, biomedical and social scientists have developed certain assumptions and preventive measures for minimizing the risks peculiar to research with humans. Some of these assumptions and procedures have been written into the research guidelines of the most diverse disciplines (see Chapter 4). The most important of these safeguards and compensations are discussed in the following sections.

## Informed Consent

In order to prevent potentially harmful research from being carried out on human beings against their will or without their knowledge, we can obviously make the consent of the subjects a criterion for the acceptability of investigations. If the contract resulting from this consent is to be considered valid, the subjects must be informed of all peculiarities of the investigation in question that might be relevant for their consent, including the procedures to be expected and their significance, possible unpleasant aspects and risks, and the purpose of the research.

This corresponds to the demands placed by the U.S. Department of Health and Human Services on research involving human subjects. The principle of informed consent applies to all investigations involving human beings, including explicitly those in the behavioral and social sciences. With certain variations, this principle is also contained in all professional and administrative guidelines for such research.

### INFORMED CONSENT IN MEDICINE

The model of informed consent originated in medical research and has been required there virtually since medicine reached the stage of experimentation (Romano, 1974). Informed consent has been a part of guidelines for medical research for more than 100 years; in some of these guidelines, it is the most important principle. However, in spite of its long history and the general—at least verbal—acknowledgment of this principle, it is still an object of discussion in all areas of medicine (D. H. Mills, 1974). Problems of interpretation arise, particularly when the patient's or subject's ability to give consent is limited or entirely lacking, as in psychiatry (Davidson, 1970), psychiatric surgery (Flor-Henry, 1975), transplant surgery (Fellner & Marshall, 1970), and pediatrics (E. B. Shaw, 1967).

### INFORMED CONSENT IN PROPORTION TO RISK

If the principle of informed consent were applied strictly to psychological research (as Baumrind applies it, 1976), entire classes of experimental and other investigations could no longer be carried out in a meaningful way. Because the risk involved in psychological experiments is usually assumed to be low in comparison with medical experiments, most psychologists consider themselves justified in applying the rule flexibly. They take it literally only when serious risks are actually to be feared (S. W. Cook, 1976, p. 212). It has been proposed by Campbell (1969) as well as Sasson and Nelson (1969) that all members of a subject pool should be told at the beginning of a semester to expect misinformation in some of the experiments. Following this, their willingness to participate should be obtained for an entire series of experiments. This could be called a flexible interpretation of the principle of informed consent, but only if there is no risk of harm in any of the experiments and if participation is really voluntary. Otherwise, the procedure proposed clearly contradicts the principle. It is generally considered unnecessary to concern oneself with consent in the case of investigations that are believed to be completely without risk. Thus, over 400,000 school children were tested for Project Talent, and their data were stored without requesting consent from them or their parents. As a rule, when nonreactive research methods are employed, it is impossible to obtain consent. For this reason such methods have hardly ever been introduced into psychological research and have already been as good as eliminated in other fields, such as anthropology (Baumrind, 1977).

## A QUESTION OF DEFINITION

The difficulty of operationalizing the principle of informed consent for psychology is no small matter. For example, how much and what kind of information do subjects need in order for us to call them "informed"? And to which subjects should the informed consent principle apply? Wolfensberger (1970) points out that some of our experiments are so complicated that hardly any colleagues not sharing our specialty are in a position to understand them. But in this connection understanding must be a prerequisite for being informed (Wolfensberger, 1967). Thus, we will have to restrict ourselves to the communication of important information. This does not mean information that is important from the standpoint of the experimenters. To them the most important aspect of a group experiment might be something that is both uninteresting and incomprehensible to the subjects, such as whether the decisions of the group members can be described with a Bayes model. Rather, it means important from the standpoint of the subjects. Thus, we must know what could be experienced by which subjects to what extent as harm, what they are able to understand in what fashion, and what kind of sense they can make out of statements of the risks involved.

## DEFINITIONS IN A HYPOTHETICAL CASE

Let us assume that we know from previous experiments that there is a risk of 1 in 40 that a subject's feeling of self-esteem will remain diminished by more than 1 scale point after 4 weeks. Let us further assume that communicating this information would not interfere with the experiment. Would it do any good to tell potential subjects about the risk? Would they understand the significance of a risk of 1 in 40? (Do smokers understand the meaning of the statement that their risk of contracting cancer is 1 in 10?) Would the subjects understand *self-esteem* in the same way as the experimenter—that is, would they think of the same internal experience that the experimenter believes is expressed in the values on the scale? Do they know how the loss in self-esteem scale points would be reflected in their experience?

There are some additional considerations. The risk is an average value and can hardly be determined for individuals. The subjects have already ventured into the laboratory situation and would find it very hard to withdraw from it. Willingness to take risks has a high social value. The subjects would like to make a good impression on the experimenter. Moreover, subjects are perhaps after all not as independent of the experimenter as the term *volunteer* would have us believe.

If it were generally possible for subjects to evaluate risks in a way that could make experimenters feel really relieved of this responsibility, and if the subjects really had the possibility of making a voluntary choice, an additional problem of representativeness would appear. Representativeness is already problematic in psychological research because of the usual means of selecting subjects. In our example, the subjects who chose to participate in the experiment after being warned of the risk would be those with a particularly high threshold of sensitivity or anxiety with regard to the experimental manipulation, that is, with regard to the reduction in self-esteem. Thus, the sample would be even less representative than is usually the case.

*FOREWARNING: A LIFTING OF RESPONSIBILITY?*

Often experimenters seem to be relieved of responsibility by virtue of having forewarned the subjects. In fact, however, in many cases the experimenters themselves have difficulty in estimating the actual average risk for subjects, to say nothing of the risk for any particular individual. But usually experimenters are, or should be, in a better position to make this assessment than are their subjects. In order to fulfill their responsibilities adequately, experimenters must do more than merely provide an optimal amount of information about the experiment. In addition, they must consider whether the social contract that they are making with each subject is just and whether the costs that they are expecting the subjects to assume (including the impossibility of calculating the risk) are commensurate with the benefits subjects can expect.

Verbal explanations to the subjects cannot relieve psychologists completely of responsibility, no matter how detailed the explanations are. Baumrind (1972, p. 1085) argues that if the subjects' consent is based on full information, including information about possible physical and psychological risks, there is no violation of important ethical principles. This shows the danger of seeing the question of correct or false information as the central ethical problem in research. In spite of the risk of sacrificing the usefulness of data gathered, the experimenter might explain all details, hypotheses, measurement procedures, etc., to the subjects before the start of an experiment. However, if the contract agreement had not already managed to create a real understanding of what it means to venture into such an unusual situation, these efforts might be in vain. As investigations have shown, subjects assume upon becoming a party to this contract that the experimenter will protect them from harm. They are so confident of this that they refrain from exploring the question of whether this is possible or whether the experimenter is competent to do so.

## ETHICS ≠ INFORMED CONSENT

Experimenters who are not oriented toward the criterion of a fair exchange should find it easy to relieve themselves of responsibility by giving information. They can fulfill the letter of the law with respect to informed consent, without really fulfilling its intent. Arellano-Galdames (1972) cites the experience of the medical researchers Lewis, McCollum, and Schwartz (1969), who found that enlightening parents about the exploratory nature of the procedure being used with their children usually does not prevent the parents from agreeing to their children's further hospitalization. The letter of the law would therefore seem to be fulfilled, but on the other hand, extending the length of stay appears to convince the parents that their children are sufficiently ill to need a longer stay. Beecher (1962, 1966) gives additional examples from medical research that illustrate the problematic nature of the concept of consent. If we wanted subjects to be truly free to make their own decisions, we would need to seek means of communication that would contribute to the subjects' freedom of choice instead of simultaneously trying to comply with and evade a regulation. In that case we would continue to explore the issue along the same lines as Berscheid, Baron, Dermer, and Libman (1973), whose experiments showed that the manner in which subjects are told about the nature of an experiment and the possible behaviors expected from them influences the subjects' readiness to participate. According to Berscheid *et al.*, another promising approach turned out to be having subjects role play before actually participating in an ethically problematic experiment, in order to provide criteria for evaluating the acceptability of the intended procedures.

The contract should include informing subjects, whenever possible, about the purpose of the research and the use intended for the data collected. In the case of applied research or research that is likely to be applied, it can be especially important for subjects to decide whether they want to contribute their data. It is not possible to allow subjects in most experimental studies the additional possibility of asking questions during the investigation without invalidating it; however, this procedure is already included in the research guidelines for many kinds of field investigations (e.g., see Campbell & Cecil, 1977, for the areas of program evaluation and survey research). This would obviously be useful for laboratory investigations as well, particularly if the subjects decided to participate in the experiment on the basis of inadequate or incomprehensible information.

## A PRESCRIPTIVE SUMMARY

In summary, we inform subjects about the goals, nature, and risks of a particular experiment as an important and effective means of protecting them from harm. We do this when the risk of harm can be calculated and the subjects can understand and evaluate its significance and consequences for themselves, assuming also that the communication of this possibility of harm is unproblematic. Without these prerequisites, however, the principle of informed consent cannot fulfill its important function to the same extent. In such cases, it is the experimenters' responsibility to weigh costs and benefits on behalf of subjects. The extent of their responsibility is determined by the parameters of the specific situation. In Chapter 1, the following parameters received special emphasis: familiarity and danger, stimulus control, reaction control, and power differential. On the one hand, merely giving detailed information cannot relieve the experimenters of their responsibility. On the other hand, such information is not necessary in order for the subject to give informed consent. If subjects have been forewarned that the giving of some misinformation is one of the rules of the game in experimenting, and if the events about which misinformation is given are unlikely to be experienced as harmful by any subject, it is possible to say that the experiment has adhered to the principle of informed consent. However, if a risk of harm can be predicted, then it is absolutely necessary to forewarn subjects accordingly. And finally, if the extent of risk cannot be estimated, it cannot be said that subjects have given their informed consent.

The voluntary nature of participation, including the freedom to leave the experimental situation at any time, is an implicit prerequisite for the validity of informed consent. Since participation often turns out not to be as clearly voluntary as it seems at first glance, this topic is treated separately in the next section.

## *The Voluntary Nature of Participation*

The voluntary nature of participation in an experiment is one of the problems that can most clearly cause a conflict between methodological and ethical demands. On the one hand, there are no regulations for professional ethics in any of the biomedical and social sciences that do not proceed from the basic assumption of voluntary participation. Moreover, there are hardly any researchers who do not accept this condition, at least in principle. On the other hand, if all participation were voluntary, there would be problems with the representative nature of the sample and in effect some research techniques would be excluded for the social sciences, for example, nonreactive procedures.

### A RELATED ISSUE OF REPRESENTATIVENESS

In psychology the representative nature of the subjects has already been questioned even apart from the issue of whether they are volunteers. According to Jung's survey (1969) of a very large data base ($N = 280,000$), 90% of all subjects in American investigations were at that time college students. Unless we intend to restrict claims for the validity of psychological theories and empirical statements to this group, this selection is certainly problematic.

### THE CHARACTER OF THE VOLUNTEER

As is clear from the results already reported of research on the subject role (Rosenthal & Rosnow, 1975; Rosnow & Rosenthal, 1976), the variable of voluntary participation is an additional selection factor. Volunteer subjects are distinguished from other students by higher average intelligence, a greater need for social recognition, and less conventional and authoritarian styles, to mention only a few of the characteristics listed by Rosenthal and Rosnow (see the section on voluntary participation in Chapter 1). Unfortunately, we do not yet know to what extent variations in experimental results can be attributed to differences in populations or how to summarize these kinds of variations for different classes of research problems. If reliable transition variables were known, we could translate the results from one population to the other and from one context to the other. We would then be able to decide before carrying out an experiment whether the data from volunteer students would be interpretable in a broader context. But at the present, we have nothing more than some reflections on what is plausible in this respect, and it is questionable whether such transition rules can ever be developed on a larger scale and in a simple enough form to be usable.

### VOLUNTEERISM: NOT NECESSARILY THE STATUS QUO

The voluntary nature of participation is often limited for a number of reasons, including the problem of representativeness and the great variance in most human modes of behavior. Menges (1973) examined 1000 published reports of experiments and determined that 60% of the subjects, rather than participating voluntarily, were fulfilling various kinds of external demands—mostly having to do with their studies—or were not even aware of their function as subjects. Jung (1969) found that only 7% of the subjects in the sample he examined were really volunteers. Among the limits on the voluntary nature of participation, he includes all requirements that students participate in an experiment in the context of a course and all policies that allow participation to satisfy course or exam requirements, including offering experiments as substitute course material, for extra course grades, etc.

As an alternative, more subtle pressure to participate in experiments, Rosenthal and Rosnow (1975, pp. 198–199) recommend using effective recruiting methods (see the section on the pursuit of equity in Chapter 1). In addition to such pressure, we must also consider the group pressure applied by participating fellow students and all the influence factors described in studies of the social psychology of the experimental setting (see Chapter 1), including especially the power differential between experimenter and subjects.

Eccles (1972, p. 844) criticized an experiment by a colleague in neurology, which demonstrates how far these "voluntary" participants are sometimes willing to go in cooperating with the experimenter. Eccles's colleague separated nerve fibers in the forearms of student subjects in order to examine the effects on the senses when only a single fiber from a bundle of nerve fibers is still functional.

In view of such dangers, Beecher (1962) demanded that college professors should not use their own students as subjects. The ethics commission of the American Psychological Association decided to include in its regulations a prohibition of course requirements that call for students to participate in experiments, but this failed because of resistance from large universities (personal communication from M. Kelty, APA member of the National Commission for the Protection of Human Subjects of Biomedical and Behavioral Research, December 1977).

## THE CASE FOR STUDENT PARTICIPATION

There are also arguments in favor of prevailing upon students to participate in investigations. These arguments include the students' obligation to make a contribution to the discipline that they are studying, the educational advantages that result, the difficulty and cost of obtaining subjects outside the university, and the even stronger self-selection in the case of other volunteers (S. W. Cook, 1976, p. 209). The self-selection versus forced conscription approaches to recruiting subjects can be seen as similar to the self-selection problems of the U.S. armed forces in times of no mandatory draft. It has long ago become clear that the caliber of military personnel drops drastically when participation is voluntary. Correspondingly, one would wonder what kinds of individuals would remain as subjects—from whom we should like to generalize—if there were no pressures at all to participate.

The routine nature of participation for students who frequently serve as subjects may have some disadvantages, but having them grow accustomed to the experimental situation as such is actually an advantage. This doubtless reduces the ethical problems connected with certain stresses and thereby reduces the experimenter's responsibility. If routine participation does not lead to the cynical attitude that is sometimes feared, it can encourage the development of the subject role into that of a research partner. In general, the experiences that have been reported with well-organized subject pools are positive (e.g., King,

1970). This is especially true when participation in experiments is integrated systematically into the educational program and is used to introduce subjects to the nature of research, as with Davis and Fernald (1975).

### VOLUNTEERISM IN THE CONTEXT OF SPECIAL GROUPS

The problem of experiments with special subject groups has attracted far more attention in biomedical research than in psychology. In particular, the problems connected with participation of persons whose ability to consent must be assumed to be limited (Lasagna, 1969) were the object of major controversies and special regulations. These special groups include children (A. Shaw, 1973), psychologically disturbed persons (Curran, 1974), and seriously ill and dying persons (Sugerman, 1972). In psychological research, such discussions have so far been limited to problems connected with child subjects (M. B. Smith, 1967).

In recent years, there has been particular interest in the use of prisoners as subjects in medical research (Jonsen, Parker, Carlson, & Emmott, 1977; Schwitzgebel, 1968). In earlier decades, no one challenged the large-scale use of prisoners for experiments in infection and radiation, for the testing of medicines and cosmetics, and for other experiments. Since then, however, such experiments have been subjected to severe restrictions. The recommendations made in 1976 by the National Commission for the Protection of Human Subjects of Biomedical and Behavioral Research were so restrictive that they were expected virtually to call a halt to all research with prisoners that did not contribute to their personal well-being or to the exploration of the conditions and circumstances of their previous lives. The basis of objection to prison experiments has been that it is impossible to speak of voluntary participation in the case of persons who are extremely dependent on material rewards, have hopes of making their imprisonment easier or shorter by means of participation, and may even be motivated by a desire to do penance (Beecher, 1970).

But there are also limits on the voluntary nature of participation for the members of institutions that are less restrictive than penal institutions. It is not unusual for soldiers to be detailed to psychological as well as medical experiments. For the members of research divisions of pharmaceutical firms, it is considered a point of honor that they make themselves available for the first experiments with new medications. And finally, employees of business and government organizations often are not aware of their roles as subjects. If we give the term *experiment* as broad an interpretation as does Wolfensberger (1970), the number of involuntary subjects becomes even greater. Wolfensberger considers many diagnostic techniques and treatments common to such fields as medicine, psychiatry, social work, and education to be tentative and experimental, lacking adequate empirical validation. He finds that "innumerable human-management and administrative practices are no more than ill-controlled experiments [p. 49]" If we were to attempt at the same time to meet demands as radical as the following, we would have to give up a large part of our present research activities: "If any sort of exploitation of the powerless is ruled out, including payment to those in financial need for acting as subjects and persuasion of students in need of recommendation and backing, then a truly cooperative enterprise can be inaugurated [M. Mead, 1969, p. 373]."

CONDITIONS THAT COMPENSATE FOR NONVOLUNTEERISM

Most researchers in psychology seem to think, surely not entirely without justification, that the danger for subjects in experiments today is relatively low, so that certain limits on the voluntary nature of participation should be acceptable. They also find it reasonable to impose on psychology students a quasi-professional obligation to participate in a certain number of experiments. (On the other hand, if we cannot simultaneously guarantee that no risk is involved, forcing students to participate in experiments might even be illegal.) On the basis of these considerations, however, justifying the risk of negative consequences for subjects with the argument that participation is voluntary seems appropriate only in those exceptional cases in which informed consent is based on a clear understanding of the conditions, a correct evaluation of the risks, and a truly voluntary decision to participate.

The following procedures can be used to compensate for the ethical problems involved in limiting the voluntary nature of participation:

1. Limiting the extent and size of incentives for participation
2. Consulting with colleagues who are not involved in the research project
3. Asking subjects to participate in the weighing of costs and benefits, perhaps in the form of preexperimental role playing
4. Allowing subjects to observe various typical experiments, perhaps in filmed versions, before they declare their readiness to participate in a series of experiments
5. Assuring subjects of their right to withdraw their consent to any particular experiment or break off participation in an experiment at any time
6. Encouraging subjects by means of a refusal model to break off participation in particularly risky experiments
7. Making another experiment available as an alternative to an experiment that could have harmful effects for certain persons

## Debriefing

Subjects in psychological experiments are frequently kept ignorant of the purpose of the experiment and the significance of the stimuli and their behavior, or given incorrect information. This suggests that after the experiment they should be fully informed of its nature. The need to inform subjects is even more urgent when an experiment has created stresses that might continue unless the experiment is explained—for example, when the subject's self-image is harmed by experimental manipulations. Only in such cases is debriefing prescribed by professional regulations. Relieving stress for subjects is the first and most important function of debriefing, but not its only function. Talking with subjects after an experiment also has two methodological functions: verifying the effectiveness of the experimental manipulations, and attempting to make the students feel obligated to keep the nature of the experiment secret so that other potential subjects do not obtain information that might affect their behavior in the experiment. Finally, an instructional function can also be ascribed to debriefing. Subjects should derive educational benefits from their participation in an experiment, particularly if they are students.

Carlson (1971) and Menges (1973) examined published reports of experiments to determine the frequency of postexperimental discussions having one or more of these purposes. According to Carlson, approximately a third of those investigations containing deceptions were reported as including debriefing procedures. Menges notes that, whereas 18.6% of the publications he reviewed mentioned deceptive measures, only 10% of all the publications indicated that debriefing was involved.

The most important function of debriefing from an ethical point of view is undoubtedly the attempt to make sure that no permanent harm to subjects will result from experimental manipulations. As the discussion of psychological harm to subjects indicates (see the section on psychological and physical harm and danger in this chapter), we cannot assume that this goal can be attained by means of simple verbal explanations. Especially when the manipulations in question change aspects of the subject's self-image, we must take into account that the resulting complex changes in perception of the self and of others may not be reversible. At any rate, their reversibility through the usual form of debriefing cannot be guaranteed for all cases. S. W. Cook (1976, p. 242) reports in this connection the case of a student who had to undergo psychotherapeutic treatment 2 years after an experiment in which he was informed of supposed homosexual tendencies, despite the debriefing that explained this experimental manipulation. Kelman (1967a) describes comparable cases.

### EXPLORING DEBRIEFING EXPERIMENTALLY

A number of empirical investigations of the effectiveness of debriefing are to be found in the literature. Milgram (1964) reported no adverse effects of his coercing subjects to administer what they believed to be electric shocks, after thorough debriefing and reassuring of the subjects. Ring *et al.* (1970) replicated the Milgram experiment and reported that no aftereffects could be clearly assessed as hazardous, although there were some indications of self-doubt, disappointment, and long-lasting problems in coming to terms with the experience. In contrast, Walster *et al.* (1967) showed that even a long and (in their opinion) atypically thorough debriefing was not able to reverse the experimental impairment of self-esteem in some subjects—those who tended in any case toward low self-evaluation.

Holmes (1976b) demonstrated the effectiveness of a debriefing procedure that he called "desensitizing." After an experiment of the Milgram type, he enlightened the first group of subjects about the gamelike character of the situation and offered them additional possibilities for justifying their behavior. He explained that their behavior was quite normal, that their actions had been harmless relative to those of other subjects, and that their obedience in the experiment did not necessarily permit conclusions about their behavior in other situations. Compared with subjects in an unstressed control group, the subjects in the first group showed no higher pulse rate, and their sense of being aroused was only slightly higher than that in the control condition. On the other hand, the subjects in Group 2, who were not debriefed until after their pulse had been measured and they had been asked some questions, showed significant differences from Group 1, as well as from the control group, on both measures. The nondebriefed subjects not only were more agitated but also expressed a higher level of anxiety, indicated less readiness to participate in a similar experiment again, and showed a greater tendency to request that the experiment in which they were participating be broken off.

While the sort of debriefing suggested by Holmes seems to be effective, a study by Ross, Lepper, and Hubbard (1975) suggests persevering effects in spite of debriefing. Some of the subjects performed a task, and others were assigned to observe them. Both performers and observers received false reports on the quality of performance. Afterward, subjects were informed about the deception, the nature of the experiment, the experimental design, etc.—in short, they were informed as completely as possible. Nevertheless, in a subsequent assessment of achievement, it turned out that the effect of the false information had by no means disappeared for the actor-subjects or the observer-subjects. Only when a discussion of the long-range effects was explicitly included in the debriefing could these effects be prevented.

It is uncertain whether in this last experiment the disappearance of the effects really means that the impressions that were formed were reversed or only that bringing up the problem caused a conscious avoidance of showing the effects in filling out the questionnaire. Quite a few cases seem to indicate therapeutically successful debriefing. However, it seems appropriate to suspect in some cases that, although no aftereffects could be detected with the instrument in question, such effects may have been present or may have shown up later, perhaps as sleeper effects. Insofar as these measurements can be considered valid, we must still keep in mind, in trying to generalize their results, that debriefing is usually carried out much less thoroughly than in the investigations described, is not individual when the experiment involves a group, and is often neglected totally. We must also remember that it is by no means obvious to the subjects that the experimenter is really telling the truth after the experiment. The debriefing could be a part of the experiment that involves new deceptions, or the experimenter—as a psychologist and a therapist—could be trying to employ a new and euphemistic explanation to improve the spirits of the patient who is so obviously anxious or suffering from damaged self-esteem.

Nevertheless, we will generally be able to assume that debriefing subjects after an experiment that was not transparent to them can remove certain undesired effects and is preferable to not debriefing. To be sure, at times we are forced to consider the possibility that debriefing itself could have negative effects (Stollack, 1967). S. W. Cook (1976, p. 241) points out that we must expect subjects to be disappointed that such respected persons as scientists employ falsehood and deceit in their work. It is not rare, he suggests, for shame and confusion to result from the revelation that one has let oneself be deceived. It does not seem misguided to take into account that self-doubts and increased distrust of others may result if experimenters do not conduct very thorough and listener-oriented conversations with the subjects and, if necessary, employ additional procedures. J. Mills (1976) proposes a manual for thorough debriefing. Besides therapeutic intervention, various kinds of catharsis suggest themselves as additional procedures. For example, Hardy (1957) asked subjects who were deceived in an Asch experiment to play the role of pseudosubjects. Whatever method is chosen, it seems inappropriate to justify ethically problematic experimental manipulations merely by reference to debriefing.

*METHODOLOGICAL FUNCTIONS OF DEBRIEFING*

The two methodological functions of debriefing will be mentioned here only in passing, although for many investigations these may be more pertinent for the investigator than the ethical functions. The first consists of ascertaining that the experimental manipulations are really successful—that is, that the conditions conceptualized as independent variables really existed for the subjects. This is not always easy to establish, partly because it is commonly believed that having allowed oneself to be deceived interferes with making a good impression. Subjects are also concerned with contributing usable data and not having their effort wasted by subsequent elimination of their contribution. Aronson and Carlsmith (1968, pp. 70–73) propose a sequential procedure for the postexperimental interview that is designed to cope with this difficulty. If anything more than simple quantitative data are presented, this is also the place for assisting subjects in interpreting their data.

The second methodological function is that of making sure that potential subjects do not obtain information that could make the validity of future experiments questionable. Aronson and Carlsmith (1968, p. 72) express optimism about the possibility of pledging subjects to silence by giving them insight into the problems involved. However, a whole series of investigations gives us cause to doubt that the relevant information is actually kept confidential. To be sure, the percentages reported vary widely. Diener, Matthews, and Smith (1972) could find only 11 of 440 control subjects who had been informed by other subjects. But using another experimental design, Newberry (1973) discovered that, depending on their experimental conditions, between 30% and 80% of the subjects who had been fed information before the experiment did not admit in the postexperimental interview that they had known something already. As was to be expected, the subjects had used their information to improve their performance in the experiment. A study by Altemeyer (1972) demonstrated the skill subjects sometimes employ in hiding their knowledge. After students had been forewarned deliberately by their fellow students, not a single one of them admitted having been let into the secret and only half of them could be identified in a blind interview.

Debriefing may also cause a methodological problem: Subjects who have been deceived in psychological experiments might react differently from naive subjects in the future. As we reported earlier in this chapter in the section on deception from the methodological perspective, there is some reason to fear this, although the problem would probably arise primarily with experiments that are very similar to the earlier experiments (Brock & Becker, 1966). This problem can be prevented, if at all, only through a rigorous and general shielding of the subjects from any kind of debriefing information. This seems neither feasible nor ethically justifiable.

## THE EDUCATIONAL FUNCTION OF DEBRIEFING

Finally, the educational function of debriefing seems to have received very little attention, as Tesch (1977) complains. And yet precisely that function might enable us to transform the exchange of costs and benefits in an experiment into a just—that is, a balanced—social contract. If subjects really gain insight and knowledge of a general psychological nature or self-knowledge through their participation in an experiment, we can speak of a benefit for the subjects themselves. Then it is not merely the benefit of some ominous scientific progress against which their costs must be weighed. To be sure, this educational function sometimes conflicts with the methodological function of ensuring that relevant information be kept confidential, at least if the debriefing is to follow the experiment immediately. And it is naturally reckoned as a cost in the experimenter's contract because of the time and effort necessary to make the experiment a scientifically or even personally useful experience for subjects. Although one of the frequently mentioned justifications for requiring students to complete a certain number of subject-hours is precisely this educational function, it is apparently quite rare that anything is undertaken that could do justice to this claim. Davis and Fernald (1975) give one of the few examples for thorough and informative debriefing. In order to ensure successful learning and assimilation of the experiments, participants in an experiment are required to compose a laboratory report that contains almost everything that would appear in a scientific publication. In addition, they report their personal experiences and evaluate the experiments. The students' evaluation of this procedure is on the whole quite positive, perhaps a little dampened by the work involved. Although the procedure is surely most useful if employed immediately, the implicit danger of information being spread would lead one to save the technique for the final stages of a research program.

## ETHICAL DILEMMAS STEMMING FROM DEBRIEFING

It has often been questioned whether debriefing is desirable in every case—not only from a methodological standpoint or one of feasibility, but also from an ethical point of view. Argyle (1962) argues that debriefing often serves functions other than benefiting the subject: "If moral attention is directed towards the consequences, there is no reason why a lengthy denouement should be given at the end of the experiment, as is often done by experimenters with guilty feelings [p. 82]." Sasson and Nelson (1969), Seeman (1969), Stollack (1967), and others point out that in some experiments there is no danger of harming the subjects until the manipulation or the reasons for the assignment to experimental conditions have been revealed. A simple example for this is informing subjects, after an attractiveness experiment, that they were assigned to the experimental group $x$ because everyone else rated them as the least attractive. D. T. Campbell (1969) considers it justified to omit debriefing when "an experimental treatment falls within the range of the respondent's ordinary experience, merely being an experimental rearrangement of normal level communications [p. 371]." If interpreted strictly, this seems to be a reasonable enough principle for any experiment from which no educational benefits are expected.

Ethical problems plainly arise when the experimenter deliberately misinforms subjects during debriefing. Carlsmith *et al.* (1976, p. 108) state that such "breaches of contract" are known, but they cite no specific experiments. The lack of transparency of the experimental situation as such is accepted by the subjects, along with a certain amount of misinformation, as the "rules of the game." When the experiment is officially over, however, the subjects need to be certain that the usual rules of social behavior apply again, that they are free to speak openly, that they can rely on what the experimenter tells them, and that everything else about this new setting is genuine. Breaking this implicit agreement even in occasional cases would make almost certain the loss of trust in experimenters, a danger that has been feared but receives little support as a general effect of experimental misinformation.

It may be clear from the discussion in this section that debriefing is generally desirable; however, communicating complete information may sometimes be unsuitable for methodological reasons and is sometimes deleterious from a moral standpoint.

## EVALUATING THE ACCEPTABILITY OF EXPERIMENTAL PROCEDURES

Only as a rare exception can we expect certainty about the consequences of experimental procedures. This is one reason why it is so hard for us to agree on the evaluation of specific research behavior and why it would still be hard even if all members of the scientific community accepted as binding a normative system oriented toward the consequences of our actions. An important additional reason why we have not agreed on such a system is that no code of normative ethics is perceived as sufficiently binding. This is true both of ethical systems oriented toward the consequences of actions and of those oriented toward the actions themselves.

Research behavior is not guided by a system of binding principles that would preserve freedom of action but still allow the deduction of sufficiently clear guidelines for the design of concrete research procedures. Nor does it seem possible to apply legal norms without ambiguity in the areas of psychological research discussed here. In the few known cases in which research psychologists have come into conflict with the law, the conflict generally did not result from procedures taken with subjects, but rather from other aspects of the research. For example, Leary was liable to legal prosecution because of possession of drugs, not because of the risks to which he subjected participants in his hallucinogenic drug experiments. Humphreys was not arrested because he secretly observed and recorded semipublic homosexual activities (Humphreys, 1970), but because he was unwilling to reveal to the police that he was a scientist. If research behavior in the social sciences were measured by legal norms that are formulated for everyday behavior, a number of experimental manipulations that are generally considered relatively harmless in the research context (examples in Kumpf & Irle, 1976, and in Silverman, 1975) could be labeled as fraud or bodily injury. But for good reason, the special nature of research behavior seems to be taken into account from a legal perspective as well. Legal norms are most likely to restrict research activities in the area of protecting privacy, particularly with regard to data protection. In field research there also seems to be an increase in problems related to social researchers' lack of legal immunity or the right to refuse testimony (cf. several contributions in the Eser & Schumann anthology, 1976). However, most of the procedures that seem problematic in the contexts discussed in this book have apparently not become legally problematic.

In the absence of binding directives for action, the scientist has considerable freedom to decide how to handle individual cases. Apparently in most cases this decision is either implicitly or explicitly based on a principle of balancing advantages against disadvantages: balancing the expected benefits of the research against the costs incurred. Possible burdens and stresses for the subjects are included among these costs, as the existing professional research guidelines demand. Might it be possible to make reliable decisions about individual cases on this basis? The following sections are devoted to examining this principle for guiding decisions. First we will consider the philosophical justification of the cost–benefit analysis. Then we will discuss the most important parameters on which such analyses would have to be based—namely, the costs for subjects and the benefits to be derived from the research project. And finally, by way of summary, we will discuss the principle of balancing costs and benefits via the concept of the experiment as a social contract between experimenter and subject, as described in Chapter 1.

## *The Philosophy of Weighing Costs and Benefits, Part 1*

Weighing costs and benefits has been a part of every version of the American Psychological Association's ethical standards up to the present. As chairman of the APA committee on ethics, S. W. Cook (1976, p. 238) has suggested that the first consideration in deciding about the acceptability of experimental procedures is whether the problem under investigation is so important and so likely to produce valuable results that possible costs to the subject are outweighed. If this is uncertain, protection of the dignity and welfare of the subject takes priority over other considerations. The formulation of the principle of weighing costs and benefits in the APA ethical standards has been modified in minor details from time to time; the first important limitation of this principle, which will be mentioned later, appeared in the 1977 version.

### UTILITARIAN ETHICS

Weighing costs and benefits is characteristic of utilitarian ethics, in which an action is judged as morally right or wrong on the sole basis of its consequences (Hoerster, 1975, p. 14). Only in the works of such classical utilitarians as Bentham and Mill is it clear which consequences can be considered positive and which negative. The criterion for evaluation is a simple hedonistic principle of maximizing pleasure or minimizing pain. Problems arise only when individual happiness and unhappiness are aggregated to produce what Bentham and Mill consider optimal, the "greatest happiness for the greatest number." Recent definitions of utilitarian ethics, since Moore's *Principia Ethica* (1903/ 1970; clearer in Moore, 1912/1975), are more complex and involve various differentiations and extensions of the principle (Foot, 1967; Höffe, 1975). Later we will consider some of these interpretations.[2] Here we must emphasize that utilitarianism is not oriented toward just any goals or values, independent of their character, but toward the principle of the Good or of Happiness or toward the fulfilling of general human needs. Thus, Nicolai Hartmann's charge that utilitarianism annihilates distinctions among values appears inappropriate (Höffe, 1977, pp. 247–248). Nor can utilitarianism be equated with the philosophical position of egotism, since it does not aim at maximizing benefits for the individual, but rather at maximizing general well-being.

*DEONTOLOGICAL ETHICS*

The extreme opposite of a utilitarian viewpoint is that of deontological ethics. Here the basic principle is that modes of behavior can be evaluated as intrinsically right or wrong (i.e., good or bad); nonteleological criteria or rules for action can be developed for classes of behavior. Frankena (1963, pp. 21–25) explains that deontological theories must contain, at least implicitly, rules or principles that apply to classes of behavior if they are to produce meaningful normative theories. According to Frankena, we can disregard moral theories for evaluating individual cases, the so-called deontological act theories, in favor of the more general deontological rule theories. The latter include a set of statements that evaluate modes of behavior in more or less general form—for example, "It is wrong to lie" or "It is wrong to frighten people." The second example shows that norms can be developed not only for modes of behavior as such but also for consequences of behavior. This makes it harder to distinguish deontological rule theories from utilitarian rule theories, in which the problem of predicting consequences is also discussed. Considered together, these two sample statements also make it clear that in some situations the two principles could conflict with each other. Suppose we are walking with a child through a dark forest and the child asks, "Are you afraid?" Let us assume that we are afraid but that at the same time we believe that confessing this would provide the child with a bad model and encourage the child's fear, thus frightening the child. This contradicts the second deontological rule, "It is wrong to frighten people." In this case, our only possibility is to violate one of the two rules, unless we allow exceptions to at least one of them. This would lead either to the

---

2. For reasons of space as well as competence, it seems appropriate to limit philosophical discussions to the essential points here. We will attempt to compensate for the inevitable simplification that results by referring the reader to relevant specialists.

principle of weighing costs and benefits (and thereby to utilitarian ethics) or to a complete hierarchical system of rules.[3]

### KANT AND DEONTOLOGICAL RULE THEORY

The classical example of a deontological rule theory is Kant's. On the basis of the self-determination of the will, he develops the principle that actions are moral only if they follow self-determined general precepts and are thus not oriented toward benefits. The central statement of the Kantian ethic, the categorical imperative, ties the moral quality of an action to the possibility of generalizing a maxim or rule for that action: "Act according to a maxim only when you can at the same time will that it shall become a universal law [Kant, 1788/1922, p. 271]." Adherents of utilitarian rule theory might justify the demand that one should not lie by arguing that lying destroys the trust necessary for the functioning of a social system. In a theory like Kant's, on the other hand, this demand would be part of a system of binding deontological judgments. Instead of being justified by any particular argument, it might be declared to be the will of God, as in the case of religious commandments.[4] In the special case of Kant's "monistic version" of a deontological theory (Frankena, 1963), the principle that one should not lie is justified by the following quasi-logical argument: It is unthinkable to make failure to keep promises (a form of lying) a general law because this would cause the practice of making promises to become meaningless. This is not meant in the utilitarian sense as a consequence of actions, but in the sense of a basic logical contradiction within the maxim.

To be sure, deontological elements also appear in more recent ethical systems, for example, Frankena's theory of obligation (1963, pp. 35–46). However, such elements are rarely named as the sole basis of moral decisions, except within religious systems.[5] The medical researcher Pappworth (1968, p. 191) formulated a typical deontological rule in the context of a discussion of ethics for scientists conducting research with humans. Pappworth's rule, reminiscent of Kant's categorical imperative, is that researchers should consider,

---

3. An incomplete hierarchical system of rules must admit exceptions that would be included in the rules of the complete system. Ross (1930) has produced a version of such a system that seems feasible for everyday use.

4. Obeying God's will is in such a context either implicitly or explicitly the basic commandment and needs no further justification for believers. Fear of divine punishment or hope for reward, on the other hand, would constitute a utilitarian or egotistical orientation.

5. Still, it does seem appropriate that the attempt is sometimes made to establish normative systems that are both abstract and precise. The systems need to be precise in order to provide guidelines for as many actual events as possible, but they also need to be abstract in order to cover classes of decisions that cannot even be anticipated when the system is inaugurated. Such guidelines would have a general and sweeping form that would still be open to amendment, much like a federal constitution.

propose, or undertake only those experiments in which they would be willing for themselves and their families and friends to participate.

## ACT VERSUS RULE UTILITARIANISM

Explicit or implicit reference to utilitarian ethics is more widespread than reference to deontological ethics. To be sure, there is competition between act utilitarianism and rule utilitarianism. As mentioned earlier, utilitarian ethics involves the evaluation of an action on the basis of its consequences with the aim of producing a predominance of good over bad results. More precisely, the aim is to produce the largest possible balance of gratification. What distinguishes act theories from rule theories is that with act utilitarianism the persons acting are relatively free to consider the individual aspects of each case; indeed, it is their responsibility to do so. In contrast, the rule utilitarian can approve an action only if it agrees with a general principle that has been found likely to produce the greatest possible benefit.

Suppose that act utilitarians and rule utilitarians are both trying to decide whether they can justify misinforming or deceiving subjects in a psychological experiment. The act utilitarian might ask: Is the benefit that we expect from this experiment (e.g., in the form of scientific progress) greater than the damage that is to be expected from the deception (e.g., in the form of distrust on the part of the subjects)? The rule utilitarian might ask: In general, is the benefit gained from an increase in the scientific worth of research to be considered greater than the benefit of interpersonal honesty? Rule utilitarians will have to decide against deception even if they believe that deception is necessary in this particular case, assuming that honesty is perceived as a higher value. On the other hand, if the validity of research is perceived as more important than honesty, a rule utilitarian will have to decide in favor of deception even if in this particular case the resulting damage might outweigh the benefits.

Let us recall again Cook's formulation of a criterion for decision: "The first consideration is whether the research problem is of sufficient importance and likely enough to produce results that will outweigh the possible cost to the research participant [S. W. Cook, 1976, p. 238]." It is now clear that this approach can be called act utilitarian. Baumrind (1976, p. 13) condemns this position most severely, suggesting that it corresponds to a presocialized stage of development. She argues that we cannot allow those making decisions to evaluate their own views as superior to views represented by a principle that they do not value highly. If this were the case, witnesses in court would have to be allowed to tell lies if lies would serve their purposes better than would the truth. This point of view places Baumrind in good company among professional philosophers (cf. Frankena, 1963; Rawls, 1955). Hoerster (1977) writes: "Like the deontological view, [the rule utilitarian view] satisfies our intuitive inclination to evaluate ethical behavior in accordance with rules. What it has in common with act utilitarianism is that it makes morality a function of the satisfaction of human interests [p. 24]." On the other hand, hardly any theoreticians favor an extreme form of act utilitarianism. Probably the process involved in most decisions must be considered a mixture of the standpoints described here, since actual decisions are oriented toward a more complex system of norms than those used in the examples. Such a mixture is anticipated implicitly by Cook's formulations and by the corresponding passages in professional guidelines.

Of course, both act utilitarianism and rule utilitarianism leave a whole series of questions unanswered. How do we know what goal we should strive for if there are no absolute values or if the level at which we agree on such values as "happiness of humanity" is too far from the level of concrete behavior? How do we determine what belongs in the classes of actions to which uniform rules for evaluation are supposed to apply? How and by whom are costs and benefits measured? What role does the validity of the measurement play in the decision?

We can make these questions more concrete by referring to experimental research. What does an experimenter hope to achieve with the experiment? What benefits can a particular research question yield with respect to these goals? How much validity can we expect from a particular experimental realization of this research question? What kinds of costs will result for others, including subjects? How can these costs be determined in general and in particular? How can these costs be balanced against alternative costs that might result (for whom?) from other research designs?

The principle of weighing costs and benefits as such seems indispensable. Hardly anyone competent in areas relevant to the questions raised here advocates a strict deontological rule approach. It does seem important, however, to seek answers to the questions or at least to determine the extent to which they can be answered. Material for tentatively answering some of these questions was assembled in Chapter 1, but the most important questions seem to be those that deal with measurement. Costs and benefits can only be balanced against each other if they are measurable. From among the varied costs and benefits of a scientific research project, we have chosen to consider in the next two sections those that are generally suggested for direct comparison in the ethical guidelines of psychological associations: the costs for the subjects and the social benefits of an experiment.

### The Costs for the Subjects

The primary means of determining the effects of experimental procedures on subjects is postexperimental questioning of subjects or otherwise testing their reactions. The second and less frequent approach is to use role playing to question persons not involved in a particular experiment about their views on doubtful procedures.

Only fragmentary results exist for these approaches; most of the results have already been mentioned in the sections on deception or misinformation, psychological and physical harm and danger, and debriefing. We will summarize the results here.

*POSTEXPERIMENTAL QUESTIONING OF SUBJECTS*

A number of systematic studies have investigated the nature and strength of the possible effects of experimental procedures and the likelihood of their occurrence. Of these only a few show results that are interesting from an ethical—as opposed to a methodological—point of view. Even these few studies were not all carried out in accordance with the methodological standards that are usually applied to experimental investigations. It is hard to generalize the results, if only because very few experimental paradigms were employed and only Milgram's was used in more than two independent studies. We will summarize the results of Abrahams (1967, cited in Walster *et al.*, 1967), Holmes (1973, 1976a, 1976b), MacKinney (1955), Milgram (1964), Ring *et al.* (1970), and Ross *et al.* (1975), and add to these findings the reports of individual cases that are scattered throughout the literature (e.g., in S. W. Cook, 1976, and in Wolfensberger, 1970), interpreting the individual reports in the light of studies of the psychology of the experiment. Though such a summary does not allow us to make statements on the empirical basis that is generally assumed, we can at least say that the weight of the evidence favors the following statements.

1. It is not known that serious, long-lasting personality disturbances requiring therapy have arisen to any large extent as a result of any kind of psychological experiment.
2. There are reports of individual disturbances requiring therapy that may have been initiated or reinforced by undergoing experiments.
3. Information or experimentally provoked behavior that cannot be reconciled with the self-image can cause prolonged changes in the self-image. Self-reproaches and irritation with oneself have been observed in this connection.
4. A great variance in reactions to experimentally induced psychological stress can be expected.
5. There is no proof that experimental deception or misinformation as such results in a generalized distrust; nor, to be sure, has the general harmlessness of such procedures been proven.
6. Subjects are more likely to react to psychological distress by blaming themselves than by blaming others. It is not known whether they would

tend more to blame others for physical harm in an experimental context, although experiments with minor mutual aggression between subjects would suggest this.
7. Subjects do not express more negative reactions to an experiment after experimental misinformation has been corrected than they do when unaware of the misinformation, assuming that the misinformation does not lead to harmful consequences.
8. There is no reason to believe that many subjects perceive the experimental control of variables per se as an unacceptable manipulation.
9. The methodological necessity of misinformation can be made understandable to subjects by careful debriefing.
10. The probability of enduring damage from psychological stress during the experiment is reduced through careful debriefing.
11. Even careful debriefing cannot eliminate the possibility of enduring damage.
12. We can often expect subjects to disguise any harm they have suffered. For that matter, it is also hard to persuade subjects to express themselves honestly with regard to other aspects of their participation in the experiment.

QUESTIONING SUBJECTS BY QUASI ROLE PLAYING

Although role playing, like postexperimental questioning, was applied in only a few investigations, the results allow us to make statements with somewhat more certainty than do the results of other questioning. As a rule, and in some cases with large numbers of subjects, several experiments are presented for evaluation. The experimental conditions that are described are varied, and the respondents include some experienced and some inexperienced subjects. Since so few role-playing investigations have been conducted, however, our summarizing statements must be tentative. They are nevertheless clearly supported by the studies of the psychology of the experiment reported in Chapter 1. The following statements are based on research by Berscheid *et al.*, 1973; Epstein *et al.*, 1973; Farr and Seaver, 1975; Shulman and Berman, 1975; and Sullivan and Deiker, 1973.

1. Psychologists judge most problematic experiments more critically than do subjects.
2. The manner in which experiments are presented influences readiness to participate. For example, if the entire course of the experiment is described, subjects evaluate it more critically than when the procedures in question are mentioned piecemeal.
3. Subjects expect high professional competence and respectful treatment from the experimenter.

4. Subjects expect the experimenter to protect them from unexpected stress and from misuse of their data.
5. Female subjects express a stronger need to be protected than do male subjects.
6. Evaluations of experimental procedures vary greatly.
7. The subjects' readiness to participate depends on what they expect their own behavior in the experiment to be.
8. A large number of subjects (between 10% and 60%) indicate that they do not wish to participate in experiments involving painful or psychologically stressful experiences.
9. Subjects expect personal questions to be asked in psychological experiments and do not perceive these as entirely unpleasant.
10. Subjects expect to be informed of the purpose of the investigation and the significance of what happened during the experiment, at least after the experiment is over.
11. Subjects do not expect to be informed of all details before the experiment.
12. Subjects evaluate deceptive procedures according to their consequences. That is, they disapprove only of those deceptions that might endanger them psychologically or physically.

RULES OF THUMB IN THE FACE OF SCANTY EVIDENCE

These conclusions are based on a certain amount of empirical evidence; however, we must remember that this evidence can be best described as indications. Still lacking is the solid empirical basis that psychologists generally consider worth striving for and have attained with respect to certain research questions. Until better empirical progress is made, it seems appropriate to employ rules of thumb, even though they are still far from being formulated in a way that makes them easy to implement. Examples of such rules follow.

1. Subjects should not feel worse after an experiment than before.
2. Experimental procedures that lie within the range of everyday experience can be considered unproblematic.
3. Misinformation or lack of transparency in an experiment is acceptable if the subjects would still agree to participate even after being fully informed and having full freedom of choice.

Until we have enough valid information about the acceptability of experimental procedures, we should also take into account those criteria that seem likely to be accepted by subjects. S. W. Cook (1976, p. 239) proposes, for example, that subjects should be asked after an experiment whether they would be willing to participate in another similar experiment. In a postexperimental survey on an investigation by Schuler and Peltzer (1978), this question was put to subjects who had participated in a decision experiment 6 weeks earlier. Their discussion partners had nonverbally expressed either friendliness or unfriendliness to them. The difference between the two groups in willingness to participate was not statistically significant. This could be explained by the fact that apparently no subject perceived the experimental events as strongly harmful and by the fact that these conditions were certainly not outside the realm of everyday experience. In any case, the difference in readiness to participate in a similar experiment was as predicted, with 79% of the subjects who received friendly treatment and 67% of the subjects with unfriendly discussion partners prepared to participate again.

## IN SEARCH OF ENLIGHTENMENT ABOUT SUBJECT REACTIONS TO EXPERIMENTS

Such approaches using pseudoobjective criteria are surely not adequate to answer the question about acceptability of procedures. The basic problem is still that we know very little about the way in which subjects experience a psychological experiment. As mentioned earlier, this may be a result of the orientation in psychology toward the recent school of behaviorism, with its general overemphasis on the parameters of external behavior. In general, we know little with any degree of certainty about how humans react to stimuli or complexes of stimuli, given that the reactions are described in terms of experiences or emotional states—that is, inner behavior—but we know even less about how subjects experience an experiment. In the first place, that question has arisen only recently. In the second place, the general tendency to emphasize external behavior in psychological research has been especially dominant in experimental psychology. It is questionable whether such a tendency is inherent in the method, or whether such a statement might even be a tautology. The experiment has shown itself to be valuable by its control of *independent* variables; limiting the *dependent* variables to "objective" measures of lesser complexity is not a necessary component of experimental research. As meaningful as it may be in many cases, this limitation places inappropriate restrictions on the answering of many urgent questions. Experience indicates that only a low percentage of the variance in reactions can be explained by the variation of the independent variables. However, this need not mean that the constellation of stimuli is ineffective. It can also be attributed to the fact that the measures chosen were not adequate to reflect the reactions.

It seems that the reluctance of experimental psychologists to employ differential and even phenomenological methods is gradually disappearing. If so, we can expect some progress in the future in such areas as the newly awakened or reawakened research on well-being (Brandstätter, 1976; Campbell, Converse, & Rogers, 1976). For example, we could attempt to train subjects to describe their feelings with honesty and precision or to fill out feeling scales. It would be necessary in this case to eliminate motives that presumably would cause interference, such as evaluation apprehension, perhaps by desensitizing subjects to interfering sources of anxiety. Or it might be possible to create demand characteristics such that honesty in expressing feelings would coincide with needs concerning self-image and evaluation, or at least not contradict them.

## THE ROLE OF DIFFERENTIAL PSYCHOLOGY

It is clear from the work of Walster *et al.* (1967) that we will not be able to manage without differential psychology. According to Walster, damage to the self-image that outlasted the experiment appeared only in those subjects whose self-evaluation was already low on the dimension in question. In addition, an investigation by Schuler in 1977 showed connections between several personality traits of a small sample of subjects and their evaluation of various experiments. Students with experience as subjects were given descriptions of 12 different experiments, representing all types of experimental procedures from actual investigations that have given rise to discussion. The following questions were answered on 5-point scales for each of the described experiments:

1. Do you consider this experiment ethically acceptable?
2. Imagine that you are a subject in this experiment: Would you find that unpleasant?
3. What is your opinion of the scientific significance of this experiment?

The factor scores of Cattell's 16 personality factors were available as differential psychological data. The first interpretations showed definite correlations between traits and evaluations. For example, there were correlation coefficients of 0.40 between factors A (schizothymia–cyclothymia) and M (praxernia–autia) on one hand and readiness to participate on the other. For students, the ethical acceptability of an experiment (Question 1) seemed to depend to some extent on its presumed scientific significance (Question 3), as the correlation of $r = .29$ indicates. However, an interesting moderating variable appeared in this context. The correlation was high for harmless experiments and low for the experiments considered problematic. That is, the students were indeed more ready to accept an experimental procedure if they considered the experiment to be significant scientifically, but only if the procedure and its consequences were considered harmless. Students were apparently not willing to allow scientific importance to outweigh questionable ethicality in the case of procedures that received a low average rating for ethical acceptability.

## A FRAMEWORK FOR ASKING RESEARCH QUESTIONS ABOUT THE SUBJECT ROLE

Many thorough investigations must be carried out if we are to begin to determine which experimental procedures are ethically acceptable. Subjects will have to be questioned on this matter and observed, and we will have to investigate in various ways how they react to these procedures, to what extent they are competent to assess risks, how they go about weighing costs and benefits, to what extent they are willing to accept imbalances in their social contract for the sake of particularly useful experiments, what kinds of short-term and long-term influences they consider to be benefits, to what extent their actual competence to act is connected with these factors, etc. No matter how extensive the data are, however, they cannot replace certain decisions. For example, should we consider only long-term damage to be an objectionable cost, or is even the evocation of temporary aversive states of mind problematic? This question must be asked and answered even before empirical investigations are undertaken. Or, how great a risk should we be prepared to accept? Is the 5% of inferential statistics an appropriate model? This question would arise even if we knew the reactions of the individual subjects. In fact, it is possible to claim that the question can be answered only after we know these reactions, since the answer depends on the kind of consequences that are to be expected. If 5% of the subjects distrust psychologists after an experiment, this may be considered tolerable; on the other hand, a suicide rate of 5% would be unacceptable.

Certain classes of feelings—such as fear, pain, hopelessness, and personal inadequacy or inferiority—are inherently aversive. There are also classes of behaviors and events that tend to elicit such feelings relatively independent of the individual personalities involved: physical injury, threats to physical existence, frustration of needs for security, rejection, disparagement, etc. Empirical investigations can clarify the relationships of the classes of events to the classes of reactions, and in many cases also the intensities of the reactions.[6] They will not, however, relieve us of the need to decide which consequences we consider acceptable and justifiable—in an absolute sense if we employ deontological rules or when balanced against benefits if our standpoint is utilitarian. The principle that the students in the preliminary investigation discussed earlier seemed to be employing might turn out to be appropriate as well as customary: a utilitarian standard until certain limits of risk and stress are reached; after that, the deontological principle that no further sacrifices be made, even for the welfare of the majority.

Thorough investigations involving subjects could be helpful in establishing a hierarchy of negative consequences. In contrast with any one-dimensional definition of negative consequences, this would have the advantage of being helpful to those weighing costs and benefits. In order to establish this hierarchy, we would need information about (*a*) the manner and intensity with which subjects view specific experimental procedures and their consequences; (*b*) the

---

6. Experiments about experiments must of course also satisfy certain preliminary ethical standards. In many extreme and unambiguous cases, experimentation is unnecessary; it would be redundant to try to answer all questions from a tabula rasa standpoint. This is because we can, and should, take advantage of whatever information is already available in the literature.

probability of these consequences occurring; (c) the variance in subject reactions to aversively experienced consequences as well as the individual probabilities of such consequences appearing; and (d) the interdependence of harmful procedures and consequences. If we succeed in constructing a hierarchy of negative consequences from our information about these parameters, experimenters and subjects could agree on amounts or limits within the hierarchy. For example, within such a hierarchy minor physical pain would have a relatively low rank. It is perceived as relatively harmless, is temporary, can be predicted on the basis of experience, and its qualities can be communicated relatively well. Subjects are legally protected in the case of lasting physical harm: The possibility of filing suit in such cases is a rather clear one, in contrast to instances of claimed psychological harm. On the other hand, the principle that a subject can discontinue participation in an experiment at any time (blatantly disregarded in Milgram's studies of obedience) should be placed very high in the hierarchy, because not following this principle amounts to the experimenter's assuming responsibility for all consequences of the original decision to participate, including unforeseeable consequences.

To a certain extent, the experimenter can also reduce the costs incurred by subjects during an experiment—for example, by compensating for unexpected stresses with especially thorough debriefing, desensitizing, or explanations. It is also possible to offer subjects various possibilities of attribution and labeling in order to relieve stress. The experimenter can demonstrate to subjects the value of the experiment and their contribution to it. Subjects can be offered possibilities for catharsis through active participation in future experiments, or the educational benefits of the experiment can be increased by such procedures as have already been mentioned.

It should be clear by now that in our current state of knowledge it is at best very difficult to determine the components of cost for the subjects in the context of the cost–benefit approach.

## The Usefulness of a Psychological Experiment

Benjamin Franklin is said to have answered the question "What is the use of a scientific discovery?" with the counterquestion "What is the use of a baby?" He must have meant something like this: The use is impossible to determine in any individual case. Perhaps it is impossible to establish the value in the majority of cases. And yet, partly because a baby (a scientific discovery) is a consequence of natural and apparently necessary human activities, it is valued without question.

### GOALS OF KNOWLEDGE

Which scientific activities we characterize as useful, relevant, or valuable depends very much on the image we have of a science and the significance that it has for us.[7] Kaminski's (1974) analysis of the discontent of his students with an educational project illustrates this. Kaminski uses a theory of action to interpret the students' reactions to a carefully worked out observation practicum. The contents of the educational presentations and the students' own activities are considered to be oriented toward a goal, in reference to a hierarchical system of spheres of action. Activities related to studies receive a large part of their valence from goal components that are connected with the studies, but they also receive part from key concepts of the students' self-images and professional goals. For example, "At some time in the course of their study of psychology, beginners may think, they will become—for example—'experts on human nature' [p. 327]."

A basic conflict results from the fact that the students' perceptions of their own roles ("subjective spheres of action") are not identical with the roles perceived or created by those who plan the course of study and teach the students ("quasi-objective spheres of action"). In the expectations of the students, psychology consists of applied psychology; that is what inspired them to choose this subject as a major. They are interested in therapeutic intervention, diagnostic competence (in the sense of knowledge of human nature), and solutions to social problems and conflicts. Many of the contents and activities of their course of study are perceived only as hindrances to reaching their actual goals and thus as "irrelevant" or "useless." On the other hand, the interest of those who are training them lies more in communicating the basis that they consider necessary for the successful application of psychological knowledge. Educators tend to be more interested in basic than in applied research. It may be that this orientation originated in the frustration of their original motives, which may have resembled those of the present generation of students. In any case, they have learned and reached some consensus about their discovery that the science of psychology is something other than the usefulness of psychological results for solutions to practical problems.

---

7. From a strict semantic standpoint, evaluations of usefulness and relevance are not identical. Here, however, they are used synonymously because in discussions of *relevance* what is normally meant is *usefulness*.

In discussing the presumed usefulness of psychological research projects or individual experiments, it might seem appropriate to consider such related problems as the regulation of research, the special interests involved in scientific work, the politics of science, the communication and especially the application of scientific results, and probably also the connection between the so-called fields of basic research and applied research. The relationships are certainly not simple, however; rather they involve complex, intricate connections. In order to concentrate on the central problem of this book, we must consider the treatment of subjects independently and largely disregard other aspects of scientific work. Only for the sake of a question that is closely related to the treatment of subjects, the principle of weighing costs and benefits, will we even take a fleeting glance at the usefulness of research.

## COMMUNICATING SCIENCE TO THE PUBLIC

Similar difficulties constantly arise in the transmission of "scientific psychology" to a public that has very specific expectations of this science in particular. In contrast, the public likes being surprised by new developments in biology, chemistry, or paleontology—perhaps because these sciences or the results that they produce and their consequences are less significant in the subjective spheres of action of laymen. In the attempt to communicate psychology to the public in the form in which psychologists as scientists understand it, we encounter the same disappointments that Kaminski describes in his students. In order for psychology to be understood properly, cognitive concepts and spheres of action must be restructured on a large scale. This is not easy to achieve and the public resists it: Defense mechanisms protect people's images of the world and their self-concepts. (The mechanisms would not be necessary if psychology played no role in the layman's subjective sphere of action.)

## PERSONAL RELEVANCE OF RESEARCH FINDINGS

In neither situation is it easy to achieve agreement on the usefulness of the results of research or of educational programs: By no means does a confrontation with competing concepts always lead to conflict-free adaptation. For example, students' anticipations may not be fulfilled. They may see the cause of this in their subjective spheres of action, blaming the way in which they formulated a problem or acted on it. However, they may also attribute the cause to any of a number of quasi-objective spheres of action and/or the persons responsible for them. If any particular person is blamed for subjective lack of progress, a conflict may arise (Kaminski, 1974, pp. 329–330).

The discussion of what methods, topic areas, theories, and results in psychological research should be considered relevant can be explained in part by the same concept—as the competition of divergent spheres of action. The persons evaluating the relevance or usefulness of a research project differ in their notions of how valid the project, its components, or even the entire discipline may be for particular aspects of the goals within their spheres of action. The less their spheres of action and goals coincide, and the less similar their evaluations of the validity of the elements of the research project with regard to these goals are, the larger the discrepancies will be between their assessments of relevance.

Naturally, if we venture to interpret the problem of usefulness in this manner, we thereby renounce all hope of unambiguous determination of usefulness. An unambiguous determination can only be made where all parameters for the determination of usefulness coincide. Thus, determining the usefulness of a research project is in the first place a matter of agreement, depending on the respective spheres of action and the components of the goals within them. Evaluating the consequences of the project for the chosen goals is a matter of semiempirical assessment and thus also a matter of agreement on data as well as on values. And finally, determining the validity of an experiment or a particular experimental procedure for the project in question is an empirical matter.

## A FORMAT FOR ASKING QUESTIONS ABOUT USEFULNESS OF RESEARCH

Considered from this standpoint, there is quite a difference between carrying out an experiment and being sure of its utility for humanity. It is no wonder that evaluations of usefulness and relevance diverge so much on a small scale, in the evaluation of individual experiments or projects, as well as on a large scale, in the evaluation of entire scientific disciplines or of scientific investigation as such. The following four questions may serve as examples of different degrees of generality in questions about usefulness in research; they are arranged in ascending order.

1. Was it necessary to deceive the subject in experiment $x$?
2. Does a particular investigation of a minority group really have the consequences intended? (Kelman, 1972, gives examples to illustrate his point that such investigations, whether they are carried out under the name of "social change" or "social control," can ultimately always be used for the purpose of oppression.)
3. From what standpoint can we call an entire branch of research such as experimental social psychology useful? (Argyris, 1975, argues that experimental social psychology in its present form improves possibilities for control and manipulation more than it helps free humanity.)
4. How "right" are the pessimists who make such claims as "The history of technology is the invention of hammers and the subsequent search for heads to bang with them [Du Mont, 1976, p. 81]"?

None of these questions has an unambiguous answer. Contrary to popular opinion, the questions at the lower levels of generality, questions 1 and 2, are by no means easier to answer than the higher-level questions. The would-be modesty of limiting ourselves to attempting to answer such lower-level questions actually assumes an implicit agreement on the higher-order questions, if the attempt to answer is to be at all meaningful. Since this agreement cannot be based on valid predictions, it depends on the conviction that the available scientific data can always be interpreted and applied in such a way that the consequences for a particular field will not contradict widely held values. This conviction cannot be based rationally on the expectation that a harmonious consensus will exist at the time when the principles are applied. This expectation may have positive psychological effects, but it at least seems more realistic to expect good results from what is sometimes called "democratic control." Democratic control implies that all those involved are as well informed as possible, so that they can assess validity. Moreover, the power differential among those involved is as small as possible, so that conflicts between competing spheres of action and goals are less likely to be solved by force.

The difficulty of predicting the consequences of a research project does not relieve us of the responsibility of taking into account all foreseeable consequences when planning the project. Nor should this difficulty be used as an argument against preferring projects with foreseeable consequences. However, it should encourage us to be cautious and skeptical, since it represents only part of the difficulty of determining a project's usefulness. Heckhausen's statement probably applies to most cases: "Relevance is an ex-post-facto criterion [1976, p. 3]."

This insight can presumably also be used as an argument in support of emphasizing basic research and avoiding an exaggerated orientation toward application. It is consistent with the call for basic research that we hear from every metatheoretical standpoint, from Kuhn (1962) to Klix (1976).

## The Philosophy of Weighing Costs and Benefits, Part 2

The presentation of some basic ethical standpoints in Part 1 of this discussion should have made it clear that we can expect agreement without conflict about the acceptability of concrete behaviors only under the following condition: All participants accept a system of normative statements as binding, with no questions asked. These would have to be statements that permit us to make unambiguous deductions of prescriptive statements on the level of concrete actions. The discussion of the acceptability of various procedures in experiments involving humans is the best indication that we cannot assume the existence of such a system in this area. To be sure, every culture has systems of norms that are relatively invariant for certain classes of behaviors; however, these are apparently not unambiguous enough or accepted generally enough that concrete research decisions based on them would be perceived as binding. Even the basic choice between deontological and utilitarian principles of action needs to be justified. If the only acceptable justification is a presumption of usefulness, we are then, by definition, already operating within a utilitarian system. In that case, we need only decide between rule utilitarianism and act utilitarianism.

Baumrind (1976) objects that the research guidelines of the American Psychological Association are based entirely on act utilitarianism. This objection is questionable, since she overlooks the part played by *implicit* rule-oriented or deontological principles in these guidelines. It does seem likely, however, that the acceptability of most concrete research procedures will be justified from the standpoint of act utilitarianism. That is, the evaluation of each individual case will depend on whether the expected benefits at least balance the expected costs. This principle seems to be supported by a relatively broad-based consensus in the scientific community.

This does not seem strange at first glance, since human action in general can be described by this principle. When people drive cars, undergo surgery, and decide for or against speed limits, they assume risks. Costs are accepted in every economic decision, in taking a job, and in choosing a partner. In every case involving decisions made of their own free will, people examine the options in order to decide whether the relationship of the benefits and the effort or risk expected is appropriate.[8]

In the case of psychological research, however, there are some special considerations. The first consists of the difficulty of determining costs and benefits. As the preceding discussion should have shown, it is not always easy to determine the costs for subjects from concrete experimental procedures. Evaluating the usefulness of an experiment is even more difficult if the considerations mentioned earlier are valid; in fact, this is impossible for most individual cases. The general conviction that the accumulation of scientific experience will tend on the whole to have positive consequences, or the conviction that knowledge in itself must be valued highly, has to compensate for the impossibility of determining the usefulness of individual experiments. Thus, the principle of weighing costs and benefits turns out to be a metaphor intended to serve as a justification and is hardly capable of preventing any concrete procedure from being implemented. This lack of empirical content for the weighing of costs and benefits is connected with other problems. The most important of these are accountability for individuals and who bears the costs and benefits.

### ACCOUNTABILITY FOR INDIVIDUALS

Let us examine the meaning of *accountability for individuals*. In all areas of life, people are constantly weighing costs and benefits, thus acting according to utilitarian principles. In almost all cases, they decide not to pay a price high enough to avoid all risks. For example, in building a bridge, investment in safety precautions is not so high that there is no risk of accidents at all. Rather, the builders allow for a certain statistical margin of safety. Often the workers are aware of this, and the danger is balanced by financial bonuses. Likewise, speed limits are not reduced to a point at which no fatal accidents are to be expected, because the economic and other costs are considered too high. Thus, everyone undergoes statistically calculable risks—but not as individuals, only as groups.

The lack of accountability for individuals, or the distribution of the risk among a large number of persons, is an important part of the justification of

---

8. We will not pursue further the psychological correlates of a cost–benefit analysis; this is merely a heuristic model.

such procedures. A yearly total of 15,000 traffic deaths seems acceptable only because it represents an unforeseeable selection from 60 million people. The decision would surely be different if it were predetermined which persons from this large number would be sacrificed for the well-being and convenience of the others. The same is true of building a bridge. If the risk of two fatal injuries were not equally distributed among all workers, but if instead it were known with certainty that persons A and B would die, the bridge would not be built. Even when great economic and scientific benefits are to be expected, sacrifices of particular lives are usually not considered acceptable. The first manned landing on the moon could have taken place years earlier and much less expensively if we had sent kamikaze astronauts to the moon instead of waiting until an automatic landing and a manned return flight were possible. Even voluntary sacrifices (which doubtless would have been made in this case) are not considered acceptable.

Various factors are relevant here: the extent of the expected benefit, the related change in given hierarchies of values (particularly clear in extreme situations such as a state of war), the extent of the costs, and the extent to which the sacrifice would be voluntary. These factors interact. Thus, for example, under normal conditions a sacrifice of one's own life is unacceptable even if voluntary, unless it is subjectively defined not as a certain sacrifice but as a risk of sacrifice, or unless it would prevent the certain death of others. It is usually acceptable to bear voluntarily a certain amount of physical pain or psychological stress. Such sacrifices, however, are criticized as unjust if they are imposed without being freely chosen.

One hundred years ago, the medical researcher von Hubbenet, weighing costs and benefits, suggested that the suffering of the victims of his experiments might well be justified by the value of his discoveries for humanity (see the section in this chapter on the history and background of ethical problems in psychological experiments). The fact that such a cost–benefit analysis is no longer considered acceptable indicates that more attention is being paid to the problem of identifying individuals and accounting for them.

*THE BEARER OF COSTS AND BENEFITS*

The second problem is who bears the costs and benefits. Generally, in decisions involving risks, the person or group that bears the costs is the same person or group that receives the benefits. For example, people who choose to do dangerous work are paid more than people who do work involving lower risks, and we assume that people who are endangered by highway traffic are the same people who benefit from highways. Therefore, decisions about such risks are usually not considered problematic. The prototype of such a decision is a person choosing between a lifelong infirmity and a risky operation: The bearer of costs and benefits is the same.

This is not true of many medical and most psychological experiments. Individuals make sacrifices for others, often not entirely voluntarily, to the extent that we can even speak of a realistic expectation of benefit. Otherwise the sacrifices are made for the idea of scientific progress. Some professional guidelines, particularly medical ones such as the "Declaration of Helsinki," consider this difference important and distinguish between therapy-related research and research that goes beyond or is unrelated to therapy for the individual involved. In carrying out research projects of the second sort, the principle of informed consent is considered more important than in therapy-related projects.

In medicine as well as in clinical psychology, experimental procedures can often be justified by a cost–benefit analysis for a single bearer. Research benefits that go beyond the welfare of an individual patient need no special justification if they do not raise the risk or the existing costs for the patient, but by no means can all investigations from these areas be included in this category. Barber et al. (1973, p. 46) interviewed medical researchers and found that 39% of them expected great benefits, 30% expected some benefits, and 31% expected no benefits for the patients in their experiments; 51% of the sample believed in great benefits for future patients. (No corresponding figures exist for research in clinical psychology.) These are very subjective estimates, and the representativeness of the sample is quite questionable, but the data at least indicate that even in clinical research the number of subjects for whom no individual benefit is expected is not marginal. Pharmacological research alone, with its great number of placebo control groups to which patients in need of treatment are assigned, contributes a considerable number of persons to this group. It seems that we often fail to uncover benefits for these patients and that we can, additionally, point to definitive harm stemming from the experiments.

### NAIVETÉ AND FALSE CALCULATIONS

In interpreting the relationship between experimenter and subject as a social contract, we pointed out that subjects tend to idealize the motives of the researcher. To be sure, the benefit of a research project for science or for humanity, which is the benefit intended in the formula for weighing costs and benefits, has turned out to be very difficult or even impossible to determine. The benefit for the experimenter, however, is quite concrete and predictable. In a number of cases, we must suspect that in reality it is this benefit that is thrown onto the scales to balance the costs for the subjects. Thus, it has become necessary to make sure that within this exchange relationship the calculable costs and benefits are distributed in a just manner. The experimenter, bound to widely accepted norms of social obligation, bears the responsibility for a just cost–benefit relationship to an extent that depends on certain characteristics of the experiment: the familiarity and danger of the situation and induced behavior, the extent of stimulus control and reaction control, and the power differential (already defined before the experiment) between experimenter and subject.

The discussion of the permissibility of sexual contact between therapist and client illustrates the possibility and danger of falsification and rationalization when calculating benefits for the various bearers of costs. An increasing number of therapists adhering to certain methods claim therapeutic value for sexual contact (Hare-Mustin, 1974). A study by Holroyd and Brodsky (1977), however, presents a different picture. Psychotherapists of all theoretical orientations were surveyed; 10.9% of the 347 males questioned admitted having had "erotic physical contact" with their patients (the percentage of female therapists was lower). However, 94% of the 347 male therapists expressed the belief that erotic contacts were rarely or never useful for patients. In a survey by Taylor and Wagner (1976), a majority of respondents considered the negative effects greater than the positive (47% as opposed to 21%). Finally, the interviews conducted by Butler (1975; cited in Holroyd & Brodsky, 1977, p. 848) indicated that even for the therapist the benefits are apparently not unalloyed in the long run; 19 of the 20 therapists who reported sexual contacts with their clients were not able to avoid subsequent fears and guilt feelings.[9]

## The Challenge of Operationalizing Ethical Principles

This discussion shows that scientific behavior can no more be described and justified with a simple act utilitarian approach than can social behavior in other areas of life. Every individual decision may be based in part on Bentham's principle of the greatest happiness for the greatest number; however, the complexity of human motives and our limited ability to obtain and integrate information prevent us from making this gigantic program of optimization anywhere near operational at the present. No one is prevented from citing Bentham's principle, which can be used to justify any sort of behavior whatsoever, and thereby claiming that the greatest happiness for the greatest number was the goal of that behavior. Instead, the basic utilitarian principle must be coupled with other imperatives because of such parameters as the difficulty of determining and assigning costs and benefits, limits on the voluntary nature of participation arising from institutional pressures and role relationships, and the difficulty of assessing the risks for subjects even when everyone is well informed. For example, in his theory of moral behavior, Frankena (1963) supplements Bentham's principle with the principles of benevolence and justice.

This is not the place to develop or even propose normative theories of be-

---

9. For a discussion of ethical problems in psychotherapy, see Van Hoose and Kottler (1977), as well as Goldiamond (1976), where a distinction is made between research and therapy. Goldiamond also analyzes the contract between therapist and client from the standpoint of learning theory.

havior, but perhaps the preceding considerations may prompt some of us to think twice before citing moral principles as justification for our actions. Some of our actions are obviously hard to justify as expressions of the honesty that is one of the most controversial virtues for psychologists. It is doubtful whether the scientific community can agree on any ethical theory that could solve the problems that have been raised. It is thus all the more necessary and meaningful to discuss possible guidelines for action. These guidelines must be abstract enough to permit flexibility in the choice of methods and concrete enough to serve as a guide in the evaluation of individual procedures. Such guidelines should not encourage irresponsible and premature evaluation of new procedures, nor should they lead to a dogmatic constraining of scientific study. A prerequisite for developing such guidelines will be the investigation of the psychology of those involved in the research process.

We can concede to scientists a certain amount of freedom of action that goes beyond the usual amount of freedom from challenge agreed upon for everyday behavior. However, this concession should not and must not stand in the way of honest and responsible behavior. Even strictly interpreted research guidelines need by no means restrict scientific progress in the long run. Suppose that it is necessary to refrain from carrying out a particular laboratory experiment that does not meet the guidelines. There is no reason to assume that the negative consequences of refraining outweigh the benefits that result when we are thereby encouraged to develop alternative research procedures.

# 3

# Ethical and Methodological Problems of Alternatives to Laboratory Experiments

The APA Committee on Ethical Standards in Psychological Research has stated that the majority of its colleagues agree that important investigations should be carried out even if harm to subjects is possible (APA, 1973, p. 59). However, the committee also points out that researchers are "ingenious enough" to conduct studies by means of alternate approaches. As an example, the committee mentions three alternate ways in which deprivation is commonly investigated: using animals, using "relatively trivial" stresses or deprivations, or studying persons who are already undergoing stress or deprivation. It is not clear from the text whether this should be understood as an observation of the status quo, as the expression of an optimistic prospect for the future, or as a morally binding judgment (as in the guidelines of *Ethical Principles in the Conduct of Research with Human Participants*). At any rate, in view of the insight that any theory or research hypothesis can be tested meaningfully in more than one particular mode, we might expect that alternatives to problematic experiments will continue to be devised.

Since its establishment as a discipline, psychology has distinguished itself by a multiplicity of methodological approaches, as is appropriate for any science that is not completely sure of its paradigms. Most of these approaches have never been considered ethically problematic—for example, questionnaire–interview research, direct participant observation, introspection and other phenomenological techniques, self-experimentation, content analyses, correlational studies, and archival research.

## THE CONFLICT BETWEEN STRENGTH OF METHOD AND ETHICAL PREFERENCE

Thus, psychological research has at its disposal a whole arsenal of methods that are not considered risky, harmful, deceptive, or manipulative. Unfortunately, however, precisely these procedures are considered to be relatively weak methodologically, to lack objectivity, or to be unsuited for permitting conclusions about cause–effect relationships. While their nonmanipulative character is their strength from an ethical standpoint, it is their weakness from a methodological one. As already indicated, the reverse is true of the experimental method: Random assignment to conditions, control of stimuli, and lack of transparency have made the experiment the most important instrument of psychological research and have caused all alternative methods to lose significance. "Psychology's divorce from philosophy has left offspring to whom only data speak," says Friedman (1967, p. 144) in describing the reluctance in his colleagues to use any methods other than the strongest available to test their theories—and it is widely believed that the most compelling data are supplied by experiments.

To be sure, it may well be that such rigorous methods, and the resulting hard data, are inappropriate for the present art of theory formulation. One could suggest that most psychological theories are formulated in a way that at best inspires empirical investigations (Harris, 1976), with precise tests being nearly impossible. But even if one views the colloquial formulation of scientific theories as a hindrance to research, that is no reason to introduce a second, avoidable weakness—that is, inadequate methodology, hence weak data.

When consideration of the experiment as a social situation and discussion of corresponding ethical problems reached the stage of a search for alternative approaches, many of the traditional methods were neglected, primarily because of the ongoing demand for tight methodology. As a consequence, two approaches rose to a certain eminence, especially in social psychology. One of these was proposed and tested explicitly as a methodological alternative to the experiment; the other can be characterized more as a directional trend than as a sharply defined approach.

The first of these alternatives, role playing, was conceived in this context primarily in order to circumvent the problem of deception of subjects. It was also argued that role playing should be considered a practicable alternative, since it is seldom clear in any case whether the behavior of experimental subjects can be considered "genuine," that is, directly influenced by the independent variables as intended by the experimenter.

On the other hand, the second approach—field research—can be traced back to more diverse roots and is more a movement than a homogeneous methodological alternative to the laboratory experiment. Ethical scruples are certainly one source of the trend, but certain other aspects were probably more influential in bringing the approach into vogue. The well-known problem of the reactive effect of measurement was given increased attention and interpreted in new ways in connection with the social psychology of psychological research. Awareness of problems with public presentation and reception of the results of psychological research increased. And, probably influenced by discussions of relevance, there was an increase in formulation of questions from various applied areas of social science, in part with explicit political reference.

While role playing as a direct alternative to the laboratory experiment will be considered more thoroughly in the following pages, only a few of the numerous field research alternatives will be discussed. What is relevant to the theme of this book is primarily the new or increasingly prominent ethical problems connected with field research, the most important of which is invasion of privacy.

## ROLE PLAYING

Kelman (1967a) suggests that role playing may be "the most promising source" of alternative research methods. Such procedures should draw on the subject's wish to contribute actively to the success of the experiment, not by attempting to produce the desired results, but by conscientiously following the experimenter's instructions (p. 9). In Kelman's view deception, manipulation, and power imbalance between the experimenter and the subject could be eliminated if role playing turned out to be morally superior and methodologically equal to the experiment, making the research situation an interaction characterized by trust and respect.

Comparative investigations testing the suitability of such procedures as role playing as substitutes for the traditional experiment were called for by Vinacke (1954) in connection with his criticism of the practice of deception. But at that time, his suggestion found even less favor than his criticism of deceptive measures as such, which at least stimulated MacKinney (1955) to question his subjects about deception. Systematic comparison of the two methods and discussion of the results began once dissatisfaction with deception as well as with other experimental procedures and their consequences had become widespread.

Before role playing was initiated and examined as an acknowledged alternative to experiments using deception, it had been used extensively (as it still is today) in the areas of therapy and education. Early on in social psychology, Janis and King (1954) studied the effect of role playing on opinion change and readiness to adopt behaviors consistent with the role playing. The subjects delivered short speeches on various topics, in each case taking a position that contradicted an opinion they had expressed before assuming the role. The subsequent measurement showed a greater change of opinion for the speaker (role player) than for passive listeners. Moreover, speakers who were satisfied with their lectures changed their opinions to a greater extent than less satisfied speakers. Similar experiments were carried out with variations on the role-playing situation, the topics, and other variables (Elms & Janis, 1965; Festinger & Carlsmith, 1959; Mann, 1956). Janis and Mann (1965) gave a particularly applicable example of the use of role playing in changing attitudes and behaviors. The technique, which had heavy smokers play the role of someone afflicted with lung cancer or of the doctor in charge, effected a reduced smoking rate.

### Empirical Answers to the Role-Playing Proposal: Consistent Problems

Role playing was proposed by Kelman (1965, 1967a) and Ring (1967) as one of several conceivable possibilities in the search for alternatives to the use of deception in deception experiments. By some of its proponents, role playing was held to be methodologically as well as ethically superior: "We believe that a role-playing subject will behave in a way that corresponds more closely to the life situation than a hoodwinked subject will [Brown, 1962, p. 74]." On the other hand, advocates of the classical experimental approach, such as Aronson and Carlsmith (1968), held that role playing lacked "experimental realism," which for them was the main prerequisite for a valid experiment. The more successful experimenters are in creating realistic conditions for the subject, they felt, the better they can predict future behavior under similar conditions. The answer of a role-playing subject, Aronson and Carlsmith argued (1968, pp. 27–28), is all too likely to reflect what the subject believes to be a reasonable answer. The subject's effort to answer appropriately could be based on the fear of making a bad impression on the experimenter or on an attempt to help. Thus, subjects tend not to give their own answers, but rather what is believed to be a "usual" answer, so that their reactions can contribute to a correct description of human behavior.

Interestingly, even Kelman (1967a) has introduced doubts into the discussion, with a report of one of his own role-playing experiments. Some of the subjects were informed that they could expect to receive electric shocks from other subjects or to administer them. Before the beginning of the experiment, they were informed that none of the measures was genuine and that they as well as the experimenter were merely supposed to act as if it were a real experiment. Kelman notes that some subjects did not believe the experimenter and wanted to know when the shock experiment would begin (p. 10). Kelman expressed doubts about the effectiveness of this procedure and warned that having subjects role play subjects might lead to a combination of the "worst of both worlds." On the other hand, he cited investigations by Rosenberg and Abelson (1960) and by Guetzkow, Alger, Brody, Noel, and Snyder (1963) that suggested the usefulness of certain variants of role playing.

Greenberg (1967) replicated an experiment by Schachter (1959) using the role-playing procedure. Schachter had observed that, when a high level of fear is induced, firstborn and only children show a stronger need for affiliation than do later-born children. Greenberg, like Kelman (1967a), told his subjects they were participating in a role-playing study. He asked them to imagine they were subjects in an important experiment. Afterward, the same threatening machines were set up as in Schachter's experiment and subjects were similarly warned that they would soon receive severe (or mild) electric shocks. The induction of fear had a lesser (not significant) effect than expected. Greenberg did not confirm Schachter's results until he had regrouped the data according to perceived fear rather than by experimental manipulations. After the regrouping, the interaction between level of fear and rank among siblings resembled that in the original experiment. Greenberg interpreted this as an indicator of the usefulness of role playing; however, it is questionable whether the regrouping of data is appropriate. This leaves room for alternative interpretations—for example, that among the firstborn (as Greenberg's data suggest) there is a particularly fearful subgroup that is not found among the later born. Thus, it seems likely that the two variables—birth order and perceived fear—were confounded. Additionally, A. G. Miller (1972a, p. 629) points out that the necessity of regrouping the subjects could be a sign that the participants were simply not able to play the roles of more or less fearful individuals. Thus, the methodological advantage of role playing is lost in this context. Moreover, given that the observer-subjects had to be subdivided into high- versus low-anxiety groups, one begins to wonder if there was any ethical advantage to the role-playing approach.

Willis and Willis (1970) compared the role-playing and deception methods directly in an experiment on conformity. The primary effect was a relationship between conformity and status of information source for naive as well as for role-playing subjects. The role-playing subjects, however, were not able to produce a more subtle interaction effect in the same way as the uninformed persons in the control group. Willis and Willis concluded cautiously from this that obvious effects could be represented adequately by role playing, but not more interesting and complicated relationships. To be sure, they added, the extent of its usefulness would have to be clarified by extensive and programmatic research.

Horowitz and Rothschild (1970) distinguished between prebriefed role playing and forewarned role playing. The first group of subjects was completely informed of all details before the experiment began; the second group was forewarned that they were to play the role of subjects, as in the Kelman and

Greenberg studies, without being given any details. Here, too, conformity was the dependent variable; it was a modification of Asch's experiment in length estimation (1952). Results from a third, "deceived" group resembled those for the forewarned group; the completely informed subjects, on the other hand, were distinctly less conforming than those in both control groups.

Essentially the same results appeared in investigations that were not conducted as role-playing studies but focused on the effect of mistrust induced in subjects. Some of these were described in the section on deception and misinformation in Chapter 2, including those by Cook *et al.* (1970), Cook and Perrin (1971), Holmes (1967), and Stricker *et al.* (1967). There the question was to what extent the validity of data is endangered by repeated participation (and debriefing) of subjects in psychological experiments and by any resulting mistrust of information and procedures in subsequent experiments. From these and other studies, it seemed legitimate to conclude that the expectation of deception in psychological experiments generally has no significant effect on the results. A difference seems most likely when negatively evaluated behavior is provoked in the subject—for example, aggressive behavior in the experiment of Turner and Simons (1974).

Readiness to conform might thus depend on the evaluation of these reactions in the specific context, assuming that the forewarning is connected in some way with the conformity-provoking stimuli. Differing meaning in context and differing evaluation could be responsible when the forewarning about deceptive measures leads to nonuniform results even with similar dependent variables. Gallo, Smith, and Mumford (1973) found no effect of previous debriefing in a Crutchfield conformity experiment and surmised that even the uninformed subjects were not naive. This should apparently be taken into account more and more in recent investigations. Stang (1976) points out an increase in the proportion of mistrustful subjects from slightly over 0 to around 50% since the mid-1950s. Allen (1966) reports that the mistrustful subjects in a similar investigation were less conforming than the uninformed but also reacted quite differently from the control subjects, who had been given no norm data. Among explanatory hypotheses offered by Allen were that negative emotional reactions to one's own deviation from the group norm could appear even when subjects knew about the deception and that perhaps the subjects were trying to play the role of "good subjects" in spite of their knowledge.

The results of the forewarning version of the role-playing paradigm also resemble results of studies on resistance to attitude-discrepant information or to attempts to persuade (e.g., McGuire & Papageorgis, 1962). According to McGuire (1969, p. 35), in most of these studies, arousing suspicion did not produce an overall significant difference. In a few studies, communication effectiveness was reduced, and in a few, the amount of change even increased.

Hardly any interaction effects of the warning were found; there were some annoying but not misleading main effects.

Finally, Darroch and Steiner (1970) found that subjects could simulate their own data in role playing better than those of other people.

Skepticism about the actual equivalence of role playing to the experiment using deception and lack of conviction about the feasibility of replacing one method with the other appear when one considers, in addition to the few investigations that were carried out to compare the two methods, those studies that were undertaken in related areas to answer other questions. A. G. Miller (1972a), after evaluating the studies of Darroch and Steiner (1970), Greenberg (1967), Horowitz and Rothschild (1970), and Willis and Willis (1970), formulated it thus: "In conclusion, the prospects for role playing as an alternative to deception are very poor [p. 634]."

Assuming that one can use the results of one method as a criterion for the other, this evaluation is still appropriate when some more recent investigations are considered. In the case of Rywick and Gaffney (1973), the effects of genuine and imaginary electric shocks on opinion formation were compared; the dependent variables for Holmes and Bennett (1974) and Houston and Holmes (1975) was the reaction to expected electric shocks. The latter comparison showed that role-playing subjects could successfully simulate the questionnaire-scale results but not the physiological responses (pulse frequency and change in skin resistance) of persons with induced anticipatory fear. Holmes and Bennett reported additionally that reactions of subjects who were told before the experiment that they would be deceived were not substantially different from those of persons who had not been informed. On the other hand, research by Hass and Grady (1975), like some earlier studies, showed that forewarned subjects were more resistant to influence than those who were uninformed about the experimental manipulations. Whereas subject involvement was an important determinant of the ability to demonstrate realistic role behavior in the study of Silverstein (1969), Spector, London, and Robinson (1972) found that the strength of role-related social motives had no relation to achievement in simulation.

Even these additional empirical comparisons have provided no unequivocal and universally valid answer about whether the experiment using deception can be replaced by role playing. A. G. Miller (1972a) emphasized that no answer can be found in this manner and that agreement of results is not an adequate criterion for equivalence. Integrating the critical thoughts of Aronson and Carlsmith (1968), D. T. Campbell (1969), Freedman (1969), McGuire (1969), and Orne (1969), Miller found the most substantial epistemological argument to be that, even when both methods attain the same results, it is not permissible to deduce similar causes. Thus, an informed subject could be inspired by the greater variety of behavioral possibilities in role playing to an even stronger orientation toward the presumed expectations of the experimenter. The subject might then behave just like a naive subject without sharing that person's experiences. Even if a series of replications showed that similar results could be expected under certain conditions, this information could only be used if one were prepared to give up expectations of unequivocal conclusions about cause–effect relationships.

Orne (1969) proposed a variant of role playing to be used as "nonexperiments" or "quasi-controls" in order to find out whether certain demand characteristics played a role in given experiments. This involves showing and explaining to the subjects the entire structure of the experiment. They are asked to provide the data that they would provide as genuine subjects. If the data from the role-playing subjects resemble those of the subjects in the experiment being compared, one possible interpretation is that the latter has recognizable demand characteristics. "Such findings merely indicate that sufficient cues are present in the situation to allow a subject to know what is expected and these could, but need not, be responsible for the data," writes Orne (1969, p. 170). Here Orne, whose intention was not actually to criticize role playing as an alternative to experiments using deception, incidentally characterizes it as the prototype of a situation that determines by means of implicit demands the behavior of persons acting in it.

## *A More Sweeping Criticism of Role Playing*

In contrast, Freedman's criticism (1969), like McGuire's (1969), emphasized the principle that questioning people is different from observing their behavior. Freedman argued that he would not even trust the opinion of his competent colleagues and thus had no reason to rely on the opinion of less experienced students. Even if role playing succeeded in producing the same results as an experiment 10 times in a row, the assumption that this would happen the next time was questionable. A professional journal, Freedman pointed out for the sake of comparison, would not be prepared to accept an eleventh article by him without data even if he had managed to confirm his hypotheses 10 times. Freedman's central criticism (1969, p. 114) is that the role-playing data, as subjects' guesses about what they would do, do not indicate how they would behave in an actual situation.

Aronson and Carlsmith (1968) had pointed out in their call for experimental realism that the quality of role-playing data is sometimes even lower than Freedman implies. That is, it is not even certain that the data reproduce the guesses of the subjects about their behavior in other situations; they could be additionally falsified by evaluation-related motives. Studies in the psychology of the experiment do indeed contain many indications that the behavior of subjects is conditioned in other ways than by the independent variables alone. It is unlikely that this could be less true of role playing than of the experiment using deception.

One can assume that subjects vary in their ability to predict their behavior in future situations and in their ability and desire to simulate the predicted behavior. Thus, the observed behavior is anything but unambiguous, and even identical results from experiment and role playing do not constitute evidence that the underlying psychological processes are identical.

The two basic components that make explanation of observed behavior less certain in role playing than in the traditional experiment are the greater freedom of behavior and the uncertainty involved in prediction. With regard to some of the other sources of error or uncertainty factors mentioned, the experiment is similarly subject to confounding or to misinterpretation of results. The extent to which content equivalence of the two methods can be assumed depends on the parameters of the experimental design and its execution by the experimenter as well as the subjects' interpretation of the experimental situation and their role in it. To be sure, one can imagine a theory of the experimental situation that specifies under what circumstances and to what extent the results can be considered equivalent or under what circumstances role playing serves the same function as actual experiments. However, as Freedman makes clear (1969, pp. 111–112), at the moment such a theory is far from being developed. On the other hand, Freedman overestimates the value of the traditional experiment as a source of knowledge when he implies that it furnishes a criterion of "genuine" behavior and thus a standard of truth: "One can never know ahead of time whether the guess is right or wrong until the people are observed in the real situation, because their actual behavior is the only standard of truth [1969, pp. 111–112]."

The structure of the experiment basically approaches our concept of explanation, but any actual laboratory experiment is merely a more or less successful simulation of behavior in nonexperimental reality and only a random sample of the many possible realizations of a research hypothesis. Subjects in classical experiments are also aware of their role—the role of the subject.

This point of view is emphasized by authors who refer to the various possibilities of role playing and distinguish, like Mixon (1977), between "active" and "nonactive" role playing or between "role playing" and "role taking." Mixon (1971) referred to the example of role playing reported by Olson and Christiansen (1966) as an indication that this method need by no means lack realism or spontaneous behavior by the actors. Olson and Christiansen had simulated an attack on an island, which was to be repelled nonviolently. The defenders of the island were committed as Quakers to pacifist ethics and had declared their belief in nonviolence. After 31 hours, the role playing was broken off—with 13 "dead."

It is evident that such "realistic" behavior must be explained differently from the correspondence (or deviation) of results of laboratory experiments with the expectations of subjects (an altogether different kind of role playing). The "phenomenology of the subject," as Bem (1967b) called the part of an experiment that actually needs to be replicated, determines whether the prognosis of one's behavior in an event that is enacted only in the mind resembles behavior in a corresponding real situation. An additional question is how accurately this behavior will be described. Generalizing Bem's argumentation (1967a, p. 536), one can say: No matter what method is used in the attempt to produce the same results as in a previous investigation, the replication can be meaningful only if the situations are experienced similarly by the subjects—not if the situations are merely defined for the experimenter by the same variables.

The emphasis on the subjects' experience leaves unresolved the problems of the relationships between language, attitudes (or opinions), and behavior. Yet this thought does remind us of the need to find out which aspects of the situation and what behavioral possibilities take precedence for the subjects, as well as how they interpret the event and their own role in it. No matter what form the actual role playing takes, limiting the discussion to the question of agreement or disagreement with the results of the experiment will not permit meaningful explanations.

### An Alternative Function for Role Playing

Mixon (1971) extended the idea of a basic difference between the traditional experiment and role playing with the suggestion that role playing be applied with a completely different purpose from that of the experiment—not as deductive testing of a hypothesis, but as an exploratory process with the goal of clarifying the determinants of action. Knowing the outcome of a particular situation, Mixon's researcher would try to invent and perfect a scenario so compelling to role-playing subjects that each of them would duplicate the outcome. As in a conventional hypothetical–deductive experiment, the subjects would not be familiar with the outcome. Unlike the researcher designing a conventional experiment, however, Mixon's investigator would focus on abstracting the situational features that determine a known outcome rather than on setting up a unique situation for the purpose of determining its outcome (1971, pp. 27–28).

Applying role playing to such explorations—an idea that is also found in the work of Harré and Secord (1972)—Mixon (1972) saw indications that the experimenter was the key variable in Milgram's study (1963). When the actors (subjects) believed that the experimenter was competent to direct activity as usual and to prevent serious injury to the victims, the percentage refusing to obey was as low as in the original experiment. On the other hand, when the actors were convinced that the "victim" would really be in danger from further "punishment," they all refused to continue cooperating. In Orne's terminology (1969), this "quasi-experiment" revealed the demand characteristics of the experiment, although this was more of an indication than a proof. Mixon's results also support the alternative explanations of the Milgram results offered in Chapter 1, not in the sense of conclusive proof, but by furnishing an empirical basis for their plausibility. Orne, too, had earlier doubted the "ecological validity" of Milgram's results because he felt that Milgram's deception of the subjects was unsuccessful (Orne & Holland, 1968).

### *Degrees of Involvement in the Role-Playing Procedure*

Hamilton (1976) took Mixon's distinction between imaginary and performed role action (Mixon, 1971) and added some dimensions and distinctions within these dimensions. For example, he distinguished between kinds of involvement on a continuum, according to whether one's own or another person's behavior was to be simulated. Hamilton argued that only a very specific kind of role playing had been tested empirically, in its use as a substitute for an experiment; the nature of the method as a whole had been misunderstood. Most important of all was to recognize the simulation character of this method and to account for what kind of reality was to be simulated in each individual case. The basic criterion, Hamilton also stressed, could not be merely the equivalence of results. As in a computer simulation, the criterion would be the functional (not technical) equivalence of the processes that bring about these results. Hamilton emphasized the possibility that cooperative effort by experimenter and subjects is what makes role-playing procedures superior to nontransparent experiments. Experimenter and subjects can attempt to create a situation as similar as possible to the reality that is to be simulated, working openly and with unrestricted communication.

### *Role Playing: Not an Unequivocal Alternative*

In summary, role playing cannot replace the traditional experiment, nor is it free from the ethical problems of the experiment. Rather, it seems meaningful to distinguish among a whole set of variants of role playing and ascribe various functions to them. In the cases where a procedure called "role playing" seems most likely to have proven itself to be a direct substitute for the experiment, the procedure probably does not deserve the name. These were the studies by Holmes and Bennett (1974), Horowitz and Rothschild (1970), and Wahl (1973), in which the subjects were forewarned that the experiment contained misinformation. Considering the special nature and nontransparency of the laboratory experiment situation for subjects, it is not surprising that they acted basically like persons without this information. To mention only a few of the possible explanations: They did not know which of the experimental measures they should consider genuine and which false; in spite of having been enlightened, they played the roles of "good" or "faithful subjects"; they believed this forewarning to be deceptive; or even the uninformed subjects were distrustful.

The possibility that the subjects could have thought the forewarning was an experimental deception should be interpreted historically: They did this because they already felt a certain distrust for psychological experiments. Or, to formulate it more neutrally, they were aware that psychological experiments often contain misinformation. If these investigations prove anything at all, it is that experiments still function even when the game rule of misinformation is not withheld from the subject.

The problem of misinformation, deception, or nontransparency cannot be completely avoided in any variation of role playing. Even when the investigation is only of an exploratory nature (as in the version of Mixon, 1972), vital information is withheld from the subjects. This version also seems particularly suited to "abstracting the determining features" (Mixon, 1971) of experiments that have already been carried out. However, this reduces ethical problems only for the investigation that clarifies the determinants of the experiment, not for the experiment itself. In the most harmless (and methodologically perhaps least productive) form of role playing, subjects need only express verbally their conjectures about how they or others would behave in the situation described. Yet even here the experimenter must withhold some information—especially the hypotheses and often the purpose of the questioning as well—in order not to completely invalidate the experiment.

Other ethical problems are not avoided, or are avoided only in part, when the involvement of role-playing subjects is comparable to that of participants in experiments. Two examples for this are the mock battle of Olson and Christiansen (1966) and Zimbardo's Stanford prison experiment (Haney et al., 1973; Zimbardo et al., 1973). Zimbardo's attempt to let students role play prisoners and guards ended in such realistic role identification that the experiment had to be broken off prematurely. The discussion of this was not much less intense than that of Milgram's deception experiments (e.g., Savin, 1973), and the objections were probably just as well founded, even though the authors believed that their experiment was justified: "While acknowledging that the Ss in the prison experiment did suffer pain and humiliation, data are presented indicating that the Ss learned a number of things about themselves and that there were no persisting negative reactions [Zimbardo, 1973, p. 243]."

Although the results of experiments cannot be considered absolute criteria of truth, the demand that the results of role-playing studies should be made standards for the results of all other methods (Forward, Canter, & Kirsch,

1976) is even less convincing. Continued development, empirical testing, and above all theoretical investigation of different versions of role playing lead us to expect expansion of what has been empirical one-sidedness. Specific areas of application for different kinds of role playing already exist, and new ones will soon appear (Cooper, 1976).

## Creative Combinations

Combinations of role playing with the classical experiment suggest themselves for many areas and problems. In decision research this can take various forms—for example, subjects imagine themselves in the role of jurors in a trial (Davis, Spitzer, Nagao, & Stasser, 1978) or of members of a disciplinary commission (Schuler & Peltzer, 1978), in order to make a decision in this function by means of free discussion. While the subjects pretend to some extent that they have these roles, the manipulation of the independent variables and the measurement of the dependent variables correspond to the usual procedures in experimental social psychology.

In these investigations, the simulation asked of the subjects was limited to imagining that their decision would have real consequences for the accused. The parameters of the decision situation that were most significant for the question being investigated were experimentally controlled: for Davis *et al.*, the basic attitude of the subjects; for Schuler and Peltzer, the style of behavior of the discussion partners. However, other proportions of role playing and experimental control are possible as long as internal validity can still be assessed and maintained.

In principle, all stages of transition between or combinations of role playing and the experiment are conceivable; optimization in individual cases requires the consideration of methodological, ethical, and economic criteria. But there is still no convincing proof that the proportion of role playing in the research situation could become so great in a large number of cases that it would completely replace the use of deception in experiments.

## FIELD RESEARCH

Field research is a second alternative to the laboratory experiment. It is more of a movement or trend than a clearly outlined approach and is easier to define in a negative than in a positive manner. Even the negative definition "nonlaboratory research" disregards the fact that sharp distinctions between the two areas cannot always be made and presumably will be even harder to make in the future. Many laboratory experiments use as independent variables selections or groupings that took place in a natural environment, while measuring the dependent variables under actual laboratory conditions. Or conversely, the effectiveness of laboratory manipulations is tested in an everyday context.

## The Frequency of Field Research

It is hard to tell how strong the trend toward field research actually is. There is little evidence for a distinct increase even within social psychology, the area that was plainly predestined for it, although such a reorientation was repeatedly predicted some time ago (e.g., McGuire, 1967). Fried, Gumpper, and Allen (1973) examined all articles that appeared in two prominent journals of social psychology between 1961 and 1970. They found very few field studies and no clear increase during this time. It seems that researchers did not begin to apply the methods made available for the initiation of field research (Campbell & Stanley, 1963; Webb *et al.*, 1966) until several years later. The more recent textbooks on research methods of social psychology pay attention to field research. Not only do they devote chapters to it, but they also point out field applications of techniques and principles presented elsewhere (e.g., Carlsmith *et al.*, 1976; and even more Selltiz, Wrightsman, & Cook, 1976). If this increased attention is a valid indicator, the actual upswing in field research could not have been expected before now.

An increased interest in field research could be traced back to many causes:

1. To start with what is most important in our context, though probably not in a broader view: Testing psychological hypotheses in everyday reality can help prevent many ethical difficulties that would arise if the same problem were being studied in the laboratory. Take the case of investigating the effects of frustrating experiences, for example. There is no need to induce frustration, thereby risking harm to the subject, if one works with people who have been frustrated by an event in their natural environment—for example, university students who were not accepted for the course of study they preferred or high school students who failed important tests or college entrance exams.

2. The next group of causes is related to the validity of the investigation. In the design of laboratory experiments, efforts focus on internal validity; empirical realization of research ideas in the field is more concerned with ensuring *external* validity. The advantage of this is that it is not necessary to reproduce the motivation of the subjects (the extent of involvement that they presumably have in an everyday context). Another important aspect is the possible complexity of connections. If a connection is not merely a simple causal relationship, but a complex network of interactions, the chance of noticing it is greater in the field than in the laboratory. Construct validity can also be improved by field investigations. Ellsworth (1977, p. 607) demonstrated again that the short-term manipulation of a condition or behavior need not be identical with

that theoretical entity on which the research hypothesis is based. For example, momentarily induced fear can have much in common with chronic anxiety. A temporarily diminished feeling of self-esteem can be experienced in ways similar to chronic low self-esteem and have similar effects. However, we do not have very much empirical evidence for this. Semantics can mislead us into drawing analogies that are theoretically unjustified. Finally, research on the social psychology of the experiment leads us to consider the possibility that arrangements for investigation outside the laboratory might be advantageous with respect to internal validity, the actual domain of the laboratory experiment, as well.

3. A third cause for the increase in exploration of areas of reality that are reduced in complexity as little as possible can be summarized as concern with what is usually called "relevance." Problems have begun more and more to be articulated in a politically or socially significant manner. The impulse toward such articulation comes from science itself, from nonscientific areas, and from areas that not too long ago were considered nonscientific. Since the early 1970s, an increasing number of people have come to believe that the social sciences are charged additionally or even primarily with the task of solving social problems. The prospect of a solution at least seems greater when these problems are investigated where they occur rather than in an artificial area of reduced reality from which it is obviously hard to generalize.

## Variations within the Field Research Theme

The possibilities, methods, and forms of field research are as various as the probable reasons for the trend. Tunnell (1977) suggests distinguishing among three "dimensions of naturalness": natural behavior, natural setting, and natural treatment. The dimension of *natural behavior* affects the dependent variable in the research plan. Behavior is considered natural when it belongs to a person's normal repertoire of behaviors and is not simply or primarily provoked or maintained for the purpose of research. The behavior of children in a play group is one example. *Natural setting* is similarly defined (under the influence of Cook & Diamond, 1972) as a context that was not established exclusively or primarily for the purpose of research—that is, almost any context outside of the laboratory. If, for example, the children in a play group are observed in kindergarten instead of in the research institute, the second dimension of naturalness is fulfilled as well as the first. The third, *natural treatment,* refers to the stimuli or events to which the subject is exposed. They are considered natural if the subjects would be under their influence even without the presence of the experimenter. To continue with our example, it might be observed that at the beginning of school interpersonal attraction in the kindergarten play group is restructured after some of the children leave the kindergarten and others enter it. In this case, all three dimensions can be called natural: behavior, context, and events.

Tunnell argues that field studies should attempt to satisfy the criterion of naturalness on all three dimensions whenever possible. He expects the discovery of new "empirical laws" to result (e.g., the structure of mutual reinforcement in certain forms of interaction), as well as higher credibility of research in the eyes of the participants (in that interest in their "real" behavior is expressed) and advantages for external validity (i.e., less severe problems with generalization).

### Deficits in the Field Research Method

To be sure, naturalness alone is by no means sufficient for attaining these goals. To begin with, each of these dimensions is coupled with a loss of experimental control. This interferes above all with internal validity, the most important condition for usable results (Cook & Campbell, 1976). Only when subjects are conscious of their role can the credibility of research be a significant issue. And it is very uncertain whether increased credibility for the subject increases internal validity more than awareness of being observed decreases it. It would also be quite premature to conclude that results can be generalized more widely merely because they took place in an environment that was considered natural rather than under the constrictions of the laboratory. Instead, the generalization problem is merely displaced. The advantage of field research is supposed to be based largely on its reflecting a complex network of interactions that characterize the specific situation being observed, but generalization is only possible to the extent that relevant dimensions and connections within this network can be discovered.

The usefulness of field research cannot, then, be guaranteed merely by seeking out natural situations as defined by these three dimensions. It might be possible, however, to attain a kind of optimal balance between control and naturalness with the aid of research planning and of techniques that were developed with this kind of data gathering in mind.

## ACTION RESEARCH

Action research is a form of field research particularly oriented toward the principle of naturalness. Lewin's field theory is usually seen as its origin (e.g., Groeben & Westmeyer, 1975, p. 186). The logic of this research can be characterized very crudely as the attempt to unite scientific action with social action. According to Chein, Cook, and Harding (1948), action research serves the needs of those who look to science as a reliable guide to effective social or political action, as well as the needs of scientists wanting to do socially useful work. Of the three causes of interest in field research noted earlier—ethical problems, methodological or validity-related issues, and relevance—action research is primarily and explicitly oriented toward a concern with relevance. Its declared goals are to change the relationship between the researcher and the subjects from a subject–object relationship to a subject–subject relationship and to conceptualize the use of research as a possibility for emancipatory changes (Haag et al., 1972). In addition, action research addresses itself to ethical problems, particularly as they are defined by Kelman (1967a, 1967b, 1972)—that is, the basic discrepancy between the experimenter's and the subject's power.

Chein et al. (1948, p. 49) describe one of their own investigations as an example of action research, even though the role of the subjects is still quite traditional. This study was designed to investigate as well as to diminish ethnic prejudice. Whenever children in play groups experienced pleasant interactions, the group leaders referred to the ethnic identity of the children in order to extinguish prejudices through positive associations. As group leaders became convinced of the effectiveness of this measure in the experimental groups, they could no longer justify omitting it in the control groups. But when they introduced the practice there as well, the experiment became useless in the sense of traditional methodology and was transformed into a socially useful activity.

Thus, validity is the weakest point of action research. Was the group leaders' impression of the effectiveness of their procedures justified? Would not more rigorous methods have illuminated the conditions of this effectiveness, thereby revealing further possibilities of generalization—and thus perhaps in the long run have brought about greater social usefulness? Is it possible that premature application amounts to a reduction of the concept of relevance to directly observable units of action? As far as we can tell, the concepts and methods of action research are not much more precise today than when the principles were first laid out by Chein et al. It is hard to see how and why the methodological problems with better-controlled research techniques—for example, the problem of the obtrusiveness of measurements or that of artifacts of regression—could be solved more effectively with informal research procedures than with those that attempt more control. We cannot yet foresee how knowledge is to accumulate more than accidentally (Backman, 1977) in this and related areas.

Even if scientific research is not to be reproduction, but rather construction, researchers cannot avoid evaluating their methods and testing the facts in the best possible way. Certainly action research seems to be an important approach, well suited to modifying the formulation of problems in the social sciences, and offering in addition through its idea of participation a radical solution to the problems of deception and of the (in-) voluntary nature of participation in research. This approach also seems likely to encourage evaluation of the consequences of research and flexible reactions to unpredictable developments. It corresponds quite well to the ideal humanistic and political image of a "democratic" science. Many of the thoughts and claims on which the approach are based will have to be incorporated into other concepts of scientific work and will surely influence the future direction of research. But, as Chein et al. pointed out in 1948 (p. 47), participant action research is more an action technique than an alternate research approach. And action research today seems as little suited to replace controlled experimental research as when its theory was formulated.

## NONREACTIVE RESEARCH METHODS

The development of nonreactive or unobtrusive measures, which are useful primarily for field application, had a completely different origin and purpose from that of action research. This approach was summarized by Webb et al. (1966). In terms of Tunnell's dimensions of naturalness, nonreactive measures are especially suited to measuring natural behavior, frequently in a natural context. The treatment dimension, in contrast, is generally manipulated by the experimenter. The fact that measurements in the social sciences are especially prone to change the object being measured was obviously decisive in determining the development of this approach.

Examples of nonreactive research procedures for the measurement of natural behavior include determining the degree of erosion of the floor covering in front of various exhibits in a museum as an indicator of interest in these objects (Webb et al., 1966, p. 2), obtaining data from archives or through concealed participant observation, analyzing sales figures, and collecting data on absence from work in a production-oriented organization as an indicator of work satisfaction (Cook & Campbell, 1976, p. 319). Behavior can also be induced in an unobtrusive manner, so that subjects are not aware of being participants in an experiment. Many of the studies that are called field experiments employ such methods. One example is the lost-letter technique (Milgram, 1969): Letters addressed to fictitious but plausible political organizations are "lost" in various parts of the city. Political positions of the finders are inferred from the percentage of letters received at the various addresses.

Another example illustrates a particular variant of nonreactive research, *participant observation*. The nonreactive element is that the observer has little or no effect on the actions of the observed persons because the observer assumes a fictitious identity. For example, Humphreys (1970) observed the sexual practices of homosexuals in public places. On such occasions he played the role of a voyeur, who was tolerated because he assumed the function of "watchqueen," or lookout. Whenever possible he noted the car licenses of the observed persons and found out their addresses in order to seek them out at their apartments after some time under the pretext of conducting an opinion poll and interview them. Humphreys' activities remained unobtrusive even when police arrested him for a short time one day. In order not to endanger his future work or the persons he had observed (social scientists have no right to refuse to testify), he kept his actual identity hidden even from the police.

Finally, a third example combines camouflage of the identity of the experimenter with provocation of behavior in a natural context. Persons in a park were interviewed in the name of a fictitious organization. A confidant of the experimenter contradicted the person who had been questioned and added insulting (in the control group neutral) remarks to his contradiction. The dependent variable was the interviewee's attitude change (Abelson & Miller, 1967).

### Recurring Criticisms

From a methodological standpoint the problems with nonreactive procedures are essentially the same as with other approaches, including experiments. Their advantage is that many events can be recorded only by employing these procedures, and many can be noted with less distortion because of them. Above all, methodological weaknesses should be suspected wherever traces of behavior are assigned the function of indicators. For example, in some cases the proportion of job fluctuation, used as an indicator of work satisfaction, actually measures this construct only to a minor extent. Rather, job fluctuation is determined more by alternative possibilities of employment, by organizational changes that take effect at the same time, by an overall change in the unemployment rate, by infrastructural measures (e.g., means of transportation), and by many other factors. Although most problems concerning the validity of nonreactive procedures resemble those for laboratory experiments, conclusions about cause–effect relationships are frequently weaker in the field than in the laboratory because of the complexity of connections. We should remember, however, that the lesser ambiguity of causal inferences drawn from laboratory experiments is generally achieved by differentiating and removing individual determinants of behavior from a complex, weblike tissue of conditions. This is hard to justify theoretically.

### A New Ethical Problem: Invasion of Privacy

Ethical problems are a different matter. A critical parameter is added to those associated with the laboratory experiment—namely, that the subjects know nothing of their role as subjects, nor do they recognize the experimenter as such. There can be no informed consent; the subjects cannot refuse to participate, nor can they break off the experiment. As a rule they cannot be debriefed after the experiment or informed of the results. In brief, no social contract has been agreed upon by experimenter and subject, and there is no particular provision for individual benefit for the subject.

The problem of invasion of privacy is relevant here. In laboratory experiments, questions are occasionally asked or behavior is provoked that would be classified as belonging to the intimate or private sphere. But unlike participants in experiments that are labeled as such, persons who unknowingly become objects of investigations in the social sciences cannot determine whether their behavior is accessible for systematic observation or not. As long as this is only a matter of observing natural behavior that does not belong to the intimate sphere, no particular problem arises, especially since such behavior can also be observed by any other person with or without a scientific interest in it. In addition, one can argue that as a rule scientific measurements do not involve collecting and interpreting individually identifiable behavioral data, but rather processing values for group characteristics. Behaviors that are considered public are generally agreed to need less protection than those assigned to the private or intimate sphere. Intrusion into areas of behavior that a person would not reveal voluntarily is difficult to justify, at least when data that identify the individual are collected at the same time.

Opinions about the legitimacy of studying behavior without informed consent depend on the kind of behavior in question (S. W. Cook, 1976). Baumrind (1977) suggests that rules for psychology and sociology should be just as strict as for anthropology, where observation without consent is more clearly considered in bad taste. This point of view, however, is relatively rare. As a rule the influential philosophical and anthropological reflections of Ruebhausen and Brim (1966) are interpreted to mean that the nature of the behavior to be observed should be of prime importance in making decisions. Ruebhausen and Brim argued that the human need to communicate is unthinkable without its counterpart, the need to conceal and keep something to oneself. The ability to choose areas in which one can withhold oneself from others has, they claimed, the same significance for well-being as does the communication of experience from other areas. The first need has just as much right to be fulfilled as the second. Kelman (1977) illustrated these principles with some examples from psychological literature. Kruse (1980) has undertaken a general analysis of various facets of the concept of privacy.

Another consideration that should influence decisions is whether invasion of privacy can harm the affected individuals. This would be likely when, as in the case of Humphreys' investigation (1970), data identifying individuals are collected and could conceivably be used by third parties as well (e.g., police or criminal authorities) in association with the other data. The possibilities of preventing this are considered later in connection with social experimentation. McGuire (1980) discusses the basic contradiction between the values of privacy and research, and some concrete situations in which a research psychologist may confront the dilemma of having to choose between conflicting responsibilities with respect to these values.

An additional variable that will influence evaluation of the justifiability of unobtrusive measures is the question of whether the behavior in question is natural or provoked by the experimenter. If we do not categorically reject the provocation of behavior in subjects who are unaware of their roles, we must consider whether a behavior is usual and public or the sort that would not appear spontaneously in such a context. Crano and Brewer (1975, p. 299) point out that especially in large cities anonymity is expected even in public. In any case, it will be necessary to calculate the risks for the subjects. It may be less problematic to ask for directions to a particular place, for example, than to provoke someone into breaking traffic laws.

## Subjects' Reactions to Nonreactive Methods

What subjects and potential subjects—that is, the public—think about nonreactive research methods is relatively unknown and hard to determine in a way that would result in definitive guidelines for action. Barnes (1977, p. 13) reports a positive reaction of those questioned after an experiment by Sissons (1971). In this experiment, 80 persons from various social classes in London were asked the way to Hyde Park. While they answered and described the route, they were secretly filmed and their answers were taped. The purpose was to study class-related modes of expression. After answering, the passersby were told by the experimenter that their answer had been recorded and were asked for some personal data. Only 1 of the 80 subjects objected to the procedure.

The findings of Wilson and Donnerstein (1976) were quite different. Students asked 172 persons their opinion of various field experiments. Four of a total of eight well-known experiments in social psychology were described to each person as examples. An amazingly high percentage of those questioned claimed that, were they to find themselves subjects in such experiments, they would be annoyed and feel that their private lives had been intruded on; that their confidence in social scientists would be thereby reduced; and that they considered the experiments illegal. Between 18% and 47% of the respondents considered the experiments unethical; even the lost-letter technique (Milgram, 1969) was considered unethical by 24%. Only every second person felt that being a subject in one of these experiments would be acceptable. In the case of the helping experiment (Piliavin & Piliavin, 1972) in which an actor collapses "bleeding" in the subway, 32% of the respondents were actually of the opinion that, assuming the experiment were illegal, they would approach a lawyer or the press about it. On the average, only a third of the respondents felt that the experiments were justified by the importance of their contribution to science.

If Wilson and Donnerstein's results are valid, continuing to conduct field experiments with nonreactive methods can hardly be justified. However, the great discrepancy between these responses and those reported by Barnes gives cause for thought. Presumably many factors influence such results—for example, the nature of the actual experiment, the population questioned, the interviewers (and their attitudes), the interview technique, the style and form of the interview, whether participation in the experiment is real or imagined, and the state of public opinion at the time (possibly influenced by newspaper articles). The acceptance of field experiments is probably reduced by the fact that the public is not aware that the data collected are normally interesting only as group characteristics.

### Nonreactive Methods in a Broader Societal Context

Thus, thorough research into public opinion is yet to come. In any case, it seems at least as important to explain principles of research in social science and benefits that can be derived from it, thereby influencing public opinion, as it is to explore public opinion. To be sure, even if these efforts are successful, there will be some limits on the applicability of nonreactive measures. In a society sensitized by Watergate and wiretapping incidents, continuing to feed mistrust and insecurity—a " 'candid camera' complex" (Crano & Brewer, 1975, p. 300)—would surely be too high a price to pay for satisfying scientific curiosity. In addition, it would also invalidate observations made by means of nonreactive methods. Wiesenthal (1974, p. 333) illustrates this fear by reporting a personal experience. Walking through a university parking lot, he saw a student working on something under the hood of her car. His first thought was that this was a helping experiment, such as those he had recently discussed with his social psychology class. Not until he had made sure that no observers with stopwatches and note pads were lurking about did he come to her aid. It was indeed a matter of a dead battery.

## SOCIAL EXPERIMENTATION

In Tunnell's terminology (1977), social experimentation usually involves the investigation of natural behavior in a natural context. However, the events—the "treatments"—do not occur naturally, but are strictly controlled. The preferred method for this approach is the experiment or quasi-experiment (as the term is used by Campbell & Stanley, 1963, or Cook & Campbell, 1976).

Social experimentation can be thought of as an alternative to the laboratory experiment. Proponents of social experimentation, like proponents of field research, are motivated by a desire to increase the relevance of research in the social sciences and to avoid the ethical and methodological problems of laboratory research. Yet they are not willing to admit new sources of error by employing "weaker" methods in the field than in the laboratory. This method, unlike role playing, for example, was indeed not developed with the intention of creating a substitute for the laboratory experiment, but rather to supplement it, extending methods of experimental design to areas of social reality that previously were not or did not seem accessible to experimental control.

Social experimentation resembles action research in its attempt to influence social realities, to actually create a scientific basis for social politics in the broadest sense. More emphatically than action research, though, social experimentation considers it possible and necessary to go beyond the intuitively phenomenological cause–effect explanations on which decisions in social politics are generally based. Its working principle closely resembles that of methods for laboratory experiments. Riecken and Boruch (1974, pp. 13–14) suggest viewing social experimentation as a cycle proceeding from problem analysis through planning, development, trial, and evaluation of an intervention, as if it were an experimental treatment. The cycle would end in implementation or replanning.

One important methodological innovation was necessary before it was possible to test hypotheses in the complex social field with experimental rigor, to create social programs or elements of them, to decide among program designs, to determine critical values of the important parameters, and to evaluate concepts or assertions of efficiency. This methodological prerequisite—presented systematically by Campbell and Stanley (1963)—was to extend experimental principles in direct or analogous form (as quasi-experimental designs) into areas of human action or social activity that are accessible only in part to traditional experimental control. While planning methods for such projects often need to be very exacting, corresponding to the complexity of the object of investigation, methods of evaluation are generally quite conventional. In the application of statistical methods, special attention up to now has been directed, not so much to the use of highly elaborate procedures, but rather to intelligent mediation between design and interpretation, as, for example, in avoiding regression artifacts (e.g., Campbell & Erlebacher, 1970).

## A Wide-Reaching Field of Application

Some of the many areas in which social experimentation can be applied (Riecken & Boruch, 1974) include educational projects (especially those for compensatory training), rehabilitation and mental health programs, pilot projects in the area of criminal law and punishment, investigations of social medicine, evaluation of the effectiveness of forms and media of communication, investigation of economic and working behavior, and comparisons of various methods of collecting, processing, and accessing data. As the examples show, the application of this approach is by no means restricted to the area that has traditionally been encompassed by psychological theories. This is surely the least of all grounds for concern, since the dissolution of boundaries between specialized fields encourages us to extend the claim of relevance of psychological theories to all social phenomena involving human experience and behavior. That in turn will necessarily extend the content of our theories to include the most important parameters of these social phenomena. Such an extension—increased inclusion of social data in psychological approaches to explanation—could also help overcome the "person-blame bias", which Caplan and Nelson (1973) consider so characteristic for psychological theories and even more for strategies of application that are fed by psychological theories: "The action (or inaction) taken will depend largely on whether causes are seen as residing within individuals or in the environment [p. 201]."

One social experimentation project that is particularly difficult and interesting from a methodological as well as a political standpoint is the New Jersey negative income tax experiment (Baratz, 1973; Kershaw, 1975; Riecken & Boruch, 1974). In New Jersey and other American states, negative taxes were imposed on families whose income was close to the poverty level. That is, the families were supported by the state with sums representing various percentages of the poverty level, ranging between $1000 and $2000 per year. The families were divided into eight experimental groups and a control group and interviewed before, after, and every 3 months during the experiment. The most salient of the numerous questions that were to be answered by this redistribution experiment were work related. Among the most interesting results was that the subsidy appeared to have no demoralizing effect on performance. Fear of such an effect was precisely why officials had decided to test the hypothesis experimentally before instituting a general program. Baratz (1973) indicates that the New Jersey experiment was not only an impressive exercise designed to test economic, psychological, and sociological hypotheses but also a demonstration of the difficulty of reconciling the criteria of scientific action with those of political action. Baratz (p. 219) found that the experiment showed what pitfalls the social scientist can expect when policy research is applied directly. In addition to the political pitfalls, the experimenters were unable to avoid immense methodological problems, including some that could be described as ethical. For example, government agencies insisted on performing their own reanalyses of one part of the data, thereby endangering confidentiality.

Another sample project, from a more restricted area that is easier to survey, is a program for special education of retarded 3- and 4-year-olds (Weikert,

1972; summary by Riecken & Boruch, 1974, p. 304). In the context of a 3-year experiment, the children were randomly assigned to three different preschool programs, including two with new training methods and (as a control group) one with traditional methods. Stanford-Binet pre- and posttest data were collected as a measure of success, supplemented with ratings by the teaching staff and outsiders. No significant difference appeared among the three training methods.

This second example involves problems that are obviously less significant than those in the first example. With good planning, these problems can be handled by methods already at the disposal of the social sciences.

Reports on the "Sesame Street" experiment (Cook, Appleton, Conner, Shaffer, Tamkin, & Weber, 1975), which was not much easier to conduct and interpret than the subsidy experiment, show that more complex tasks exist in the area of education as well. For example, it would be difficult to evaluate the effects of so-called orientation grades in the transition between German elementary school and high school. The attempt in one West German state to answer this question by popular vote rather than to seek a scientific solution reminds us that values and political influence still define the possibilities open in the field much more than they do for laboratory research. The example of the preschool experiment also illustrates that intervention previously called by a different name is now included under the label "social experimentation." What these projects have in common, reduced to the lowest common denominator, is that they are carried out in essentially unaltered areas of social reality and that rigorous experimental methods are applied.

## *New Ethical Dilemmas*

The drawback of this rigor is the appearance of new ethical problems, or the intensification of problems that also exist in laboratory research. One of these is random distribution, which can interfere with social ties and lead to great burdens on certain individuals.

Sometimes it is merely a matter of comparing treatment groups, as in the case of the preschool experiment. But assigning some of the subjects to an untreated control group, as in the case of the negative taxes, leads to a particular sort of ethical problem that is basically identical with the one mentioned in connection with placebo groups and untreated control patients in pharmacological research. Campbell (1976) argues that it is defensible to assign persons at random to an untreated control group even if they fail to receive a benefit that they would have received in one of the experimental groups. (This benefit, indeed, is only demonstrated to be such after the results are analyzed.) It is not defensible, however, to do so when it can be foreseen that the distribution will cause the subjects some direct loss. The majority of Campbell's colleagues probably take a similar view. The New Jersey negative income tax experiment shows that the problem is somewhat more complicated, since failing to receive a benefit can certainly be experienced as a loss by those affected. Although in both cases $15 per interview was paid as an honorarium, 26% of the respondents from the control group were lost in the course of the experiment, compared with 7% from the best-paid experimental group. Campbell himself (1976, pp. 16–17) assumes that disappointment about the relative deprivation of the control families contributed to this.

In some cases it will be necessary to work with quasi-experimental designs that manage to dispense with control groups. In general, it is a matter of one-sided tests of presumably positive treatment conditions, the lack of which causes the persons in the control group no absolute disadvantage. If according to a consensus of experts, however, a relative disadvantage can be expected for the untreated groups, the program can be generally introduced, instead of being tested first by an experiment (Campbell, 1976, p. 18).

## Invasion of Privacy Surfaces Again

Another ethical problem resulting from social experimentation is invasion of privacy. In order to measure the success of social programs, it is generally necessary to collect data on the participants, often for an extended period. These data concern participants' economic and social status, their home and family relationships, and their mental and physical well-being. If the data are collected by direct questioning and observation, subjects can refuse to cooperate whenever they object, at least to the extent that they are aware that these particular data are being collected. Here, however, one must consider certain difficulties that are familiar to social scientists and arise from differential status, limited possibilities of articulation, and a frequent incapacity to judge the purpose, meaning, and risks of the investigation. In addition, the possibility of refusal to cooperate introduces self-selection into a random sample, creating a methodological problem.

In connection with the necessary protection of privacy, the question arises to what extent confidentiality can be guaranteed for future use of the data. Especially when extensive social programs are evaluated, there is some interest in analyzing the data in various ways and relating them to each other and to other data. They must be stored for extended periods and may be accessible to a variety of persons and interest groups. If as much of the information could reasonably be considered confidential as in the New Jersey negative income tax experiment, serious conflicts of goals arise. The identifiability of individuals opens the possibility of damage to reputation or economic disadvantage, perhaps even extortion or prosecution. As Campbell reports (1976, pp. 11–12), the district attorney's office of one of the states included in the subsidy experiment demanded the disclosure of data in order to expose tax and subsidy fraud. Negotiations were necessary in order to persuade the officials to refrain from legal procedures and from demanding to see the relevant data. In many areas, it makes no sense at all to carry out research projects—for example, on drug use or criminal behavior—unless the confidentiality of data and the immunity of the participating researchers have been established (see various contributions in Eser & Schumann, 1976).

In case of doubt, procedures should be taken that protect respondents from misuse of their data. These include such simple procedures as refraining as much as possible and reasonable from collecting incriminating information, not registering the identity of individual persons at all, or destroying the keys that connect individuals with data as soon as possible. Campbell and Cecil (1977) survey various data security procedures, some of which were developed in response to the appearance of such problems in social experimentation projects. The examples they cite underline the importance of developing research methodology, not only for accomplishing scientific tasks, but also for solving social or ethical problems resulting from research.

## *Ensuring Confidentiality*

One of the many possibilities for safeguarding data is to "contaminate" them with random errors. If the means and deviations are preserved, the data are still usable on the group level but no longer on an individual basis. When known changes are made in the distributions, such as adding a small random error with the mean of 0 to each individual value, all necessary statistical comparisons of groups of data and persons can be performed even though no individual value can be interpreted. Boruch (1972) describes a variation of this procedure, the "contamination method," which makes it impossible for the interviewer to interpret each individual answer without invalidating the data as a whole (when the random sample is large enough).

The respondent receives two dice and instructions to roll them before answering each question. If the dice show a double one, double two, or double three, the respondent is to answer untruthfully; with any other combination of spots the respondent is to tell the truth. If the probability of a lie (one-twelfth) and the percentage of positive answers in the random sample are known, an estimate of the actual frequencies can be calculated very simply. This procedure is especially appropriate in the case of sensitive questions that may not be answered honestly, such as questions about drug use, criminal actions, or deviant sexual behavior.

Presumably this procedure is not yet usable in actual research. Respondents who do not understand statistics probably do not trust the procedure and may be even more suspicious of it than of unfalsified questioning by name. On the other hand, if they do know something about statistics, the questionnaire cannot consist entirely of potentially incriminating questions, since it would then be obvious to them that the researchers could also calculate the probability that they have a police record or something else to hide. And even one-twelfth, added to the usual error of measurement for questionnaires, is probably not a large enough increase in error to prevent attempts at interpretation on an individual basis. Moreover, the procedure might on occasion be the respondents' first clue to the intimate nature of the questions and might thereby raise their threshold of responsiveness. Some of these reasons were probably responsible when a test of the method with students produced no higher honesty quotients than questioning by name (Berman, McCombs, & Boruch, 1977). Students probably also have relatively few inhibitions about answering intimate questions.

The example of the contamination method was mentioned here even though in this form it apparently does not serve the intended purpose. (It does, on the other hand, function quite well in the contamination of stored data.) Like all other methods, those used to ensure confidentiality also require critical testing and development. In its cleverness and originality, however, the example seems very well suited to demonstrate that humanizing research (and thereby perhaps also society) need not mean anxiously avoiding research innovations, as humanistic psychologists and their critics alike sometimes seem to fear. It can also be achieved, probably even more effectively, through creative development of new approaches and methods.

## FIELD RESEARCH: A SUPPLEMENT RATHER THAN A SUBSTITUTE

Approaches in field research, as suggested earlier in the chapter, seem suited to furthering progress or development of solutions in three problem areas: overcoming the methodological weaknesses of laboratory experiments, preventing ethical problems connected with these experiments, and, finally, reducing the lack of relevance that research in the social sciences has been so often accused of in recent years. It should be obvious from the preceding remarks that none of these goals can be reached automatically by shifting the research context from the laboratory to the field. No kind of validity, whether internal, external, or construct validity, can reach a respectable or even an adequate level merely through that shift. The ethical problems found in laboratory research will not vanish with the shift, and even demands for relevance could be satisfied by that simple action only if they were meant very superficially in the first place. On the contrary, new methodological as well as ethical problems are appearing in field research; new ideas and methods for dealing with them need to be developed.

Nor is social experimentation a substitute for the traditional laboratory experiment, but rather a supplement, an extension of its domain with the help of methodological principles that were developed and tested in laboratory research. This approach is probably the most promising of the three discussed—the most effective as well as the one that can have the strongest influence on psychological thought. The scientific status of psychological theories could change if the theories took into account social realities and were tested in the social domain. Gergen (1973b) suggested with regard to psychological research in general that the empirical testing of hypotheses changes reality and thus does not constitute a test of theory in the traditional sense. This seems most valid for those areas in which intervention research is about to take over.

Aside from the alternatives already mentioned, still others are likely to be used and further developed in the near future. The opinion leaders of the discipline have opened the doors for methodological pluralism (Herrmann, 1976; McGuire, 1973). Indeed, Kuhn (1962) describes pluralism as characteristic of that stage of dissatisfaction that encourages creativity and precedes agreement on revolutionary new paradigms. This is a good time for scientists who are aware of their ethical responsibilities. As long as it is clear that there are many ways to realize a research idea empirically, it should be possible to choose approaches that do justice not only to high methodological standards but also to high moral standards.

# 4

# The Codification of Ethical Principles for Psychological Research

Scientists usually consider it their primary obligation to contribute to the accumulation of knowledge. This is how their task is defined, and the primary criterion for selecting future scientists is their ability to make such a contribution. Today this obligation is not considered apart from responsibility for the foreseeable consequences of scientific research. This responsibility, in turn, is viewed in the context of the norms that generally govern human behavior. Unlike scientists from other disciplines, scientists studying humans have one further responsibility: to carry out their research in accordance with the norms that regulate the conduct of humans with each other in their own culture and society. For example, in an age in which individual human life is accorded low value, it would be considered legitimate to sacrifice the health and life of individuals for the well-being of the majority.[1] In contrast, in an age of generally high moral expectations of behavior towards one's fellow human beings, research activities involving humans would be subject to relatively severe restrictions. Thus, professional regulations in one of the research areas cannot include just any principles. Their contents and the stringency of their ethical demands are determined and limited by generally accepted concepts of morality.

1. Even though individual views and ideological positions on this subject may vary considerably, actions tend to correspond to the accepted norms. The question of the correspondence of attitudes and actions is also a question of social power. Thus, the norms for scientific research need not reflect the general values of a majority. Under some circumstances, they merely reflect the values of an elite defined by power.

Within the range established by these limits, however, ethical guidelines for research may not merely reflect general concepts, but through modifications and restrictions, they may even have a certain innovative character. Not only is art formed by the aesthetic perceptions of the majority, but it also affects these perceptions in turn. Similarly, research guidelines could have the effect of changing existing standards in the direction of their own deviation from the average value of the distribution of existing cultural standards, assuming that a high value is placed on scientific research.

A professional code of ethics is dependent on the norms of an entire society. In specific details, it reflects the values of the scientific community to which it applies. But even when this community is called upon to make these values explicit, as in the case of the APA ethical principles, the resulting code will not necessarily reflect the opinion of the majority, nor will it represent the lowest common denominator of attitudes in the profession. It is likely to contain a bias in the direction of attitudes that are considered socially more valuable. Why should this be so? It may well be that the more stringent ethical requirements are more readily articulated, and overtly valued more highly, than are lenient ethical rules. Thus, the resulting regulations will deviate from the center of the distribution of actual opinions, in the direction of greater ethical stringency. This assumption can be supported only by informal impressions. However, this principle does seem to characterize some of the codes adopted during the 1970s. It is also plausible to suppose that attitudes, if only by means of behavior, will approach the more stringent norms.

## THE FUNCTIONS OF ETHICAL GUIDELINES

The codification of ethical research principles is an attempt to balance two occasionally contradictory interests or needs: the need to contribute to the accumulation of knowledge and the need to avoid harming others. A number of existing codes discuss the obligation of contributing to scientific knowledge, but this cannot be their main goal. Rather, it is necessary to emphasize the other side of the conflict. As mentioned earlier, psychologists are selected for their profession, not because of their commitment to social and ethical principles, but because of their interest and competence in conducting research. Therefore, the dedication to producing scientific knowledge is the side of the conflict that can go without discussion.

### *Intrusion of Personal Motives into Science*

If we are willing to consider the psychology of scientific work, however, we cannot fail to detect a certain idealization of the pursuit-of-knowledge side of the conflict. "Scientific interest," "the search for truth," or "furthering knowledge" is revealed upon closer examination to consist to a considerable extent of pursuing such thoroughly prosaic motives as the desire to become established professionally and attain social recognition. Thus, the conflict is in part reduced to a conflict between the pursuit of one's own goals and the consideration of the interests of others. The power possessed by experimenters in their roles as scientists and college teachers, compared with the power of their subjects, combines with the usual lack of transparency of investigations for the subjects to create a particular responsibility for experimenters. They must weigh costs and benefits for themselves and for their subjects. In a contract between well-informed persons of equal status, on the other hand, both partners would make their own decisions, or the decision would be made jointly. Moreover, the structure of rewards for scientific research is not exactly designed to contribute to the balance of this social contract. Thus, a further function of professional ethical obligations, or another perspective on the basic function, is the correction of the system of rewards. Although no one is directly accused of submitting to temptation, the act of codification does express a certain distrust or uncertainty as to whether the "iron law of morals" within us all offers adequate assurance that we will all evaluate research procedures in the same way.

One could also view the development of guidelines as a consequence of the rapid growth of the institution of science. Its size and complexity have now reached a stage at which it no longer seems adequate or even feasible to rely on informal regulation or to expect implicit standards to be accepted as obvious. The growth of the institution called science makes it harder to survey and regulate by means of informal agreement, and perhaps the mechanisms of socialization are no longer as definite and coherent as they once were.

## Maintaining a Public Image

The demonstration of goodwill to the outside world is surely an independent function of ethical principles for research. This intention is formulated in an explanation of the code proposed for the British Psychological Society (see Appendix): "At the very least there is no harm in putting our house in order and being seen to do so [British Psychological Society, 1977, p. 25]." At a time of increasing demands for public control of science, this gesture can help prevent attacks that stem either from general distrust or from the exaggeration of individual incidents in the public press. If at the same time, the existence of the regulations actually manages to prevent such individual incidents, then the goal is doubly served.

To be sure, the formulation of regulations could produce the opposite effect. It could awaken the public distrust that it is supposed to appease. It is probably an exaggeration, however, to fear that formulating ethical guidelines for research could encourage anti-intellectual and antipsychological attitudes and thereby bring about a setback for the social sciences (Kerlinger, 1972). Short-term effects of this sort probably cannot be prevented, since topics that can cause a public sensation always tend to be discovered by newspaper writers who want to stir up resentment. However, experiences from the field of medicine indicate that long-term negative effects are not to be expected. There is no reason to avoid publicity if the development and application of research guidelines is handled responsibly; on the other hand, it is also unnecessary to seek it out too energetically. For this and other reasons, it would be helpful if the negative correlation between enthusiasm for research and sensitivity to ethical problems (see the section in Chapter 2 on the demography of ethical commitment) were to change to a positive relationship.

### Self-Regulation or State Regulation?

Some of the dangers to which subjects in medical experiments might be subjected are prohibited by law. In extreme cases psychological experiments would also come into conflict with relatively unambiguous legal regulations. For the usual range of psychological experiments, however, the law is irrelevant. Legal liability is hard to establish in such cases, and there is considerable room for interpretation. This is true of the United States (Silverman, 1975) as well as the Federal Republic of Germany (Kumpf & Irle, 1976). The reasons for this lie not only in the comparative harmlessness of psychological research procedures but also in the insensitivity of our laws to psychological damage.

In the area of psychological therapy, as in medicine, a more critical attitude toward the appropriateness of therapeutic procedures appears to be developing (Roston & Sherrer, 1973; Van Hoose & Kottler, 1977). Thus, we can also expect effects on research within the area of psychological therapy. On the other hand, there is little evidence at the moment that concern about possible harm to subjects in other areas of psychological research has reached the point where research would be affected. It is true that the voluntary establishment of restrictions by the research community itself could serve to prevent this function from being assumed by the state, which can probably not be expected to have as much insight into the actual risks and necessities as the researchers themselves have. But it should be clear that voluntary limitations protect us from government regulation only if they are stricter than the current legal norms. In any case, if professional regulations are also to describe a kind of legal free zone—that is, the extent and forms of the special behavior scientists are permitted in order to fulfill their tasks—then unilateral regulations by professional committees cannot replace agreements between representatives of the profession and legal bodies.

Finally, the regulations serve to inform members of the scientific community about the extent to which their projects correspond to official norms. This can serve to reduce insecurity about the likelihood of subsequent difficulties. If we manage to establish professional regulations that ensure legal acceptability, then researchers who orient themselves by these guidelines are afforded considerable security in this area as well.

### Enforcement of Regulations

To what extent can professional codifications of ethical research principles fulfill their functions? As with all normative systems, this depends on the sanctions and on the enforceability of such sanctions. This is of course especially true for the functions of control and guidance, and less so for the functions of information and security. Part of the control can be exercised by committees even before the investigations are carried out, as in regional or intrauniversity consultation on the planning of projects or preliminary review by the organizations financing the research. Journals that publish results have considerable power of control. If they make observance of ethical principles a prerequisite for publication, as is literally stipulated by the journals published by the APA, this might be the strongest incentive for recalcitrant social scientists to go along with the guidelines.

However, we should not fail to emphasize that, whenever possible, research regulations should be based on a consensus by scientists; the scientific community should take responsibility for formulating them. No less insight and prudence are required to establish and enforce these criteria than are needed to evaluate the appropriateness of scientific methods. The establishment and enforcement of research principles by a government bureaucracy would be a function of political zeal rather than of self-control on the part of the scientists themselves. This would presumably tend more to bring scientific innovation to a standstill than to fulfill the intended purpose of protecting subjects.

## THE HISTORY OF REGULATIONS FOR RESEARCH WITH HUMANS

Ethical principles for medical therapy and research have been formulated and revised repeatedly since the beginning of the nineteenth century. The version used at present, however, was not developed until after World War II, which is also when the ethical principles governing psychological research were first developed. In spite of all the differences, the formulations contained in the medical guidelines can be considered the predecessors and parallels of those for psychology. Both the common background of moral and philosophical views and the immediate incentive stemming from research-connected crimes committed in German concentration camps led to similarities in the development and tightening up of regulations.

## The Beginnings of Medical Ethics

The first substantial contribution to medical ethics since the code of Hammurabi in the East and the oath of Hippocrates in the West seems to have been the book *Medical Ethics* by the English doctor Percival, published in 1803.[2] There is an occasional tendency in medicine to call every attempt at a new treatment an experiment; however, if we disregard this liberal definition of research, we can say that systematic experimentation was not yet widespread in the early nineteenth century. Percival devoted most of his attention to the obligation to use appropriate medical treatments. Little was said about the relationship between doctor and patient. Since the Nuremburg trials, all medical guidelines have included as a basic principle that the patient or subject should be fully informed of all impending procedures and risks. Percival, however, merely remarked that the friends of the patient should be informed in case of dangerous illness and that the patient should be informed if absolutely necessary (Katz, 1970, p. 299).

Percival's book was the basis for the first "Code of Ethics of the American Medical Association" in 1847, as well as its later versions in 1903 and 1912 (Katz, 1970, p. 312). In 1946, influenced by reports on the medical experiments that took place in Germany during the war, the American Medical Association (AMA) established three requirements for the ethical conduct of experiments: voluntary consent by the subject, preliminary experimentation with animals to determine the danger involved, and appropriate protection and management by medical personnel (Judicial Council of the AMA, 1946, p. 1090). In subsequent years, this preliminary statement by the AMA was refined, extended, and tightened up by national associations and by the World Medical Association.

On August 19, 1947, the Nuremberg military trials (*United States* v. *Karl Brandt et al.*) culminated in death sentences for seven and with prison terms for another nine of the defendants, accused of war crimes and crimes against humanity. The defendants had been charged with carrying out medical experiments on a disputed but undoubtedly large number of persons. These experiments were described by the military tribunals as "murders, brutalities, tortures, atrocities, and other inhumane acts [Ladimer, 1955, p. 488]." Some of the experiments that the physicians had conducted "in the interest of science and the people" included experiments in pressure chambers, freezing experiments, infection of subjects with malaria and typhoid fever, experiments with

---

2. The doctor's name was Thomas Percival, according to Katz (1970, p. 299) and Romano (1974, p. 129). Ladimer (1955, p. 487), however, calls him James Percival.

different toxins, and experiments involving infections in wounds that were inflicted for the purpose of the experiment (*Trials of War Criminals before the Nuremberg Military Tribunals,* 1948, excerpted in Katz, 1972, pp. 292–306). The defense argued that similar experiments had been carried out by doctors in other countries. They managed to call into question the concepts of "voluntary participation" and "information about risks" by pointing out that prisoners had "volunteered" for equally dangerous experiments. It was documented by Mitscherlich and Mielke (1960) that some of the experiments had actually made a contribution to medical knowledge and that the physicians involved had indeed carried out the experiments from a sense of duty. The state had instigated the experiments and protected the physicians, who were allegedly convinced that the experiments were a necessary part of the German struggle for existence (Katz, 1972, p. 304).

## THE NUREMBERG CODE

The 10 rules that have become known as the "Nuremberg code" were developed in connection with the Nuremberg trials (Katz, 1972, pp. 305–306). They can be seen as the basis of all subsequent guidelines that deal with any kind of experimentation with human subjects. These 10 conditions for the acceptability of an experiment are summarized here:

1. Participation entirely voluntary, full information about risks.
2. Humanitarian purpose, not attainable in any other way.
3. Solid background of relevant knowledge, including information from experiments with animals.
4. Avoidance of unnecessary physical and psychological harm.
5. No reason to expect the experiments to result in death or disablement.
6. Risk proportional to the humanitarian significance of the problem.
7. Appropriate precautions to prevent harmful effects.
8. Experimenters who are highly qualified in their branch of science.
9. Freedom of subjects to discontinue participation in the experiment.
10. Provision that the experimenter should discontinue the experiment if there is danger of unforeseen negative consequences for the subjects.

It was clear that these regulations would not be able to prevent a new catastrophe like that of Nazi Germany and that the Nazi experiments would not have been prevented even if these rules had existed earlier. Yet a certain amount of protection was expected from the rules, especially wherever the use of institutionalized subjects cannot be observed or modified effectively from the outside—for example, for the mentally retarded, the severely ill, and prisoners (Alexander, 1966). The regulations do not mention the treatment of special groups, however, and have nothing to say about the problem of limitations on ability to consent and the resulting apportioning of responsibility.

The first and basic principle of the Nuremberg code makes voluntary participation and informed consent irrevocable prerequisites for the acceptability of medical experiments. This should guarantee that the unequal relationship between doctor and patient will not be exploited and should offer protection from all consequences that could otherwise result. This first principle, then, functions approximately as a gatekeeper or filter. More recently, the principle of informed consent has been fundamental in the regulations of the World Medical Association (e.g., World Medical Association, 1955). Since the "Declaration of Helsinki" (1964), the principle has also influenced the regulations of many national medical associations.

## American Developments

Through the regulations of the National Commission for the Protection of Human Subjects of Biomedical and Behavioral Research, the principle of informed consent also attained a position in the social sciences, particularly in psychology, that has made this principle the object of pronounced controversy. As mentioned already, the requirement that subjects be fully informed would make it hard to carry out certain major categories of experiments meaningfully, especially in social and personality psychology, where the reactivity of research methods plays an important role. It has been argued that such a requirement does not fit the field: The dangers of psychological experiments for the subjects are far fewer than those of medical experiments. While medical experiments almost always involve certain risks, in many psychological experiments the subjects undergo almost no risk. By this argument, the obligation to inform psychological subjects fully is justifiable only for those experiments involving risks and should be made dependent on the risk in the individual experiment.

### THE NATIONAL COMMISSION

The National Commission was created by the National Research Act in 1974. The task of this commission was to propose means of ensuring protection of subjects to the secretary of the Department of Health, Education, and Welfare (HEW, later known as the Department of Health and Human Services, or HHS). The areas involved—the biomedical and social sciences—included almost all research areas in which humans are used as subjects. The commission consisted of 11 scientists from all branches of the humanities, including philosophy and theology. It was stipulated that only 5 of these 11 members should have had experience in working with subjects. The members were nominated by their professional organizations and appointed by the secretary.

In addition to developing general ethical guidelines, the commission was charged with developing recommendations for work with any specific research areas, methods, and subject groups (e.g., prisoners) that might seem especially problematic from an ethical point of view. This included such issues as the selection of subjects, the conditions under which subjects are considered capable of giving their consent, the procedures by which research in institutions is evaluated, research with children, experiments with prisoners, and psychosurgery (National Commission, 1977c).

The work of the commission and its recommendations were accompanied by a lively discussion in the scientific community (Levine, 1976). Still, it was clear that the recommendations were to serve as the basis of legal regulations. Public research funds have been granted partly on the basis of observance of these guidelines (Lowe, 1975; National Commission, 1977a; National Research Act, 1974).

Controversies have generally been in regard to the pronounced ethical stringency of the guidelines developed by the commission. If earlier discussions of ethics are any indication, this stringency was probably not matched by the views of the average scientist in the disciplines in question. For example, the regulations proposed for research involving prisoners (National Commission, 1976) would amount to restricting experiments to those from which direct benefits for the subjects could be expected. This would exclude many of the numerous medical, nutritional, cosmetic, and psychophysiological experiments that have previously been conducted with prisoners. Experimenters have been glad to avail themselves of these potential subjects, who are generally willing and live under all sorts of controlled conditions.

Another object of criticism was the danger that the research process would be bureaucratized. It was feared that this bureaucratization would be particularly encouraged by the existence of institutional review boards established in response to the commission's requirements (National Commission, 1978). These boards were created to review all projects in which humans function as research objects, before these projects begin. They examine all proposed procedures and are entitled to suggest modifications. It was intended and recommended that the rules be applied as flexibly as possible in individual cases. Nevertheless, researchers feared that projects would be delayed and that the boards might lack sufficient insight into the problems of research in their own specific disciplines, since no more than two-thirds of the members were to be involved in research themselves and members were to be chosen from as many different disciplines as possible (Herbert, 1977).

## MIXING MEDICINE AND PSYCHOLOGY

The fact that the regulations of the National Commission did not distinguish between medical research and research in the social sciences was the focus of much criticism by psychologists. Even harsher criticism arose as researchers in other fields became aware of the commission's recommendations. The political scientist De Sola Pool (1980) called "the proposed regulation absurd, revolutionary, and unconstitutional [p. 61]." Regulations prescribing general preexperimental briefing of subjects do not yet exist in psychology. Most research psychologists would perceive such regulations as unacceptable and unnecessary restrictions of their research possibilities. The rules that were established by the HEW were understandably designed flexibly enough to leave the decision about the admissibility of deceptive procedures up to the institutional review boards, which examine individual cases (personal communication from M. Kelty as representative of the National Commission, December 1977). Reactions to the verdicts of the boards have so far varied considerably from region to region, which does indeed suggest differences in the way rules are applied; however, differences in the acceptance of the various boards by researchers are undoubtedly influenced by the extent to which the critics are personally affected by committee decisions.

## THE BELMONT REPORT AND THE 1981 HHS POLICY AMENDMENTS

The National Commission was disbanded in the fall of 1978. Its final report, the Belmont Report, included a general statement on the problem of protecting subjects, based on two volumes of testimony from numerous experts (National Commission, 1979, appendixes 1 and 2). Instead of recommending specific procedures, the commission suggested that the secretary of Health, Education, and Welfare accept the entire report as a part of HEW's official policy.

The Belmont Report has three main sections on (*a*) boundaries between practice and research; (*b*) basic ethical principles; and (*c*) applications. The first section is concerned with problems that arise in drawing boundaries between research and application, especially when new methods are being tested by means of practical application. It is not proposed that each individual deviation from standard procedures become the object of evaluation, even though it might be described colloquially as an experiment; however, all procedures that would normally be called "research" are to be evaluated.

The basic ethical principles referred to in the second section are respect for persons, beneficence, and justice. *Respect for persons* refers to the basic conviction that individuals should be treated as autonomous agents and that anyone whose autonomy is limited needs special protection. The two other basic principles are reminiscent of Frankena's theory of obligation. *Beneficence* (in Frankena's theory, *benevolence*) means essentially the attempt to ensure the well-being of the persons who entrust themselves to researchers as subjects, or, more precisely, to avoid harming subjects and to maximize their benefits. *Justice* is understood to mean distributional fairness.

In the third section, on applications, the following requirements are discussed: informed consent, assessment of risks and benefits, and selection of subjects. The basic components of informed consent are sufficient information, the ensuring of comprehension, and voluntariness (absence of undue influence). General suggestions for a systematic assessment of risks and benefits include determining the validity of the presuppositions of the research. Just as the principle of respect for persons is reflected in informed consent and the principle of beneficence is reflected in assessment of risks and benefits, the principle of justice is involved in the selection of subjects for research. In choosing subjects and in determining who will benefit from the research, particular attention is to be paid to principles of fairness—for example, that the same social groups should be involved in both cases.

The Belmont Report, along with the request that it be adopted in its entirety by HEW as a statement of the department's policy, was made available for public comment by the Department of Health, Education, and Welfare (1979). On January 26, 1981, the final ruling on this issue appeared in the *Federal Register* (Department of Health and Human Services, 1981). There the department announced its new policy for the protection of human research subjects, justifying it on the basis of the recommendations of the national commission and of a second commission, the President's Commission for the Study of Ethical Problems in Medicine and Biomedical and Behavioral Research, and on the basis of the public discussion of the Belmont Report.

For this ruling, the department also relied on experience with the work of the institutional review boards. It was now clear that the boards would be unreasonably burdened by the requirement to evaluate all research in the biomedical and social sciences and thus would be prevented from giving thorough attention to the evaluation of the genuinely important cases. Thus, the regulations make an explicit exception for research that involves no more than normal everyday risk for the participants. There is also a category of "expedited review" for cases of insignificant risk and for minor changes in already approved projects. Specifically, the new regulations (Department of Health and Human Services, 1981, p. 8366) accomplish the following:

1. Exempt from coverage most social, economic, and educational research in which the only involvement of human subjects will be in one or more of the following categories:
   a. the use of survey and interview procedures;
   b. the observation of public behavior; or
   c. the study of data, documents, records, and specimens.
2. Require board review and approval of research involving human subjects if it is supported by department funds and does not qualify for exemption from coverage by these regulations.
3. Require only expedited review for certain categories of proposed research involving no more than minimal risk and for minor changes in research already approved by an institutional review board.
4. Provide specific procedures for full and for expedited board review.

5. Designate basic elements of informed consent that are necessary as a prerequisite for humans to participate as subjects in research and additional elements of informed consent that may be added when they are appropriate.
6. Indicate circumstances under which an institutional review board may approve withholding or altering some or all of the elements of informed consent otherwise required to be presented to research subjects.
7. Establish review board membership requirements.
8. Establish regulations that, to the extent possible, are congruent with Food and Drug Administration final regulations to be published on informed consent and institutional review board activities.

The HHS ethics regulations took effect on July 27, 1981. They apply only to research projects sponsored by HHS. For other projects, review by an institutional review board or some other effective procedure for protecting subjects is strongly recommended.

The institutional review boards owe their existence to the national commission and to HEW (HHS); the influence of the department on recent APA guidelines for professional ethics has been less prescriptive, but noticeable. To the extent that the codes of most other professional organizations and scientific societies are oriented around the APA code, the decisions of the department and its various committees are likely to influence international developments as well.

## APA CODES OF ETHICS

The APA, the largest professional association of psychologists in the world, founded a Committee on Scientific and Professional Ethics in 1938. The preparation of written rules began in 1947, on the basis of the problematic cases that had been reported by the members. The committee's proposals were discussed frequently in *American Psychologist* and *Psychological Bulletin* (summarized by APA, 1952). The extensive proposal for "Ethical Standards in Research" was published in 1950 and 1951; this code was accepted in 1953. It related ethical standards to six areas: public responsibility, professional relationships, client relationships, research, writing and publishing, and teaching.

The discussion of ethical standards in research was divided into sections on research planning, execution, and reporting; on responsibility for the interpretation of research results to the public; and on the relationship of psychologists to their subjects. The section on conduct with subjects established the researcher's responsibility for the objects of research, whether animals or humans. In the context of the fundamental idea of weighing costs and benefits, three principles were presented, concerning misinformation and negative consequences, confidentiality of data, and fulfilling responsibilities as promised.

As Vinacke (1954) complained, there has been a tendency to consider the APA ethical standards nonbinding and sometimes even to ignore them. The principle of weighing costs and benefits has been used to justify this practice. In fact, the 1951 APA guidelines suggested that temporary deception, withholding of information, and even exposing subjects to psychological stress can be justified if the research problem is significant and can be examined only in the way proposed (APA, 1951, pp. 441–442). Psychologists, of course, are no more likely to decide that their own research projects are a priori worthless than are scientists in other disciplines. In planning a project, too, researchers generally make methodological decisions that allow them to conclude that their research question cannot be explored just as well or better in any other way. Moreover, who would take on the task of proving the opposite? By this reasoning, justifying the measures taken with subjects is not difficult.

True, the "Ethical Standards" stated that decisions involving the weighing of subject costs against research benefits are often difficult. The discrete formulation "if ever" was used to express doubts about whether potential harm to subjects is ever justified by research benefits (APA, 1951, p. 441). However, this latter formulation seems to have been ahead of the spirit of the times, in view of the subsequent appearance of problem cases, such as the experiments of Bergin (1962), Berkun (1962), Bramel (1962), and Milgram (1963), which were discussed in Chapter 2.

## Modern Experimentation Provokes New Ethical Concerns

On the one hand ahead of their time and on the other hand not binding enough, the "Ethical Standards" of 1951 and 1953 led a shadowy existence until the discovery of the conceptual and methodological problems of experimentation awakened increased concern about ethical problems as well. At first, the "Ethical Standards" were adjusted to reality. In 1959 a new version appeared in which the responsibility for subjects was reduced to taking precautions against harmful aftereffects. Whereas in the 1951 version, psychologists had been discouraged from carrying out experiments whenever harmful aftereffects could be expected, by the time of the 1959 version (APA, 1959, p. 282), tolerance for experiments with possible harmful aftereffects had increased and the question now was what to do about these aftereffects. The first answer was to make informed consent of subjects (or their representatives) and voluntary participation a requirement wherever serious aftereffects were possible. In addition, psychologists were instructed to remove negative consequences of experimental procedures with dispatch. However, both of these requirements were formulated only in regard to aftereffects, as if psychologists must attempt to deal with the problem of negative consequences only when the consequences are expected to continue after the experiment is over. Moreover, even in 1959 psychologists must have understood the dynamics of the relationship between experimenter and subject better than to believe that the mere fact that participation is voluntary relieves the experimenter of responsibility. Thus, the impression that the regulations were developed to justify the actions of researchers is strengthened. As pointed out in the sections of Chapter 2 on safeguards and compensations for subjects, it is not always easy for subjects or their representatives to assess risks. Finally, the obligation to remove harmful aftereffects as soon as permitted by the design of the experiment [APA, 1959, p. 282] expresses not only considerable optimism about the therapeutic competence of experimental psychologists, but also considerable tolerance of research designs that do not "permit" the removal of aftereffects for a long time or perhaps not at all.

In 1951 the principle of responsibility for subjects had been discussed in a general section called "Protecting the Subject's Welfare." In 1959 the only treatment of such matters was in a section called "Harmful Aftereffects." The 1963 revision of "Ethical Standards" returned this principle to a general section, this time called "Research Precautions." By virtue of its place in this general section, the obligation of responsibility seemed again, as in the 1951 version, to refer to more than just aftereffects. The authors, however, did not return to the more stringent formulations of 1951: The wording and sense of the individual paragraphs were basically unchanged from the 1959 version (APA, 1963).

### A Stringent New Code: 1973

The crucial revision of the code was not published until 1973, under the title *Ethical Principles in the Conduct of Research with Human Participants*. It referred explicitly to an HEW ruling that grants for research involving risks for human subjects must be to researchers connected with institutions that can and do agree to be responsible for protecting the subjects (APA, 1973, p. 3).

Before the new code was accepted by the association, new examples of problematic experiments were collected, thousands of questionnaires were sent to APA members, and two preliminary versions were made available to all members and discussed in detail (APA, 1971; Cook, Hicks, Kimble, McGuire, Schoggen, & Smith, 1972). The investment of time in collection, evaluation, and dissemination justified the proud statement that the APA was the first and only association with a set of ethical principles developed by means of empirical procedures and with participation by members (APA, 1973, p. 3).

The fact that the participation was not without conflict was shown by the

# APA Codes of Ethics

heated discussion of the basic question of whether ethical regulations are necessary at all, as well as the discussion of the basic principles underlying the code and of individual points and formulations (see Chapter 2). The compromise that arose in this fashion was basically identical with the second preliminary version. It was an extensive and carefully considered presentation of 10 principles that were explained and discussed by means of sample cases. Its length was quite substantial, considering that these regulations were concerned only with research, not with the profession in general.

## THE PRINCIPLES

The 10 principles contained the following key concepts (for the exact wording see the Appendix):

Preamble: Careful consideration of the decision to undertake research. Basic responsibility of the psychologist to subjects, concern for their dignity and welfare.

1. Experimenters are obligated to comply with the rules and to weigh scientific and humane values. If their evaluation suggests a deviation from the rules, they must seek advice and observe safeguards.
2. Experimenters are responsible for their own actions as well as those of co-workers. The co-workers themselves are also responsible.
3. Participants (i.e., subjects) are to be informed of whatever is relevant to participation. Further explanations must be given if desired by subjects. Failure to do this increases the experimenter's responsibility.
4. Openness and honesty are essential characteristics of the relationship. When exceptions are necessary, experimenters must ensure understanding and restore the quality of the relationship.
5. Subjects must be free to decline or discontinue participation, particularly subjects who are dependent on the experimenter. Limitation of this freedom increases the experimenter's responsibility.
6. Clear and fair agreement must be reached on the responsibilities of both partners. Promises must be kept.
7. Experimenters must protect subjects from physical and mental harm and danger. In case of risk, they must provide information, obtain consent, and use procedures for minimizing distress. Procedures that cause serious and lasting harm may not be used.
8. Experimenters must provide debriefing, removal of misconceptions. Delay or omission increases the experimenter's responsibility to ensure that no damaging consequences occur.
9. Experimenters must detect and remove or correct undesirable consequences for subjects, including long-term aftereffects.
10. Confidentiality of experimental data must be maintained. Experimenters must reveal risks in this regard as a part of informed consent.

According to the preamble, these 10 rules were to be interpreted and applied in the light of the explanations and the discussion of sample cases that accompany the rules. Most of the individual statements in this version were more clearly binding than in earlier versions (e.g., "the investigator is required to...," "... is responsible for...," "... has the obligation to..."). The total number of responsibilities also increased; according to the authors of the document, it increased to the point of exhaustive coverage.

The explanatory comments and sample cases accompanying the rules made it clear that the rules could only be applied appropriately when connections among the individual principles were considered, as well as the particular methodological requirements of the individual case. However, only in extreme cases did the conclusions in the comments lack ambiguity. For example, one planned study was rejected as "unethical" because it was designed to test experimentally the effects of long-term protein deprivation on the intellectual development of children (APA, 1973, pp. 34–35). The rejection was relatively easy here because it was already known (from nonexperimental research!) that harmful effects on the experimental group were highly likely. Thus, the experiment would be of questionable scientific value *and* would cause great and irreparable damage. Even so, the justification given for rejection in this clear-cut case is primarily that "there is no adequate justification for the conduct of research which risks human life or potentiality when the results can only affirm a deleterious reaction [p. 25]." We cannot help asking: And if no research existed on this topic?

The rules seem less clear in their application to examples more typical of experimental research in psychology. One of the critical incidents reported by APA members was an experiment with first-year college students who were given a test. In order to examine the effect of success and failure on subsequent problem solving, the test was said to be a measure of intelligence and the participants were informed either of very high or very low scores. The subjects were debriefed immediately after the experiment. In the discussion of this case, it was argued that the acceptability of this experiment could be determined only if it were known whether it was carried out in a methodologically sound manner, whether the subjects would have been allowed to discontinue participation, whether the experimenter would have been able to deal with any stress reactions that might have occurred, and other considerations. But above all, the significance of the research question was considered the important criterion for whether such stressful deception was justified (APA, 1973, p. 38).

### INTERPRETING THE RULES THROUGH A COST-BENEFIT ANALYSIS

Thus, the basic principle of weighing costs and benefits determines the interpretation of the rules. Imperatives that seem at first glance to have the character of categorical rules are limited through the explanatory notes of the guidelines. More generally, such rules rank second in importance relative to the need to weigh costs and benefits.[3] The result is that unambiguous judgments on the basis of the 1973 code would be possible only in extreme cases. This result could be partly attributable to the manner in which the code was developed, in that some of the standpoints represented in the discussion of the basis for the code and of the specific principles proposed were very extreme. Though presumably only the views of individuals, they received particularly effective publicity. For example, Baumrind (1971, 1972) basically rejected the legitimacy of deception research and argued in favor of a general prohibition of misinformation. This would have turned out to be, in effect, the prohibition of entire, traditional domains of research. Gergen (1973a), on the other hand, considered ethical restrictions as signaling the end of freedom of research. He predicted that creating them would invite caustic criticism from students and laymen, and he warned of the danger of snooping and control by nonprofessionals. He felt that restrictions would be justified only if harmful consequences of particular experimental measures had already been demonstrated and standard procedures for the measurement of side effects and aftereffects existed.

It is quite easy to see how those attempting to reconcile such divergent standpoints can be tempted on the one hand to formulate strict regulations but on the other hand to place sufficient limits on their application to make it impossible to argue that the regulations will prevent important research. Thus, it is fairly easy to establish rules acceptable to all participants, but only at the expense of clarity in the rules.

An alternative possibility would be to forgo acceptance of the regulations by the proponents of extreme standpoints and instead to make the fairness of the contract between subject and experimenter the central theme. In such a situation, the unconditional obligation to reveal information could be dispensed with. The preexperimental agreement would then include both an agreement to dispense with full information and a guarantee of freedom from negative consequences (to the extent that they can be predicted, of course). If, however, there were sufficient risk of negative consequences, it would have to be communicated to the subjects. The extent of risk considered sufficient for this would have to be determined, and the researcher would be responsible for weighing the risk against the benefit for the subjects involved. It seems desirable to create a hierarchy of ethical principles (see the section on asking research questions about the subject role in Chapter 2) in which one of the major principles would be the subject's right to discontinue participation in the experiment. To be sure, this principle was stated very clearly in the 1973 APA rules (No. 5), but it was qualified by the statement that the investigators' responsibil-

---

3. As mentioned earlier, the experiment can best be seen as a social contract between experimenter and subject, and in this context, the principle of weighing costs and benefits is actually indispensable. A resulting complication, however, is the question of the inequality in who bears the costs and who receives the benefits.

ity is increased if they have limited this freedom for the subjects. The implication here is that the investigators do have the authority to prevent subjects from discontinuing participation when they please.

### CONTINUED AMBIGUITY IN IMPLEMENTATION

In recent years psychologists have engaged in the discussion of several critical research projects without having been able to arrive at unanimous decisions about the ethical questions involved. This shows that there is also considerable uncertainty about how to evaluate investigations that were carried out after the American code of ethics took effect. To give just one example: Koocher (1977) attacked Middlemist, Knowles, and Matter, who had undertaken a field study to investigate the inhibition of autonomous bodily functions through increased arousal. They had used a mirror to observe the users of public urinals, either with or without the presence of another person at the urinal. The result confirmed the hypothesis: It is more difficult to urinate when someone is standing nearby. Koocher saw this as an obvious invasion of privacy and did not consider the study valuable enough to justify the offense. He also raised the question of the responsibility of the APA journals to enforce the code of ethics by adhering to their stated rules for accepting publications. (The study was published in the *Journal of Personality and Social Psychology.*) Middlemist *et al.* (1977) justified their work in two ways. First, they had observed "public behavior," which needed no protection. And second, in planning this study, they had indeed considered ethical problems, although they had not reported the results of their considerations in detail. After all, the rules merely require that one consider such matters, not that the considerations be published. Technically this is correct, but at the same time, such an attitude would seem to circumvent the spirit of the law.

One innovation of the 1973 APA code is that the term *participants* was used instead of *subjects*. This change in terms is understandable and perhaps also useful, given that *subjects* connotes *subordinates* or *vassals,* but it creates a confusion that can be resolved only in the context of the report on the investigation. The problem is that *participants* includes not only the subjects but everyone who participates in an experiment, including experimenters and their assistants.[4]

---

4. Actually the term *objects* would correspond better to the subject role in the research process, but that would sound even more offensive than *subjects*. Calling the "objects" "participants in the experiment" or even "partners in the experiment" not only is less precise but even sounds opportunistic, as if the researchers were trying to show how democratic their concepts of the research process were and how highly they valued their subjects as individuals. Such euphemisms do not relieve experimenters of the obligation to treat human beings as such even when they are objects of psychological investigation. A more justifiable compromise might be to take over the term *respondent,* which is common in the Campbell school. To be sure, it is not generally familiar and is also less clear to laymen, but at least it would have the advantage of applying to a wide range of research in psychology as well as in related disciplines, such as anthropology.

## Later Modifications

These criticisms of the APA ethical standards should not mislead the reader into thinking that the regulations were unwelcome. On the contrary, the code must be considered sound in its fundamental concepts and timely as a substantial innovation for psychological research. The same is true of the later revisions.

The 1977 version (APA, 1977) added two regulations to the 1973 version's 10 principles for the conduct of research. One was concerned with research with animals; the second required that pharmacological investigations take place only in clinics or comparable settings (see Appendix). The crucial revisions, however, were two minor changes in the language or content of the 10 already established principles.

The first of these changes consisted of omitting the last sentence of Principle 5 (1973 version, see Appendix; 9e in 1977 version, also in Appendix). This sentence had implicitly allowed limitations on the subjects' freedom to discontinue their participation in the research at any time: "The decision to limit this freedom increases the investigator's responsibility to protect the participant's dignity and welfare." In the new version, several examples made it clear that when the subject is dependent on the researcher in certain ways, the researcher is obligated to observe this principle with particular care. The examples included subjects who were students, clients, or employees of the experimenter. Let us consider the interpretation of Principle 1 (1973 version, see Appendix; 9a in 1977 version, also in Appendix). Principle 1 can be interpreted as prohibiting deviations from individual rules when the rules are unambiguous and lack clauses providing for exceptions. If this interpretation is correct, the omission of the last sentence of Principle 5 should have very clear consequences. For example, Milgram's obedience experiments (from 1963 on) could not be carried out in the same form today without being clear violations of the guidelines (Principle 5/9e).

The second crucial revision was so inconspicuous linguistically that it could almost be overlooked. The last sentence in Principle 7 in the 1973 version read: "A research procedure may not be used if it is likely to cause serious and lasting harm to participants." In the 1977 version, as Principle 9g, it read: "A research procedure *must* not be used if it is likely to cause serious *or* lasting harm to *a* participant [italics added]." Assuming a correct understanding of the language, these changes have three implications. First, the prohibition involved in "must not" is somewhat more forceful in tone than the prohibition in "may not." Second, the rule is violated if a procedure causes serious *or* lasting harm; either one alone is sufficient to constitute a problem. And third, a research procedure is considered inadmissible if it can be expected to endanger even a single subject (the singular "a participant" instead of the plural "participants" in the earlier version). If interpreted strictly, this rule could indeed be an impediment to some research projects. For example, an experiment would violate the rule if someone were seriously frightened during the experiment, even if no negative postexperimental consequences could be determined. On the other hand, if slight but lasting harm can be expected for even a single subject, the experiment likewise constitutes a violation of the principle.[5]

In the case of harm to subjects as well as in the case of limiting subjects' freedom, our deductions are correct only if Principle 1 (9a) is not used for a general exculpation. Still other problems are connected with applying the last sentence in Principle 7 (9g). It is difficult to predict the nature of the harm that might occur and even to define the terms in the rule. What is meant by "likely"? How is "harm" to be defined? When is harm "serious"? When can we speak of "lasting"? So much room for interpretation remains that unambiguous evaluation is difficult or impossible in many cases. To be sure, the APA code is no different on this point from most other fundamental regulations in various spheres of life. It is precisely those spheres of action such as scientific work that are complex and subject to change, in which more concrete instructions for behavior would probably serve no useful purpose. The basic thoughts and principles are doubtless more crucial than are detailed guides for action.

After a further revision in 1979, the 1981 version of "Ethical Principles of Psychologists" was adopted (APA, 1981). Like the earlier codes, it is merely a reworked form of the crucial 1973 revision. The changes in Principle 9, "Research with Human Participants," not only are in keeping with the spirit of the times, but also seem to reflect experience with the application of the earlier codes, which was in part quite rigorous.

The timely call for consideration of "alternative directions in which research energies and resources might be invested [preamble to Principle 9, p. 637]" is new. Another innovation is the prudent suggestion that "subjects at risk" be distinguished from "subjects at minimal risk" (Principle 9b, pp. 637–638). This addition made it possible to exempt the researcher from the obligation to establish an explicit agreement with subjects in cases of minimal risk (Principle 9d, p. 638). A further innovation consists of the admonition to provide special safeguarding procedures for children or other persons with limited ability to understand the situation (Principle 9d, p. 638). In addition to the possibility of exculpation through "great potential benefit" (when subjects are fully informed and give voluntary consent), dangerous research procedures can now also be considered appropriate if their use would preserve the subjects from even greater harm. A final addition is the suggestion that the participant be informed of procedures for contacting the experimenter in the case of any stresses that might appear after the experiment (these last two additions from Principle 9g, p. 638).

---

5. This interpretation of Principle 7 (9g) assumes that Principle 1's recognition of the possibility of deviation from rules (1973 version; 9a in the 1977 version) cannot be used for a general exculpation. In other words, it assumes that deviations from clearly stated rules that lack exceptions are prohibited.

In addition, some linguistic changes were made. In part, these changes increase the precision of the guidelines (e.g., Principle 9e on the use of concealment or deception); in part, their effect is to moderate the tone of the guidelines and reduce some of the harshness of the earlier versions. Instead of a "justification" the experimenter has the responsibility of providing an "explanation" to the subjects (Principle 9e), and in Principle 9f the experimenter is said to have a "position of authority or influence over the participant" rather than a "position of power" (both p. 638). Principle 9l of the 1977 version, on investigations involving drugs, was deleted. An entire principle (Principle 10) is now dedicated to the care and use of animals in research (previously Principle 9k).

### INTERPRETATION CONTINUES TO BE THE CENTRAL CHALLENGE

It is hoped that some future version of the APA *Casebook on Ethical Standards of Psychologists* will give more productive examples for the interpretation of the ethical principles—that is, for their application to sample cases—than the current version (APA, 1974), which is based on the "Ethical Standards" of 1963. In the 1974 version, the only example for the section on research ethics is the case of a psychologist who sent sample tests to colleagues with the request that they be completed and returned anonymously; the ethical problem identified was that he did not want to tell the respondents what was supposed to be measured by the test until they had taken it. The APA committee assembled an extensive collection of critical incidents in the process of preparing the 1973 code of ethics. This should make it possible to choose more relevant examples for a new casebook. After all, the effect of the code must depend to a large extent on the models furnished by the concrete examples chosen for abstract rules.

The APA Board of Scientific and Ethical Responsibility in Psychology has decided to investigate systematically the effects of increasing the stringency of the ethical guidelines and the effects of the measures undertaken to ensure that the guidelines are followed. However, S. W. Cook, source of this information (personal communication, October 1977), warns that it will be difficult to determine the effects of the APA guidelines. Activity with a similar aim on the part of HHS and other institutions makes it hard to ascribe causal connections. If changes have arisen, we must be content in some cases to attribute them to a combination of various procedures.

## OTHER CODES OF ETHICS: A COMPARATIVE SURVEY

The APA code of ethics has been discussed here at relatively great length. It is the most extensive and most thoroughly elaborated codification of ethical principles in psychology that has ever existed. In addition, it is relevant for the greater part of contemporary empirical psychological research. Finally, these regulations have served as models for codification in other countries and will presumably continue to do so to an even greater extent in the future. Discussions of ethical problems in psychological research have appeared in professional journals and taken place at professional conventions primarily in the United States. To a certain extent, they have occurred also in Great Britain and in some other English-speaking countries or countries in which research is published in English. Discussion of these questions has recently begun in other European countries and will probably lead to agreement on new responsibilities for researchers.

In the summer of 1977, the author wrote to every professional organization for psychology that could be identified throughout the world and asked for information on the status of the development of ethical codes in their countries. The existence of valid ethical codes was reported and documented for the following countries: the Federal Republic of Germany, Berufsverband Deutscher Psychologen (German Association of Professional Psychologists), 1978; Great Britain, British Psychological Society, 1977; Canada, Canadian Psychological Association (code identical with that of the APA), 1973; the Netherlands, Nederlands Instituut van Psychologen (Netherlands Association of Psychologists), 1976; Poland, Polskie Towarzystwo Psychologiczne (Polish Psychological Association), 1971; Austria, Berufsverband Österreichischer Psychologen (Austrian Association of Professional Psychologists), 1976: Sweden, Swedish Council for Social Science Research, 1975, and Johansson, 1976; Switzerland, Schweizerische Gesellschaft für Psychologie (Swiss Psychological Association), 1974, adopted by the Schweizerische Gesellschaft für Psychologie und ihre Anwendungen (Swiss Professional Association for Applied Psychology), 1976; and the United States, American Psychological Association, 1973, 1977, and 1981. In 1981 an additional code was received from France, Société Française de Psychologie (French Psychological Society), 1960. Most of the codes were labeled as preliminary, still under development, or about to be revised.[6]

---

6. The Berufsverband Deutscher Psychologen represents the interests of professional psychologists in Germany; the Deutsche Gesellschaft für Psychologie (German Psychological Association) represents the psychologists who are active in teaching and research. In 1980 the Deutsche Gesellschaft für Psychologie, which previously did not have its own ethical code, chose the 1979 version of the APA rules to serve as its preliminary ethical guidelines. A commission composed of representatives of both German psychological associations was formed in the same year to work out a joint formulation of new ethical principles.

The Schweizerische Gesellschaft für Psychologie represents the Swiss psychologists who are active in teaching and research; the Schweizerische Gesellschaft für Psychologie und ihre Anwendungen, which represents the interests of Swiss professional psychologists, adopted the ethical code of the Schweizerische Gesellschaft für Psychologie in 1976.

The Swedish code, adopted for a trial period in 1975, was revised in 1981. The revised version was not yet available in translation when this volume went to press, but will be available beginning in 1982 from the Swedish Council for Research in the Humanities and Social Sciences.

## Other Codes of Ethics: A Comparative Survey 187

It seems inappropriate to discuss all existing codes in detail here, especially since such a survey would probably be outdated soon. Instead, the following pages will provide a rough overview in the form of a table summarizing briefly which ethical principles are currently considered by the various professional organizations to be the most important and worthy of attention for psychological research. This presentation is severely limited by the following considerations:

1. The codes are structured in such a way that they are hard to compare. Some make a clear distinction between research problems and other problem areas; some do this to a lesser extent or not at all. For example, in the code of the Netherlands, the relationship of the psychologist to subjects is treated in combination with the relationship to clients.

2. Some codes imply, assume, or state in a general preamble principles that are articulated separately in other codes. The psychologist's obligation to work with the best and safest methods available is one such principle.

3. The extent to which the principles are formulated in a general manner varies considerably. In some codes many principles are listed in detail; in others the statements of responsibilities are kept very general and their implications are sometimes unclear. An extreme example: In the preliminary (1975) version of the Swedish code reproduced in the Appendix of this book, five rules are stated and supplemented by the comment that they should be interpreted in the context of the APA principles as well as in the context of the Swedish Social Science Research Council's *Etiska problem i psykologisk–pedagogisk forskning* (Ethical Problems in the Conduct of Psychological and Educational Research).

4. The presentation in the table does not do justice to the differences in the basic positions taken by the codes. For example, the British version is distinguished by a stronger emphasis on considering risks when evaluating the acceptability of research procedures. In most other codes, the expectation of benefit from the research is emphasized more heavily.

5. Not only basic positions, but also individual principles are limited in ways not reflected in the table, either through supplementary notes directly following the principles or by general statements at the beginning of the code.

For these reasons, the summary in Table 2 must be presented with reservations. It can serve only as a general orientation and cannot substitute for reading the codes reproduced in the Appendix.

**TABLE 2**
**Ethical Principles in Europe and America**[a]

| Principle | United States, 1973 & Canada (U.S., 1977) | United States, 1981 | Federal Republic of Germany, 1978 | Great Britain, 1977 | Netherlands, 1976 | Austria, 1976 | Poland, 1971 | Sweden, 1975 | Switzerland, 1974 | France, 1960 |
|---|---|---|---|---|---|---|---|---|---|---|
| Commitment to regulations and committees | | X | | | | | | | | |
| Research for benefit of humanity | X | X | | X | X | X | | | X | X |
| Consider alternative research directions | | X | | | | | | | | X |
| Responsibility to maintain competence | X | X | X | X | X | X | | | | |
| Provide safety measures | X | X | X | X | X | X | X | | X | |
| Weigh scientific and humane values | X | X | X | X | X | X | | | | |
| Obtain advice in difficult cases | X | X | X | X | X | X | | X | | |
| Experimenter bears basic responsibility | X | X | X | X | X | X | X | X | X | |
| Responsibility for co-workers | X | X | | | X | | | | | |
| Omissions increase responsibility | X | X | | X | | | X | | | |
| Minimal-risk criteria | X | X | | X | | | | | | X |
| Give information relevant to participation | | X | | | | | | | | |
| Open, fair agreement | X | X | X | X | X | X | X | X | | |
| Reduced obligations if risk minimal | X | X | | X | X | | | | | |
| Voluntary participation (with exceptions) | X | X | | X | | | | | | |

| | | | | | | | |
|---|---|---|---|---|---|---|---|
| Voluntary participation (no exceptions) | (X) | | | | X | | |
| Freedom to discontinue (with exceptions) | X | | | | | | |
| Freedom to discontinue (no exceptions) | (X) | | | X | X | | |
| Special responsibility to dependents and subordinates | X | | | X | X | | |
| Keep promises | X | | | | | | |
| Avoid physical harm | X | X | | X | X | X | X |
| Avoid psychological harm | X | X | | X | X | X | X |
| Avoid insult to dignity/self-respect | X | X | | X | X | X | |
| No permanent harm (with exceptions) | X | X | | X | | | X |
| No permanent harm (no exceptions) | (X) | | | | | | |
| Safeguards for children or handicapped | | X | | | | | |
| Discontinue if unexpectedly stressful | | | X | | | | |
| Tolerance for stress as criterion | | | | | | X | |
| Conduct drug experiments only in clinics | X | | | | | | |
| Obtain consent in case of risk | X | | X | X | X | X | |
| Debriefing (unless harmful) | X | X | | X | X | X | |
| Ensure understanding | X | | | X | X | | |
| Responsibility for quasi-therapeutic intervention | X | | | X | X | | |
| Protect privacy | X | | X | X | X | | X |
| Confidentiality of data | X | X | X | X | X | X | X |

*(continued)*

**TABLE 2 (Continued)**

| Principle | United States, 1973 & Canada (U.S., 1977) | United States, 1981 | Federal Republic of Germany, 1978 | Great Britain, 1977 | Netherlands, 1976 | Austria, 1976 | Poland, 1971 | Sweden, 1975 | Switzerland, 1974 | France, 1960 |
|---|---|---|---|---|---|---|---|---|---|---|
| Security of stored data | X | X | | | | | | X | | X |
| Endangered confidentiality increases obligation to inform | X | X | | | | | | | X | |
| Inform of concealed observation | | | X | | X | X | | | | X |
| Subject can have data destroyed | | | X | | | X | | | | |
| Interpretable as psychologist–client relationship | | | X | X | X | X | | | | X |
| Consult or refer to professionals in case of difficulties | | | X | | | | | | | |
| Inform subjects about experimenter and institute | | | | X | | | | | | |
| Rules for special research methods | | | | X | | | | | | |
| Address subjects' personal needs | | | | | X | | | | | |
| Subjects' right to complain | | | | X | X | X | | | | X |
| Facilitate later contact | | X | | | | | | | | |
| Representatives for persons not capable of making contracts | | | X | X | | | | X | | |
| Caution when informing parents of results | | | | X | | | | | | |

| | | | | | | | | |
|---|---|---|---|---|---|---|---|---|
| Consider idiosyncratic effects on individuals | (X) | | | X | | | | |
| Communicate goals to subjects | X | | | | X | | | |
| Inform of possible use of data | | | | X | X | | X | |
| Inform of results | | | | X | X | X | | |
| Consider social consequences of research | X | | | | X | | | |
| Follow-up in field research | | | | | | | | X |
| Obligation to publish results | | | | X | | | | X |
| Prevent misinterpretation of results | X | X | | X | X | X | | X |
| Honesty in research and publication | X | X | | | | | X | |
| Economical use of resources | | | X | | | | | |
| Ethical obligations to animals | X | X | | | | X | X | |
| Urge colleagues to obey rules | X | X | | X | | | X | |
| Development of regulations | | X | | | | | X | |

[a] The Appendix contains only the sections of the codes that are relevant to research, insofar as this distinction can be made. It includes the preambles or general sections if they make explicit statements about research. Thus in some exceptional cases, this table contains more information than the Appendix. This occurs when individual principles, although explicitly related to research, are included in sections that are not relevant to research and are too long to reproduce in the Appendix, such as sections on therapy. The order in which the principles appear is approximately that of the APA codes of 1973 and 1977. Only explicitly formulated principles or elements of such principles are taken into account; they need not have appeared as individual regulations in the code, however. These principles are marked with an X in the columns of the countries in whose codes they are included. The X in parentheses represents the APA code of 1977.

# Appendix

United States (1973) and Canada, American Psychological Association (and
  Canadian Psychological Association)
  Ethical Principles in the Conduct of Research with Human Participants
United States (1977), American Psychological Association
  Ethical Standards of Psychologists
United States (1981), American Psychological Association
  Ethical Principles of Psychologists
Federal Republic of Germany, Berufsverband Deutscher Psychologen
  Berufsethische Verpflichtungen für Psychologen
    (Ethical Obligations of Professional Psychologists)*
Great Britain, British Psychological Society
  Ethical Principles for Research with Human Subjects
Netherlands, Nederlands Instituut van Psychologen
  Professional Code for Psychologists*
Austria, Berufsverband Österreichischer Psychologen
  Berufsverpflichtungen für Psychologen
    (Obligations of Professional Psychologists)*
Poland, Polskie Towarzystwo Psychologiczne
  Psychologist's Ethical Code*
Sweden, Swedish Council for Social Science Research
  Ethical Principles in the Conduct of Psychological and Educational Research
    with Human Participants*
Switzerland, Schweizerische Gesellschaft für Psychologie; Schweizerische
  Gesellschaft für Psychologie und ihre Anwendungen
  Code déontologique
    (Deontological Code)*
France, Société Française de Psychologie
  Projet de code de déontologie à l'usage des psychologues
    (Proposed Deontological Code for Psychologists)*
(Copyrights held by the respective national associations; for sources, see the list of references)

*The translators of these codes are as follows: Margaret Woodruff for the German, Austrian, Swiss, and French codes; H. Jacobs for the Dutch code; B. Rosemann for the Polish code; U. Enderlein for the Swedish code.

# USA (1973) AND CANADA: ETHICAL PRINCIPLES IN THE CONDUCT OF RESEARCH WITH HUMAN PARTICIPANTS[1]

## American Psychological Association

The decision to undertake research should rest upon a considered judgment by the individual psychologist about how best to contribute to psychological science and to human welfare. The responsible psychologist weighs alternative directions in which personal energies and resources might be invested. Having made the decision to conduct research, psychologists must carry out their investigations with respect for the people who participate and with concern for their dignity and welfare. The Principles that follow make explicit the investigator's ethical responsibilities toward participants over the course of research, from the initial decision to pursue a study to the steps necessary to protect the confidentiality of research data. These Principles should be interpreted in terms of the contexts provided in the complete document offered as a supplement to these Principles.

1. In planning a study the investigator has the personal responsibility to make a careful evaluation of its ethical acceptability, taking into account these Principles for research with human beings. To the extent that this appraisal, weighing scientific and humane values, suggests a deviation from any Principle, the investigator incurs an increasingly serious obligation to seek ethical advice and to observe more stringent safeguards to protect the rights of the human research participant.

2. Responsibility for the establishment and maintenance of acceptable ethical practice in research always remains with the individual investigator. The investigator is also responsible for the ethical treatment of research participants by collaborators, assistants, students and employees, all of whom, however, incur parallel obligations.

3. Ethical practice requires the investigator to inform the participant of all features of the research that reasonably might be expected to influence willingness to participate and to explain all other aspects of the research about which the participant inquires. Failure to make full disclosure increases the investigator's responsibility to maintain confidentiality, and to protect the welfare and dignity of the research participant.

4. Openness and honesty are characteristics of the relationship between investigator and research participant. When the methodological requirements of a study necessitate concealment or deception, the investigator is required to ensure the participant's understanding of the reasons for this action and to restore the quality of the relationship with the investigator.

---

[1] Copyright 1973 by the American Psychological Association. Reprinted by permission of the publisher and author.

5. Ethical research practice requires the investigator to respect the individual's freedom to decline to participate in research or to discontinue participation at any time. The obligation to protect this freedom requires special vigilance when the investigator is in a position of power over the participant. The decision to limit this freedom increases the investigator's responsibility to protect the participant's dignity and welfare.

6. Ethically acceptable research begins with the establishment of a clear and fair agreement between the investigator and the research participant that clarifies the responsibilities of each. The investigator has the obligation to honor all promises and commitments included in that agreement.

7. The ethical investigator protects participants from physical and mental discomfort, harm and danger. If the risk of such consequences exists, the investigator is required to inform the participant of that fact, to secure consent before proceeding, and to take all possible measure to minimize distress. A research procedure may not be used if it is likely to cause serious and lasting harm to participants.

8. After the data are collected, ethical practice requires the investigator to provide the participants with a full clarification of the nature of the study and to remove any misconceptions that may have arisen. Where scientific or humane values justify delaying or withholding information, the investigator acquires a special responsibility to assure that there are no damaging consequences for the participant.

9. Where research procedures may result in undesirable consequences for the participant, the investigator has the responsibility to detect and remove or correct these consequences, including, where relevant, long-term aftereffects.

10. Information obtained about the research participants during the course of an investigation is confidential. When the possibility exists that others may obtain access to such information, ethical research practice requires that this possibility, together with the plans for protecting confidentiality, be explained to the participants as a part of the procedure for obtaining informed consent.

## USA (1977):
## ETHICAL STANDARDS OF PSYCHOLOGISTS
## (1977 REVISION)[1]
## (SEE ESPECIALLY PRINCIPLE 9)

American Psychological Association

### Preamble

*Psychologists respect the dignity and worth of the individual and honor the preservation and protection of fundamental human rights. They are committed to increasing*

---
[1] Copyright 1977 by the American Psychological Association. Reprinted by permission of the publisher and author.

knowledge of human behavior and of people's understanding of themselves and others and to the utilization of such knowledge for the promotion of human welfare. While pursuing these endeavors, they make every effort to protect the welfare of those who seek their services or of any human being or animal that may be the object of study. They use their skills only for purposes consistent with these values and do not knowingly permit their misuse by others. While demanding for themselves freedom of inquiry and communication, psychologists accept the responsibility this freedom requires: competence, objectivity in the application of skills and concern for the best interests of clients, colleagues, and society in general. In the pursuit of these ideals, psychologists subscribe to principles in the following areas: 1. Responsibility, 2. Competence, 3. Moral and Legal Standards, 4. Public Statements, 5. Confidentiality, 6. Welfare of the Consumer, 7. Professional Relationships, 8. Utilization of Assessment Techniques, and 9. Pursuit of Research Activities.

## Principle 1. Responsibility

In their commitment to the understanding of human behavior, psychologists value objectivity and integrity, and in providing services they maintain the highest standards of their profession. They accept responsibility for the consequences of their work and make every effort to insure that their services are used appropriately.

*a.* As scientists, psychologists accept the ultimate responsibility for selecting appropriate areas and methods most relevant to these areas. They plan their research in ways to minimize the possibility that their findings will be misleading. They provide thorough discussion of the limitations of their data and alternative hypotheses, especially where their work touches on social policy or might be construed to be detriment of persons in specific age, sex, ethnic, socioeconomic or other social groups. In publishing reports of their work, they never suppress disconfirming data. Psychologists take credit only for the work they have actually done.

Psychologists clarify in advance with all appropriate persons or agencies the expectations for sharing and utilizing research data. They avoid dual relationships which may limit objectivity, whether political or monetary, so that interference with data, human participants, and milieu is kept to a minimum.

*b.* As employees of an institution or agency, psychologists have the responsibility of remaining alert to and attempting to moderate institutional pressures that may distort reports of psychological findings or impede their proper use.

*c.* As members of governmental or other organizational bodies, psychologists remain accountable as individuals to the highest standards of their profession.

*d.* As teachers, psychologists recognize their primary obligation to help others acquire knowledge and skill. They maintain high standards of scholarship and objectivity by presenting psychological information fully and accurately.

*e.* As practitioners, psychologists know that they bear a heavy social responsibility because their recommendations and professional actions may alter the lives of others. They are alert to personal, social, organizational, financial, or political situations or pressures that might lead to misuse of their influence.

*f.* Psychologists provide adequate and timely evaluations to employees, trainees, students, and others whose work they supervise.

## Principle 2. Competence

*The maintenance of high standards of professional competence is a responsibility shared by all psychologists in the interest of the public and the profession as a whole. Psychologists recognize the boundaries of their competence and the limitations of their techniques and only provide services, use techniques, or offer opinions as professionals that meet recognized standards. Psychologists maintain knowledge of current scientific and professional information related to the services they render.*

*a.* Psychologists accurately represent their competence, education, training and experience. Psychologists claim as evidence of professional qualifications only those degrees obtained from institutions acceptable under the Bylaws and Rules of Council of the American Psychological Association.

*b.* As teachers, psychologists perform their duties on the basis of careful preparation so that their instruction is accurate, current and scholarly.

*c.* Psychologists recognize the need for continuing education and are open to new procedures and changes in expectations and values over time. They recognize differences among people, such as those that may be associated with age, sex, socioeconomic, and ethnic backgrounds. Where relevant, they obtain training, experience, or counsel to assure competent service or research relating to such persons.

*d.* Psychologists with the responsibility for decisions involving individuals or policies based on test results have an understanding of psychological or educational measurement, validation problems and other test research.

*e.* Psychologists recognize that their effectiveness depends in part upon their ability to maintain effective interpersonal relations, and that aberrations on their part may interfere with their abilities. They refrain from undertaking any activity in which their personal problems are likely to lead to inadequate professional services or harm to a client; or, if engaged in such activity when they become aware of their personal problems, they seek competent professional assistance to determine whether they should suspend, terminate or limit the scope of their professional and/or scientific activities.

## Principle 3. Moral and Legal Standards

*Psychologists' moral, ethical and legal standards of behavior are a personal matter to the same degree as they are for any other citizen, except as these may compromise the fulfillment of their professional responsibilities, or reduce the trust in psychology* or psychologists held by the general public. Regarding their own behavior, psychologists should be aware of the prevailing community standards and of the possible impact upon the quality of professional services provided by their conformity to or deviation from these standards. Psychologists are also aware of the possible impact of their public behavior upon the ability of colleagues to perform their professional duties.

*a.* Psychologists as teachers are aware of the diverse backgrounds of students and, when dealing with topics that may give offense, treat the material objectively and present it in a manner for which the student is prepared.

*b.* As employees, psychologists refuse to participate in practices inconsistent with legal, moral and ethical standards regarding the treatment of employees or of the public. For example, psychologists will not condone practices that are inhumane or that result in illegal or otherwise unjustifiable discrimination on the basis of race, age, sex, religion, or national origin in hiring, promotion, or training.

*c.* In providing psychological services, psychologists avoid any action that will violate or diminish the legal and civil rights of clients or of others who may be affected by their actions.

As practitioners, psychologists remain abreast of relevant federal, state, local, and agency regulations and Association standards of practice concerning the conduct of their practice. They are concerned with developing such legal and quasilegal regulations as best serve the public interest and in changing such existing regulations as are not beneficial to the interests of the public and the profession.

*d.* As researchers, psychologists remain abreast of relevant federal and state regulations concerning the conduct of research with human participants or animals.

## Principle 4. Public Statements

Public statements, announcements of services, and promotional activities of psychologists serve the purpose of providing sufficient information to aid the consumer public in making informed judgments and choices. Psychologists represent accurately and objectively their professional qualifications, affiliations, and functions, as well as those of the institutions or organizations with which they or the statements may be associated. In public statements providing psychological information or professional opinions or providing information about the availability of psychological products and services, psychologists take full account of the limits and uncertainties of present psychological knowledge and techniques.

*a.* When announcing professional services, psychologists limit the information to: name, highest relevant academic degree conferred, date and type of certification or licensure, diplomate status, address, telephone number, office hours, and a brief listing of the type of psychological services offered. Such statements are descriptive of services provided but not evaluative as to their quality or uniqueness. They do not contain testimonials by quotation or by implication. They do not claim uniqueness of skills or methods unless determined by acceptable and public scientific evidence.

*b.* In announcing the availability of psychological services or products, psychologists do not display any affiliations with an organization in a manner that falsely implies the sponsorship or certification of that organization. In particular and for example, psychologists do not offer APA membership or fellowship as evidence of qualification. They do not name their employer or professional associations unless the services are in fact to be provided by or under the responsible, direct supervision and continuing control of such organizations or agencies.

*c.* Announcements of "personal growth groups" give a clear statement of purpose and the nature of the experiences to be provided. The education, training and experience of the psychologists are appropriately specified.

*d.* Psychologists associated with the development or promotion of psychological devices, books, or other products offered for commercial sale make every effort to insure that announcements and advertisements are presented in a professional, scientifically acceptable, and factually informative manner.

*e.* Psychologists do not participate for personal gain in commercial announcements recommending to the general public the purchase or use of any proprietary or single-source product or service.

*f.* Psychologists who interpret the science of psychology or the services of psychologists to the general public accept the obligation to present the material fairly and accurately, avoiding misrepresentation through sensationalism, exaggeration or superficiality. Psychologists are guided by the primary obligation to aid the public in forming their own informed judgments, opinions and choices.

*g.* As teachers, psychologists insure that statements in catalogs and course outlines are accurate and sufficient, particularly in terms of subject matter to be covered, bases for evaluating progress, and nature of course experiences. Announcements or brochures describing workshops, seminars, or other educational programs accurately represent intended audience and eligibility requirements, educational objectives, and nature of the material to be covered, as well as the education, training and experience of the psychologists presenting the programs, and any fees involved. Public announcements soliciting subjects for research, and in which clinical services or other professional services are offered as an inducement, make clear the nature of the services as well as the costs and other obligations to be accepted by the human participants of the research.

*h.* Psychologists accept the obligation to correct others who may represent the psychologist's professional qualifications or associations with products or services in a manner incompatible with these guidelines.

*i.* Psychological services for the purpose of diagnosis, treatment or personal advice are provided only in the context of a professional relationship, and are not given by means of public lectures or demonstrations, newspaper or magazine articles, radio or television programs, mail, or similar media.

## Principle 5. Confidentiality

*Safeguarding information about an individual that has been obtained by the psychologist in the course of his teaching, practice, or investigation is a primary obligation of the psychologist. Such information is not communicated to others unless certain important conditions are not met.*

*a.* Information received in confidence is revealed only after most careful deliberation and when there is clear and imminent danger to an individual or to society, and then only to appropriate professional workers or public authorities.

*b.* Information obtained in clinical or consulting relationships, or evaluative data concerning children, students, employees, and others are discussed only for professional purposes and only with persons clearly concerned with the case. Written and oral reports should present only data germane to the purposes of the evaluation and every effort should be made to avoid undue invasion of privacy.

*c.* Clinical and other materials are used in classroom teaching and writing only when the identity of the persons involved is adequately disguised.

*d.* The confidentiality of professional communications about individuals is maintained. Only when the originator and other persons involved give their express permission is a confidential professional communication shown to the individual concerned. The psychologist is responsible for informing the client of the limits of the confidentiality.

*e.* Only after explicit permission has been granted is the identity of research subjects published. When data have been published without permission for identification, the psychologist assumes responsibility for adequately disguising their sources.

*f.* The psychologist makes provisions for the maintenance of confidentiality in the prevention and ultimate disposition of confidential records.

## Principle 6. Welfare of the Consumer

*Psychologists respect the integrity and protect the welfare of the people and groups with whom they work. When there is a conflict of interest between the client and the psychologist's employing institution, psychologists clarify the nature and direction of* their loyalties and responsibilities and keep all parties informed of their commitments. Psychologists fully inform consumers as to the purpose and nature of an evaluative, treatment, educational or training procedure, and they freely acknowledge that clients, students, or participants in research have freedom of choice with regard to participation.

*a.* Psychologists are continually cognizant of their own needs and of their inherently powerful position *vis a vis* clients, in order to avoid exploiting their trust and dependency. Psychologists make every effort to avoid dual relationships with clients and/or relationships which might impair their professional judgment or increase the risk of client exploitation. Examples of such dual relationships include treating employees, supervisees, close friends or relatives. Sexual intimacies with clients are unethical.

*b.* Where demands of an organization on psychologists go beyond reasonable conditions of employment, psychologists recognize possible conflicts of interest that may arise. When such conflicts occur, psychologists clarify the nature of the conflict and inform all parties of the nature and direction of the loyalties and responsibilities involved.

*c.* When acting as a supervisor, trainer, researcher, or employer, psychologists accord informed choice, confidentiality, due process, and protection from physical and mental harm to their subordinates in such relationships.

*d.* Financial arrangements in professional practice are in accord with professional standards that safeguard the best interests of the client and that are clearly understood by the client in advance of billing. Psychologists are responsible for assisting clients in finding needed services in those instances where payment of the usual fee would be a hardship. No commission, rebate, or other form of remuneration may be given or received for referral of clients for professional services, whether by an individual or by an agency. Psychologists willingly contribute a portion of their services to work for which they receive little or no financial return.

*e.* The psychologist attempts to terminate a clinical or consulting relationship when it is reasonably clear that the consumer is not benefiting from it. Psychologists who find that their services are being used by employers in a way that is not beneficial to the participants or to employees who may be affected, or to significant others, have the responsibility to make their observations known to the responsible persons and to propose modification or termination of the engagement.

### Principle 7. Professional Relationships

*Psychologists act with due regard for the needs, special competencies and obligations of their colleagues in psychology and other professions. Psychologists respect the prerogatives and obligations of the institutions or organizations with which they are associated.*

   *a.* Psychologists understand the areas of competence of related professions, and make full use of all the professional, technical, and administrative resources that best serve the interests of consumers. The absence of formal relationships with other professional workers does not relieve psychologists from the responsibility of securing for their clients the best possible professional service nor does it relieve them from the exercise of foresight, diligence, and tact in obtaining the complementary or alternative assistance needed by clients.

   *b.* Psychologists know and take into account the traditions and practices of other professional groups with which they work and cooperate fully with members of such groups. If a consumer is receiving services from another professional, psychologists do not offer their services directly to the consumer without first informing the professional person already involved so that the risk of confusion and conflict for the consumer can be avoided.

   *c.* Psychologists who employ or supervise other professionals or professionals in training accept the obligation to facilitate their further professional development by providing suitable working conditions, consultation, and experience opportunities.

   *d.* As employees of organizations providing psychological services, or as independent psychologists serving clients in an organizational context, psychologists seek to support the integrity, reputation and proprietary rights of the host organization. When it is judged necessary in a client's interest to question the organization's programs or policies, psychologists attempt to effect change by constructive action within the organization before disclosing confidential information acquired in their professional roles.

   *e.* In the pursuit of research, psychologists give sponsoring agencies, host institutions, and publication channels the same respect and opportunity for giving informed consent that they accord to individual research participants. They are aware of their obligation to future research workers and insure that host institutions are given adequate information about the research and proper acknowledgement of their contributions.

   *f.* Publication credit is assigned to all those who have contributed to a publication in proportion to their contribution. Major contributions of a professional character made by several persons to a common project are recognized by joint authorship, with the experimenter or author who made the principal contribution identified and listed first. Minor contributions of a professional character, extensive clerical or similar nonprofessional assistance, and other minor contributions are acknowledged in footnotes or in an introductory statement. Acknowledgement through specific citations is made for unpublished as well as published material that has directly influenced the research or writing. A psychologist who compiles and edits material of others for publication publishes the material in the name of the originating group, if any, and with his/her own name appearing as chairperson or editor. All contributors are to be acknowledged and named.

*g.* When a psychologist violates ethical standards, psychologists who know first-hand of such activities should, if possible, attempt to rectify the situation. Failing an informal solution, psychologists bring such unethical activities to the attention of the appropriate local, state, and/or national committee on professional ethics, standards, and practices.

*h.* Members of the Association cooperate with duly constituted committees of the Association, in particular and for example, the Committee on Scientific and Professional Ethics and Conduct, and the Committee on Professional Standards Review, by responding to inquiries promptly and completely. Members taking longer than 30 days to respond to such inquiries shall have the burden of demonstrating that they acted with "reasonable promptness." Members also have a similar responsibility to respond with reasonable promptness to inquiries from duly constituted state association ethics committees and professional standards review committees.

### Principle 8. Utilization of Assessment Techniques

*In the development, publication, and utilization of psychological assessment techniques, psychologists observe relevant APA standards. Persons examined have the right to know the results, the interpretations made, and, where appropriate, the original data on which final judgments were based. Test users avoid imparting unnecessary information which would compromise test security, but they provide requested information that explains the basis for decisions that may adversely affect that person or that person's dependents.*

*a.* The client has the right to have and the psychologist has the responsibility to provide explanations of the nature and the purposes of the test and the test results in language that the client can understand, unless, as in some employment or school settings, there is an explicit exception to this right agreed upon in advance. When the explanations are to be provided by others, the psychologist establishes procedures for providing adequate explanations.

*b.* When a test is published or otherwise made available for operational use, it is accompanied by a manual (or other published or readily available information) that fully describes the development of the test, the rationale, and evidence of validity and reliability. The test manual explicitly states the purposes and applications for which the test is recommended and identifies special qualifications required to administer the test and to interpret it properly. Test manuals provide complete information regarding the characteristics of the normative population.

*c.* In reporting test results, psychologists indicate any reservations regarding validity or reliability resulting from testing circumstances or inappropriateness of the test norms for the person tested. Psychologists strive to insure that the test results and their interpretations are not misused by others.

*d.* Psychologists accept responsibility for removing from clients' files test score information that has become obsolete, lest such information be misused or misconstrued to the disadvantage of the person tested.

*e.* Psychologists offering test scoring and interpretation services are able to demonstrate that the validity of the programs and procedures used in arriving at interpretations are based on appropriate evidence. The public offering of an automated test interpretation service is consultation. The psychologist makes every effort to avoid misuse of test reports.

## Principle 9. Pursuit of Research Activities

*The decision to undertake research should rest upon a considered judgment by the individual psychologist about how best to contribute to psychological science and to human welfare. Psychologists carry out their investigations with respect for the people who participate and with concern for their dignity and welfare.*

*a.* In planning a study the investigator has the responsibility to make a careful evaluation of its ethical acceptability, taking into account the following additional principles for research with human beings. To the extent that this appraisal, weighing scientific and humane values, suggests a compromise of any principle, the investigator incurs an increasingly serious obligation to seek ethical advice and to observe stringent safeguards to protect the rights of the human research participants.

*b.* Responsibility for the establishment and maintenance of acceptable ethical practice in research always remains with the individual investigator. The investigator is also responsible for the ethical treatment of research participants by collaborators, assistants, students, and employees, all of whom, however, incur parallel obligations.

*c.* Ethical practice requires the investigator to inform the participant of all features of the research that might reasonably be expected to influence willingness to participate, and to explain all other aspects of the research about which the participant inquires. Failure to make full disclosure imposes additional force to the investigator's abiding responsibility to protect the welfare and dignity of the research participant.

*d.* Openness and honesty are essential characteristics of the relationship between investigator and research participant. When the methodological requirements of a study necessitate concealment or deception, the investigator is required to insure as soon as possible the participant's understanding of the reasons for this action and of a sufficient justification for the procedures employed.

*e.* Ethical practice requires the investigator to respect the individual's freedom to decline to participate in or withdraw from research. The obligation to protect this freedom requires special vigilance when the investigator is in a position of power over the participant, as, for example, when the participant is a student, client, employee, or otherwise is in a dual relationship with the investigator.

*f.* Ethically acceptable research begins with the establishment of a clear and fair agreement between the investigator and the research participant that clarifies the responsibilities of each. The investigator has the obligation to honor all promises and commitments included in that agreement.

*g.* The ethical investigator protects participants from physical and mental discomfort, harm, and danger. If a risk of such consequences exists, the investigator is required to inform the participant of that fact, secure consent before proceeding, and take all possible measures to minimize distress. A research procedure must not be used if it is likely to cause serious or lasting harm to a participant.

*h.* After the data are collected, the investigator provides the participant with information about the nature of the study and to remove any misconceptions that may have arisen. Where scientific or human values justify delaying or withholding information, the investigator acquires a special responsibility to assure that there are no damaging consequences for the participant.

*i.* When research procedures may result in undesirable consequences for the individual participant, the investigator has the responsibility to detect and remove or correct these consequences, including, where relevant, long-term after effects.

*j.* Information obtained about the individual research participants during the course of an investigation is confidential unless otherwise agreed in advance. When the possibility exists that others may obtain access to such information, this possibility, together with the plans for protecting confidentiality, be explained to the participants as part of the procedure for obtaining informed consent.

*k.* A psychologist using animals in research adheres to the provisions of the Rules Regarding Animals, drawn up by the Committee on Precautions and Standards in Animal Experimentation and adopted by the American Psychological Association.

*l.* Investigations of human participants using drugs should be conducted only in such settings as clinics, hospitals, or research facilities maintaining appropriate safeguards for the participants.

## REFERENCES

*Psychologists are responsible for knowing about and acting in accord with the standards and positions of the APA, as represented in such official documents as the following:*

American Association of University Professors. Statement on Principles on Academic Freedom and Tenure. *Policy Documents & Report,* 1977, 1-4.

American Psychological Association. *Guidelines for Psychologists for the Use of Drugs in Research.* Washington, D.C.: Author, 1971.

American Psychological Association. *Principles for the Care and Use of Animals.* Washington, D.C.: Author, 1971.

American Psychological Association. Guidelines for conditions of employment of psychologists. *American Psychologist,* 1972, 27, 331-334.

American Psychological Association. Guidelines for psychologists conducting growth groups. *American Psychologist,* 1973, 28, 933.

American Psychological Association. *Ethical Principles in the Conduct of Research with Human Participants.* Washington, D.C.: Author, 1973.

American Psychological Association. *Standards for Educational and Psychological Tests.* Washington, D.C.: Author, 1974.

American Psychological Association. *Standards for Providers of Psychological Services.* Washington, D.C.: Author, 1977.

Committee on Scientific and Professional Ethics and Conduct. Guidelines for telephone directory listings. *American Psychologist,* 1969, 24, 70-71.

## USA (1981): ETHICAL PRINCIPLES OF PSYCHOLOGISTS (1981 REVISION)[1]

American Psychological Association

### Preamble

*Psychologists respect the dignity and worth of the individual and strive for the preservation and protection of fundamental human rights. They are committed to increasing knowledge of human behavior and of people's understanding of themselves and others and to the utilization of such knowledge for the promotion of human welfare. While pursuing these objectives, they make every effort to protect the welfare of those who seek their services and of the research participants that may be the object*

---

[1]Copyright 1981 by the American Psychological Association. Reprinted by permission of the publisher and author.

of study. They use their skills only for purposes consistent with these values and do not knowingly permit their misuse by others. While demanding for themselves freedom of inquiry and communication, psychologists accept the responsibility this freedom requires: competence, objectivity in the application of skills, and concern for the best interests of clients, colleagues, students, research participants and society. In the pursuit of these ideals, psychologists subscribe to principles in the following areas: 1. Responsibility, 2. Competence, 3. Moral and Legal Standards, 4. Public Statements, 5. Confidentiality, 6. Welfare of the Consumer, 7. Professional Relationships, 8. Assessment Techniques, 9. Research with Human Participants, and 10. Care and Use of Animals.

Acceptance of membership in the American Psychological Association commits the member to adherence to these principles.

Psychologists cooperate with duly constituted committees of the American Psychological Association, in particular, the Committee on Scientific and Professional Ethics and Conduct, by responding to inquiries promptly and completely. Members also respond promptly and completely to inquiries from duly constituted state association ethics committees and professional standards review committees.

### *Principle 1: Responsibility*

In providing services, psychologists maintain the highest standards of their profession. They accept responsibility for the consequences of their acts and make every effort to insure that their services are used appropriately.

*a.* As scientists, psychologists accept responsibility for the selection of their research topics and the methods used in investigation, analysis, and reporting. They plan their research in ways to minimize the possibility that their findings will be misleading. They provide thorough discussion of the limitations of their data, especially where their work touches on social policy or might be construed to the detriment of persons in specific age, sex, ethnic, socioeconomic or other social groups. In publishing reports of their work, they never suppress disconfirming data, and they acknowledge the existence of alternative hypotheses and explanations of their findings. Psychologists take credit only for work they have actually done.

*b.* Psychologists clarify in advance with all appropriate persons and agencies the expectations for sharing and utilizing research data. They avoid relationships which may limit their objectivity or create a conflict of interest. Interference with the milieu in which the data are collected is kept to a minimum.

*c.* Psychologists have the responsibility to attempt to prevent distortion, misuse, or suppression of psychological findings by the institution or agency of which they are employees.

*d.* As members of governmental or other organizational bodies, psychologists remain accountable as individuals to the highest standards of their profession.

*e.* As teachers, psychologists recognize their primary obligation to help others acquire knowledge and skill. They maintain high standards of scholarship by presenting psychological information objectively, fully, and accurately.

*f.* As practitioners, psychologists know that they bear a heavy social responsibility because their recommendations and professional actions may alter the lives of others. They are alert to personal, social, organizational, financial, or political situations and pressures that might lead to misuse of their influence.

## Principle 2: Competence

*The maintenance of high standards of competence is a responsibility shared by all psychologists in the interest of the public and the profession as a whole. Psychologists recognize the boundaries of their competence and the limitations of their techniques. They only provide services and only use techniques for which they are qualified by training and experience. In those areas in which recognized standards do not yet exist, psychologists take whatever precautions are necessary to protect the welfare of their clients. They maintain knowledge of current scientific and professional information related to the services they render.*

*a.* Psychologists accurately represent their competence, education, training, and experience. They claim as evidence of educational qualifications only those degrees obtained from institutions acceptable under the Bylaws and Rules of Council of the American Psychological Association.

*b.* As teachers, psychologists perform their duties on the basis of careful preparation so that their instruction is accurate, current, and scholarly.

*c.* Psychologists recognize the need for continuing education and are open to new procedures and changes in expectations and values over time.

*d.* Psychologists recognize differences among people, such as those that may be associated with age, sex, socioeconomic, and ethnic backgrounds. When necessary, they obtain training, experience, or counsel to assure competent service or research relating to such persons.

*e.* Psychologists responsible for decisions involving individuals or policies based on test results have an understanding of psychological or educational measurement, validation problems, and test research.

*f.* Psychologists recognize that personal problems and conflicts may interfere with professional effectiveness. Accordingly, they refrain from undertaking any activity in which their personal problems are likely to lead to inadequate performance or harm to a client, colleague, student, or research participant. If engaged in such activity when they become aware of their personal problems, they seek competent professional assistance to determine whether they should suspend, terminate, or limit the scope of their professional and/or scientific activities.

### Principle 3: Moral and Legal Standards

*Psychologists' moral and ethical standards of behavior are a personal matter to the same degree as they are for any other citizen, except as these may compromise the fulfillment of their professional responsibilities, or reduce the public trust in psychology and psychologists. Regarding their own behavior, psychologists are sensitive to prevailing community standards and to the possible impact that conformity to or deviation from these standards may have upon the quality of their performance as psychologists. Psychologists are also aware of the possible impact of their public behavior upon the ability of colleagues to perform their professional duties.*

*a.* As teachers, psychologists are aware of the fact that their personal values may affect the selection and presentation of instructional materials. When dealing with topics that may give offense, they recognize and respect the diverse attitudes that students may have toward such materials.

*b.* As employees or employers, psychologists do not engage in or condone practices that are inhumane or that result in illegal or unjustifiable actions. Such practices include but are not limited to those based on considerations of race, handicap, age, gender, sexual preference, religion, or national origin in hiring, promotion, or training.

*c.* In their professional roles, psychologists avoid any action that will violate or diminish the legal and civil rights of clients or of others who may be affected by their actions.

*d.* As practitioners and researchers, psychologists act in accord with Association standards and guidelines related to the practice and to the conduct of research with human beings and animals. In the ordinary course of events psychologists adhere to relevant governmental laws and institutional regulations. When federal, state, provincial, organizational, or institutional laws, regulations, or practices are in conflict with Association standards and guidelines, psychologists make known their commitment to Association standards and guidelines, and wherever possible work toward a resolution of the conflict. Both practitioners and researchers are concerned with the development of such legal and quasi-legal regulations as best serve the public interest, and they work toward changing existing regulations that are not beneficial to the public interest.

### Principle 4: Public Statements

*Public statements, announcements of services, advertising, and promotional activities of psychologists serve the purpose of helping the public make informed judgments and choices. Psychologists represent accurately and objectively their professional qual-*

ifications, affiliations, and functions, as well as those of the institutions or organizations with which they or the statements may be associated. In public statements providing psychological information or professional opinions or providing information about the availability of psychological products, publications, and services, psychologists base their statements on scientifically acceptable psychological findings and techniques with full recognition of the limits and uncertainties of such evidence.

   *a.* When announcing or advertising professional services, psychologists may list the following information to describe the provider and services provided: name, highest relevant academic degree earned from a regionally accredited institution, date, type and level of certification or licensure, diplomate status, APA membership status, address, telephone number, office hours, a brief listing of the type of psychological services offered, an appropriate presentation of fee information, foreign languages spoken, and policy with regard to third-party payments. Additional relevant or important consumer information may be included if not prohibited by other sections of these Ethical Principles.

   *b.* In announcing or advertising the availability of psychological products, publications, or services, psychologists do not present their affiliation with any organization in a manner that falsely implies sponsorship or certification by that organization. In particular and for example, psychologists do not state APA membership or fellow status in a way to suggest that such status implies specialized professional competence or qualifications. Public statements include, but are not limited to, communication by means of periodical, book, list, directory, television, radio, or motion picture. They do not contain: (i) a false, fraudulent, misleading, deceptive, or unfair statement; (ii) a misinterpretation of fact, or a statement likely to mislead or deceive because in context it makes only a partial disclosure of relevant facts; (iii) a testimonial from a patient regarding the quality of a psychologist's services or products; (iv) a statement intended or likely to create false or unjustified expectations of favorable results; (v) a statement implying unusual, unique, or one-of-a-kind abilities; (vi) a statement intended or likely to appeal to a client's fears, anxieties, or emotions concerning the possible results of a failure to obtain the offered services; (vii) a statement concerning the comparative desirability of offered service; (viii) a statement of direct solicitation of individual clients.

   *c.* Psychologists do not compensate or give anything of value to a representative of the press, radio, television, or other communication medium in anticipation of or in return for professional publicity in a news item. A paid advertisement must be identified as such, unless it is apparent from the context that it is a paid advertisement. If communicated to the public by use of radio or television, an advertisement shall be prerecorded and approved for broadcast by the psychologist, and a recording of the actual transmission shall be retained by the psychologist.

   *d.* Announcements or advertisements of "personal growth groups," clinics, and agencies give a clear statement of purpose and a clear description of the experiences to be provided. The education, training, and experience of the staff members are appropriately specified.

*e.* Psychologists associated with the development or promotion of psychological devices, books, or other products offered for commercial sale make reasonable efforts to insure that announcements and advertisements are presented in a professional, scientifically acceptable, and factually informative manner.

*f.* Psychologists do not participate for personal gain in commercial announcements or advertisements recommending to the public the purchase or use of proprietary or single-source products or services when that participation is based solely upon their identification as psychologists.

*g.* Psychologists present the science of psychology and offer their services, products, and publications fairly and accurately, avoiding misrepresentation through sensationalism, exaggeration, or superficiality. Psychologists are guided by the primary obligation to aid the public in developing informed judgments, opinions, and choices.

*h.* As teachers, psychologists insure that statements in catalogs and course outlines are accurate and not misleading, particularly in terms of subject matter to be covered, bases for evaluating progress, and the nature of course experiences. Announcements, brochures, or advertisements describing workshops, seminars, or other educational programs accurately describe the audience for which the program is intended as well as eligibility requirements, educational objectives, and nature of the materials to be covered. These announcements also accurately represent the education, training, and experience of the psychologists presenting the programs, and any fees involved.

*i.* Public announcements or advertisements soliciting research participants in which clinical services or other professional services are offered as an inducement, make clear the nature of the services as well as the costs and other obligations to be accepted by the participants of the research.

*j.* Psychologists accept the obligation to correct others who represent that psychologist's professional qualifications, or associations with products or services, in a manner incompatible with these guidelines.

*k.* Individual diagnostic and therapeutic services are provided only in the context of a professional psychological relationship. When personal advice is given by means of public lecture or demonstration, newspaper or magazine articles, radio or television programs, mail, or similar media, the psychologist utilizes the most current relevant data and exercises the highest level of professional judgment.

*l.* Products that are described or presented by means of public lectures or demonstrations, newspaper or magazine articles, radio or television programs, or similar media meet the same recognized standards as exist for use in the context of a professional relationship.

## Principle 5: Confidentiality

Psychologists have a primary obligation to respect the confidentiality of information obtained from persons in the course of their work as psychologists. They reveal such information to others only with the consent of the person or the person's legal representative, except in those unusual circumstances in which not to do so would result in clear danger to the person or to others. Where appropriate, psychologists inform their clients of the legal limits of confidentiality.

*a.* Information obtained in clinical or consulting relationships, or evaluative data concerning children, students, employees, and others, are discussed only for professional purposes and only with persons clearly concerned with the case. Written and oral reports present only data germane to the purposes of the evaluation and every effort is made to avoid undue invasion of privacy.

*b.* Psychologists who present personal information obtained during the course of professional work in writings, lectures, or other public forums either obtain adequate prior consent to do so or adequately disguise all identifying information.

*c.* Psychologists make provisions for maintaining confidentiality in the storage and disposal of records.

*d.* When working with minors or other persons who are unable to give voluntary, informed consent, psychologists take special care to protect these persons' best interests.

## Principle 6: Welfare of the Consumer

Psychologists respect the integrity and protect the welfare of the people and groups with whom they work. When there is a conflict of interest between a client and the psychologist's employing institution, psychologists clarify the nature and direction of their loyalties and responsibilities and keep all parties informed of their commitments. Psychologists fully inform consumers as to the purpose and nature of an evaluative, treatment, educational or training procedure, and they freely acknowledge that clients, students, or participants in research have freedom of choice with regard to participation.

*a.* Psychologists are continually cognizant of their own needs and of their potentially influential position vis-a-vis persons such as clients, students, and subordinates. They avoid exploiting the trust and dependency of such persons. Psychologists make every effort to avoid dual relationships which could impair their professional judgment or increase the risk of exploitation. Examples of such dual relationships include but are not limited to research with and treatment of employees, students, supervisees, close friends, or relatives. Sexual intimacies with clients are unethical.

*b.* When a psychologist agrees to provide services to a client at the request of a third party, the psychologist assumes the responsibility of clarifying the nature of the relationships to all parties concerned.

*c.* Where the demands of an organization require psychologists to violate these Ethical Principles, psychologists clarify the nature of the conflict between the demand and these principles. They inform all parties of psychologists' ethical responsibilities, and take appropriate action.

*d.* Psychologists make advance financial arrangements that safeguard the best interests of and are clearly understood by their clients. They neither give nor receive any remuneration for referring clients for professional services. They contribute a portion of their services to work for which they receive little or no financial return.

*e.* Psychologists terminate a clinical or consulting relationship when it is reasonably clear that the consumer is not benefiting from it. They offer to help the consumer locate alternative sources of assistance.

## *Principle 7: Professional Relationships*

*Psychologists act with due regard for the needs, special competencies, and obligations of their colleagues in psychology and other professions. They respect the prerogatives and obligations of the institutions or organizations with which these other colleagues are associated.*

*a.* Psychologists understand the areas of competence of related professions. They make full use of all the professional, technical, and administrative resources that serve the best interests of consumers. The absence of formal relationships with other professional workers does not relieve psychologists of the responsibility of securing for their clients the best possible professional service nor does it relieve them of the obligation to exercise foresight, diligence, and tact in obtaining the complementary or alternative assistance needed by clients.

*b.* Psychologists know and take into account the traditions and practices of other professional groups with whom they work and cooperate fully with such groups. If a person is receiving similar services from another professional, psychologists do not offer their own services directly to such a person. If a psychologist is contacted by a person who is already receiving similar services from another professional, the psychologist carefully considers that professional relationship and proceeds with caution and sensitivity to the therapeutic issues as well as the client's welfare. The psychologist discusses these issues with the client so as to minimize the risk of confusion and conflict.

*c.* Psychologists who employ or supervise other professionals or professionals in training accept the obligation to facilitate the further professional development of these individuals. They provide appropriate working conditions, timely evaluations, constructive consultation and experience opportunities.

*d.* Psychologists do not exploit their professional relationships with clients, supervisees, students, employees, or research participants sexually or otherwise. Psychologists do not condone nor engage in sexual harrassment. Sexual harrassment is defined as deliberate or repeated comments, gestures, or physical contacts of a sexual nature that are unwanted by the recipient.

*e.* In conducting research in institutions or organizations, psychologists secure appropriate authorization to conduct such research. They are aware of their obligation to future research workers and insure that host institutions receive adequate information about the research and proper acknowledgement of their contributions.

*f.* Publication credit is assigned to those who have contributed to a publication in proportion to their professional contribution. Major contributions of a professional character made by several persons to a common project are recognized by joint authorship, with the individual who made the principal contribution listed first. Minor contributions of a professional character and extensive clerical or similar nonprofessional assistance may be acknowledged in footnotes or in an introductory statement. Acknowledgement through specific citations is made for unpublished as well as published material that has directly influenced the research or writing. A psychologist who compiles and edits material of others for publication publishes the material in the name of the originating group, if appropriate, with his/her own name appearing as chairperson or editor. All contributors are to be acknowledged and named.

*g.* When psychologists know of an ethical violation by another psychologist, and it seems appropriate, they informally attempt to resolve the issue by bringing the behavior to the attention of the psychologist. If the misconduct is of a minor nature and/or appears to be due to lack of sensitivity, knowledge, or experience, such an informal solution is usually appropriate. Such informal corrective efforts are sensitive to any rights to confidentiality involved. If the violation does not seem amenable to an informal solution, or is of a more serious nature, psychologists bring it to the attention of the appropriate local, state, and/or national committee on professional ethics and conduct.

### *Principle 8: Assessment Techniques*

*In the development, publication, and utilization of psychological assessment techniques, psychologists make every effort to promote the welfare and best interests of the client. They guard against the misuse of assessment results. They respect the client's right to know the results, the interpretations made and the bases for their conclusions* and recommendations. Psychologists make every effort to maintain the security of tests and other assessment techniques within limits of legal mandates. They strive to assure the appropriate use of assessment techniques by others.

*a.* In using assessment techniques, psychologists respect the right of clients to have a full explanation of the nature and purpose of the techniques in language that the client can understand, unless an explicit exception to this right has been agreed upon in advance. When the explanations are to be provided by others, the psychologist establishes procedures for insuring the adequacy of these explanations.

*b.* Psychologists responsible for the development and standardization of psychological tests and other assessment techniques utilize established scientific procedures and observe the relevant APA standards.

*c.* In reporting assessment results, psychologists indicate any reservations that exist regarding validity or reliability because of the circumstances of the assessment or the inappropriateness of the norms for the person tested. Psychologists strive to insure that the results of assessments and their interpretations are not misused by others.

*d.* Psychologists recognize that assessment results may become obsolete. They make every effort to avoid and prevent the misuse of obsolete measures.

*e.* Psychologists offering scoring and interpretation services are able to produce appropriate evidence for the validity of the programs and procedures used in arriving at interpretations. The public offering of an automated interpretation service is considered as a professional-to-professional consultation. The psychologist makes every effort to avoid misuse of assessment reports.

*f.* Psychologists do not encourage or promote the use of psychological assessment techniques by inappropriately trained or otherwise unqualified persons through teaching, sponsorship, or supervision.

## Principle 9: Research with Human Participants

The decision to undertake research rests upon a considered judgment by the individual psychologist about how best to contribute to psychological science and human welfare. Having made the decision to conduct research, the psychologist considers alternative directions in which research energies and resources might be invested. On the basis of this consideration, the psychologist carries out the investigation with respect and concern for the dignity and welfare of the people who participate, and with cognizance of federal and state regulations and professional standards governing the conduct of research with human participants.

*a.* In planning a study, the investigator has the responsibility to make a careful evaluation of its ethical acceptability. To the extent that the weighing of scientific and human values suggests a compromise of any principle, the investigator incurs a correspondingly serious obligation to seek ethical advice and to observe stringent safeguards to protect the rights of human participants.

*b.* Considering whether a participant in a planned study will be a "subject at risk" or a "subject at minimal risk," according to recognized standards, is of primary ethical concern to the investigator.

*c.* The investigator always retains the responsibility for insuring ethical practice in research. The investigator is also responsible for the ethical treatment of research participants by collaborators, assistants, students, and employees, all of whom, however, incur similar obligations.

*d.* Except for minimal risk research, the investigator establishes a clear and fair agreement with the research participants, prior to their participation, that clarifies the obligations and responsibilities of each. The investigator has the obligation to honor all promises and commitments included in that agreement. The investigator informs the participant of all aspects of the research that might reasonably be expected to influence willingness to participate, and explains all other aspects of the research about which the participant inquires. Failure to make full disclosure prior to obtaining informed consent requires additional safeguards to protect the welfare and dignity of the research participant. Research with children or participants who have impairments which would limit understanding and/or communication, requires special safeguard procedures.

*e.* Methodological requirements of a study may make the use of concealment or deception necessary. Before conducting such a study, the investigator has a special responsibility to: (i) determine whether the use of such techniques is justified by the study's prospective scientific, educational, or applied value; (ii) determine whether alternative procedures are available that do not utilize concealment or deception; and (iii) insure that the participants are provided with sufficient explanation as soon as possible.

*f.* The investigator respects the individual's freedom to decline to participate in or to withdraw from the research at any time. The obligation to protect this freedom requires careful thought and consideration when the investigator is in a position of authority or influence over the participant. Such positions of authority include but are not limited to situations when research participation is required as part of employment or when the participant is a student, client, or employee of the investigator.

*g.* The investigator protects the participants from physical and mental discomfort, harm, and danger that may arise from research procedures. If risks of such consequences exist, the investigator informs the participant of that fact. Research procedures likely to cause serious or lasting harm to a participant are not used unless the failure to use these procedures might expose the participant to risk of greater harm, or unless the research has great potential benefit and fully informed and voluntary consent is obtained from each participant. The participant should be informed of procedures for contacting the investigator within a reasonable time period following participation should stress, potential harm, or related questions or concerns arise.

*h.* After the data are collected, the investigator provides the participant with information about the nature of the study and attempts to remove any misconceptions that may have arisen. Where scientific or humane values justify delaying or withholding information, the investigator incurs a special responsibility to monitor the research and to assure that there are no damaging consequences for the participant.

*i.* Where research procedures result in undesirable consequences for the individual participant, the investigator has the responsibility to detect and remove or correct these consequences, including long-term effects.

*j.* Information obtained about the research participant during the course of an investigation is confidential unless otherwise agreed upon in advance. When the possibility exists that others may obtain access to such information, this possibility, together with the plans for protecting confidentiality, is explained to the participant as part of the procedure for obtaining informed consent.

### *Principle 10: Care and Use of Animals*

*An investigator of animal behavior strives to advance our understanding of basic behavioral principles and/or to contribute to the improvement of human health and welfare. In seeking these ends, the investigator insures the welfare of the animals and treats them humanely. Laws and regulations notwithstanding, the animal's immediate protection depends upon the scientist's own conscience.*

*a.* The acquisition, care, use, and disposal of all animals is in compliance with current federal, state or provincial, and local laws and regulations.

*b.* A psychologist trained in research methods and experienced in the care of laboratory animals closely supervises all procedures involving animals and is responsible for insuring appropriate consideration of their comfort, health, and humane treatment.

*c.* Psychologists insure that all individuals using animals under their supervision have received explicit instruction in experimental methods and in the care, maintenance, and handling of the species being used. Responsibilities and activities of individuals participating in a research project are consistent with their respective competencies.

*d.* Psychologists make every effort to minimize discomfort, illness, and pain to the animals. A procedure subjecting animals to pain, stress, or privation is used only when an alternative procedure is unavailable and the goal is justified by its prospective scientific, educational, or applied value. Surgical procedures are performed under appropriate anesthesia; techniques to avoid infection and minimize pain are followed during and after surgery.

*e.* When it is appropriate that the animal's life be terminated, it is done rapidly and painlessly.

## Notes

This version of the Ethical Principles of Psychologists (formerly entitled Ethical Standards of Psychologists) was adopted by the American Psychological Association's Council of Representatives on January 24, 1981. The revised Ethical Principles contain both substantive and grammatical changes in each of the nine ethical principles constituting the Ethical Standards of Psychologists previously adopted by the Council of Representatives in 1979, plus a new tenth principle entitled Care and Use of Animals. Inquiries concerning the Ethical Principles of Psychologists should be addressed to the Administrative Officer for Ethics, American Psychological Association, 1200 Seventeenth Street, N.W., Washington, D.C. 20036.

These revised Ethical Principles apply to psychologists, to students of psychology, and to others who do work of a psychological nature under the supervision of a psychologist. They are also intended for the guidance of nonmembers of the Association who are engaged in psychological research or practice.

Any complaints of unethical conduct filed after January 24, 1981, shall be governed by this 1981 revision. However, conduct (a) complained about after January 24, 1981, but which occurred prior to that date, and (b) not considered unethical under prior versions of the principles but considered unethical under the 1981 revision, shall not be deemed a violation of ethical principles. Any complaints pending as of January 24, 1981, shall be governed either by the 1979 or by the 1981 version of the Ethical Principles, at the sound discretion of the Committee on Scientific and Professional Ethics and Conduct.

## FEDERAL REPUBLIC OF GERMANY (1978): BERUFSETHISCHE VERPFLICHTUNGEN FÜR PSYCHOLOGEN[1] (ETHICAL OBLIGATIONS OF PROFESSIONAL PSYCHOLOGISTS)

### (EXCERPTS)

Berufsverband Deutscher Psychologen
(German Association of Professional Psychologists)

### A. General Principles

*I. GENERAL CONDUCT OF PSYCHOLOGISTS*

Psychologists respect the dignity and worth of the individual; they bear in mind that all human beings have an equal claim to this respect. Psychologists respect the right of all human beings to live according to their convictions and assume responsibility for themselves. In every professional activity, psychologists are concerned with the welfare of the people who are affected by the practice of their profession. They are aware of their obligation to serve individuals and the society in which they live. Psychologists claim their right to freedom of research and communication but at the same time always remain conscious of the responsibility that this freedom imposes on them with respect to the integrity of their goals and the quality of their work.

Psychologists undertake no tasks that violate these basic maxims. They make sure that their services are not used by others in a way that violates these maxims.

*II. GENERAL PRINCIPLES FOR THE WORK OF PSYCHOLOGISTS*

In the interest of the people involved and in the interest of the progress of their discipline, psychologists strive for a high quality of work in their professional activity, whether research, teaching, or practice. Because of the rapid development of psychology, they have a particular responsibility to continue their education and work toward a mutually productive relationship between basic research and practice.

The difficulties associated with verifying many psychological statements increase the responsibility of psychologists and reinforce their need to seek a solid foundation for their work.

Moreover, psychologists are always aware of the special responsibility that

---

[1] These excerpts from Berufsethische Verpflichtungen für Psychologen, herausgegeben vom (edited by the) Berufsverband Deutscher Psychologen, Heilsbachstrasse 22, D-5300 Bonn 1, Federal Republic of Germany.

results from the particularly direct and lasting manner in which the practice of psychology affects the lives of other human beings.

*a.* Psychologists allow their work to be guided only by objective considerations, not by such irrelevant personal evaluations as their liking for the persons involved.

*b.* In their work psychologists take into account the limitations of their means and of their own competence.

*c.* Psychologists always aim to employ those techniques that can be considered soundest in view of the current state of the discipline.

*d.* In their attempt to perform their activities in the best possible way, psychologists consider the possibility of working with other professionals from their own area and related areas, especially when they are forced to recognize the limits of their own competence.

*e.* Psychologists are responsible for seeing to it that external working conditions satisfy the requirements that must be made of professional work.

*f.* Psychologists do not engage in psychological activities such as diagnosis, individual counseling, or treatment that should only be given in the context of an individual professional relationship to the client, by means of media such as newspapers and magazines, radio, or television, nor by means of correspondence alone.

*g.* In the interest of improving both their manner of working and the knowledge on which their work is based, psychologists strive to evaluate or have someone evaluate the success of their work with appropriate methods.

*h.* Psychologists help prevent the incompetent exercise of psychological activities or undertakings that are called psychological. If they find out in any manner that a colleague is practicing in a way that does not correspond to the basic principles of this code, they will first attempt on their own to see that this is stopped. Should that not be possible in an informal manner, the designated authorities in organizations for psychologists should be informed of the questionable behavior. The unprofessional practice of an activity that is presented as psychological by non-psychologists is also to be brought to the attention of these authorities. (The procedures to be taken by these authorities in such cases have not yet been determined.)

## B. Special Principles

### III. PRINCIPLES FOR RESEARCH

Psychological research must stay within certain limits with regard to its goals and methods. These limitations result from the need to be considerate of the people (or animals) involved in research.

*a.* In every psychological research project, whether basic or applied, psychologists will be guided in the planning and execution of their investigations by the principles of scientific methodology that are appropriate for the problem under investigation.

*b.* In particular, basic and applied psychological research should be designed to minimize the possibility of inappropriate, misleading interpretations of the results.

*c.* In the planning and execution of investigations, psychologists attempt to exclude all conditions from which harmful aftereffects for the subjects could result. If they decide for important reasons to carry out research in which there is a possibility of certain harmful aftereffects, they must inform subjects of this possibility explicitly. Psychologists should use these subjects only if they have stated explicitly, as a completely free choice, that they are prepared to undergo this risk.

*d.* Research situations that are physically or psychologically stressful for subjects may be created only when it is a matter of important scientific problems that cannot be investigated in any other manner, and only under the condition that subjects are willing to submit to such stresses. The stresses may not injure the dignity of the subject, must be kept within reasonable limits, and can be introduced only if all possible precautionary measures have been taken.

*e.* If subjects are to be observed during an investigation in a manner that is not obvious (for example, by means of one-way windows or similar devices) or if their behavior is to be recorded by means of a camera or tape recorder, they should be informed of this intention ahead of time and their consent should be obtained.

Researchers may deviate from this principle only if the investigation of scientifically significant questions makes this unavoidably necessary. In this case, however, subjects are to be informed as soon as possible that their behavior was observed or recorded, and in what manner. Subjects have the right to have the data destroyed if they do not approve of the observation or recording even after being presented with the reasons for its scientific necessity. In the case of subjects who cannot make such decisions for themselves, appropriate agreements are to be made with those responsible for them.

*f.* Psychologists take into account that under some circumstances subjects may see their relationship as a therapist-client relationship, or that it can unintentionally develop into such a relationship. In this case the approach described in section B,I is applicable.

*g.* The law for the protection of animals applies to work with animals in psychological research. Experiments connected with considerable harm to an animal always need the approval of the highest governmental veterinary authorities.

*h.* In the evaluation and interpretation of data from investigations nothing may be omitted or disguised that would modify the results of the investigation or their interpretation.

## GREAT BRITAIN (1977): ETHICAL PRINCIPLES FOR RESEARCH WITH HUMAN SUBJECTS[1]

British Psychological Society

Psychologists are committed to increasing the understanding that people have of their own and others' behaviour in the belief that this understanding ameliorates the human condition and enhances human dignity. These ethical values must characterize not only applications of psychological knowledge but also the means of obtaining knowledge. Performing an investigation with human subjects may occasionally require an ethical decision concerning the balance between the interests of the subject and the humane or scientific value of the research.

Psychologists require an atmosphere of free inquiry and communication without misrepresentation of their knowledge and methods by others. Psychologists must match this freedom with ethical concern, competence, objectivity and the non-wasteful use of material resources and human resources. Psychologists have an obligation to prevent misuse through personal influence, public statement and professional sanction. Psychologists can and should promote the public understanding of psychological knowledge in such a way as to prevent its misuse or render misuse ineffective.

The psychologist has a general obligation to make the results of his research available to other psychologists, to related scientists, and to allied professions. No psychologist should seek to restrict the availability or publication of his own or colleagues' research without seeking the opinion of experienced and disinterested colleagues. Until such publication has permitted the verification of results and the evaluation of their apparent implications by the scientific community, psychologists have an obligation to resist the premature citation of results in wider discussions on policy, and especially their premature use in policy formulation. This general principle does not prevent a psychologist from undertaking explicitly confidential research on restricted topics (e.g. for commercial development or national security) where that research does not violate these principles.

The following set of ethical principles is issued by the British Psychological

---

[1] Reprinted by permission of the British Psychological Society.

Society in the belief that a detailed list of prescribed and proscribed procedures would be impractical. It is the Society's belief that the degree of awareness and responsibility that follows from adherence to this general set of principles will serve to raise standards in psychological science and will safeguard the welfare of human subjects who contribute to it. While it would be appropriate to use this set of principles as an indication of the level of awareness that a psychologist should display, the psychologist's compliance with these principles can only be determined by those of his peers who are experienced with the problems which the principles encompass. Accordingly, the principles should not be used as a substitute for a considered judgement in which a case is examined on its merits in all aspects. The principles place reliance upon the opinion of the psychological community as an extension of the individual investigator's ability to anticipate the ethical issues raised and to assess the extent to which any consequences for the subject may be serious. The opinion of colleagues should also assist the investigator in determining whether the research is justified scientifically or pragmatically.

Scientific justification involves the assessment of both the conceptual importance of the potential results and their usefulness to mankind. Pragmatic justification involves assessing, for example, the likely effects of participants' guesses about the objectives of the research upon public attitudes to psychological inquiry in general and upon local voluntary participation in particular.

1. Whenever possible the investigator should inform the subjects of the objectives, and, eventually, the results of the investigation. Where this is not possible the investigator incurs an obligation to indicate to the subject the general nature of the knowledge achieved by such research and its potential value to people, and to outline the general values accepted by psychologists as listed in the introduction to these principles. The investigator's name, status and employer or affiliation should be declared.

2. In all circumstances the investigator must consider the ethical implications and the psychological consequences for his subjects of the research he is carrying out. The investigator must actively consider, by proper consultation, whether local cultural variations, special personality factors in the subjects or variations in his procedure from procedures reported previously may introduce unexpected problems for the subject.

3. An investigator should seek the opinion of experienced and disinterested colleagues whenever his research requires or is likely to involve:

(a) Deception concerning the purpose of the investigation or the subject's role in it.
(b) Deception concerning the basis of subject selection.
(c) Psychological or physiological stress.
(d) Encroachment upon privacy.

Geographical and institutional isolation of the investigating psychologist increases rather than decreases the need to seek colleagues' opinions.

4. Deception of subjects, or withholding of relevant information from them, should only occur when the investigator is satisfied that the aims and objects of his research or the welfare of his subjects cannot be achieved by other means. Where deception has been necessary, revelation should normally follow participation as a matter of course. Where the subject's behaviour makes it appear that revelation could be stressful or, when to reveal the objectives or the basis of subject selection would be distressing, the extent and timing of such revelation should be influenced by consideration for the subject's psychological welfare. Where deception has been substantial, the subject should be offered the option of withholding his data, in accordance with the principle of participation by informed consent.

5. In proportion to the risks of stress or encroachment upon privacy the investigator incurs an obligation to emphasize to the subject at the outset his volunteer status and his right to withdraw, irrespective of whether or not payment or other inducement is offered, and to describe precisely the demands of the investigation.

Wherever a situation turns out to be more stressful for an individual subject than anticipated by the investigator or than might be reasonably expected by the subject from his introduction, the investigator has an obligation to stop the investigation and consult an experienced and disinterested colleague before proceeding.

6. In proportion to the risks under 3 (a)–(d) and to the personal nature of the information involved the investigator incurs an obligation to treat data as confidential and to conceal identities when reporting results.

7. Studies on non-volunteers, based upon observation or upon records (whether or not explicitly confidential) must respect the privacy and psychological well-being of the subjects.

8. Investigators have the responsibility to maintain the highest standards of safety in procedure, equipment and premises.

9. Where research involves infants and young children as subjects, consent should be obtained from parents or from those *in loco parentis,* according to the foregoing principles. In the case of children of appropriate age, the informed consent of subjects themselves should also be obtained in advance. In research involving children caution should be exercised when discussing results of research with parents, teachers or others *in loco parentis* since evaluative statements may carry unintended weight.

10. If a subject solicits advice concerning educational, personality or behavioural problems, extreme caution should be exercised and if the problem is serious the appropriate source of professional advice should be recommended.

11. It is the investigator's responsibility to ensure that research executed by associates, employees or students conforms in detail to the ethical decision taken in the light of the foregoing principles.

12. A psychologist who believes that another psychologist or related investigator may be conducting research not in accordance with the foregoing principles has the obligation to encourage the investigator to re-evaluate the research in their light, if necessary consulting a responsible senior colleague as a source of further opinion or influence.

## NETHERLANDS (1976):
## PROFESSIONAL CODE FOR PSYCHOLOGISTS[1,2]
## (EXCERPTS)

Nederlands Instituut van Psychologen
(Netherlands Association of Psychologists)

### 0. Basic Concepts and Scope of this Professional Code

0.1. As and from January 1, 1976, the Code shall be binding on all members of "Nederlands Instituut van Psychologen" (Netherlands Association of Psychologists), hereinafter to be referred to as N.I.P., except inasfar as it concerns those articles that actually are, or shall be, incompatible with Dutch law.

0.2. Wherever in this Code mention shall be made of "psychologist", or of "he" or "him" respectively, the provision in question shall be taken to apply to all N.I.P.-members, irrespective of sex.

0.3. In all his professional dealings, the psychologist shall be invariably mindful and indeed abide by the ethical principles and aims as laid down in the Preamble; moreover, in the exercise of his profession he shall, apart from the precepts and principles contained in the present Code, also be guided by the specific rules of behaviour obtaining for the various specializations that have been added to this Code.

0.4. In the exercise of his function, the psychologist shall invariably give due consideration to the consequences any of his professional actions may have for his fellow-men, Society at large, as well as any new developments that may occur in it.

---

[1]These excerpts are from the official English version of the code, translated by H. Jacobse, which was sent to the author in response to his inquiry; an even more detailed Dutch version also exists (Beroepsethiek voor Psychologen, 1976).

[2]Reprinted by permission of the Nederlands Instituut van Psychologen.

As well as he can, and with regard to his special knowledge, he shall publicly draw attention to and describe any structural problems and situations that, in his judgment, are prejudicial to human well-being; it shall be incumbent on him to contribute his share towards their solution or improvement.

0.5. The psychologist is bound to foster and develop his own professional ability and to keep abreast of the latest developments in psychology. He shall do everything in his power to ensure that his methods of investigation and patient care shall be constant objects of critical re-assessment, whilst he generally shall make every effort to contribute his share towards the development of psychology as a science.

0.6. The psychologist shall deem himself bound to observe the precepts of the present Code, not merely in regard of the subjects directly concerned, but also of groupings or individuals liable to either directly or indirectly experience the consequences of his professional actions.

## *1. Entering into Professional Relationships*

### 1.1. ACCEPTABILITY

Before accepting a commission or responding favourably to a request for assistance, or undertaking to carry out an investigation, the psychologist is to make sure that adequate conditions have been created to enable him to behave towards all persons directly or indirectly concerned, in a manner agreeable to the precepts of the professional code and particularly also towards his clients' direct relations as also towards persons employed in a subordinate capacity in any organization or agency in which he, too, holds an appointment.

### 1.2. EFFICIENCY

The psychologist is not to enter upon any sort of investigation, or to commence any therapy or give any professional advice, before having duly ascertained whether the procedures or methods selected by him will contribute towards the solution of the problem, as also whether adequate possibilities exist of carrying the envisaged therapeutic measures into effect and for introducing such changes in the client system as shall be necessary for the solution of the problem.

### 1.3. VALUES AND AIMS

Whenever the system of values of those with whom the psychologist entertains professional relations should differ from his own views on issues affecting the nature of his services or the use that might be made of those services, he is bound to divulge these in good time and present them for discussion to the other parties concerned.

*1.4. PERSONAL LIMITATIONS*

In considering whether or not to accept a commission, or to accede to a request for assistance or commence an investigation, the psychologist shall carefully and critically consider his own limitations, indeed if necessary consult other experts or refer his client to other, more competent, specialists.

Similar limitations may among other things concern his professional qualifications and ability, his social and ethical views with reference to his potential clients and the means at his disposal for the performance of his task.

*1.5. INFORMATION AND FREEDOM OF PARTICIPATION*

The psychologist shall take special care to assure that client or clients shall be properly informed on the nature of their rights and obligations under the present professional code, as also the rules of conduct to which the psychologist considers himself bound.

*1.6. RISKS*

On entering on any professional relation, suitable measures shall be taken by the psychologist to ensure that he may timely recognize and protect his clients from any injurious effects they may suffer as a result of his work or, respectively, make sure that similar injurious effects shall be offset by a reasonable measure of compensation.

*1.7. PAYMENTS ARRANGEMENTS*

The psychologist shall see to it that his payments arrangements are such as to ensure that less substantial individuals, groupings and institutions shall in an equal measure be able to avail themselves of his services as persons more fortunate in this respect.

*1.8. INDEMNIFICATIONS*

The psychologist shall see to it that any arrangements concluded with test persons or informants engaged for the purpose of scientific or applied research shall be of such a nature that, in their own discretion and opinion, the advantages to be gained by their co-operation will outweigh the disadvantages and risks involved in such co-operation. Possible remunerations should not be such as to disproportionately influence their willingness to co-operate.

*1.9. LIABILITY TO ACCOUNT*

The psychologist shall keep notes of his professional dealings to the extent that, in case of a dispute, he shall be in a position to duly inform any competent body on his working methods and the considerations on which his conclusions, procedures and advice were grounded.

*1.10. REFUSAL TO ACCEPT A COMMISSION*

The psychologist shall refuse to accept any commission of which he has good reasons to believe that its performance will bring him in collision with the code of his profession.

## 2. Relations with Clients, Client Groups and Test Persons

### 2.1. INFORMATION TO WHICH CLIENTS AND TEST PERSONS ARE ENTITLED

The psychologist shall provide all those whom he has accepted to enter into a professional relation, either for research or therapeutic purposes, with a truthful account of his researches or treatment, respectively. This account may deal with:

— the procedures with which client, respectively test person, will be directly or indirectly confronted;
— the sort of data that will be collected on him;
— the amount of time and trouble he will have to spend in the course of the treatment or research in question;
— the agencies that may in some way be interested in the research or treatment, and their motives;
— the objectives, both direct and indirect, for which data are to be collected;
— the context within which the research or treatment is to take place; should this happen to be a decision-making process, the position of the psychologist and of the subject within this process;
— what type of information, bearing on himself or the system or organization concerned he, or other persons, may expect to receive on the termination of the investigation or treatment in respect of results achieved;
— possible (side)-effects of the investigation, respectively treatment, notably in as far as they are likely to induce a better insight into own possibilities;
— to what extent and in what manner the confidential character of the data obtained, as also the reports based on them, are to be respected;
— the existence of a Right of Complaint, and the manner in which it operates.

2.1.2. For the purpose of any scientific investigation it shall solely be permissible to withold from a test person the type of information he is entitled to by virtue of art. 2.1.1., respectively to temporarily supply him with deceptive information, so to deviate from the provisions laid down in art. 2.2.1., provided the following conditions are met:

1. The investigation concerns an important problem or objective, the reali-

zation or solution of which the investigator demonstrably could not possibly achieve in any other way.
2. It may in all reason be assumed that test person, after having been acquainted with the actual procedures followed will approve of the information having been withheld or the type of deception practised.
3. Test person is, at the earliest convenience, to be provided with the actual facts, after which he is to be offered the opportunity of withdrawing from the investigation any data that should by then have been obtained on him.

## 2.2. FREEDOM OF PARTICIPATION

*2.2.1.* It shall not be permissible to have any person participate in any investigation, or to submit to any therapy, without his express consent; all this in compliance with the provisions of 2.2.5. and with the understanding that participation in any psychological investigation as part of selective or screening procedures, is to be deemed to take place with the implied consent of the subject concerned.

*2.2.2.* On entering on any professional relations (including the recruiting of test persons for the purpose of scientific investigations), the psychologists shall attempt to create such conditions as are likely to ensure that any decision to take part in an investigation, respectively the preparedness to submit to a therapy or, if necessary, his assistance in the procedures of which it constitutes part, shall be made in complete freedom.

*2.2.3.* The psychologist shall show every possible diligence in guarding the right of any persons taking part in an investigation or submitting to a therapy, to refuse their co-operation and to see to it that his clients or test persons shall be duly acquainted with this right.

*2.2.4.* The psychologist recognizes the right of clients or test persons to refuse their further co-operation at any time in the course of any investigation or treatment.

The application of sanctions should only be considered if, inasmuch this shall have been agreed upon beforehand.

*2.2.5.* Whenever any subject of an intended investigation or treatment should, owing to any circumstances, be incapable of making a well-considered and free decision either to assist or not to assist in the investigation, respectively to submit to the treatment, it shall be incumbent on the psychologist to defer this decision and/or refer it to any persons or institutions charged with looking after the subject's well-being.

*2.2.6.* If entrusted with a commission for an investigation or treatment by any organizations or social institutions, the psychologist may, without prejudice to his own responsibilities as stipulated sub 1.1 and 1.6. of the present code, consider the power of decision regarding the participation of any individuals to be delegated to such agencies or persons as must, by virtue of their status in those organizations or institutions, be considered to represent these individuals.

2.2.7. The psychologists shall be only permitted to demand of somebody that he, in connexion with his special training or education, supply certain information, assist in any investigation or submit to any treatment, if and insofar it will be likely to greatly contribute towards the attainment of the goal that this person hopes to achieve via this training.

2.3. CONFIDENTIALITY AND RIGHT OF COMPLAINT

2.3.1. In entering into any investigatory or therapeutical relation, the psychologist actually enters into a relationship of confidentiality with the persons or groups of persons concerned—a relationship which entails an obligation to secrecy as well as the right to claim exemption if anyone should demand to divulge any data that are to be considered confidential.

Unless a client should expressly object to it, the psychologist shall, however, be entitled for the purpose of furthering the development and testing of scientifically and ethically justifiable methods and procedures, to discuss confidential information on a confidential basis with colleagues.

2.3.2. In his reports to third parties, the psychologist is to confine himself to supplying only such information as shall be essentially necessary in order to obtain a suitable answer to the problem in hand and that in unmistakable terms whilst clearly indicating the scope of the advice.

2.3.3. The client shall have the right to be informed by the psychologist on the substance and results of any investigation bearing on him personally and carried out for the use of non-professional third parties. If, after having consulted the psychologist, a client will expressly desire this, the psychologist is bound to refrain from reporting his findings to third parties.

2.3.4. Any client, group of clients or test persons shall have the right to lodge a complaint with a competent body (Board of Control), whenever he should be of opinion that either in the course of, or as a result of, the investigation or treatment, aftercare or advice, the psychologist has failed to act correctly (in contravention of the present Code).

2.4. INVESTIGATORY AND THERAPEUTICAL METHODS AND PROCEDURES

2.4.1. The psychologist shall refrain from resorting to methods of investigation that are likely to undermine the sense of self-respect of his subjects or to further encroach upon their private life than shall be warranted for the purpose of the investigation.

2.4.2. The psychologist shall see to it that, within the scope of the methods used by him, persons of equal ability shall also have equal chances, irrespective of any ethnical differences, or differences of class, age, skin colour, sex, sexual preferences, religious or political views or otherwise.

2.4.3. The deliberate exposing of clients or test persons to negative experiences shall be only permissible, provided the following conditions have been met:

1. Client or test person has voluntarily and deliberately given his consent;
2. Certainty exists that client or test person shall not suffer injury as a result of similar experiences;
3. Client or test person is fully aware of the fact that he can revoke his collaboration at any given moment;
4. Psychologist has taken suitable measures to remove or eliminate time reveal themselves; (sic)
5. The aim of the investigation or treatment is of great consequence and could not be achieved in any other way;
6. Other, independent experts were consulted on the subject.

2.4.4. Whenever, for reasons of a technical nature, some of the test persons are to be denied a potentially beneficial experience or treatment, the investigator is to do everything in his power to offset this with some positive experience or therapy.

2.4.5. As soon as an investigation or treatment shall have been completed, the psychologist is bound to:

*a.* immediately rectify any misunderstanding that may have arisen in consequence of any test or therapeutic procedures in the client, respectively test person, or in any other persons involved;
*b.* take due measures to neutralize any injurious side effects likely to result for the client system or the clients.

## 3. Filing of Psychological Data, Reports, and Dossiers

3.1. The psychologist shall satisfy himself that, in case of any data or results collected by him (or digests thereof) being kept for later reference (e.g., in files or data banks), this shall be done in such a way as to rule out any unwarranted use (including any such use as for which client or test person has not given his consent).

3.2. Whenever data are to be kept for storage, the psychologist shall, if so arranged beforehand, notify his client or test person of this with due regard to art. 2.2.5. and 2.2.6., as well as inform him on the possible use to which these data may be put, so that he shall on these grounds be able to refuse his co-operation in this respect.

3.3. If so desired by him, the client or test person shall be given a guarantee that any data collected on him shall be removed from a data bank whenever he should make a request to this effect.

3.4. The psychologist shall make all necessary arrangements to ensure that he will be duly informed in case of any use being made of the data stored for purposes other than for which they had been left in his charge. If necessary, he shall still request his client's or test person's written consent to this effect.

3.5. The psychologist reserves to himself the right, at any moment he should deem this necessary, to have removed from the data bank any data previously supplied by him if, in his judgment, the further storage thereof may bring him into conflict with the ethics of his profession.

3.6. The psychologist is to make sure that any data, or compilations thereof, shall be available to colleagues at cost price but, otherwise, shall be inaccessible to any unauthorized persons.

3.7. In the absence of sufficient guarantees to ensure that the provisions of the art. 3.1. to 3.6. inclusive, shall be properly met, the psychologist shall proceed to destroy the data concerned, once his commission has been completed.

## AUSTRIA (1976): BERUFSVERPFLICHTUNGEN FÜR PSYCHOLOGEN[1] (OBLIGATIONS OF PROFESSIONAL PSYCHOLOGISTS)

## (EXCERPTS)

Berufsverband Osterreichischer Psychologen
(Austrian Association of Professional Psychologists)

### A. General Principles

Psychologists are concerned with the welfare and dignity of the people who are affected by their professional activities; they are conscious of their obligation to serve individuals and the society in which they live.

Psychologists are aware of the special responsibility that results from the

[1] By permission of the Berufsverband Österreichischer Psychologen.

direct and lasting manner in which the practice of psychology affects the lives of other human beings.

1. Psychologists allow their work to be guided only by objective considerations, not by personal evaluation or liking.

2. Psychologists take into account the limitations of their means and of their own competence.

3. Psychologists always aim to employ those methods that can be considered soundest in view of the current state of the discipline.

4. In the attempt to perform their activities in the best possible way, psychologists consider the possibility of working with other professionals from their own area and related areas.

5. Psychologists are responsible for seeing to it that their work cannot be hampered by inadequate working conditions.

6. In the interest of improving both their manner of working and the knowledge on which their work is based, psychologists strive to evaluate the success of their work with appropriate methods.

## B. Principles for Research

1. Psychological research must stay within certain limits with regard to its goals and methods. These limitations result from the need to be considerate of the people (or animals) involved in research.

2. In the planning and execution of investigations, psychologists must exclude all conditions from which harmful aftereffects for the subjects could result. If they decide for important reasons to carry out research in which there is a possibility that they might be responsible for certain harmful aftereffects, they must inform subjects of this possibility explicitly. Psychologists may ask for the cooperation of these subjects only if they have stated explicitly, in unrestricted freedom, that they are prepared to undergo this risk.

3. Research situations from which one can expect unusual physical or psychological stresses for subjects may be created only when it is a matter of important problems that cannot be investigated in any other manner, and only under the condition that subjects are willing to expose themselves to such stresses. The stresses may not injure the dignity of the subject, must be kept within reasonable limits, and can be induced only if all appropriate precautionary measures have been taken. These precautionary measures include if necessary an examination and checkup by a physician for the persons involved.

4. If subjects are to be observed during an investigation in a manner that is not obvious (for example, by means of one-way windows or similar devices), or if their behavior is to be recorded audiovisually, they should be informed of this intention ahead of time and their consent should be obtained.

Researchers may deviate from this principle only if the investigation of scientifically significant questions makes this unavoidably necessary. In this case, however, subjects are to be informed as soon as possible that their behavior was observed or recorded, and in what manner. Subjects have the right to have the data destroyed if they do not approve of the observation or recording even after being presented with the reasons for its scientific necessity. In the case of subjects who cannot make such decisions for themselves, appropriate agreements are to be made with those responsible for them.

5. For psychological research involving animals the regulations in the relevant laws are applicable.

## POLAND (1971): PSYCHOLOGIST'S ETHICAL CODE[1,2]

### (EXCERPTS)

Polskie Towarzystwo Psychologiczne
(Polish Psychological Association)

### Research Activity

14. Scientific solidity requires that all psychologists must be absolutely honest both when they gather or elaborate materials and when they give interpretations. It is inadmissible to bend the facts to hypotheses and to conceal or change the data in order to get desirable results or for any other reasons.

15. The psychologist avoids experiments that can cause suffering or damage to the subject. When such experiments are necessary, the psychologist is obliged to inform the subject and get his agreement.

16. Each examination in which a pharmacological remedy is used must be under the control of a competent specialist and in such circumstances that enable to watch the subject's state of health.

17. Using animals in experiments—if it is not necessary for a special important goal—the psychologist avoids to cause pain.

18. The psychologist may keep secret the real aim of an experiment to the subject, if the research requires it. In principle, however, when the experiments are over, he announces the real aim.

19. The psychologist is obliged to give real and comprehensive information about sources he has used. When he has used in his publication or research

---

[1] Translated by B. Rosemann.
[2] Reprinted by permission of the Polskie Towarzystwo Psychologiczne.

work the materials of other authors or the help and consultation of other persons, he has no right to conceal it.

20. The psychologist uses in his elaboration the results got by a collective body, provided that each member of this collectivity has been informed. He is also obliged to mention the names of all of them.

21. When the psychologist presents the results of his own research, he produces also suitable documents, if necessary.

22. The psychologist does not figure on any publication or paper in which he has not taken part. He does not present his contribution to a work in a way that is out of accord with his real contribution to this work.

23. When it is necessary to quote concrete empirical materials in a publication, the psychologist eliminates all details that allow the identification of examined persons.

## SWEDEN (1975):
## ETHICAL PRINCIPLES IN THE CONDUCT OF PSYCHOLOGICAL AND EDUCATIONAL RESEARCH WITH HUMAN PARTICIPANTS[1,2]

## Swedish Council for Social Science Research

The responsibility for ethical considerations always rests with the individual investigator. In planning any study the investigator should weigh the expected value of the research against possible damaging consequences for the research participants and any third party, taking into account short-range as well as long-term aftereffects.

The natural basis for ethical appraisal of psychological and educational re-

[1] This code appeared in a paper by Johansson (1976). It was applied to the fields of psychology and education during a trial period and is now subject to a thorough revision and amplification. The new code will retain the same basic aim: to achieve balance between society's demand for research and the individual's right to privacy and personal integrity, but it will be designed for application to the whole field of research in the humanities and social sciences. It will include eight rules and two recommendations, the former of which will be grouped under four headings: Openness, Self-determination, Confidentiality, and Autonomy. U. Enderlein translated the 1975 code.

An English translation of the new code will be available in 1982 from the Swedish Council for Research in the Humanities and Social Sciences, P.O. Box 6712, S-113 85 Stockholm, Sweden.

[2] Reprinted by permission of the Swedish Council for Research in the Humanities and Social Sciences.

search is the requirement that research participants should not be exposed to physical or mental danger or humiliation and that they should, as far as possible, be protected from discomfort and inconvenience.

In order to satisfy the basic requirement the following principles—intended to serve as guide-lines for prereview of research projects—regulate the relations between the investigator and the research participants. Should there be a conflict between ethical principles and methodological requirements, the reason for a deviation from the principle in question should be carefully explained and weighed against the value of the planned study. When in doubt the investigator should seek advice, in the first place by consulting his colleagues. The principles that follow should be interpreted in terms of the contexts provided in "Etiska problem i psykologisk-pedagogisk forskning" ("Ethical Problems in the Conduct of Psychological and Educational Research") drawn up by the Social Science Research Council's committee on research ethics and in "Ethical Principles in the Conduct of Research with Human Participants" published by the American Psychological Association.

1. Research participants and, in the case of minors, also parents/persons acting *in loco parentis* should be informed in advance of all features of the research that reasonably might be expected to influence their willingness to participate.

2. After imparting the said information the investigator should obtain the consent of the individual to participate in the research. The way in which this is done must allow the individual full liberty of choice. In the case of minors the consent of parents/persons acting *in loco parentis* should be obtained in addition to the consent of the minor.

3. Research participants should be informed in advance of their freedom to discontinue participation at any time.

4. Strict confidentiality must be observed when registering and storing personal data. Reports of the results should be in terms that make it impossible to identify individual research participants.

5. The investigator is responsible for reporting, as far as possible, the results of the study to the research participants and others directly involved in the research.

## SWITZERLAND (1974):
## CODE DÉONTOLOGIQUE[1]
## (DEONTOLOGICAL CODE)

Schweizerische Gesellschaft für Psychologie and
Schweizerische Gesellschaft für Psychologie und
ihre Anwendungen
(Swiss Psychological Association and
Swiss Professional Association for Applied Psychology)

### 1. General Principles

Psychologists contribute to the growth of knowledge and to our understanding of ourselves and others. They respect the dignity of others; they refrain from actions or words that could lower this dignity; they recognize that everyone has the right to be respected.

1.2. Psychologists care about the well-being of everyone who consults them; they make certain that they do not harm anyone with whom they have professional contact.

1.3. Of necessity psychologists carry out their activities in a society with explicit and implicit norms. They do not aim for social adaptation in the sense of a simple accommodation to these norms, but rather consider that other forms of adaptation can exist.

1.4. Psychologists are free to point out problems that the norms of behavior and social values may create from a psychological standpoint. They can propose appropriate modifications of these norms and values. They favor the creation of environments that contribute to the growth of each individual.

1.5. Psychologists practice their profession—research, teaching, or consultation—in complete freedom. They are aware of the responsibility that this freedom brings, especially with regard to the integrity of their goals, the quality of their work, their attitudes, and their objectivity. They refuse to undertake tasks that conflict with the present code.

1.6. Psychologists are careful not to interfere with the freedom of others. They particularly respect the rights of others to inform themselves, to evaluate, and to make decisions.

### 2. Competence and Responsibility

2.1. Psychologists avoid all ambiguities as to their qualifications, their training, their goals, and the goals of the organizations with which they are as-

---

[1] By permission of the Schweizerische Gesellschaft für Psychologie and the Schweizerische Gesellschaft für Psychologie und ihre Anwendungen.

sociated. They do not allow their qualifications, training, or goals to be misused by others.

They discourage the professional practice of psychology by persons who lack proper qualifications.

2.2. Psychologists force themselves to be aware of the structure of their own personality. They take into account the limits of their professional knowledge, of their competence, and of the methods that they use; they attempt to progress in these areas.

2.3. Psychologists refrain from offering services or methods that are beyond the limits of their knowledge and competence. If need be, they will call on qualified colleagues for assistance.

## 3. The Relationship Between Psychologists and Their Clients

3.1. Before accepting any fees, psychologists must make known to their clients the general conditions under which they are willing to work and the extent of the services they provide. They inform the client of all factors that could possibly influence their relationship.

3.2. When psychologists establish professional relationships with persons referred by third parties, they will ask those who request their assistance to define their position and their relationship to and responsibility toward the clients. As for the psychologists themselves, they will make clear to the referring colleagues their function and role with respect to the clients as well as the nature and limits of the services they provide. If a conflict arises between psychologists and third parties, especially those who have referred clients to the psychologists, the psychologists will attempt above all to safeguard the interests of their clients.

3.3. Psychologists will not impose their services on others.

3.4. Psychologists are obliged to professional secrecy. They demand the same discretion from their colleagues, assistants, and employees.

Aside from legal obligations, psychologists can be released from their obligation to secrecy only by those whom the secret concerns.

3.5. The information and results obtained by psychologists in the course of their work, along with any interpretations or reports that may be drawn from them, are also subject to the rule concerning professional secrets. This information cannot be divulged to anyone without the approval of the one concerned. Psychologists are obliged to explain to their clients any limitations on the rule of professional secrecy.

3.6. Psychologists can use the information or results of psychological consultations for teaching or publication only if the anonymity of their clients is guaranteed. In doubtful cases psychologists will seek the explicit consent of their clients.

## 4. Methods

4.1. It is essential that psychologists have control over the choice and implementation of methods used in their practice, research, or teaching.

4.2. Psychologists do not leave up to non-psychologists the burden and responsibility for the choice of methods.

4.3. Psychologists do not use psychodiagnostic methods or other procedures in a professional setting without adequate training and experience.

Psychologists discourage the use of psychodiagnostic methods and procedures by persons who are insufficiently qualified.

## 5. Research and Teaching of Psychology

5.1. The rules of this code are to be applied by analogy to ethical problems that arise in psychological research or in teaching psychology. In the context of their training the students should be made aware of the ethical implications of their activities.

5.2. Psychology students are to abide by this code, as do professional psychologists. Instructors are obliged to inform the students early in their course of study about the contents and implications of this code.

5.3. Psychologists bear the responsibility for all steps taken during their research. Situations that are harmful to the subjects are not acceptable.

5.4. All those who make significant contributions to a publication are to receive credit.

## 6. Rules for Application

6.1. The present code is supplemented by a set of rules for application.

# FRANCE (1960):
# PROJET DE CODE DE DÉONTOLOGIE À L'USAGE DES PSYCHOLOGUES[1]
# (PROPOSED DEONTOLOGICAL CODE FOR PSYCHOLOGISTS)

## (EXCERPTS)

Société Française de Psychologie
(French Psychological Society)

## 1. Scientific Knowledge

1.0 Whatever psychologists choose as their specialty (research, practice, or teaching), they should be concerned with the existence, development, and dissemination of information about studies in psychology, in the social sciences, and in all other areas of science. Thus they should accept all the rules and requirements of these fields.

1.1 All psychologists should be concerned with studying and applying readily communicable and verifiable methods and criteria for *testing a hypothesis*. This is an essential basis for an effective deontological code and the only one that will, by its very nature, prevent or limit whenever possible the recourse to principles or procedures justified only by tradition.

1.2 Precise and absolute *honesty* is a fundamental requirement for communication.

The same is true for *publication of research*, which is indispensable for the continued development of research, and which prevents its falsification or its dissemination in spurious forms.

1.3 *Special Principles*

1.31 As *researchers*, psychologists should choose their fields of research as best they can according to their judgment of its scientific interest, avoiding all lesser motives. They should publish complete reports of their work, never discarding without explanation any data that could modify the interpretation of the results.

1.32 As *teachers*, psychologists should accept as their primary duty the formation and training of their students at the highest level possible, both in terms of scholarship and of techniques, in close conjunction with current research.

---

[1] By permission of the Société Française de Psychologie.

1.33 In their *practice,* psychologists should be dedicated to making as great a contribution as possible to scientific advancement. They should be concerned with verifying and controlling the validity of their techniques and of the basis of these techniques and should not encourage disdain for such an approach, either actively or passively.

## 9. The Relationship with the Subjects in Scientific Research

9.0 Subjects of study may be clients or patients of a professional psychologist, or they may be exclusively objects of a study.

In either case, though in varying degrees, the desired effect is to make a contribution to knowledge. That contribution should be safeguarded. The subject, whether an individual or a group, should be assured of complete protection.

9.1 *Safeguarding the subject's contribution to knowledge*

9.10 Psychologists should avoid any step that could compromise a future or related study. This holds true for all techniques: diagnostic, psychographic or psychometric, sociometric, and experimental.

9.11 The effectiveness of these techniques can depend in part on the subject's not being aware of their use. They should not be published or described in popular magazines in a form that could compromise their effectiveness. Access to tests, materials, or experimental procedures of this sort should be limited to specialists who are capable of ensuring that they are used appropriately.

9.111 *Items* resembling items in tests that are actually used can be published as examples in popular articles and elsewhere, but only specialized publications should publish tests that are actually used, or authentic test items.

9.112 Psychologists are responsible for controlling the instructional use of tests, experimental procedures, and other methods, for their value could be compromised by revealing their specific contents or their underlying principles to the public.

9.12 Analogous principles apply to every psychological or social-psychological study. Psychologists should refrain from any study of the so-called "scorched earth" variety (in which observation becomes impossible anywhere that they have set foot). On the contrary, they should endeavor to conduct their observations in such a way as to facilitate further studies of their own or studies by other psychologists, and to facilitate rather than hinder readiness to cooperate with psychological research in the various environments that they have explored.

### 9.2 *Protection of subjects*

9.20 Individuals or groups of subjects should be protected from any injurious effect of research, either present or future, direct or indirect. In every instance, therefore, psychologists should examine carefully every conceivable injurious effect and eliminate the possible causes.

9.21 If psychologists are investigating a major problem that cannot be approached by another method, they may be obliged to cause subjects to experience frustrations, *stresses,* or minor physical or psychological harm. Such methods may possibly result in a subject's suffering from *delusions* or errors in judgment. Only if the problem is a major one and cannot be explored in another fashion are these methods acceptable. These methods should not be used except under the following strictly-defined conditions, which concern possible aftereffects.

9.22 Theoretically all *aftereffects* must be eliminated. In extreme cases, when the possibility of aftereffects cannot be entirely excluded scientifically, the project should be undertaken only if the subjects are informed in detail of that possibility, are personally capable of evaluating and coming to a decision about the matter, and then are still willing to be volunteers. The criteria for eligibility, particularly with respect to age, are strict and exclude adolescents in particular. The research design should be drawn up in such a way that doubtful factors are eliminated as soon as possible.

9.23 *Roles involving deception* ("accomplices in an experiment") in intensive role-playing situations should not be given to subjects, especially not to children, unless the absence of any injurious effect can be ensured (for example, the effect on sincerity or personal identity).

9.24 *Participant observation* is only to be used for strictly scientific purposes, and those who are observed should remain anonymous in any ensuing reports.

9.25 The same applies to *concealed observation, whether auditory or visual.* The essential condition is the absolute protection of subjects from any harm and even from any possible effects, by means of anonymity and secrecy.

9.26 In the *selection of subjects* for observation or experimentation, subjects should be examined carefully enough to eliminate from the sample any subjects who might suffer trauma from the proposed project.

9.27 Psychologists who use *animals* in their research should follow the rules employed by physiological laboratories using animals.

### 9.3 *Services rendered to subjects in connection with scientific research*

9.30 In every possible case during the course of research projects, psychologists should not fail to render service to the subjects.

9.31 *Experimental intervention research involving a natural group* should be accompanied by whatever practical follow-up assistance is needed for the group affected by the intervention.

9.32 In general, any study or observation conducted solely for the purpose of research could bring to light the need for consultation or treatment of a subject. This must be recommended to the parties involved and if possible carried out by the observer—should he be competent to do so—or by a person or institute to which he sends them, without the observer's being able to derive any profit from this treatment.

# References

Abelson, R. P., & Miller, J. C. Negative persuasion via personal insult. *Journal of Experimental Social Psychology*, 1967, 3, 321–333.

Abrahams, D. The effect of concern on debriefing following a deception experiment. Unpublished master's thesis, University of Minnesota, 1967. Cited in E. Walster, E. Berscheid, D. Abrahams, & V. Aronson, Effectiveness of debriefing following deception experiments. *Journal of Personality and Social Psychology*, 1967, 6, 371–380.

Adair, J. C., & Epstein, J. Verbal cues in the mediation of experimenter bias. *Psychological Reports*, 1968, 22, 1045–1053.

Adams, J. S. Inequity in social exchange. In L. Berkowitz (Ed.), *Advances in experimental social psychology* (Vol. 2). New York: Academic Press, 1965.

Adorno, T. W. *Einleitung in die Musiksoziologie.* Hamburg: Rowohlt, 1971.

Alexander, L. Limitations of experimentation on human beings with special reference to psychiatric patients. *Diseases of Nervous System,* Monograph Supplement, 1966, 27, 61–65.

Allen, V. L. Effect of knowledge of deception on conformity. *Journal of Social Psychology*, 1966, 69, 101–106.

Altemeyer, R. A. Subject pool pollution and the postexperimental interview. *Journal of Experimental Research in Personality*, 1972, 5, 79–84.

Amelang, M., & Aevermann, D. Forschungsbezogene Verhaltensweisen und Einstellungen von Wissenschaftlern. *Psychologische Rundschau*, 1976, 28, 71–95.

American Psychological Association, Committee on Ethical Standards for Psychology. Ethical standards in research. *American Psychologist*, 1951, 6, 436–443.

American Psychological Association. Discussion on ethics. *American Psychologist*, 1952, 7, 425–455.

American Psychological Association. Ethical standards of psychologists. *American Psychologist*, 1959, 14, 279–282.

American Psychological Association, Committee on Ethical Standards of Psychology. Ethical standards of psychologists. *American Psychologist*, 1963, 18, 56–60.

American Psychological Association, Committee on Ethical Standards in Psychological Research. Proposed ethical principles. *APA Monitor*, July 1971, 2, 9–28.

American Psychological Association, Committee on Ethical Standards in Psychological Research. *Ethical principles in the conduct of research with human participants.* Washington, D.C.: Author, 1973.

American Psychological Association. *Casebook on ethical standards of psychologists.* Washington, D.C.: Author, 1974.

American Psychological Association. *Ethical standards of psychologists (1977 revision).* Washington, D.C.: Author, 1977.

American Psychological Association. Ethical principles of psychologists. *American Psychologist,* 1981, 36, 633–638.

Arellano-Galdames, F. J. Some ethical problems in research on human subjects. (Doctoral dissertation, University of New Mexico, 1972).

Argyle, M. *Report to the council of the British Psychological Society on my dealings with the A.P.A. Committee on Scientific and Professional Ethics and Conduct.* Oxford, June 24, 1960.

Argyle, M. Experimental studies of small groups. In A. T. Welford (Ed.), *Society: Problems and methods of study.* London: Routledge & Kegan Paul, 1962.

Argyris, C. Some unintended consequences of rigorous research. *Psychological Bulletin,* 1968, 70, 185–197.

Argyris, C. Dangers in applying results from experimental social psychology. *American Psychologist,* 1975, 30, 469–485.

Aronson, E., & Carlsmith, J. M. Experimentation in social psychology. In G. Lindzey & E. Aronson (Eds.), *The handbook of social psychology* (Vol. 2). Reading, Mass.: Addison-Wesley, 1968.

Asch, S. E. *Social psychology.* Englewood Cliffs, N.J.: Prentice-Hall, 1952.

Backman, W. Do it yourself sociology (Review of *Doing social life* by Lofland). *Contemporary Psychology,* 1977, 22, 562–564.

Baratz, S. S. Applying the behavioral sciences to the needs of public policy making. *Professional Psychology,* 1973, 4, 216–223.

Barber, B., Lally, J. J., Makarushka, J. L., & Sullivan, D. *Research on human subjects.* New York: Russell Sage Foundation, 1973.

Barber, T. X., & Silver, M. J. Fact, fiction, and the experimenter bias effect. *Psychological Bulletin,* 1968, 70, 1–29.

Barnes, J. A. *The ethics of inquiry in social science.* Delhi: Oxford Univ. Press, 1977.

Baumrind, D. Some thoughts on ethics of research: After reading Milgram's "Behavioral study of obedience." *American Psychologist,* 1964, 19, 421–423.

Baumrind, D. Principles of ethical conduct in the treatment of subjects: Reaction to the draft report of the Committee on Ethical Standards in Psychological Research. *American Psychologist,* 1971, 26, 887–896.

Baumrind, D. Ethical standards in psychological research. *American Psychologist,* 1972, 27, 1083–1086.

Baumrind, D. Nature and definition of informed consent in research involving deception. Paper prepared for the National Commission for the Protection of Human Subjects of Biomedical and Behavioral Research, University of California, 1976.

Baumrind, D. Snooping and duping: The application of the principle of informed consent to field research. Paper presented at the meeting of the Society for Applied Anthropology, University of California, San Diego, 1977.

Beecher, H. K. *Experimentation in man.* Springfield, Ill.: Thomas, 1959.

Beecher, H. K. Some fallacies and errors in the application of the principle of consent in human experimentation. *Clinical Pharmacology and Therapeutics,* 1962, 3, 141–145.

Beecher, H. K. Ethics and clinical research. *New England Journal of Medicine,* 1966, 274, 1354–1360.

Beecher, H. K. *Research and the individual.* Boston: Little, Brown, 1970.

Beecher, H. K. Deciding about qualifications of investigators? In J. Katz (Ed.), *Experimentation with human beings*. New York: Russell Sage Foundation, 1972.
Bem, D. J. Reply to Judson Mills. *Psychological Review*, 1967, 74, 536–537. (a)
Bem, D. J. Self-perception: An alternative interpretation of cognitive dissonance phenomena. *Psychological Review*, 1967, 74, 183–200. (b)
Benson, J. K., & Smith, J. O. The Harvard Drug Controversy—A case study of subject manipulation and social structure. In J. Katz (Ed.), *Experimentation with human beings*. New York: Russell Sage Foundation, 1972.
Bergin, A. E. The effect of dissonant persuasive communications upon changes in a self-referring attitude. *Journal of Personality*, 1962, 30, 423–436.
Berkun, M. M., Bialek, H. M., Kern, R. P., & Yagi, K. Experimental studies of psychological stress in man. *Psychological Monographs*, 1962, 76 (15, Whole No. 534).
Berman, J., McCombs, H., & Boruch, R. Notes on the contamination method: Two small experiments in assuring confidentiality of responses. *Sociological Methods & Research*, 1977, 6, 45–61.
Berscheid, E., Baron, R. S., Dermer, M., & Libman, M. Anticipating informed consent: An empirical approach. *American Psychologist*, 1973, 28, 913–925.
Berufsverband Deutscher Psychologen. Berufsethische Verpflichtungen für Psychologen. Mimeographed, 1978.
Berufsverband Österreichischer Psychologen. Berufsverpflichtungen für Psychologen. Mimeographed, 1976.
Biermann, H. R., Miller, E. R., Dod, K. S., Kelly, K. H., Byron, R. L., & Black, D. H. *American Journal of Roentgenology*, 1951, 66, 555.
Boring, E. G. A history of introspection. *Psychological Bulletin*, 1953, 50, 169–190.
Boring, E. G. The nature and history of experimental control. *American Journal of Psychology*, 1954, 67, 573–589.
Boring, E. G. *A history of experimental psychology*. New York: Appleton, 1957.
Boring, E. G. Perspective: Artifact and control. In R. Rosenthal & R. L. Rosnow (Eds.), *Artifact in behavioral research*. New York: Academic Press, 1969.
Boruch, R. Relations among statistical methods for assuring confidentiality of social research data. *Social Science Research*, 1972, 1, 403–414.
Bramel, D. A dissonance theory approach to defensive projection. *Journal of Abnormal and Social Psychology*, 1962, 64, 121–129.
Bramel, D. Selection of a target for defensive projection. *Journal of Abnormal and Social Psychology*, 1963, 66, 318–324.
Brandstätter, H. Wohlbefinden und Unbehagen: Entwurf eines Verfahrens zur Messung von situationsabhängigen Stimmungen. Paper presented at the thirtieth annual convention of the Deutsche Gesellschaft für Psychologie, 1976. (Shortened version in W. Tack, *Bericht über den 30. Kongress der deutschen Gesellschaft für Psychologie in Regensburg*. Göttingen: Hogrefe, 1977.)
Brehm, J. W. *A theory of psychological reactance*. New York: Academic Press, 1966.
British Psychological Society, Scientific Affairs Board. *Ethical principles for research with human subjects*. Originally published as part of the following article: Ethics of investigations with human subjects: A set of principles proposed by the Scientific Affairs Board. *Bulletin of the British Psychological Society*, 1977, 30, 25–26.
Brock, T. C., & Becker, L. A. "Debriefing" and susceptibility to subsequent experimental manipulations. *Journal of Experimental Social Psychology*, 1966, 2, 314–323.
Brown, R. Models of attitude change. In R. Brown, E. Galanter, E. H. Hess, & G. Mandler (Eds.), *New directions in psychology*. New York: Holt, 1962.
Bunge, M. *Scientific research* (Vols. 1, 2). New York: Springer, 1967.
Buss, A. The emerging field of the sociology of psychological knowledge. *American Psychologist*, 1975, 30, 988–1002.

Butler, S. Sexual contact between therapists and patients. Unpublished doctoral dissertation, California School of Professional Psychology, 1975.

Campbell, A., Converse, P. E., & Rogers, W. L. *The quality of American life.* New York: Russell Sage Foundation, 1976.

Campbell, D. T. Factors relevant to the validity of experiments in social settings. *Psychological Bulletin,* 1957, *54,* 297–312.

Campbell, D. T. Prospective: Artifact and control. In R. Rosenthal & R. Rosnow (Eds.), *Artifact in behavioral research.* New York: Academic Press, 1969.

Campbell, D. T. Protection of the rights and interests of human subjects in program evaluation, social indicators, social experimentation, and statistical analysis based upon administrative records. Paper prepared for the National Commission for the Protection of Human Subjects of Biomedical and Behavioral Research, Northwestern University, Evanston, Illinois, 1976.

Campbell, D. T., & Cecil, J. S. Protection of the rights and interests of human subjects in the areas of program evaluation, social experimentation, social indicators, survey research, secondary analysis of research data, and statistical analysis of data administrative records (third draft). Unpublished manuscript, Northwestern University, Evanston, Illinois, 1977.

Campbell, D. T., & Erlebacher, A. How regression artifacts in quasi-experimental evaluations can mistakenly make compensatory education look harmful. In J. Hellmuth (Ed.), *Disadvantaged child* (Vol. 3). New York: Brunner, Mazel, 1970.

Campbell, D. T., & Stanley, J. C. Experimental and quasi-experimental design for research on teaching. In N. L. Gage (Ed.), *Handbook of research on teaching.* Chicago: Rand McNally, 1963.

Caplan, N., & Nelson, S. D. On being useful: The nature and consequences of psychological research on social problems. *American Psychologist,* 1973, *28,* 199–211.

Carlsmith, J. M., Ellsworth, P. C., & Aronson, E. *Methods of research in social psychology.* Reading, Mass.: Addison-Wesley, 1976.

Carlson, R. Where is the person in personality research? *Psychological Bulletin,* 1971, *75,* 203–219.

Carver, C. S. Physical aggression as a function of objective self-awareness and attitudes toward punishment. *Journal of Experimental Social Psychology,* 1975, *11,* 510–519.

Chein, J., Cook, S. W., & Harding, J. The field of action research. *American Psychologist,* 1948, 43–50.

Cherry, F., Mitchell, H., & Nelson, D. A. Helping or hurting? The aggression paradigm. *Proceedings of the 81st Annual Convention of the American Psychological Association.* Montreal, Canada, 1973, *8,* 117–118.

Coe, W. C., Kobayashi, K., & Howard, M. L. Experimental and ethical problems of evaluating the influence of hypnosis in antisocial conduct. *Journal of Abnormal Psychology,* 1973, *82,* 476–482.

Cook, S. W. Comments on ethical considerations in "Self-control techniques as an alternative to pain medication." *Journal of Abnormal Psychology,* 1975, *84,* 169–171.

Cook, S. W. Ethical issues in the conduct of research in social relations. In L. Selltiz, L. S. Wrightsman, & S. W. Cook (Eds.), *Research methods in social relations.* New York: Holt, 1976.

Cook, S. W., Hicks, L. H., Kimble, G. A., McGuire, W. J., Schoggen, P. H., & Smith, M. B. Ethical standards for research with human subjects (draft). *APA Monitor,* 1972, *3,* I-XIX.

Cook, T. D., Appleton, H., Conner, R., Shaffer, A., Tamkin, G., & Weber, S. J. *Sesame Street revisited: A case study in evaluation research.* New York: Russell Sage Foundation, 1975.

Cook, T. D., Bean, J. R., Calder, B. J., Frey, R., Krovety, M., & Reisman, S. R. Demand characteristics and three conceptions of the frequently deceived subject. *Journal of Personality and Social Psychology,* 1970, *3,* 185–194.

Cook, T. D., & Campbell, D. T. The design and conduct of quasi-experiments and true experiments in field settings. In M. D. Dunnette (Ed.), *Handbook of industrial and organizational psychology.* Chicago: Rand McNally, 1976.

Cook, T. D., & Diamond, S. An introduction to field experiments. Unpublished manuscript, Northwestern University, 1972.

Cook, T. D., & Perrin, B. F. The effects of suspiciousness of deception and the perceived legitimacy of deception on task performance in an attitude change experiment. *Journal of Personality,* 1971, *39,* 204–224.

Cooley, C. H. *Human nature and the social order.* New York: Schocken Books, 1967. (Originally published, 1902.)

Cooper, J. Deception and role playing: On telling the good guys from the bad guys. *American Psychologist,* 1976, *31,* 605–610.

Cox, D. E., & Siprelle, C. N. Coercion in participation as a research subject. *American Psychologist,* 1971, *26,* 726–731.

Crano, W. D., & Brewer, M. B. *Einführung in die sozialpsychologische Forschung.* Cologne: Kiepenheuer & Witsch, 1975.

Cronbach, L. J. Response sets and test validity. *Educational and Psychological Measurement,* 1946, *6,* 475–494.

Curran, W. J. Ethical and legal considerations in high risk studies of schizophrenia. *Schizophrenia Bulletin,* 1974, *10,* 74–92.

Darroch, R. K., & Steiner, I. D. Role playing: An alternative to laboratory research? *Journal of Personality,* 1970, *38,* 302–311.

Davidson, H. A. Legal and ethical aspects of psychiatric research. *American Journal of Psychiatry,* 1970, *126,* 237–240.

Davis, J., & Fernald, P. Psychology in action: Laboratory experience versus subject pool. *American Psychologist,* 1975, *30,* 523–524.

Davis, J. H., Spitzer, C. E., Nagao, D. H., & Stasser, G. Bias in social decisions by individuals and groups: An example from mock juries. In H. Brandstätter, J. H. Davis, & H. Schuler (Eds.), *Dynamics of group decisions.* Beverly Hills: Sage, 1978.

Declaration of Helsinki (Editorial). *English Journal of Medicine,* 1964, *271,* 473–474.

Department of Health, Education, and Welfare, Office of the Secretary. Protection of human subjects: Notice of report for public comment. *Federal Register,* 18 April 1979, *44* (76), 23192–23197.

Department of Health and Human Services, Office of the Secretary. Final regulations amending basic HHS policy for the protection of human research subjects: Final rule. *Federal Register,* 26 January 1981, *46* (16), 8366–8391.

De Sola Pool, I. The new censorship of social research. *The Public Interest,* 1980, *59,* 57–66.

Diener, E., Matthews, R., & Smith, R. Leakage of experimental information to potential future subjects by debriefed subjects. *Journal of Experimental Research in Personality,* 1972, *6,* 264–267.

Du Mont, M. Social science versus privacy. *Journal of Humanistic Psychology,* 1976, *16,* 81.

Duval, S., & Wicklund, R. A. *A theory of objective self-awareness.* New York: Academic Press, 1972.

Eccles, J. Animal experimentation versus human experimentation. In J. Katz (Ed.), *Experimentation with human beings.* New York: Russell Sage Foundation, 1972.

Edwards, A. L. *The social desirability variable in personality assessment and research.* New York: Dryden, 1957.

Ellsworth, P. C. From abstract ideas to concrete instances. *American Psychologist,* 1977, *32,* 604–615.

Elms, A. The crisis of confidence in social psychology. *American Psychologist,* 1975, *30,* 967–976.

Elms, A., & Janis, I. Counter-norm attitudes induced by consonant versus dissonant role-playing. *Journal of Experimental Research in Personality,* 1965, *1,* 50–60.

Epstein, Y. M., Suedfeld, P., & Silverstein, S. J. Subjects' expectations of and reactions to some behaviors of experimenters. *American Psychologist,* 1973, *28,* 212–221.

Errera, P. Statement based on interviews with forty "worst cases" in the Milgram obedience experiments. In J. Katz (Ed.), *Experimentation with human beings.* New York: Russell Sage Foundation, 1972.

Escalona, S. K. Feeding disturbances in very young children. *American Journal of Orthopsychiatry,* 1945, *15,* 76–80.

Eser, A., & Schumann, K. F. (Eds.). *Forschung im Konflikt mit Recht und Ethik.* Stuttgart: Enke, 1976.

Farr, J., & Seaver, W. Stress and discomfort in psychological research: Subject perceptions of experimental procedures. *American Psychologist,* 1975, *30,* 770–773.

Farr, R. M. Experimentation: A social psychological perspective. *British Journal of Social and Clinical Psychology,* 1976, *15,* 225–238.

Fellner, C. H., & Marshall, J. P. Kidney donors: The myth of informed consent. *American Journal of Psychiatry,* 1970, *126,* 1245–1251.

Festinger, L. Laboratory experimentation. In L. Festinger & D. Katz (Eds.), *Research methods in the behavioral sciences.* New York: Holt, 1953.

Festinger, L. *A theory of cognitive dissonance.* Stanford: Stanford Univ. Press, 1957.

Festinger, L., & Carlsmith, J. M. Cognitive consequences of forced compliance. *Journal of Abnormal and Social Psychology,* 1959, *58,* 203–210.

Fillenbaum, S. Prior deception and subsequent experimental performance: The faithful subject. *Journal of Personality and Social Psychology,* 1966, *4,* 532–537.

Fillenbaum, S., & Frey, R. More on the "faithful" behavior of suspicious subjects. *Journal of Personality,* 1970, *38,* 43–51.

Fine, R. H., & Lindskold, S. Subjects' experimental history and subject-based artifact. *Proceedings of the Annual Convention of the American Psychological Association,* 1971, *6,* 289–290.

Fishbein, M., & Ajzen, I. Attitudes and opinions. *Annual Review of Psychology,* 1972, *23,* 487–544.

Flanagan, M. F. The evils of researchers. *American Psychologist,* 1973, *28,* 531.

Flor-Henry, P. Psychiatric surgery 1936–1973: Evolution and current perspectives. *Canadian Psychiatric Association Journal,* 1975, *20,* 157–167.

Flugel, J. C. *A hundred years of psychology.* Andover: Chapel River Press, 1933.

Foot, P. (Ed.). *Theories of ethics.* Oxford: Oxford Univ. Press, 1967.

Forward, J., Canter, R., & Kirsch, N. Role-enactment and deception methodologies: Alternative paradigms. *American Psychologist,* 1976, *31,* 595–604.

Foxman, J., & Radtke, R. C. Negative expectancy and the choice of an aversive task. *Journal of Personality and Social Psychology,* 1970, *3,* 253–257.

Frank, J. D. Experimental studies of personal pressure and resistance: I. Experimental production of resistance. *Journal of General Psychology,* 1944, *30,* 23–41.

Frankena, W. K. *Ethics.* Englewood Cliffs, N.J.: Prentice-Hall, 1963.

Freedman, J. Role playing: Psychology by consensus. *Journal of Personality and Social Psychology,* 1969, *13,* 107–114.

Fried, S. B., Gumpper, D. C., & Allen, J. C. Ten years of social psychology: Is there a growing commitment to field research? *American Psychologist,* 1973, *28,* 155–156.

Friedman, N. *The social nature of psychological research: The psychological experiment as a social interaction.* New York: Basic Books, 1967.

Gadlin, H., & Ingle, G. Through the one-way-mirror: The limits of experimental self-reflection. *American Psychologist,* 1975, *30,* 1003–1009.

Gallo, P. S., Smith, S., & Mumford, S. Effects of deceiving subjects upon experimental results. *Journal of Social Psychology,* 1973, *89,* 99–107.

Gergen, K. J. The codification of research ethics: Views of a doubting Thomas. *American Psychologist*, 1973, 28, 907–912. (a)
Gergen, K. J. Social psychology as history. *Journal of Personality and Social Psychology*, 1973, 26, 309–320. (b)
Gergen, K. J. Experimentation in social psychology: A reappraisal. Invited address to Division 8 at the meeting of the American Psychological Association, Chicago, 1975.
Gibbons, F. X. Sexual standards and reactions to pornography: Enhancing behavioral consistency through self-focused attention. *Journal of Personality and Social Psychology*, 1978, 36, 976–987.
Gibby, R. G., & Stotsky, B. A. The relationship of Rorschach free association to inquiry. *Journal of Consulting Psychology*, 1953, 17, 359–364.
Glover, W. E., Greenfeld, A. D., & Shanks, R. G. The contribution made by adrenaline to the vasodilatation in the human forearm during emotional stress. *Journal of Physiology*, 1962, 164, 422–429.
Goldberg, L. R. Grades as motivants. *Psychology in the School*, 1965, 2, 17–24.
Goldiamond, I. Protection of human subjects and patients: A social contingency analysis of distinctions between research and practice, and its implications. *Behaviorism*, 1976, 4, 1–41.
Gould, A., & Shotter, J. *Human action and its psychological investigation*. London: Routledge & Kegan Paul, 1977.
Grabitz-Gniech, G. Versuchspersonenverhalten: Erklärungsansätze aus Theorien zum sozialen Einfluss. *Psychologische Beiträge*, 1972, 14, 541–549.
Graumann, C. F., & Métraux, A. Die phänomenologische Orientierung in der Psychologie. In K. Schneewind (Ed.), *Wissenschaftstheoretische Grundlagen der Psychologie*. Munich: Ernst Reinhard Verlag, 1977.
Greenberg, S. M. Role playing: An alternative to deception? *Journal of Personality and Social Psychology*, 1967, 7, 152–157.
Groeben, N., & Westmeyer, H. *Kriterien psychologischer Forschung*. Munich: Juventa, 1975.
Guetzkow, H., Alger, C. F., Brody, R. A., Noel, R. C., & Snyder, R. C. *Simulation in international relations*. Englewood Cliffs, N.J.: Prentice-Hall, 1963.
Haaf, G. Dollars, Drogen und Gehirne. *Die Zeit*, 1977, 35, 41.
Haag, F., Krüger, H., Schwärzel, W., & Wildt, J. (Eds.). *Aktionsforschung—Forschungsstrategien, Forschungsfelder und Forschungspläne*. Munich: Juventa, 1972.
Hamilton, V. L. Role play and deception: A re-examination of the controversy. *Journal of the Theory of Social Behaviour*, 1976, 6, 233–250.
Hamsher, J. H., & Reznikoff, M. Ethical standards in psychological research and graduate training: A study of attitudes within the profession. *Proceedings of the 75th Annual Convention of the American Psychological Association*, 1967, 2, 203–204.
Haney, C., Banks, W. C., & Zimbardo, P. G. International dynamics in a simulated prison. *International Journal of Criminology and Penology*, 1973, 1, 69–97.
Hardy, K. R. Determinants of conformity and attitude change. *Journal of Abnormal and Social Psychology*, 1957, 54, 289–294.
Hare-Mustin, R. T. Ethical considerations in the use of sexual contact in psychotherapy. *Psychotherapy: Theory, Research & Practice*, 1974, 11, 308–310.
Harré, R., & Secord, P. G. *The explanation of social behaviour*. Oxford: Blackwell, 1972.
Harris, R. J. The uncertain connection between verbal theories and research hypotheses in social psychology. *Journal of Experimental Social Psychology*, 1976, 12, 210–219.
Hartshorne, H., & May, M. A. *Studies in deceit*. New York: Macmillan, 1928.
Hass, R. G., & Grady, K. Temporal delay, type of forewarning, and resistance to influence. *European Journal of Social Psychology*, 1975, 11, 459–469.
Heacock, D., Thurber, S., & Vale, D. Shock elicited oppression by human subjects. *Journal of Social Psychology*, 1975, 95, 55–59.

Heckhausen, M. Relevanz der Psychologie als Austausch zwischen naiver und wissenschaftlicher Verhaltenstheorie. *Psychologische Rundschau,* 1976, 28, 1–11.
Hendrick, C., & Jones, R. A. *The nature of theory and research in social psychology.* New York: Academic Press, 1972.
Herbert, W. Commission drafts rules for local research review. *APA Monitor,* December 1977, p. 9.
Herrmann, T. *Die Psychologie und ihre Forschungsprogramme.* Göttingen: Hogrefe, 1976.
Hillis, J. W., & Wortman, C. B. Some determinants of public acceptance of randomized control group experimental designs. *Sociometry,* 1976, 39, 91–96.
Hoerster, N. Preface to G. Moore, *Grundprobleme der Ethik.* Munich: Beck, 1975.
Hoerster, N. *Utilitaristische Ethik und Verallgemeinerung* (2nd ed.). Freiburg: Karl Alber, 1977.
Höffe, O. (Ed.). *Einführung in die utilitaristische Ethik.* Munich: Beck, 1975.
Höffe, O. (Ed.). *Lexikon der Ethik.* Munich: Beck, 1977.
Hofstätter, P. R. *Gruppendynamik: Kritik der Massenpsychologie.* Hamburg: Rowohlt, 1957.
Holmes, D. S. Amount of experience in experiments as a determinant of performance in later experiments. *Journal of Personality and Social Psychology,* 1967, 7, 403–407.
Holmes, D. S. Effectiveness of debriefing after a stress-producing deception. *Journal of Research in Personality,* 1973, 7, 127–138.
Holmes, D. S. Debriefing after psychological experiments: I. Effectiveness of postdeception dehoaxing. *American Psychologist,* 1976, 31, 858–867. (a)
Holmes, D. S. Debriefing after psychological experiments: II. Effectiveness of postdeception desensitizing. *American Psychologist,* 1976, 31, 868–875. (b)
Holmes, D. S., & Bennett, D. H. Experiments to answer questions raised by the use of deception in psychological research. *Journal of Personality and Social Psychology,* 1974, 29, 358–367.
Holroyd, J. C., & Brodsky, A. M. Psychologists' attitudes and practices regarding erotic and nonerotic physical contact with patients. *American Psychologist,* 1977, 32, 843–849.
Holzkamp, K. *Theorie und Experiment in der Psychologie.* Berlin: Walter de Gruyter & Co., 1964.
Holzkamp, K. Zum Problem der Relevanz psychologischer Forschung für die Praxis. *Psychologische Rundschau,* 1970, 21, 1–22. (a)
Holzkamp, K. Wissenschaftstheoretische Voraussetzungen kritisch-emanzipatorischer Psychologie. *Zeitschrift für Sozialpsychologie,* 1970, 1, 5–21. (b)
Holzkamp, K. *Kritische Psychologie.* Frankfurt: Fischer, 1972.
Homans, G. C. *Social behavior—its elementary forms.* New York: Harcourt, 1961.
Hormuth, S. E. Drive theory and self-focused attention: An experimental comparison. *Journal of European Social Psychology,* in press.
Horowitz, J. A. Effects of volunteering, fear arousal, and number of communications on attitude change. *Journal of Personality and Social Psychology,* 1969, 11, 34–37.
Horowitz, J. A., & Rothschild, B. H. Conformity as a function of deception and role playing. *Journal of Personality and Social Psychology,* 1970, 14, 224–226.
Houston, B. K., & Holmes, D. S. Role playing versus deception: The ability of subjects to simulate self-report and physiological responses. *Journal of Social Psychology,* 1975, 96, 91–98.
Hull, C. L. *Principles of behavior.* New York: Appleton, 1943.
Hume, D. An inquiry concerning human understanding (1748). In T. H. Green & T. H. Grose (Eds.), *The philosophical works of David Hume* (Vol. 4). Aalen: Scientia, 1964.
Humphreys, L. *Tearoom trade—impersonal sex in public places.* Chicago: Aldine, 1970.
Hyman, H. H. *Interviewing in social research.* Chicago: Univ. of Chicago Press, 1954.
Janis, I. L., & King, B. T. The influence of role playing on opinion change. *Journal of Abnormal and Social Psychology,* 1954, 49, 211–218.
Janis, I. L., & Mann, L. .Effectiveness of emotional role playing in modifying smoking habits and attitudes. *Journal of Experimental Research in Personality,* 1965, 1, 84–90.
Johansson, G. Ethical principles in the conduct of psychological and educational research with

human participants (ethical code of the Swedish Council for Social Science Research) (U. Enderlein, translator.) In Comments on the ethical conduct and application of psychological research. Revised version of a paper given at the Twenty-first International Congress of Psychology in Paris, 1976. (A revised version of the code will be available in 1982 from the Swedish Council for Research in the Humanities and Social Sciences, formerly Swedish Council for Social Science Research.)

Jones, R. A., & Cooper, J. Mediation of experimenter effects. *Journal of Personality and Social Psychology,* 1971, *20,* 70–74.

Jonsen, A. R., Parker, M. L., Carlson, R. J., & Emmott, C. B. Biomedical experimentation on prisoners. *Ethics in Science and Medicine,* 1977, *4,* 1–28.

Jourard, S. M. *Project replication: Experimenter–subject acquaintance and outcome in psychological research.* Unpublished manuscript, University of Florida, 1968. Cited by R. Rosenthal, Interpersonal expectations: Effects of the experimenter's hypothesis. In R. Rosenthal & R. Rosnow (Eds.), *Artifact in behavioral research.* New York: Academic Press, 1969.

Judicial Council of the AMA. Requirements for experiments on human beings: Report of the Judicial Council adopted by AMA House of Delegates. *Journal of the American Medical Association,* 1946, *132,* 1090.

Jung, J. Current practices and problems in the use of college students for psychological research. *Canadian Psychologist,* 1969, *10,* 280–290.

Kaminski, G. Studieren als Handeln und als Trauern. *Psychologische Beiträge,* 1974, *16,* 310–337.

Kant, I. *Kritik der praktischen Vernunft* (B. Cassirer, Ed., Vol. 4). Berlin: Cassirer, 1921. (Originally published, 1788.)

Katz, J. The education of the physician-investigator. In P. Freund (Ed.), *Experimentation with human subjects.* London: Allen & Unwin, 1970.

Katz, J. *Experimentation with human beings.* New York: Russell Sage Foundation, 1972.

Kaufmann, H. The price of obedience and the price of knowledge. *American Psychologist,* 1967, *22,* 321–322.

Kelman, H. Manipulation of human behavior: An ethical dilemma for the social scientist. *Journal of Social Issues,* 1965, *11,* 31–46.

Kelman, H. Human use of human subjects: The problem of deception in social psychological experiments. *Psychological Bulletin,* 1967, *1,* 1–11. (a)

Kelman, H. Psychological research on social change: Some scientific and ethical issues. *International Journal of Psychology,* 1967, *2,* 301–313. (b)

Kelman, H. *A time to speak: On human values and social research.* San Francisco: Jossey-Bass, 1968.

Kelman, H. C. The rights of the subject in social research: An analysis in terms of relative power and legitimacy. *American Psychologist,* 1972, *27,* 989–1016.

Kelman, H. C. Was deception justified—and was it necessary? Comments on "Self-control techniques as an alternative to pain medication." *Journal of Abnormal Psychology,* 1975, *84,* 172–174.

Kelman, H. C. Privacy and research with human beings. *Journal of Social Issues,* 1977, *33,* 169–195.

Kennedy, J. L. Experiments on "unconscious whispering." *Psychological Bulletin,* 1938, *35,* 5–26.

Kennedy, J. L. A methodological review of extrasensory perception. *Psychological Bulletin,* 1939, *36,* 59–103.

Kerlinger, F. N. Draft report of the APA Committee on Ethical Standards in Psychological Research: A critical reaction. *American Psychologist,* 1972, *27,* 894–896.

Kershaw, D. N. The New Jersey negative income tax experiment: A summary of the design, operations, and results of the first large-scale social science experiment. In G. M. Lyons (Ed.), *Social research and public policies.* Hanover, N.H.: Dartmouth College Public Affairs Center, 1975.

Kiesler, C. A., Pallak, M. S., & Kanouse, D. E. Interactive effects of commitment and dissonance. *Journal of Personality and Social Psychology*, 1968, *8*, 331–338.

King, D. The subject pool. *American Psychologist*, 1970, *25*, 1179–1181.

Klinger, E. Modeling effects on achievement imagery. *Journal of Personality and Social Psychology*, 1967, *7*, 49–62.

Klix, F. Aspekte des Erkenntnisfortschritts in der psychologischen Grundlagenforschung. *Zeitschrift für Psychologie*, 1976, *184*, 17–36.

Klüver, J., & Krüger, H. Aktionsforschung und soziologische Theorien. In F. Haag, H. Krüger, W. Schwärzel & J. Wildt (Eds.), *Aktionsforschung—Forschungsstrategien, Forschungsfelder und Forschungspläne*. Munich: Juventa, 1972.

Koch, S. Epilogue. In S. Koch (Ed.), *Psychology: A study of science*. New York: McGraw-Hill, 1959.

Koocher, G. P. Bathroom behavior and human dignity. *Journal of Personality and Social Psychology*, 1977, *35*, 120–121.

Kruglanski, A. W. The human subject in the psychology experiment: Fact and artifact. In L. Berkowitz (Ed.), *Advances in experimental social psychology* (Vol. 8). New York: Academic Press, 1975.

Kruse, L. *Privatheit als Problem und Gegenstand der Psychologie*. Bern: Huber, 1980.

Kudirka, N. K. Defiance of authority under peer influence. Unpublished doctoral dissertation, Yale University, 1965.

Kuhn, T. S. *The structure of scientific revolutions*. Chicago: Univ. of Chicago Press (Phoenix Edition), 1962.

Külpe, O. *Grundriss der Psychologie*. Leipzig: Wilhelm Engelmann, 1893.

Kumpf, M., & Irle, M. Juristische Probleme bei sozialpsychologischen Experimenten. Paper presented at the thirtieth annual convention of the Deutsche Gesellschaft für Psychologie, 1976. (Shortened version in W. Tack, *Bericht über den 30. Kongress der deutschen Gesellschaft für Psychologie in Regensburg*. Göttingen: Hogrefe, 1977.)

Ladimer, J. Ethical and legal aspects of medical research on human beings. *Journal of Public Law*, 1955, *3*, 457–511.

Lange, F. A. *Geschichte des Materialismus* (2nd ed., H. Cohen, Ed.). Iserlohn: Baedeker, 1881. (Originally published, 1866 [Vol. 1]/1875 [Vol. 2].)

Lantin, Sr., P. T., Geronimo, A., & Calilong, V. *American Journal of Medical Science*, 1963, *245*, 239.

Lasagna, L. Special subjects in human experimentation. *Daedalus*, 1969, *98*, 449–462.

Lazarsfeld, P. F. *Training guide on the controlled experiment in social research*. Columbia University, Bureau of Applied Social Research, 1948.

Levendusky, P., & Pankratz, L. Self-control techniques as an alternative to pain medication. *Journal of Abnormal Psychology*, 1975, *84*, 165–168.

Levine, R. J. Ethische Regeln für Humanexperimente: Spannungen zwischen der biomedizinischen Forschergemeinschaft und der US-Bundesregierung. In A. Eser & F. Schumann (Eds.), *Forschung im Konflikt mit Recht und Ethik*. Stuttgart: Ferdinand Enke Verlag, 1976.

Lewin, K. *Die Entwicklung der experimentellen Willenspsychologie und die Psychotherapie*. Leipzig: Hirzel, 1929.

Lewin, K. *A dynamic theory of personality*. New York: McGraw-Hill, 1935.

Lewis, M., McCollum, T., & Schwartz, A. H. Informed consent in pediatric research. *Children*, 1969, *16*, 143–148.

Lindzey, G., & Aronson, E. (Eds.). *The handbook of social psychology*. Reading, Mass.: Addison-Wesley, 1968.

Lowe, C. U. The National Commission for the Protection of Human Subjects of Biomedical and Behavioral Research. In National Academy of Sciences, *Experiments and research with humans: Values in conflict*. Washington, D.C.: Author, 1975.

Lützenkirchen, W. Laser-Gase-Mikrowellen. *Augsburger Allgemeine*, May 9, 1977.

McGuire, W. J. Some impending reorientations in social psychology: Some thoughts provoked by Kenneth Ring. *Journal of Experimental and Social Psychology*, 1967, 3, 124–139.

McGuire, W. J. Personality and attitude change: An information-processing theory. In A. G. Greenwald, T. C. Brock, & T. M. Ostrom (Eds.), *Psychological foundations of attitudes*. New York: Academic Press, 1968.

McGuire, W. J. Suspiciousness of experimenter's intent. In R. Rosenthal & R. Rosnow (Eds.), *Artifact in behavioral research*. New York: Academic Press, 1969.

McGuire, W. J. Social psychology. In P. C. Dodwell (Ed.), *New horizons in psychology* (Vol. 2). Middlesex: Penguin, 1972.

McGuire, W. J. The yin and yang of progress in social psychology: Seven koan. *Journal of Personality and Social Psychology*, 1973, 26, 446–456.

McGuire, W. J. The value of privacy versus the need to know. In W. C. Bier (Ed.), *Privacy: A vanishing value?* New York: Fordham Univ. Press, 1980.

McGuire, W. J., & Papageorgis, D. Effectiveness of forewarning in developing resistance to persuasion. *Public Opinion Quarterly*, 1962, 26, 24–34.

Mackinney, A. C. Deceiving experimental subjects. *American Psychologist*, 1955, 10, 133.

Makarushka, J. L., & Lally, J. J. Medical schools, clinical research, and ethical leadership. *Journal of Medical Education*, 1974, 49, 411–418.

Mann, J. H. Experimental evaluations of role playing. *Psychological Bulletin*, 1956, 53, 227–234.

Masling, J. The influence of situational and interpersonal variables in projective testing. *Psychological Bulletin*, 1960, 57, 65–85.

Masling, J. Role-related behavior of the subject and psychologist and its effects upon psychological data. In D. Levine (Ed.), *Nebraska Symposium on Motivation* (Vol. 14). Lincoln: Univ. of Nebraska Press, 1966.

May, W. W. On Baumrind's four commandments. *American Psychologist*, 1972, 27, 899–900.

Mead, G. H. *Mind, self, and society*. Chicago: Univ. of Chicago Press, 1934.

Mead, M. Research with human beings: A model derived from anthropological field practice. *Daedalus*, 1969, 98, 361–386.

Menges, R. J. Openness and honesty versus coercion and deception in psychological research. *American Psychologist*, 1973, 28, 1030–1034.

Mertens, W. *Sozialpsychologie des Experiments*. Hamburg: Hoffmann & Campe, 1975.

Middlemist, R. D., Knowles, E. S., & Matter, C. F. What to do and what to report: A reply to Koocher. *Journal of Personality and Social Psychology*, 1977, 35, 122–124.

Milgram, S. Behavioral study of obedience. *Journal of Abnormal and Social Psychology*, 1963, 67, 371–378.

Milgram, S. Issues in the study of obedience: A reply to Baumrind. *American Psychologist*, 1964, 19, 848–852.

Milgram, S. Some conditions of obedience and disobedience to authority. *Human relations*, 1965, 18, 57–75.

Milgram, S. The lost-letter technique. *Psychology Today*, June 1969, pp. 30–33, 66, 68.

Milgram, S. *Obedience to authority: An experimental view*. New York: Harper, 1974.

Miller, A. G. Role playing: An alternative to deception? A review of the evidence. *American Psychologist*, 1972, 27, 623–636.

Miller, A. G. The social psychology of the research situation. In B. Seidenberg & A. Snadowsky (Eds.), *Social psychology*. New York: Free Press, 1976.

Miller, A. G., & Minton, H. L. Machiavellianism, internal–external control, and the violation of experimental instructions. *Psychological Record*, 1969, 19, 369–380.

Miller, G. A., Galanter, E., & Pribram, K. H. *Strategien des Handelns*. Stuttgart: Klett, 1973.

Mills, D. H. Whither informed consent? *Journal of the American Medical Association*, 1974, 229, 305–310.

Mills, J. A procedure for explaining experiments involving deception. *Personality and Social Psychology Bulletin,* 1976, *2,* 3–13.
Minor, M. W. Experimenter-expectancy effect as a function of evaluation apprehension. *Journal of Personality and Social Psychology,* 1970, *15,* 326–332.
Mitscherlich, A., & Mielke, F. (Eds.). *Medizin ohne Menschlichkeit.* Frankfurt: Fischer, 1960.
Mixon, D. Behavior analysis treating subjects as actors rather than organisms. *Journal of the Theory of Social Behaviour,* 1971, *1,* 19–31.
Mixon, D. Instead of deception. *Journal of the Theory of Social Behaviour,* 1972, *2,* 145–177.
Mixon, D. On the difference between active and non-active roleplaying methods. *American Psychologist,* 1977, *32,* 676–677.
Moore, G. E. *Principia Ethica.* Stuttgart: Reclam, 1970. (Originally published, 1903.)
Moore, G. E. *Grundprobleme der Ethik.* Munich: Beck, 1975. (Originally published, 1912.)
National Commission for the Protection of Human Subjects of Biomedical and Behavioral Research. *Research involving prisoners* (HEW Publication No. (OS) 76-131/132). Washington, D.C.: U.S. Government Printing Office, 1976.
National Commission for the Protection of Human Subjects of Biomedical and Behavioral Research. *Charter.* January 19, 1977. (a)
National Commission for the Protection of Human Subjects of Biomedical and Behavioral Research. *Psychosurgery* (HEW Publication No. (OS) 77-0001/2). Washington, D.C.: U.S. Government Printing Office, 1977. (b)
National Commission for the Protection of Human Subjects of Biomedical and Behavioral Research. *Summary of commission activities: Factsheet.* Ca. November 1977. (c)
National Commission for the Protection of Human Subjects of Biomedical and Behavioral Research. *Institutional review boards* (HEW Publication No. (OS) 78-0008). Washington, D.C.: U.S. Government Printing Office, 1978.
National Commission for the Protection of Human Subjects of Biomedical and Behavioral Research. *The Belmont report: Ethical principles and guidelines for the protection of human subjects of research* (HEW Publication No. (OS) 78-0012; Appendix 1 No. (OS) 78-0013; Appendix 2 No. (OS) 78-0014). Washington, D.C.: U.S. Government Printing Office, 1979.
*National Research Act.* Public Law 93-348. Title II—*Protection of human subjects of biomedical and behavioral research* (Part A). July 12, 1974.
Nederlands Instituut van Psychologen. *Professional code for psychologists* (official shortened English version of *Beroepsethiek voor Psychologen*). (H. Jacobse, translator.) Amsterdam: Author, 1976.
Neuhäusler, A. *Grundbegriffe der philosophischen Sprache.* Munich: Ehrenwirth, 1963.
Newberry, B. H. Truth telling in subjects with information about experiments: Who is being deceived? *Journal of Personality and Social Psychology,* 1973, *25,* 369–374.
Newcomb, T. M. *The acquaintance process.* New York: Holt, 1961.
Nuttin, J. M. *The illusion of attitude change: Towards a response contagion theory of persuasion.* New York: Academic Press, 1975.
Olson, T., & Christiansen, G. *The Grindstone experiment: Thirty-one hours.* Toronto: Canadian Friends Service Committee, 1966.
Orne, M. T. The demand characteristics of an experimental design and their implications. Paper read at the meeting of the American Psychological Association, Cincinnati, 1959.
Orne, M. T. On the social psychology of the psychological experiment: With particular reference to demand characteristics and their implications. *American Psychologist,* 1962, *17,* 776–783.
Orne, M. T. Demand characterisitcs and the concept of quasicontrols. In R. Rosenthal & R. Rosnow (Eds.), *Artifact in behavioral research.* New York: Academic Press, 1969.
Orne, M. T., & Evans, F. J. Social control in the psychological experiment: Antisocial behavior and hypnosis. *Journal of Personality and Social Psychology,* 1965, *1,* 189–200.

Orne, M. T., & Holland, C. C. On the ecological validity of laboratory deceptions. *International Journal of Psychiatry,* 1968, *6,* 282-293.

Pappworth, M. H. *Menschen als Versuchskaninchen: Experiment und Gewissen.* Zurich: Albert Müller, 1968. (Originally published as *Human Guinea Pigs,* Boston: Beacon Press, 1967.)

Pfungst, O. *Clever Hans (The horse of Mr. van Osten): A contribution to experimental, animal, and human psychology.* New York: Holt, 1911. (German original, 1907.)

Piliavin, J. A., & Piliavin, J. M. Effect of blood on reactions to a victim. *Journal of Personality and Social Psychology,* 1972, *23,* 353-361.

Polskie Towarzystwo Psychologiczne. *Psychologist's ethical code (Kodeks Etyczny Psychologa).* (B. Rosemann, translator.) 1971.

Pongratz, L. J. *Problemgeschichte der Psychologie.* Bern: Franke Verlag, 1967.

Rawls, J. Two concepts of rules. *Philosophical Review,* 1955, *64,* 3-32.

Rawls, J. Justice as fairness. *Philosophical Review,* 1958, *67,* 164-194.

Remington, C. L. An experimental study of man's genetic relationship to great apes, by means of interspecific hybridization. In J. Katz (Ed.), *Experimentation with human beings.* New York: Russell Sage Foundation, 1972.

Resnick, J. H., & Schwartz, T. Ethical standards as an independent variable in psychological research. *American Psychologist,* 1973, *28,* 134-139.

Rice, S. A. Contagious bias in the interview: A methodological note. *American Journal of Sociology,* 1929, *35,* 420-423.

Riecken, H. W. A program for research on experiments in social psychology. In P. Wuebben, B. Straits, & G. Schulman (Eds.), *The experiment as a social occasion.* Berkeley, Cal.: Glendessary Press, 1974. (Originally published, 1958; 1962.)

Riecken, H. W., & Boruch, R. F. (Eds.). *Social experimentation: A method for planning and evaluating social intervention.* New York: Academic Press, 1974.

Ring, K. Experimental social psychology: Some sober questions about some frivolous values. *Journal of Experimental and Social Psychology,* 1967, *3,* 113-123.

Ring, K., Wallston, K., & Corey, M. Mode of debriefing as a factor affecting subjective reaction to a Milgram-type obedience experiment: An ethical inquiry. *Representative Research in Social Psychology,* 1970, *1,* 67-88.

Rogers, C. R., & Skinner, B. F. Some issues concerning the control of human behavior. *Science,* 1956, *124,* 1057-1066.

Romano, J. Reflections on informed consent. *Archives of General Psychiatry,* 1974, *30,* 129-135.

Rosenberg, M. J. When dissonance fails: On eliminating evaluation apprehension from attitude measurement. *Journal of Personality and Social Psychology,* 1965, *1,* 28-42.

Rosenberg, M. J. The conditions and consequences of evaluation apprehension. In R. Rosenthal & R. Rosnow (Eds.), *Artifact in behavioral research.* New York: Academic Press, 1969.

Rosenberg, M. J., & Abelson, R. P. An analysis of cognitive balancing. In M. J. Rosenberg, C. I. Hovland, W. J. McGuire, R. P. Abelson, and J. W. Brehm, *Attitude organization and change.* New Haven: Yale Univ. Press, 1960.

Rosenthal, R. *Experimenter effects in behavioral research.* New York: Appleton, 1966.

Rosenthal, R. Covert communication in the psychological experiment. *Psychological Bulletin,* 1967, *67,* 356-367.

Rosenthal, R. Interpersonal expectations: Effects of the experimenter's hypothesis. In R. Rosenthal & R. Rosnow (Eds.), *Artifact in behavioral research.* New York: Academic Press, 1969.

Rosenthal, R., & Fode, K. L. The effect of experimenter bias on the performance of the albino rat. *Behavioral Science,* 1963, *8,* 183-189. (a)

Rosenthal, R., & Fode, K. L. Three experiments in experimenter bias. *Psychological Reports,* 1963, *12,* 491-511. (b)

Rosenthal, R., & Rosnow, R. L. (Eds.). *Artifact in behavioral research*. New York: Academic Press, 1969.
Rosenthal, R., & Rosnow, R. L. *The volunteer subject*. New York: Wiley, 1975.
Rosnow, R. L., & Aiken, S. L. Mediation of artifacts in behavioral research. *Journal of Experimental Social Psychology*, 1973, *9*, 181–201.
Rosnow, R. L., & Davis, D. J. Demand characteristics and the psychological experiment. *Etcetera: A Review of General Semantics*, 1977, *34*, 301–313.
Rosnow, R. L., Goodstadt, B. E., Suls, J. M., & Gitter, A. G. More on the social psychology of the experiment: When compliance turns to self-defense. *Journal of Personality and Social Psychology*, 1973, *27*, 337–343.
Rosnow, R. L., & Rosenthal, R. The volunteer subject revisited. *Australian Journal of Psychology*, 1976, *28*, 97–108.
Ross, D. *The right and the good*. Oxford: Oxford Univ. Press, 1930.
Ross, L., Lepper, M. R., & Hubbard, M. Perseverance in self-perception and social perception: Biased attributional processes in the debriefing paradigms. *Journal of Personality and Social Psychology*, 1975, *32*, 880–892.
Roston, R. A., & Sherrer, C. W. Malpractice: What's new? *Professional Psychology*, 1973, *4*, 270–276.
Rowland, L. W. Will hypnotized persons try to harm themselves or others? *Journal of Abnormal and Social Psychology*, 1939, *34*, 114–117.
Rubin, Z. Designing honest experiments. *American Psychologist*, 1973, *28*, 445–448.
Ruebhausen, O. M., & Brim, O. G. Privacy and behavioral research. *American Psychologist*, 1966, *21*, 423–437.
Rywick, T., & Gaffney, M. Imagined versus real aversive stimulation. *Perceptual and Motor Skills*, 1973, *35*, 742.
Sader, M. *Psychologie der Gruppe*. Munich: Juventa, 1976.
Sasson, R., & Nelson, T. M. The human experimental subject in context. *Canadian Psychologist*, 1969, *10*, 409–437.
Savin, H. B. Professors and psychological researchers: Conflicting values in conflicting roles. *Cognition*, 1973, *2*, 147–149.
Schachter, S. *The psychology of affiliation*. Stanford: Stanford Univ. Press, 1959.
Schneewind, K. A. (Ed.). *Wissenschaftstheoretische Grundlagen der Psychologie*. Munich: Reinhardt, 1977.
Schuler, H. *Sympathie und Einfluss in Entscheidungsgruppen*. (*Zeitschrift für Sozialpsychologie*, Beiheft 1 [monograph supplement].) Bern: Huber, 1975.
Schuler, H., & Peltzer, U. Friendly versus unfriendly nonverbal behavior: The effects on partners' decision-making preferences. In H. Brandstätter, J. H. Davis, & H. Schuler (Eds.), *Dynamics of group decisions*. Beverly Hills: Sage, 1978.
Schultz, D. P. The human subject in psychological research. *Psychological Bulletin*, 1969, *72*, 214–228.
Schweizerische Gesellschaft für Psychologie. *Code déontologique*. 1974.
Schwitzgebel, R. K. Ethical problems in experimentation with offenders. *American Journal of Orthopsychiatry*, 1968, *38*, 738–748.
Seeman, J. Deception in psychological research. *American Psychologist*, 1969, *24*, 1025–1028.
Selltiz, L., Wrightsman, L. S., & Cook, S. W. (Eds.). *Research methods in social relations*. New York: Holt, 1976.
Shapiro, A. K. A contribution to a history of the placebo effect. *Behavioral Science*, 1960, *5*, 109–135.
Shapiro, A. K., & Struening, E. L. The use of placebos: A study of ethics and physicians' attitudes. *Psychiatry in Medicine*, 1973, *4*, 17–29.

Shaw, A. Dilemmas of "informed consent" in children. *New England Journal of Medicine*, 1973, 289, 885–890.

Shaw, E. B. Informed consent. *American Journal of the Diseases of Children*, 1967, 114, 590.

Shulman, A. D., & Berman, H. J. Role expectations about subjects and experimenters in psychological research. *Journal of Personality and Social Psychology*, 1975, 32, 368–380.

Sigall, H., Aronson, E., & Van Hoose, T. The cooperative subject: Myth or reality? *Journal of Experimental Social Psychology*, 1970, 6, 1–10.

Sigall, H., Page, R., & Brown, A. C. Effort expenditure as a function of evaluation and evaluator attractiveness. *Representative Research in Social Psychology*, 1971, 2, 19–25.

Silverman, J. Nonreactive methods and the law. *American Psychologist*, 1975, 30, 764–769.

Silverman, J., Shulman, A. D., & Wiesenthal, D. L. Effects of deceiving and debriefing psychological subjects on performance in later experiments. *Journal of Personality and Social Psychology*, 1970, 14, 203–212.

Silverstein, S. Attitudinal congruency and anticipation of feedback as variables affecting the comparability of deception and role-playing experimental procedures. Unpublished doctoral dissertation, University of Connecticut, 1969.

Sinick, D. Comments on the "use of human subjects in psychological research." *American Psychologist*, 1954, 9, 489.

Sissons, M. The psychology of social class. In Open University, *Understanding society: A foundation course, Units 14–18: Money, wealth, and class*. Bletchley: Open University Press, 1971.

Skinner, B. F. *The behavior of organisms: An experimental analysis*. New York: Appleton, 1938.

Smith, E. E. The power of dissonance techniques to change attitudes. *Public Opinion Quarterly*, 1961, 25, 626–639.

Smith, M. B. Conflicting values affecting behavioral research with children. *American Psychologist*, 1967, 22, 377–382.

Société Française de Psychologie. Projet de code de déontologie à l'usage des psychologues. *Psychologie Française*, 1960, 1, 3–27.

Spector; D., London, P., & Robinson, J. P. Role-playing performance as a function of incentive condition and two social motives. *Journal of Personality and Social Psychology*, 1972, 23, 328–332.

Stang, D. J. Ineffective deception in conformity research: Some changes and consequences. *European Journal of Social Psychology*, 1976, 6, 353–369.

Stanton, F., & Baker, K. H. Interviewer bias and the recall of incompletely learned materials. *Sociometry*, 1942, 5, 123–134.

Steiner, I. D. The evils of research: Or what my mother didn't tell me about the sins of academia. *American Psychologist*, 1972, 27, 766–768.

Stollack, G. E. Obedience and deception research. *American Psychologist*, 1967, 22, 678.

Stricker, L. J. The true deceiver. *Psychological Bulletin*, 1967, 68, 13–20.

Stricker, L. J., Messick, S., & Jackson, D. N. Suspicion of deception: Implications for conformity research. *Journal of Personality and Social Psychology*, 1967, 5, 379–389.

Stricker, L. J., Messick, S., & Jackson, D. Evaluating deception in psychological research. *Psychological Bulletin*, 1969, 71, 343–351.

Sugerman, A. Psychopharmacological research concerned with the dying patient. *Journal of Thanatology*, 1972, 2, 858–864.

Sullivan, D. S., & Deiker, T. E. Subject–experimenter perceptions of ethical issues in human research. *American Psychologist*, 1973, 28, 587–591.

Swedish Council for Social Science Research. See Johansson, 1976.

Szent-Györgyi. *Lancet*, 1961, 1, 1394.

Taylor, B. J., & Wagner, N. N. Sex between therapists and clients: A review and analysis. *Professional Psychology*, 1976, 7, 593–601.

Tesch, F. E. Debriefing research participants: Though this be method there is madness to it. *Journal of Personality and Social Psychology*, 1977, 35, 217–224.
Thibaut, J. W., & Kelley, H. H. *The social psychology of groups*. New York: Wiley, 1959.
Thomae, H. Phänomenologie und Statistik in der Psychologie der Entscheidung. In H. Thomae (Ed.), *Die Motivation menschlichen Handelns*. Cologne: Kiepenheuer & Witsch, 1965.
Thomas, W. J., & Znaniecki, F. *The Polish peasant in Europe and America*. Boston: Badger, 1918.
Thorndike, E. L. Animal intelligence. *Psychological Review*, Monograph Supplement 2, 1898.
Timaeus, E. *Experiment und Psychologie*. Göttingen: Hogrefe, 1974.
Titchener, E. B. Simple reactions. *Mind*, 1895, 7, 115–121. (a)
Titchener, E. B. The type-theory of the simple reaction. *Mind*, 1895, 4, 506–514. (b)
Titchener, E. B. *Experimental psychology*. New York: Macmillan, 1901.
Tolman, E. C. *Operational behaviorism and current trends in psychology*. Berkeley: Univ. of California Press, 1950. (Originally published, 1936.)
Tunnell, G. B. Three dimensions of naturalness: An expanded definition of field research. *Psychological Bulletin*, 1977, 84, 426–437.
Turner, C. W., & Simons, S. L. Effects of subject sophistication and evaluation apprehension on aggressive responses to weapons. *Journal of Personality and Social Psychology*, 1974, 30, 341–348.
Van Hoose, W. H., & Kottler, J. A. *Ethical and legal issues in counseling and psychotherapy*. San Francisco: Jossey-Bass, 1977.
Veressayev, V. The memoirs of a physician. In J. Katz (Ed.), *Experimentation with human beings*. New York: Russell Sage Foundation, 1972, 284–291.
Vinacke, W. Deceiving experimental subjects. *American Psychologist*, 1954, 9, 155.
Wahl, J. M. The utility of deception: An empirical analysis. Unpublished manuscript prepared for the Symposium on Ethical Issues in the Experimental Manipulation of Human Beings, Western Psychological Association, Oregon, 1972.
Wahl, J. M. Role playing versus deception: Differences in experimental realism as measured by subjects' level of involvement and level of suspicion. *Dissertation Abstracts International*, 1973, 33, 4497.
Walster, E., Berscheid, E., Abrahams, D., & Aronson, V. Effectiveness of debriefing following deception experiments. *Journal of Personality and Social Psychology*, 1967, 6, 371–380.
Watson, J. B. Psychology as the behaviorist views it. *Psychological Review*, 1913, 20, 158–177.
Watson, J. B., & Rayner, R. Conditioned emotional reactions. *Journal of Experimental Psychology*, 1920, 3, 1–14.
Watzlawick, P., Beavin, J. H., & Jackson, D. D. *Menschliche Kommunikation—Formen, Störungen, Paradoxien*. Bern: Huber, 1969.
Webb, E. W., Campbell, D. T., Schwartz, R. D., & Sechrest, L. *Unobtrusive measures: Nonreactive research in the social sciences*. Chicago: Rand McNally, 1966.
Weber, S. J., & Cook, T. D. Subject effects in laboratory research: An examination of subject roles, demand characteristics, and valid inferences. *Psychological Bulletin*, 1972, 77, 273–295.
Weikert, D. P. Relationship of curriculum, teaching, and learning in preschool education. In J. C. Stanley (Ed.), *Preschool programs for the disadvantaged*. Baltimore, Md.: Johns Hopkins Press, 1972.
West, S. G., Gunn, S. P., & Chernicky, P. Ubiquitous Watergate: An attributional analysis. *Journal of Personality and Social Psychology*, 1975, 32, 55–65.
Wicklund, R. A. Objective self-awareness. In L. Berkowitz (Ed.), *Advances in experimental social psychology* (Vol. 8). New York: Academic Press, 1975.
Wicklund, R. A. Die Aktualisierung von Selbstkonzepten in Handlungsvollzügen. In S.-H. Filipp (Ed.), *Selbstkonzept-Forschung: Probleme, Befunde, Perspektiven*. Stuttgart: Klett, 1979. (a)
Wicklund, R. A. The influence of self-awareness on human behavior. *American Scientist*, 1979, 67, 187–193. (b)

Wiesenthal, D. L. Reweaving deception's tangled web. *Canadian Psychologist*, 1974, *15*, 326–336.
Willis, R. H., & Willis, Y. A. Role playing versus deception: An experimental comparison. *Journal of Personality and Social Psychology*, 1970, *16*, 472–477.
Wilson, D. W., & Donnerstein, E. Legal and ethical aspects of nonreactive social psychology research: An examination into the public mind. *American Psychologist*, 1976, *31*, 765–773.
Windelband, W. *Lehrbuch der Geschichte der Philosophie* (15th ed., H. Heimsoeth, Ed.). Tübingen: Mohr, 1957.
Wolfensberger, W. Ethical issues in research with human subjects. *Science*, 1967, *155*, 47–51.
Wolfensberger, W. Ethical issues in research with human subjects. In D. P. Schultz (Ed.), *The science of psychology: Critical reflections*. New York: Appleton, 1970.
Woodworth, R. S. *Contemporary schools of psychology*. New York: Roland Press, 1931.
World Medical Association, Committee on Medical Ethics. Principles for those in research and experimentation. *World Medical Journal*, 1955, *2*, 14–15.
Wundt, W. *Beiträge zur Theorie der Sinneswahrnehmung*. Leipzig: Winter, 1862.
Wundt, W. *Zur Psychologie und Ethik*. Leipzig: Reclam, 1911.
Zimbardo, P. G. On the ethics of intervention in human psychological research: With special reference to the Stanford prison experiment. *Cognition*, 1973, *2*, 243–256.
Zimbardo, P. G., Haney, C., Banks, W., & Jaffe, D. The mind is a formidable jailer: A Pirandellian prison. *The New York Times Magazine*, 1973, *60*, 38–60.

# Subject Index

**A**

Acceptability, *see* Effects; Evaluation; Procedures
Accountability, for individuals, 130–131
Action
   research, 13, 42, 150–152, 157
   sphere, *see* Sphere of action
   type, 36–37
Advice, *see* Consultation, with professionals, on difficult cases
Aftereffects, of experimental procedures, 90, *see also* Effects
Agreement, between experimenter and subject, *see* Contract
Altering object of observation, through observation, *see* Measurement
Alternative research methods, 11–13, 43, 58, 74, 78, 134–163, *see also* Research
American Psychological Association, *see* Codes for research
Animals
   ethical obligations, 191
Anthropology, 5, 154
   eliminating nonreactive research methods, 100

Application of manipulative techniques outside research, 97
Artifact
   experimenter, *see* Experimenter
   of regression, 151
Assessment, *see* Evaluation
Attitude
   change, 96–97
   of researchers, 67–76
Austrian ethical code, *see* Codes for research
Awareness, of ethical problems, in biomedical and social sciences, *see* History

**B**

Bearer of costs and benefits, identity, *see* Costs and benefits
Behavior, normative theories, *see* Normative theories of behavior
Behavioral control, 95–98, *see also* Control
Behaviorism, 6, 13, 15–19, 25
Belmont Report, 174–175
Benefits, 151, 154, 181, *see also* Costs and benefits
   educational, 92, 105, 111–112, 151
   system for researchers, 74–75, 167

261

Benevolence, 48, 133
Biomedical research, see Research
Briefing, preexperimental, 111, 139–142, 170, 174, see also Debriefing; Forewarning; Informed consent
British ethical code, see Codes for research

## C

Canadian ethical code, see Codes for research
Categorical imperative, 116
Causal relationship, 1–2, 7–11, 44–45, 136, 142, 148, 157–158
Caution when informing parents of results, 190
Chronology, 8
Codes of ethics, see Codes for research
Codes for research, 68, 103, 165–242, see also History
  in Austria, 186, 188–191, 231–233
  biomedical, 170–176
  in Canada, 186, 188–191
  Department of Health, Education, and Welfare/Health and Human Services, 172–176, 178, 185
  enforcement, 169
  in Federal Republic of Germany, 186, 188–191, 218–221
  in France, 186, 188–191, 239–242
  functions, 166–169
  in Great Britain, 186–191, 221–224
  international, 185–242
  interpretation, 180–182, 185
  National Commission for the Protection of Human Subjects of Biomedical and Behavioral Research, 172–176
  in Netherlands, 186–191, 224–231
  in Poland, 186, 188–191, 233–234
  process of developing, see Codification
  in Sweden, 186–191, 234–235
  in Switzerland, 186, 188–191, 236–238
  in United States, 74
    American Medical Association, 170
    American Psychological Association, 82, 93, 136, 176–217
Codification, 166
Coercion, see Voluntary participation; Volunteer subjects
Cognitive revolution, 6
Colleagues urged to obey rules, 191

Commitment
  to regulations and committees, 167–169
  to research, 72–73, 166–168, see also Demography of ethical commitment
Communication
  of goals, to subjects, 191
  of science, to public, 127
  theory, as perspective on experimental situation, 41
Communicative influence, 39–42
Compensation for risks in experiments, 56, 98–113
Complexity, 1–5, 8–9, 11–13, 19, 36–37, 148–150, 153
Confidentiality, see Data
Conflict between methodological and ethical norms, 1–5, 41, 57, 59, 74–75, 80, 103, 136–137, see also Ethics; Methodological issues
Consent of subjects, see Informed consent; Voluntary participation
  limitations on ability, 99–103, 106, 171–173
Consequences, see Effects
Consultation, with professionals, on difficult cases, 190
Contract, social, 5, 39, 48–65, 72–73, 81–82, 86, 101–102, 111, 154, 181
  breach, 112
  fair exchange, 48, 56–57, 181, 188
  partner, 58–60, 96, 167
Contributions, see Costs and benefits
Control, 122, 149–153, see also Behavioral control; Experiment; Experimenter
  lacking for subjects, 38–39
Costs and benefits, 48–51, 72–73, 87, 89, 92–93, 101, 111–134, see also Benefits
  analysis, 55–61, 68–71, 114–118, 129–133, 167, 176–177, 180–182
  criteria, 117–118
  difficulty of determining, 49, 118–129, 133
  for experimenters, 49, 56
  identity of bearer, 87–88, 131–132, 181
  individual versus collective, 87, 173
  for subjects, 49, 56, 118–125, 173
Course
  credits, 49, 54
  requirements, 44
Covariation, 8
Cover story, 77

## Subject Index

Covert observation, see Observation
Critical theory, 13

### D

Danger, 73-75, 86-97, 177-183, see also Harm to subjects
  of experimental situation, 52-55, 88, 103, 132
  of induced behavior, 52-55, 88-89, 103, 132
  physical, 88
  psychological, 88-89
  misuse, 121, 160-162
  protection, 113, 161-162, 179, 189-191
Debriefing, 78, 82, 89, 95, 107-113, 120-121, 154, 179-180, 189, see also Briefing, preexperimental; Forewarning
  diffusion of information, 111-112
  effectiveness, 95, 108-113
  effects, 108-113
  ethical issues, 112-113
  experimental investigation, 108-110
  frequency, 108
  functions, 107-112, 125
  methodological issues, 110-111
  misuse for further deception, 112-113
Deceptive research procedures, 5, 10, 34, 41-45, 60-61, 64, 67, 74-86, 90-93, 100-101, 103, 108, 117, 119-121, 128, 174, 180-181, see also Debriefing; Informed consent; Misinformation
  consequences, 80-82, 117, 119-120, 136-142
  conventions, 81-82
  frequency, 77
  passive versus active, 79-80
Declaration of Helsinki, 172
Delegation of responsibility, see Responsibility
Demand characteristics, 13, 20-23, 33, 37-40, 78, 123, 142-145
Demography of ethical commitment, 72, see also Commitment, to research; History
Deontological ethics, 48, 65, 68, 115-117, 124, 129
  act theories, 115
  rule theories, 85, 116-117, 180
Department of Health, Education, and Welfare, 172, 174-176, 178, see also Department of Health and Human Services

Department of Health and Human Services, 172, 175-176, 185, see also Department of Health, Education, and Welfare
Dependence, 53-54, 183, 189
Deprivation, 55
Desensitizing, 109
Diagnostic competence as form of social control, 45-48
Differential psychology, of subject, see Effects; Subject
Discontinuation
  of participation, in an experiment, by a subject, 63-64, 93-94, 103, 107, 109, 125, 171, 179-183
Dishonesty, see Deceptive research procedures
Distrust, 63, 78, 84, 119, 146, see also Trust
Drug experiments, 96-97
Dutch ethical codes, see Codes for research

### E

Effects, 88, 92-93, 118-125, 152-153, see also Aftereffects, of experimental procedures; Debriefing; Deceptive research procedures; Experimenter
  of different procedures on different subjects, 5, 94, 122-123
  guinea pig, 22
  Hawthorne, 22
  placebo, 21
Egotism, 115
Equity theory, 48, see also Contract, social
Error, see Measurement
Ethics, 4-5, 48, 65, 114-118, 129-134, 165-166, see also Conflict between methodological and ethical norms; Demography of ethical commitment
  connaturalism, 31-32
  norms for research, 4, 31-32, 64-65, 124, 129-134, 165-191
    binding, 113-114
    hierarchy, 181
  problems in research, 67-163
Evaluation
  apprehension, see Subject
  of effects, 55-56, 64-65, 67-68, 80-82, 86, 88-89, 113-134, 157, 160, see also Effects
  by experimenters, power, 45-46

Evaluation (*cont'd*)
  program, 102, 157–158
  of risks, *see* Risks
  by subjects
    of acceptability of behavior of scientists, 119–125
    of research procedures, 82–83, 88, 90–92, 99, 118–119, 123–125, 155–156, *see also* Procedures
Exchange, 48, 72, *see also* Costs and benefits; Justice
Expectations, *see* Subject
Experiment
  function, 10–11
  preferred research method, 5–15, 143–147
  procedures, *see* Procedures
  realism, 138
  replacement through role playing, *see* Role playing
  situation
    communication, 41
    growing accustomed, 105–106
    influence, 40
    peculiarities, 32, 51–52
    rules of the game, 45, 82, 103, 112
    social contract, 39, 48–65
    social interaction, 20, 32, 36–37, 42, 51–54, 68
    transparency, 39, 45, 57, 61, 69, 81–82, 110–111, 136, 145, 167
Experimental intervention research, *see* Social experimentation
Experimenter
  artifact, 43
  control measures, 29–30
  influence, 47–48, 61–64
    effects, 27–32
    expectancy effects, 27–32, 34–36
  motives, 30–32, 47, 132, 166–167
  power of control, 44–45, *see also* Behavioral control
  psychology, 25–32
  as quasi-subject, 31
  responsibility, 44–47
  role definition, 62–63
Exporting methods, *see* Application of manipulative techniques outside research

**F**

Fair exchange, *see* Contract, social; Exchange
Familiarity
  experimental behavior, 52–55, 103, 132
  experimental situation, 52–55, 103, 132
Fear of death, experimentally induced, 73–74, 87
Field research, 9, 43, 58, 136–137, 147–156, 162–163
  frequency, 148–150
  problems, 150
Forewarning, 101–102, *see also* Briefing, preexperimental
Freedom to discontinue participation, *see* Discontinuation
French ethical code, *see* Codes for research
Functionalism, 17

**G**

Generalizing from subject behavior, 64
German ethical codes, *see* Codes for research
Goals of research, *see* Research
Guidelines for research, *see* Codes for research
Guinea pig effect, *see* Effects

**H**

Habituation, *see* Experiment
Harm to subjects, 4–5, 67–75, 82, 86–96, 100, 112–114, 135, 166–168, 170–171, 179–183, *see also* Consequences; Danger; Evaluation; Hierarchy, of negative consequences; Procedures; Risks; Safeguards against harming subjects
  kinds, 88–89
  long-term negative consequences, 109, 119
  permanent, 108, 189
  physical, 88
  psychological, 88–89
Hawthorne effect, *see* Effects
Hedonistic principle, 114
Hierarchy
  of ethical principles, 125
  of negative consequences, 124–125
History, *see also* Materialistic–behavioristic tradition

## Subject Index

awareness of ethical problems in biomedical and social sciences, 68–76, 169–176
biomedical research, 68–75, 169–176
ethical codes for research with humans, 74, 76, 169–176
subject role, 15–19
Homosexuality, 87, 94–95, 113, 152–153
Honesty, 5, *see also* Deceptive research procedures; Misinformation
in publication, 191
in research, 179

### I

Identity
bearer of costs and benefits, *see* Costs and benefits
surrendering by subjects, 44
Image, public, of psychologists, 167–168
Incentives, *see* Benefits; Costs and benefits
Information about experiments, 111, 170–172, 179, 181, 188, 190–191, *see also* Informed consent
restricting for subjects, 5, 44–45, 73, 85
Informed consent, 42, 60, 86, 99–103, 154, 179, 188, *see also* Briefing; Consent; Debriefing; Forewarning; Information about experiments; Misinformation
Interaction between subject and experimenter, *see* Experiment; Relationship of subject and experimenter
Interest of researchers in ethical questions, 71–76, *see also* Commitment; Demography of ethical commitment; History
Interpretation of results, need for correctness, 191
Intervention research, *see* Social experimentation
Introspection, 15–18
Invasion of privacy, *see* Privacy
Investments, *see* Costs and benefits
Involuntary participation, 35–36, 41, 73

### J

Justice
cost–benefit relationship, 52, 56–57, 101, 111, 132–133, *see also* Costs and benefits
as exchange, 48, 101–102, 132–133
Justification of research procedures, 56–60, 68–71, 89, 91–92, 110–114, 156–157, *see also* Procedures

### L

Law, *see* Natural law
Legal immunity, 113–114
Legally problematic procedures, 113–114
Legal norms, 113–114
Legal perspective on special nature of research behavior, 113–114, 168–169
Legal prosecution, 113
Legal regulations, 113–114, 168–169
Limitations on ability to consent, *see* Consent, of subjects

### M

Manipulation of subjects, 5, 8—10, 19, 41, 44–45, 67, 77–78, 87–88, 90–91, 96–98, 108, 137, *see also* Application of manipulative techniques outside research
verifying effectiveness, 90, 108–110
Materialistic–behavioristic tradition, 17, *see also* Behaviorism
Measurement
effect of purpose of observation, 4
imprecision, 14–16
reactive effect, 1–4, 15–16, 22–23, 76–77, 137, 151, 172, *see also* Nonreactive research methods
Medical research, *see* Research
Methodological issues, 5–6, 78, 84–85, 93–96, 135–163, *see also* Conflict between methodological and ethical norms; Procedures
Methods, choice, 31, 43
Misinformation, 81–82, *see also* Deceptive research procedures; Information about experiments
Mistrust, *see* Distrust
Model of thought based on analysis of variance, 11
Moral behavior, theory, 133

Morality, see Ethics
Motives, see Experimenter; Subject

**N**

Naiveté of subjects, see Subjects
National Commission for the Protection of Human Subjects of Biomedical and Behavioral Research, see Codes for research
Natural law, 48
Naturalness, dimensions, 149–150, 152, 156
Nonreactive research methods, 40, 100, 104, 152–156, see also Measurement
Normative statements, system, 129, 169
Normative theories of behavior, 133–134
Norms, see Contract; Ethics; Legal norms; Normative statements; Normative theories of behavior; Social obligation norms
Nuremberg
  code, 171–172
  trials, 70, 170–171

**O**

Obedience, 38–39, 45–48, 51–52, 60–64
Object of investigation, 4–5, see also Subject
Observation, 7–8, 76–77, see also Measurement; Nonreactive research methods
  covert, 64, 78, 152, 190
  methods, 7–8, 14–15
  participant, 152–154

**P**

Pain, 55, 67, 91
Participant observation, see Observation
Participatory research, 41–42
Peculiarities
  of experimental situation, see Experiment
  of research with humans, see Research
Perceptions, see Experimenter; Relationship of subject and experimenter; Subject
  of experimenter by subject, 46–48
  of subject by experimenter, 47
Personality
  change, 94–97, 119
  disturbance, 119

Phenomenology, see Subject
Philosophy, 4–5, see also Costs and benefits; Ethics
  practical, 4, 48
Placebo effect, see Effects
Polish ethical code, see Codes for research
Postexperimental contact, 190
Postexperimental investigation of effects, 118–121, 124–125
Power
  differential, 20, 32–35, 38–39, 41–42, 44–48, 50–56, 69, 103, 105, 133, 137, 151–152, 167
  of experimenter, see Experimenter
Prevention of harm to subjects, see Safeguards against harming subjects
Principles, see Codes for research; Ethics
Privacy, 113, 189, see also Data
  invasion, 56, 86, 91, 137, 153–156, 160–161, 182
Procedures, see also Justification of research procedures
  acceptability, 64–65, 80–83, 90–91, 97–99, 102–103, 113–136, 154–156, 169–173, 177–182
  problems, 75–98, 105–106, see also Ethics
  taxonomy, 86, 124–125
Profits, see Benefits; Costs and Benefits
Program evaluation, see Evaluation
Promises, to subjects, 189
Protection
  expectation by subjects, 121
  from misuse of data, see Data
  need by subjects, 121
  of privacy, 189, see also Privacy
  from stress, see Stress
Psychology
  of experiment, see Social psychology of the experiment
  of experimenter, see Experimenter
  of scientific work, 25–26, 30–32
  of subject, see Subject
Publication of results
  obligation, 191

**Q**

Quasiexperimental design, 9, 156–160, see also Experiment

## Subject Index

Quasiobjective sphere of action, *see* Sphere of action
Quasi-role-playing, 119–121, *see also* Role playing
Quasitherapeutic responsibility, *see* Responsibility
Questioning of subjects, *see* Postexperimental investigation of effects; Quasi-role-playing

### R

Reaction control, 52–55, 103, 132
Reactions, *see* Effects; Subject
Reactivity, *see* Measurement; Nonreactive research methods
Realism, *see* Experiment
Refusal, 63–64
Regression artifact, *see* Artifact
Regressive behavior, 51–52
Regulations, *see* Codes for research; History; Legal regulations
Reinforcement, 97–98, *see also* Experimenter; Stimulus-response concept
  power, 53–57
Relationship of subject and experimenter, 20, 24–25, 36–37, 39, 41–46, 51–52, 172
  as social contract, 5, 72–73, 81–82, 111, 124–125, 132–133, 154, 181, *see also* Contract, social
Relevance, 125–129, 149–152, 157–158, 162, *see also* Benefits
Renunciation of autonomy, 45–46
Representativeness, *see* Validity
  of behavior in experiments, 12
  of environment in experiments, 12
  of experience in experiments, 12
  of subjects in experiments, 12, 44, 101, 104–105
Representatives for persons not capable of making contracts, 190
Research, *see also* Alternative research methods; Experiment; Methods; Procedures
  biomedical, 68–75, 86–87, 98–99, 106, 169–176
  codes, *see* Codes for research
  consequences, *see* Effects
  empirical realization of ideas, 148–149
  goals, 118, 125–129
  with humans, 1–5, 98–99
  norms, *see* Ethics
  situation, *see* Experiment
  in social sciences, *see* Research, with humans
  view of human nature, 5–6, 15–19
Researcher, *see* Experimenter
Resources, economical use, 191
Respondents, 182
Response
  bias, 21–22
  sets, 21–22
Responsibility
  delegation, 39, 51–52
  to dependents and subordinates, 179
  increased, if information omitted, 101–103
  quasitherapeutic, for intervention, 47
  of researchers for human subjects, 4–5, 44, 46–48, 57–60, 62–63, 78, 83, 92–93, 96, 101–103, 105, 149, 166–167, 176–183, 188–191
  of subject, 46–48, 104–105, 179
Restriction of freedom, 97
Rewards, *see* Benefits; Costs and benefits
Risks, *see also* Costs and benefits
  competence to assess
    of experimenters for subjects, 100–103
    of subjects, 100–103, 124
  decisions, 130–132
  difficulty in determining, 133, 178
  of harm to subjects, 42, 73–75, 86–89, 91–93, 98–103, 107, 130–132, 154–155, 171–172, 179–181, 188
  minimal-risk criteria, 99–100
Role, *see* Experimenter; Relationship of subject and experimenter; Subject
  inequality, *see* Power, differential
Role playing, 68, 102, 107, 137–147
  active versus nonactive, 143
  equivalence to deception experiment, 42–43, 141–147
  exploratory process, 102, 144–145
  imaginary versus performed, 145
  variations in behavior, 143
Rosenthal effect, *see* Effects
Rules, *see* Codes for research; Legal regulations
  of the game, *see* Experiment
Rule utilitarianism, *see* Utilitarian ethics

## S

Safeguards against harming subjects, 98–113, 125, 171–181, 188
  for children and handicapped, 189
Science, 127, see also Experiment; Research
Scientific revolution, 12
Scientist, see Experimenter
Self-awareness theory, 38
Self-concept
  change, as result of experiment, 49, 108–110, 119, 123
  as determinant of subject behavior, 2–3, 37–39, 50, 89, 123, 126–127, 143
Self-doubt, 90, 92
Self-esteem, change, as result of experiment, 38–39, 49–50, 86, 89, 100–101, 110, 149
Self-evaluation, 37–38, 90, see also Evaluation
Self-image, see Self-concept
Sexual contact between therapist and client, 133
Situational cues, see Demand characteristics
Social contract, see Contract, social; Relationship of subject and experimenter
Social desirability, 21–22, 34, 38, 45
Social experimentation, 96–97, 156–162
Social obligation norms, 4, 48, 64–65, 116, 132
Social psychology of the experiment, 39–43, 49, 105, 137, 142–143, 149, see also Experiment
Sphere of action, 2–3, 31, 126–127
  quasiobjective, 47, 126–127
  subjective, 47, 126–127
Stimulus control, 5, 52–55, 96, 103, 132, 136
Stimulus-response concept, 11, 19
Stress, 55, 67, 69, 88, 105, 121, 125, 188, see also Danger; Harm to subjects; Risks
  long-lasting, 108–109, 178–179, 189
  psychological, 119–121
Structuralism, 17
Students as subjects, see Subject
Subject
  artifacts, 15–16, 43
  concept, see Subject, in-role behavior
  expectations, 46–48, 51–52, 120–125
  harm, see Harm to subjects
  history, see History
  idiosyncratic reactions to experimental procedures, 15, 90–91, 94–95, 122–123
  in-role behavior, 15–26, 33–40, 46, 51–53, 61–64, 105, 143–146, 153–155
    apprehensive, 22, 33–38, 40, 45–47, 78, 123, 138, 142–143
    faithful, 33–39, 44–45, 83, 146
    good, 20–22, 33–40, 140, 146
    negativistic, 33–40
  manipulation, 143
  motives, 15, 21–25, 36–40, 49–52, 65, 141–144
  naiveté, 132
  phenomenology, 144
  pool, 100, 106
  representativeness, see Representativeness
  right to complain, 190
  special groups, 106–107, 171–173
  student, 104–107
  as term, 51, 182
  understanding to be ensured, 82–83
Submissiveness, see Obedience
Swedish ethical codes, see Codes for research
Swiss ethical code, see Codes for research
Symbolic interactionism, 36–37
System of normative statements, see Normative statements

## T

Taxonomy, see Procedures
Testing of psychological hypotheses in an everyday context, 148
Theories, 2–4, 65, see also Ethics
Therapy, 69, see also Sexual contact between therapist and client
Transparency, see Experiment
Trust, 44, 47–48, 51–52, see also Distrust
  breach, 52, 112
  loss, 78, 89, 112–113, 155–156

## U

United States, ethical codes, see Codes for research
Unobtrusive measures, see Nonreactive research methods
Usefulness of research, 125–129, see also Research
Utilitarian ethics, 48, 65, 114–115, 117–118, 124, 129–130, 133

## V

Validity, 9–11, 81, 84, 95, 104, 111, 117–118, 127, 143, 151, 153, 162
  construct, 9, 148, 162
  ecological, 145
  external, 9, 11, 37, 46, 148, 162
  internal, 9, 37, 43–47, 61, 76–77, 80, 147–151, 162
  statistical conclusion, 9
Values
  changes in structure, 165–166
  judgments, *see* Evaluation
Voluntary participation, 23–24, 35, 69, 91, 98–107, 170–173, 178–185, 188–189, *see also* Consent of subjects; Informed consent; Involuntary participation; Volunteer subjects
  compensations for limits, 107–108
  extent, 41, 44, 57, 104–105, 151–156, 171–175
Volunteer subjects
  ability to consent, 91
  characteristics, 23–24, 104

## W

Well-being research, 122